ROBERT GOURLAY
Statistical Account of Upper Canada

Abridged and with an Introduction by
S. R. MEALING

The Carleton Library No. 75
McClelland and Stewart Limited

THE CARLETON LIBRARY
A series of Canadian reprints and new
collections of source material relating
to Canada, issued under the editorial
supervision of the Institute of Canadian
Studies of Carleton University, Ottawa.

DIRECTOR OF THE INSTITUTE
Davidson Dunton

GENERAL EDITOR
Michael Gnarowski

EXECUTIVE EDITOR
James H. Marsh

EDITORIAL BOARD
B. Carman Bickerton *(History)*
Dennis Forcese *(Sociology)*
J. George Neuspiel *(Law)*
Thomas K. Rymes *(Economics)*
Derek G. Smith *(Anthropology)*
Michael S. Whittington *(Political Science)*

0-7710-9775-1

The Canadian Publishers
McClelland and Stewart Limited
25 Hollinger Road, Toronto

Printed and bound in Canada

Table of Contents

From *Statistical Account of Upper Canada*, II:

Review:

Parliament and the People:

Principles and Proceedings of the Inhabitants of the District of Niagara: (II, 579-88, 591-94, 609-12)   366

Introduction to the Carleton Library Edition

I

The author of the *Statistical Account of Upper Canada* has attracted more attention than the book itself. Ever since his banishment from the province in August 1819, Robert Gourlay's misfortunes have overshadowed his accomplishments. He lived for eighty-five busy years, the first thirty-three of them markedly successful: he was a highly competent tenant farmer with an income of about £500 a year,[1] the prospect of a decent inheritance and some reputation as a writer on agriculture, taxation and the poor laws. A combination of lawsuits and illness then, in 1811, began to turn his life into a tragedy.[2] By the summer of 1817, when he first came to Upper Canada, his finances were tangled and his prospects in England were declining. Nevertheless, he was still a vigorous, purposeful, capable and solvent man. His twenty-seven months in the province, which fixed his place in history, distorted and embittered the rest of his life.

Disapproving of the administration, he attacked the Tory oligarchy and became its best-publicized victim. Twice acquitted of libel, he was charged under the Sedition Act, denied bail, brought to trial after eight months in jail had damaged his capacity to defend himself, and banished. His conviction was legal under the Act, but only, as a committee of the Assembly was later to admit, "by a most lawyer-like and quibbling construction" of its terms.[3] The Act, passed in 1804 to exclude Irish rebels after the rising of 1798, was admitted by the Chief Justice to be a bad piece of legislation; Gourlay had laughed when the possibility of a charge under it was first raised.[4] It became a target for reformers and was repealed in 1829. Gourlay's banishment stood until, as the culmination of a long campaign of self-justification, he returned to petition against it. Even then the last Assembly of Upper Canada moved only in grudging terms, after a bitter seven-hour debate and by the Speaker's casting vote, to "enable the said Robert Gourlay to return and reside in the Province, if he shall think fit."[5] His petition did not succeed until Upper Canadian Toryism had been defeated by more formidable opponents. The first Assembly of the united Canadas finally moved an address to rescind his banishment, expressed its "reprobation of all the acts of unparalleled injustice under which he had suffered," and, with apologies for his "22 years of complicated misery," recommended a pension.[6] Long before Dent and Riddell identified his persecution as the Family Compact's critical error in public relations,[7] Gourlay's political martyrdom had received official sanction.

He invited martyrdom, both by the intemperance of his language before his trials and by his self-dramatization afterwards. He was an inveterate and pugnacious controversialist, with the habit of making highly personal accusations in print. He quarreled with his first patron, the agronomist Arthur Young, who had published some of his notes without permission, although with acknowledgement. In Fifeshire, where he first farmed one of his father's estates, an argument with the Earl of Kellie over farmer's income tax became a bitter personal quarrel. In Wiltshire, where he was a tenant of the Duke of Somerset, he won a lawsuit against his landlord but jeopardized his tenancy,[8] finding time also to be expelled from the Bath and Wiltshire Agricultural Societies and to conduct a quarrel (which was composed before he left for Upper Canada) with his father. He maintained against his opponents a flow of invective, not especially imaginative but shrewdly chosen to offend. Richard Cartwright was "Smellfungus"; Chief Justice Powell was "Pawkie"; Samuel Street – a New Englander but no Puritan – was "heir direct of the blue-laws"; John Bethune was "the *priest* of Augusta" – an unmistakable insult for an Anglican from a Presbyterian.[9] In the *Statistical Account* his most common target was John Strachan, who appears variously as a "contemptible miscreant," "a hand, malignant and ungentlemanly," the author of "12 pages of scandal and . . . 32 falsehoods," and who was reminded both of his stature and of his Presbyterian origins by the epithets "the Dominie of Little York" and "a monstrous little fool of a parson."[10] Strachan was certainly Gourlay's enemy and may have been directly responsible for his first arrest;[11] what Gourlay particularly resented was that Strachan, alone among his antagonists, managed to publish his version of the quarrel first.[12] Counting pamphlets but excluding letters and petitions, Gourlay published more than eighty titles during his lifetime, over half of them vituperative defences of his own conduct. Any persistent reader of Gourlay will feel some of the Attorney-General's regret that in Niagara jail he was allowed "pen, ink, paper and too much latitude in the exercise of those materials."[13]

His most spectacular bids for public attention, however, were not in print. His celebrated whipping of Henry Brougham, because that future Lord Chancellor had not been active enough in petitioning for him, amounted to no more than a couple of taps on the shoulder with a riding crop; it won him little sympathy, but nearly four years' imprisonment. More successful was the device of getting himself enrolled as a pauper in his old Wiltshire parish, where the spectacle of him breaking flints under an umbrella attracted parliamentary notice.[14] Characteristically, he sued the parish overseer for six shillings, being met by a demand for the return of the parish hammer. He took to law as readily as to print: he sued a farmer who stoned him off his land (with no damage done) and he sued a man who tore down a placard he had put up in a tavern.[15] His campaign for recognition in fact called attention to his eccentricity quite as much as to his grievances. It invited the contemporary judgement that "when sane, he was a very reasonable man,"[16] just as it has invited the assessments that he was "an interesting subject for those interested in abnormal psychology" and that he had "little that was helpful to offer Upper Canada."[17] He accepted the labels "reformer" and "radical," but it had to be "one of my own sort . . . I am known, both in England and in Scotland, for my peculiar opinions."[18] He was proud of being solitary and aggrieved, "as proud of his record as Saint Paul was of his dozen-odd whippings."[19]

II

Gourlay's original purposes in coming to Upper Canada were to produce his *Statistical Account,* to promote British emigration to the province and to recover his fortunes as an entrepreneur of settlement. It took him less than six months to conclude that his real task there was "a call for inquiry into corruption, mismanagement, and mis-rule."[20] This was unfortunate, for he was a tactless politician. Prophetic though some of his views on colonial government were,[21] he was also a confused political theorist. On the one hand, he was a believer in natural rights, especially in the right of the people to choose and change their rulers, and in the perfectibility of human nature: mankind was naturally good, "when not crossed by tyranny or ruined by bad example."[22] The accumulation of wealth and power in the hands of a few was "the perpetual source of oppression and neglect to the mass of mankind."[23] On the other hand, he believed that abuses in government were ineradicable; they stemmed from the inherent vices of man, which were bound to be reflected by any set of governors, however chosen.[24] He reconciled these propositions by a faith in the improving powers of education and, more especially, in the widespread distribution of property:

> God instituted property, and clearly tells us that, by the proper use of it, we can rise to excellence; but without property, or the chance of acquiring it, no good can be expected of us.[25]

All this was commonplace in the tradition of agrarian radicalism, but it left Gourlay with a relatively innocuous programme of direct political action. He rejected both violence and political parties: "England does not contain a more resolute foe to riot than myself; or a person so completely alone in political concerns."[26] Back in North America by 1837, he not only condemned Mackenzie's rebellion but sent warnings of proposed American assistance to it.[27] All three of his attempts at election (for Fifeshire in 1832 and 1846, for Oxford, Canada West, in 1858) were as an independent candidate. His political method relied entirely on the rights of assembly and petition. "By systematic petitioning: – by every parish petitioning the king or parliament for a specific and well-defined object," the people themselves could accomplish "any rational change."[28] On his own showing, this meant asking government to act against the interests of those who selfishly controlled it; it turned out to be a fruitless programme, but he could think of nothing else. He was not democrat enough to attempt an experiment in "convention rule."[29] Towards the end of his campaign in Upper Canada he discovered a faith in the Assembly's powers of supply. Then he urged meetings of constituents to instruct their representatives, but by the time the first such "purse-string" meeting was held at St. Catharines on 26 December 1818, the Niagara justices had issued an order requiring him to leave the province.

The importance of his reforming campaign is hard to judge, since the reality and extent of his popular support remain in question. He certainly found a response in Upper Canada which his pamphleteering had never met in Great Britain. His questionnaire on the state of the province revealed issues on which Upper Canadians were more than ready to speak: the slow rate of economic growth, the dearth of capital and immigrants, the bad roads, the manifold sins of inefficiency, favoritism and policy in land-granting. The unresponsiveness of government to complaints and the rival ambitions of the two houses of the legislature had already strained relations between them; just before his arrival the legislature had been prorogued as the only way to avoid an open breach.[30] The call for a commission of inquiry into the affairs of the province, which his second "Address to the Resident Land-Owners of Upper Canada" made in February 1818, was echoed next month in the Assembly. The Administrator of the province, Colonel Samuel Smith, was concerned enough to warn the Secretary of State: "My Lord, this man's insignificance is no security against the mischief he may generate."[31] The province seemed to be fertile ground for a campaign on the issues that aroused Gourlay most. Moreover, he began with the support of the local powers of the Niagara district. The Dicksons, Clarks and Hamiltons, to all of whom he was related through his wife, were pillars of the emerging Compact but restive under the policy of excluding American settlers. William Dickson alone had 94,035 acres on the Grand River, from which he could expect no early profit unless immigrants were encouraged.[32] He had just been removed from the commission of the peace for his persistence in administering the oath of allegiance to American applicants for land.[33] With a power base and a popular grievance to exploit, Gourlay would appear to have had the materials for a reform movement; it has been argued that the township and district meetings which he organized were in fact the model for later reform organizations.[34] They were enough to alarm the Attorney-General. "They seem to me dangerous in this country," John Beverley Robinson wrote to Colonel Smith, "chiefly from their example, as they point the mode by which popular movements on pretences less specious than the present can be effected."[35] Gourlay's arrests for libel were an attempt to silence him before he went any further.

It is questionable that he had much further to go. The Upper Canadian Convention of Friends to Enquiry, which met at York for four days in July 1818, had no programme beyond petitioning for an inquiry; the question debated was whether it should be requested of the Prince Regent or of the new Lieutenant-Governor, Sir Peregrine Maitland. Of the twenty-five district representatives projected, fifteen had been chosen and fourteen appeared.[36] The report of the convention dwells principally on the peaceable intentions and respectable character of its members, half of whom were local magistrates. Gourlay's own speech reads like an apology for the poor turn-out: dark machinations "had held back that frank and confiding support for the cause, which certainly would have prevailed throughout, from the unbiassed feelings of the people."[37] It may be doubted that such meetings were worth the Act soon passed to outlaw them, particularly since Strachan and Robinson were already on record as believing that Gourlay's influence was declining.[38] It may be doubted, too, that any further action against Gourlay himself was necessary to confirm his political failure. The nabobs of Niagara, however, were finding him an embarassment. It was William Dickson, making his peace with the York Compact, who arranged for an accusation under the Sedition Act. Neither Maitland nor his executive had a hand in this,[39] although the Chief Justice was one of three judges who signed an opinion beforehand that such an accusation would be founded in law.[40] The Attorney-General had no option but to prosecute. Duty alone, however, can hardly explain his continuing with the prosecution in spite of Gourlay's visible incapacity in the court-room. No court record of the trial survives; it has been thought significant that the clerk of the court was the Chief Justice's son.[41] As Gourlay said, "What are laws without morals?"[42]

III

Gourlay was no political revolutionary, but it was by a sound instinct that Upper Canadian Tories identified him as an enemy. A full list of the things that he wanted to reform in the world would read like a catalogue of human miseries; perhaps a full list of his solutions would resemble a catalogue of human folly. He had however a consistent focus on the relief of poverty. That was the deepest and the most constantly preoccupying of his concerns. His diet in Coldbath Fields prison, he noted, was better than that of the poor in Wiltshire.[43] Only ignorance was worse than poverty, but poverty was its cause.[44] The root of the trouble was simply the maldistribution of land. Agricultural labourers in England had been forced into an "abyss of misery and degradation" by having their small holdings taken away from them.[45] His quarrel with the poor laws was that they merely kept labourers alive in a state of landless dependence. He proposed an elaborate and highly bureaucratic scheme for their regeneration. The government, at what he described as trifling expense, would buy a hundred acres in every parish in England and rent half-acre allotments to the poor until they had sufficiently demonstrated their industry to receive ownership. The tenant of an allotment who kept it "in good garden culture" would become a "parish-holder"; after saving a hundred pounds in a government bank he could become a "cottage-holder"; after two consecutive years without receiving parish relief he would become a "freeman," able to vote in parish elections and to pasture a cow on common land; another sixty pounds in the bank would make him a "parish freeholder," eligible to hold parish office and no longer obliged to pay rent for his half-acre.[46] Until late in his career, Gourlay's preoccupation with rural poverty blinded him to the processes of industrialization and urban growth. One of the advantages he claimed for his plan of allotments was that city dwellers might be induced to return to villages of fifty or a hundred inhabitants, quite large enough to secure "every good of combination."[47] When he turned his attention to the improvement of cities, his concern was to preserve a rural atmosphere: he advocated fountains in Central Park and the pasturing of sheep on Boston Common.[48] Given his way, and if human nature had lived up to his expectations, he would have arrested the industrial growth and upset the aristocratic government of England, to produce a property-owning although certainly not an egalitarian democracy.

If that Arcadian ideal was impracticable in England, it might be attained in the colonies. Gourlay came to Upper Canada as an ardent advocate of emigration, not primarily for the sake of colonial development, but for the relief of poverty in Great Britain. Among the first generation of enthusiasts for that solution, he was unusual in recognizing the need that it implied for a re-planning of colonial land policy. In the *Statistical Account* he proposed a single land board for all of British North America, to keep land-granting apart from local politics.[49] Eventually he seems to have decided that it would have to be done by imperial legislation.[50] In Upper Canada he was the first to publicize the idea of selling the Crown Reserves.[51] The central feature in his plan was a land tax, applied with "no distinction whatever between wild and cultivated lands, public or private property, that of residents or absentees."[52] The revenue would not only make other forms of taxation unnecessary, it would pay for emigration. England alone could spare fifty thousand people a year, and Ireland just as many; even the most destitute could be transported without misery and settled in comfort, to be regenerated by the ownership of land.[53] He drew the line at convicts, at least before his own imprisonment in England.[54] The hints he gave for making the sale and taxation of land bear the cost of migration drew Edward Gibbon Wakefield's acknowledgement as the source of his own plan for systematic colonization; when the two met in 1838 Wakefield assured him that a colony in Australia had been founded on his principles.[55] He intended an additional volume of the *Statistical Account* to elaborate a scheme of emigration and land-granting, but never wrote it.

Gourlay had more personal if equally unfulfilled plans for Upper Canadian lands. Seven years before his arrival, he had bought five hundred acres from William Dickson, beside the 866 acres in Dereham Township that his wife already had from her uncle, Robert Hamilton.[56] By his own account, he first thought of coming to the province "solely with a view to ascertain whether it would be prudent to remove my family thither."[57] He had hopes of removing more than his family. Ultimately, he did succeed in organizing seventeen emigration societies in Fifeshire, none of which kept up its dues for as long as six months.[58] He made two unsuccessful applications for more land, being put off the second time with a reference, which he publicly resented, to "your means to become a useful settler".[59] How much land he asked for is not recorded; presumably it was more than the twelve hundred acres that was the standard maximum for an individual applicant of respectable character but no special influence. His application was of course rejected because he had so conspicuously lived up to his reputation as a radical. The reference to his means was however better founded than the Clerk of the Executive Council knew: by the end of 1817 his father's estates had been sold in bankruptcy, the rent on his Wiltshire farm was in arrears and a fresh lawsuit was pending.[60] He did not have the capital to manage the settlement of any extensive tract of land, nor did he have any interest in commercial enterprises that might have provided it for him, as for his Niagara relations. His only non-agricultural private project was to found a newspaper.[61] It seems, too, that his acknowledged expertise in British farming would have been a dubious asset in Upper Canadian conditions.[62] If he had in fact devoted himself to organizing a settlement, he would most probably have paralleled the career not of a Colonel Talbot or a John Galt but of a William Berczy, unable to collect his debts, confirm his titles or regain in the New World the standing he could no longer afford in the Old.[63]

IV

But Gourlay was tough. It is a tribute to his resilience that he was able to salvage some considerable part of his original intentions and to publish the *Statistical Account*. It was a help that he had been raised in a flourishing tradition of practical scholarship, both among the radical writers of his father's acquaintance and at St. Andrew's. Since Gregory King and the other "political arithmeticians" of the late seventeenth century, Britain had seen more writers on commerce, agriculture and taxation than on political theory. Behind the economic theories of Dean Tucker, Adam Smith and David Ricardo there was a host of compilers – some scholarly, some polemical, some mere hacks. Most of their works have passed readily into limbo: T. Janssen's *General Maxims of Trade* (1713), M. Postlethwayt's *Universal Dictionary of Trade and Commerce* (1751), George Bridges' *Plain Dealing, or the whole Method of Wool Smuggling clearly Discovered* (1744), E. Wade's *Proposal for Improving and Adorning the Island of Great Britain* (1755), John Arbuthnot's *Prices of Provisions and the Size of Farms, with Remarks on Population* (1773), R. Whitworth, *The Advantages of Inland Navigation* (1766), J. Bannister's *Synopsis of Husbandry* (1799). Their common assumption was that the systematic assemblage of information was of practical use, especially for the framing of public policy. Smith and Bentham articulated their faith in defining political economy as "a branch of the art of legislation, the knowledge of the best use to be made of the national wealth."[64] Gourlay joined this host in 1799, when Arthur Young at the Board of Agriculture employed him to survey the conditions of farm labourers in Lincoln and

Rutland. By the time that he began his attacks on farmer's income tax and the poor laws, the tradition had produced great names: Young himself on agriculture, George Chalmers on commerce, Malthus on population, Bryan Edwards on the West Indian trade, John Phillips on inland navigation, Charles Jenkinson on the coinage, Patrick Colquhoun on policing London, William Marshall on landed property.[65] The most remarkable of these productions, at least for sheer industry, was under way. Thomas Tooke's *History of Prices* did not begin to appear until 1838, but its author was already pouring out evidence to parliamentary committees on the grain trade and on bullion. Parliamentary fact-finding was entering upon its Utilitarian heyday. It had received the stimulus of the fifteen reports of the Commission on Public Accounts for which Lord Shelburne had been responsible.[66] And the persistence of a clerk in the House of Commons, John Rickman, had been rewarded with the inauguration of a national census.[67]

Nowhere was this tradition of applied scholarship stronger, and nowhere was it more directed towards the problems of agriculture, than in Scotland. Moreover, since the first treatise on Scottish agriculture in 1696, it had had an increasing statistical emphasis.[68] The official census of population was anticipated by nearly half a century in the work of Alexander Webster in 1755. Webster's distinctive contribution was to use ministers of religion as a source of local information. The method did not, in his hands, yield impeccably accurate results;[69] but it was the precedent for Sir John Sinclair of Ulbster, the founder with Arthur Young of the Board of Agriculture. When Sinclair began his *Statistical Account of Scotland* there was already in print the ambitious *Present State of Husbandry in Scotland* (4 volumes, 1778-84), the result of a survey made by Andrew Wight of Ormiston for the Board of Commissioners for Forfeited Estates. Unlike Wight or Young, Sinclair did not rely mainly on his own observations. He devised a set of questions to standardize the information supplied him by parish ministers. The resulting twenty-one volumes (1791-99) were a land-mark in the history of statistical inquiry. He extended the method, during the first of his two terms as President of the Board of Agriculture, into a system of county reports which were the basis for his *General Review of Agriculture*.

Gourlay, an opponent of enclosures, was no disciple of the man who promoted the general Enclosure Bill of 1796 and who was an evicting landlord on a large scale in Caithness. Still, he adopted Sinclair's method of inquiry. The idea of writing an account of Upper Canada at all apparently occured to him, not long before he sailed, from reading James Melish, *Travels through the United States of America*.[70] The list of queries that he drew up during his passage of the Atlantic, however, was based on Sinclair's. In particular, his famous thirty-first question, on what most retarded the development of the province, reflected Sir John's last heading: "Means by which their situation could be meliorated." In Upper Canada he could not expect an educated and sympathetic body of clergy. The one report that he did get from a Presbyterian clergyman supports his decision to rely on other sources of information.[71] He proposed a series of township meetings to answer his queries. His first "Address to the Resident Land-Owners of Upper Canada" contains a hint that he recognized the political implications of such meetings,[72] but there is no reason to doubt that his main purpose was still to collect information and it is hard to see what alternative method was open to him. Previous surveys of the province had generally been travellers' accounts or topographical sketches. Their information on settlement was relatively unsystematic; in some cases their desire to attract immigrants made it suspect. Moreover, when Gourlay began his inquiry they were too old to be informative. The best were still four travellers' accounts from the 1790's. The most recent dated from 1813; it was by Michael Smith, an American immigrant who had expected the war of 1812 to turn out differently, and is remarkable chiefly for its insistence that Upper Canadian bears were edible.[73] Gourlay had good reason to think that an up-to-date guide to settlers was necessary and that it could not be based on personal observation. He did make three tours that covered most of the settled parts of the province, but these merely supplemented his questionnaire.

v

As it was published in 1822, the *Statistical Account* was not the book that Gourlay had intended. Altogether fifty-seven township meetings were held in response to his questionnaire. They produced reports from nearly all the settled townships of Niagara and Gore, and from about half of those in the London and Western districts. Eastward from the head of Lake Ontario, however, he got only scattered responses. Of nineteen townships in Newcastle only Haldimand replied, from Midland's twenty-two only Kingston and five of its neighbours, from Johnstown's twenty-two only Wolford and Landsdown, from the Eastern District's twelve only Charlottenburg. From the Home District with nearly sixty surveyed townships and from Ottawa with eleven he got no reports at all. Even if politics had not interfered, the results of his survey would have been uneven. The replies from townships had not always paid close attention to his questions, those on land prices being a particular disappointment to him.[74]

Most of the deficiencies in the work, however, were the result of Gourlay's state of mind. "Not only the bitterest words, but the most direct and pointed personalities," he wrote, "are justifiable in the exposure of public crime."[75] Resentment of his treatment in Upper Canada, grief over his first wife's death, irritation with the difficulties of finding a publisher and the continuing entanglements of his finances, all made the composition of an orderly and thorough work impossible. Perhaps the sheer untidy multiplicity of his opinions would have made it impossible in any case. Apart from drawing up statistical tables for each district reporting, he attempted little analysis of the township reports. He tabulated the replies to his thirty-first question, but his commentary merely uses them as a point of departure for an attack on the exclusion of American settlers.[76] He made only intermittent efforts to disentangle subjects from one another: the fullest account of his father's affairs appears under the heading, "Explanation of the Map, Etc."[77] The *General Introduction* contains a supplementary index, because he went on writing after the first one had been compiled. A large part of that introductory volume, and for students of Gourlay the most valuable part, turned into a recapitulation of his earlier criticisms of the poor laws and his schemes to re-organize rural life in England. His complaints, his politics and his projects for social reform are well under control in the first volume of the *Account* itself; elsewhere, they run riot.

The work was part of his campaign for recognition. John Beverley Robinson, in London when it appeared, was happy to find it "the most absurd thing you ever saw," and to note that Gourlay's accusations of corruption were not based on the township reports themselves.[78] The account has been characterized as "a verbose and redundant three-volume tirade in which his original purposes were heavily overlaid by calls for political reform and still more by a consuming interest in self-justification."[79] Gourlay's own judgement of it was similar:

> That book was composed while I was in a fever and wholly distorted in its arrangements by grievous occurrences in its progress through the press. . . . The first volume was intended for separate publication, but the greatest misfortune of my life disabled me from sending it forth till it appeared a year afterwards with others, which at first was not contemplated and which were produced by a mere series of impulses. It was a most unfortunate publication.[80]

Nevertheless, the resulting compendium of information was without precedent and remained without rival in the history of Upper Canada. For the Niagara District, where he had the fullest response, its continued usefulness has been strikingly demonstrated.[81] For the province as a whole, it was a remarkable pioneering inquiry, quite beyond comparison with the competitors that the decade of the 1820's produced in some numbers. His exact contemporary James Cawdell, who was also diverted from settlement schemes to political criticism, wrote only a trivial *Memorial*.[82] More typical were the casual advice and unsystematic information of Charles Stuart's *The Emigrant's Guide to Upper Canada* (1820), William Watson's *Emigrant's Guide to the Canadas* (1822), or William Bell's *Hints to Emigrants* (1824). The shrewd and entertaining but snobbish and personal *Sketches of Upper Canada* by John Howison (1821) are easier reading than Gourlay, but they contain remarkably little solid information for any assessment of the province as a place to settle. Slighter still were Henry John Boulton's partisan *Short Sketch of Upper Canada* (1826); Charles Fothergill's ramshackle *Sketch of Upper Canada* (1822); or the half-humorous, half scatter-brained *Statistical Sketches of Upper Canada for the Use of Emigrants* published by Gourlay's champion in the legislature, William Dunlop, in 1832. Another radical Scot, John M'Taggart, was a better observer and a saner critic than Gourlay, as well as a longer resident in the province. So was E. A. Talbot; but neither of their books show any comparable appreciation of orderly statistical investigation.[83] The same comments apply to the *Statistical Account's* nearest counterparts for the other British North American provinces: Joseph Bouchette's on Lower Canada, Haliburton's on Nova Scotia and Peter Fisher's on New Brunswick.[84] Fisher intended a statistical account, but the New Brunswick Agricultural and Emigrant Society first took over the project and then neglected it.[85]

Gourlay's work was therefore unique; and unique in a double sense, for he did not undertake another statistical inquiry. In 1836 he proposed one for Ohio, but nothing came of it.[86] Nor did he receive encouragement for a proposal, made in 1845, to write another for the Province of Canada.[87] Incomplete and distorted though it is, the *Statistical Account* stands as his best memorial and his most important legacy.

This abridgement reduces the *Statistical Account* to about one-quarter of its original length. The *General Introduction* has been the most heavily cut of the three volumes, eliminating from it most of Gourlay's political apology. From the first volume of the *Account* itself, the township reports have been retained in full, with Gourlay's district summaries and statistical tables. Those "Sketches of Upper Canada" dealing with climate, wild life and other matters not closely related to Gourlay's interests have been omitted. The "Sketches" are not by Gourlay; he received them from Barnabas Bidwell of Kingston,[88] who had been unable to get them published and whose own work they no doubt are. The historical survey that occupies half the second volume of the *Account* has been omitted altogether. The review of Upper Canadian legislation has been cut, although its principal subjects are represented. Gourlay's narrative of his Upper Canadian agitation has been shortened, not severely. Throughout, most of the documents that Gourlay printed extensively have been left out and wherever possible repetitions have been excised. The temptation to re-arrange the *General Introduction* and the second volume of the *Account* into a series of coherent essays on Gourlay's favorite subjects has been resisted. The necessary re-shuffling of short extracts would have raised insoluble problems about preserving their context. It would in any case have totally misrepresented his mind and work. Two concessions to the reader's convenience have been made: Gourlay's introduction to the "Sketches" and the township reports has been moved so as to stand next to them; and the draft petition to the Prince Regent has been similarly moved from the first volume to end the second, immediately after the minutes of meetings that endorsed it. The table of contents gives the original page numbers of all extracts. The *Account* was published with sheets of errata; the text here reproduced has been corrected in accordance with them. One elision has been bridged by an explanation in square brackets; the others are marked by dots. It has not been possible to reproduce the original type faces, for which modern ones have been substituted. There are no changes in the spelling, capitalization or punctuation of the original text. The notes, unless they conclude [Ed.], are Gourlay's own.

S. R. MEALING
Ottawa, 1973

*Footnotes to the Introduction**

* References to the *Statistical Account*, passages included in the abridged text, occur in footnotes 4, 9, 10, 20, 21, 22, 25, 36, 42, 46, 47, 49, 52, 53, 54, 57, 71, 72, 74, 76.

1 Robert Gourlay, *The Banished Briton and Neptunian: being a Record of the Life, Writings, Principles and Projects of Robert Gourlay, Esquire* (Boston, 1843), No. 7, p. 68.

2 Ontario Archives, Gourlay Papers. Jean Gourlay to Mrs. Henderson, 5 December 1811.

3 *Debates of the Legislative Assembly of United Canada*, Vol. I: *1841*, edited by E. Nish (Montreal, 1970), p. 1004. Debate of 16 September 1841.

4 Toronto Public Library, W. D. Powell Papers. Powell to Gore, 18 January 1819; Robert Gourlay, *Statistical Account of Upper Canada* (London, 1822), II, 483*.

5 *The Banished Briton*, No. 5, pp. 50-6.

6 *Debates of the Legislative Assembly of United Canada*, I, 1003-4.

7 J. C. Dent, *The Story of the Upper Canadian Rebellion* (Toronto, 1885), I, 46-7, W. R. Riddell, "Robert (Fleming) Gourlay as Shown by his Own Records," Ontario Historical Society, *Papers and Records*, XIV (1916), 5.

8 L. D. Milani, "Robert Gourlay, Gadfly," *Ontario History*, LXIII (1971), 233-42.

9 *Statistical Account* I, 553; II, 483*, 516-17*.

10 *Ibid.*, I, 458*; II, XV-XVI, 564-66*, 573*.

11 G. W. Spragge (ed.), *The John Strachan Letter Book, 1812-34* (Toronto, 1946), p. 163. Strachan to Colonel Harvey, 22 June 1818.

12 Under his brother's name. James Strachan, *A Visit to the Province of Upper Canada in 1819* (Aberdeen, 1820), pp. 189-201.

13 *Niagara Spectator*, 29 July 1819. Letter of Bartimus Ferguson.

14 Gourlay's accounts of this incident are in *The Banished Briton*, No. 30, and in his *An Appeal to the Common Sense, Mind, and Manhood of the British Nation* (London, 1826). The whipping of Brougham is described at length in L. D. Milani, *Robert Gourlay, Gadfly* (Toronto, 1971), pp. 233-38.

15 Milani, p. 255.

16 Joseph Hume in the House of Commons, 12 March 1824. *Parliamentary Debates*, 2nd series, X, 9556.

17 A. Dunham, *Political Unrest in Upper Canada, 1815-36* (Carleton Library ed: Toronto, 1963), p. 51; G. M. Craig, *Upper Canada: The Formative Years, 1784-1841* (Toronto, 1963), p. 93.

18 *Statistical Account*, I, ccxxii.

19 Robert Gourlay, *Canada and the Corn Laws; or No Corn Laws, No Canada* (Edinburgh, 1852), p. 12.

20 Robert Gourlay, *General Introduction to the Statistical Account of Upper Canada* (London, 1822), p. xxxvi.*

21 *Ibid.*, p. cccxxxviii*.

22 *Ibid.*, p. ciii; and see *Statistical Account*, II, 306-7*.

[23] *General Introduction,* p. clxxix.

[24] *Ibid.*, p. ccclxxxiv; *Statistical Account,* II, 532.

[25] *General Introduction,* p. clxiv*

[26] *Ibid.*, p. ccxii; and see *Statistical Account,* I, ccxxii.

[27] *The Banished Briton,* No. 4, pp. 14-16, 48.

[28] *General Introduction,* p. cxxxvi.

[29] *Pace* S. D. Clark, *Movements of Political Protest in Canada 1640-1840* (Toronto, 1959), p. 431.

[30] Public Archives of Canada, Q322-1, 129-41. Gore to Bathurst, 9 April 1817.

[31] Public Archives of Canada, Q324-1, 22. Samuel Smith to Bathurst, 23 February 1818.

[32] H. V. Nelles, "Loyalism and Local Power: The District of Niagara, 1792-1837," *Ontario History,* LVIII (1966), 102.

[33] Public Archives of Canada, Upper Canada Sundries. Dickson to Cameron, 27 April 1817.

[34] E. Jackson, "The Organization of Upper Canadian Reformers, 1818-67," *Ontario History,* LIII (1961), 95-115.

[35] On 29 June 1818. Printed in E. A. Cruikshank, "The Government of Upper Canada and Robert Gourlay," Ontario Historical Society, *Papers and Records,* XXIII (1926), 152.

[36] *Statistical Account,* II, 576-77*.

[37] Robert Gourlay, *Chronicles of Canada: being a Record of Robert Gourlay, Esquire* (St. Catharines, 1842), p. 17.

[38] *The John Strachan Letter Book,* pp. 171, 182. Strachan to Colonel Harvey, 27 July and 8 December 1818. Ontario Historical Society, *Papers and Records,* XXIII (1926), 151. Robinson to Colonel Smith, 29 June 1818.

[39] Ontario Historical Society, *Papers and Records,* XIV (1916), 97. Maitland to Goulburn, 22 July 1822. And see F. M. Quealey, "The Administration of Sir Peregrine Maitland, Lieutenant-Governor of Upper Canada, 1818-1828" (Ms. Ph. D. thesis: University of Toronto, 1968), p. 183.

[40] Public Archives of Canada, Upper Canada Sundries. Memorandum by Powell, William Campbell and D'Arcy Boulton, 10 November 1818.

[41] Milani, p. 213.

[42] *Statistical Account,* II, 300*.

[43] Milani, p. 240.

[44] *The Banished Briton,* No. 13, p. 120.

[45] Robert Gourlay, *A Specific Plan for Organizing the People and for obtaining Reform Independent of Parliament – to The People of Fife – to The People of Britain* (London, 1809), p. 84.

[46] *General Introduction,* p. cxliii*.

[47] *Ibid.*, p. clx.*

[48] Robert Gourlay, *Plans for Beautifying New York, and for Enlarging and Improving the City of Boston* (Boston, 1844).

[49] *General Introduction,* p. cccxxxix.*

[50] Robert Gourlay, *Mr. Gourlay's Addresses, etc., to the Electors of Fife* (Cupar, 1847).

[51] L. F. Gates, *Land Policies of Upper Canada* (Toronto, 1968), p. 20.

[52] *General Introduction*, p. ccclxxxii*.

[53] *Ibid.*, pp. xviii, ccc, iv.

[54] *Statistical Account*, II, 392-93.*

[55] *The Banished Briton*, No. 2, p. 27. See also Wakefield's letter to Lord Howick, 8 January 1831; F. L. Pritchard (ed.), *The Collected Works of Edward Gibbon Wakefield* (Glasgow, 1968), p. 47; *ibid.*, pp. 14-16; R. C. Mills, *The Colonization of Australia, 1829-42: The Wakefield Experiment in Empire Building* (London, 1915), pp. 136-39; H. I. Cowan, *British Emigration to British North America: The First Hundred Years* (Toronto, rev. ed. 1961), p. 96; P. Bloomfield, *Edward Gibbon Wakefield* (London, 1961), p. 194.

[56] *The Banished Briton*, No. 4, p. 41.

[57] *General Introduction*, pp. v-vi*.

[58] *The Banished Briton*, No. 23, p. 268.

[59] *The Banished Briton*, No. 19, p. 208, John Small to Gourlay, 6 January 1818.

[60] *Appeal to the Common Sense of the British Nation*, p. 75; *The Banished Briton*, No. 19, p. 210.

[61] Ontario Archives, Gourlay Papers, Prospectus for *The Commonwealth and Canadian Farmer's Joint Stock Press*, 1842. See also *Chronicles of Canada*, p. 29. For *The United Labourer*, projected in Fife in 1828, see *The Banished Briton*, No. 23, p. 276.

[62] K. Kelly, "The Transfer of British Ideas on Improved Farming to Ontario during the First Half of the Nineteenth Century," *Ontario History*, LXIII (1971), 103-11.

[63] See L. R. Betcherman, "William von Moll Berczy," *Ontario History*, LIV (1962), 57-68.

[64] E. Halévy, *The Growth of Philosophic Radicalism*, translated by M. Morris (London, 1928), pp. 107-8.

[65] A. Young, *Tour through the Southern Counties of England and Wales*, (London, 1768), *Six Months' Tour through the North of England* (4 vols., London, 1770), *Travels in France* (2 vols., Bury St. Edmunds, 1792), and above all the forty-six volumes of *Annals of Agriculture* (1784-1815); G. Chalmers, *Estimate of the Comparative Strength of Great Britain* (London, 1794); Bryan Edwards, *History, Civil and Commercial, of the British Colonies in the West Indies* (London, 1793); J. Phillips, *Treatise on Inland Navigation* (London, 1785) and *History of Inland Navigation* (London, 1792); C. Jenkinson, *Treatise of the Coinage of the Realm* (London, 1805); P. Colquhoun, *Treatise on the Police of the Metropolis* (London, 1795); W. Marshall, *The Landed Property of England* (London, 1804).

[66] J. E. D. Binney, *British Public Finance and Administration, 1774-92* (Oxford, 1958), pp. 7-15.

[67] See O. Williams, *Life and Letters of John Rickman* (London, 1908).

[68] James Donaldson's *Husbandry Anatomized*. J. E. Handley, *Scottish Farming in the Eighteenth Century* (London, 1953), p. 116.

[69] F. F. Darling (ed.), *West Highland Survey: An Essay in Human Ecology* (London, 1955), p. 72.

[70] Milani, p. 75.

[71] *Statistical Account*, I, 507-19*.

[72] *General Introduction*, p. clxxxvii*.

[73] For extensive bibliographies, see G. M. Craig (ed.), *Early Travellers in the Canadas* (Toronto, 1955), pp. 287-97, and N. Story, *The Oxford Companion to Canadian History and Literature* (Toronto, 1967), pp. 606-9. Of the books published before 1820, one may reckon only seven as worth notice. The travellers were the Duke de Larochefoucauld (1799), the American J. C. Ogden (1799), and the British visitors Patrick Campbell (1793) and Isaac Weld (1799). Of the two surveys by officials, D. W. Smith's in 1799 was a careful work, while D'Arcy Boulton's in 1805 was much slighter. A number of diaries and private letters were far more informative about life in the province, but none had yet been published.

[74] *Statistical Account*, I, 273*.

[75] *General Introduction*, p. ccxxxiv.

[76] *Statistical Account*, II, 416ff*.

[77] *Ibid.*, II, v-xiii.

[78] Public Archives of Canada, Upper Canada Sundries. Robinson to Major Hillier, 10 April 1822.

[79] G. Bloch, "The Visions of Robert Gourlay" (Ms. M.A. thesis: Carleton University, 1973), p. 30.

[80] Gourlay to Joseph Hume, 1 April 1823. Quoted in W. R. Riddell, "Robert (Fleming) Gourlay," Ontario Historical Society, *Papers and Records*, XIV (1916), 72-3.

[81] R. L. Gentilcore, "The Niagara District of Robert Gourlay," *Ontario History*, LIV (1962), 229-36.

[82] A. Shortt, "The Memorial of J. M. Cawdell," *Canadian Historical Review*, I (1920), 289-301.

[83] John M'Taggart, *Three Years in Canada: an Account of the Actual State of the Country in 1826-7-8* (2 vols., London, 1829); E. A. Talbot, *Five Years' Residence in the Canadas: Including a Tour through Part of the United States of America in the year 1823* (2 vols., London, 1824).

[84] Joseph Bouchette, *Topographical Description of the Province of Lower Canada* (London, 1815); Thomas Chandler Haliburton, *Historical and Statistical Account of Nova Scotia* (2 vols., Halifax, 1829); Peter Fisher, *Sketches of New Brunswick* (Saint John, 1825).

[85] K. N. Windsor, "Historical Writing in Canada to 1920," in C. F. Klinck (ed.), *Literary History of Canada* (Toronto, 1965), p. 210.

[86] Robert Gourlay, *Proposals for Drawing up and Publishing a Statistical Account of Ohio; under the direction of its legislature* (Cleveland, 1836).

[87] Milani, p. 260.

[88] The father of the better-known reform politician, Marshall Spring Bidwell. Barnabas Bidwell was to provoke the "alien question" in 1821, when he was elected to the Assembly but unseated as an American citizen. He had come to Upper Canada in 1810 after being accused of misusing public funds as attorney-general of Massachusetts. The only literary work that he acknowledged the authorship of was a tragedy, *The Mercenary Match*, written when he was a student at Yale. He is also reputed to have written a number of essays on civic duties which appeared in the *Upper Canada Herald* and were published anonymously as *The Prompter* (Kingston, 1821).

Suggestions for Further Reading

W. R. Riddell, "Robert (Fleming) Gourlay, as Shown by His Own Records," Ontario Historical Society, *Papers and Records,* XIV (1916), 5-133, is still the most painstakingly documented account of Gourlay's experiences in Upper Canada, although not the most readable. E. A. Cruikshank, "The Government of Upper Canada and Robert Gourlay", *ibid.*, XXIII (1926), 65-179, remains helpful chiefly for the documents that it prints. William Smith's essay in his *Political Leaders of Upper Canada* (Toronto, 1931), which also appeared in *Queen's Quarterly*, XXXIV (1926), 149-68, is comparatively sketchy but more evaluative. The two most balanced and readable short accounts are Aileen Dunham, *Political Unrest in Upper Canada, 1815-1836* (Carleton Library No. 10: Toronto, 1963), pp. 51-60, and G. M. Craig, *Upper Canada: The Formative Years, 1784-1841* (Canadian Centenary Series: Toronto, 1963), pp. 93-100. S. D. Clark, *Movements of Political Protest in Canada, 1640-1840* (Toronto, 1959), pp. 331-48, 464-68, makes higher claims for the importance of Gourlay's political agitation. So does E. Jackson, "The Organization of Upper Canadian Reformers, 1818-67," *Ontario History*, LIII (1961), 95-115. There is no recent study of Gourlay's popular influence to compare with E. A. Cruikshank, "Post-War Discontent at Niagara in 1818", Ontario Historical Society, *Papers and Records*, XXIX(1933), 14-46. No published work pays as much attention to Gourlay's emphasis on social and economic reform as to his politics. The story of his whole life has been told in a thorough and sympathetic biography, Lois D. Milani's *Robert Gourlay, Gadfly* (Toronto, 1971). For an example of the use that can be made of the *Statistical Account*, see R. L. Gentilcore, "The Niagara District of Robert Gourlay," *Ontario History*, LIV (1962), 229-36.

General Introduction.

Statement.

To The Editors of British News-Papers.

GENTLEMEN,

Craigrothie, Fifeshire, Jan. 3, 1820.

I LANDED at Liverpool, from Quebec, the 2d December, and have since learned, that, during the last two years, my name has frequently appeared in your columns, connected with certain political movements in Upper Canada. By consulting the files of various newspapers, I have discovered that very great mistakes have prevailed as to Canadian affairs, and that calumnies, both false and malignant, have been propagated with regard to me.

As a specimen of these, it has been published that I was "One of the worthies who escaped from Spa-fields;" and attempts have been made to impress a belief on the public mind, that my operations in Canada were connected with the schemes of Messrs. Cobbett and Hunt in England. The very contrary of all this is true.

In consequence of unavoidable change of fortune, I went out to Upper Canada, where I had many friends, in the summer of 1817, solely with a view to ascertain whether it would be prudent to remove my family thither. My intention of going there was announced more than a year before I set out, and my wish was not to be more than six months from home.

Though a sincere friend to parliamentary reform in this country, I had repeatedly published, before going abroad, my opinion of the impropriety of holding large irregular meetings for that purpose, and particularly reprobated those of Spa-fields. No man can shew that I was ever connected in politics with a single individual in Britain; and it must be well remembered in Wiltshire, that I stood forward in opposition to Messrs. Cobbett and Hunt, at the county meeting held there in 1816, when their object was to run down the property-tax. So very decided and serious was I on that occasion, that I caused to be stuck up in every corner of the county a placard, declaring, that, *"by a well modified property-tax, and by that alone, could the country be preserved in peace."*

In Upper Canada my efforts had no view whatever to a

reform of parliament. The people there have a perfect representation, and before long they will make a better use of it than they have hitherto done. Soon after my arrival in that country, I viewed it as the most desirable place of refuge for the redundant population of Britain, and I conceived schemes for promoting a grand system of emigration. Nothing could be more palpably innocent than my first proposals, yet they were opposed, and from reflections springing out of the nature of this opposition, I became convinced, that without parliamentary inquiry into the state of the Province, every effort towards liberal improvement would be futile and vain. I prolonged my stay till the meeting of the Provincial parliament, that I might press a reference of certain matters to the Prince and Parliament at home. A vote of inquiry was carried in the Commons House of Assembly; but immediately afterwards a dispute having arisen between that body and the Legislative Council, the parliament was suddenly prorogued, its business unfinished.

At this juncture, and without the slightest idea of evil, I advised the people to raise a subscription, and send home Commissioners to intreat attention from the Throne to the affairs of the Province. It was necessary to hold a meeting of Deputies for the purpose in view, and to this meeting I inadvertently gave the name of *Convention*, a name in every-day use over America, and applied to all sorts of meetings, both civil and sacred. On this occasion, it proved to be –

    _____"A word of fear,
Unpleasant to the guilty ear."

The Executive of Upper Canada took alarm. In some districts, where the people had little information from newspapers, the most outrageous opposition was set on foot by creatures in office; and, to cause a general panic, I was twice arrested, and held to bail for appearance to answer charges of seditious libel.

Notwithstanding all this, respectable Deputies were chosen throughout the greater part of the Province, and they met openly in Convention at York, the capital. By this time, the Duke of Richmond and his son-in-law had been announced as Governor and Lieutenant-Governor of the Canadas. I conceived favourable impressions of their liberality, and judging that the agitation excited, could not fail to impress serious notions of the importance of *inquiry*, advised the Convention to refer its cause to the Lieutenant-Governor and General Assembly. After this, I stood two *trials*, and was twice honourably acquitted. The people were now sanguine that all would go well, when, to their astonishment, the Lieutenant-Governor having met the parliament, hinted that sedition existed, and procured a law to prevent, in future, meetings by deputy. The discontent created by these measures, libelling the most loyal men, and without any proof of necessity circumscribing general liberty, was universal; yet, nothing more was resolved on by the people, but to clear the House of Assembly, at next election, of members who had balked their expectations. To me, who indulged the anxious hope of being allowed to develop my views, and point out a practicable plan, by which many thousands of the idle poor of England could be annually transported into Canada, with profit to the nation, and comfort to themselves, the disappointment was cruelly provoking; but it was far from rendering me hopeless of ultimate success. I had resolved to establish myself in the Province as a land-agent, &c. and was now treating for a house in which to commence business, when, lo! I was arrested by the Sheriff, carried before a party of my most virulent political enemies, and served with an order to quit the Province, merely because a wretch was found base enough to swear that I was a seditious person.

To have obeyed this order would have proved ruinous to the business, for which, at great expense, and with much trouble, I had qualified myself: it would have been a tacit acknowledgment of guilt, whereof I was unconscious; it would have been a surrender of the noblest British right: it would have been holding light my natural allegiance: it would have been a declaration that the Bill of Rights was a Bill of Wrongs. I resolved to endure any hardship rather than to submit voluntarily. Although I had written home that I meant to leave Canada for England in a few weeks, I now acquainted my family of the cruel delay, and stood my ground, till I was a second time arrested, and forthwith committed to remain in jail for eight months, without bail or mainprize.

The impressions made on the public by this strange proceeding were such, that it was intimated from various quarters, that if I chose, the jail should be pulled down for my relief, a step which, of course, I opposed.

My enemies, now feeling that they had gone too far, laboured, by artful addresses to the Lieutenant-Governor, to impress an opinion upon the public mind that some of my writings were seditious; but this conduct only exposed to fuller view the malevolence by which they were actuated. All hope of convicting me of crime seemed to die away, and after three months confinement, it was whispered that I should not be tried for sedition, but, simply, for not having obeyed the order to quit the Province. This I could not believe possible. In the mean time, I instituted a suit for false imprisonment, and wrote off to various quarters for legal advice. From Montreal – From Edinburgh – from London, the replies of most respectable lawyers were uniform, that my imprisonment was illegal; and the late Sir Arthur Piggott declared, that not only should the Chief Justice of Upper Canada have granted my liberty, applied for by writ of *Habeas Corpus*, but that a good action lay against the magistrates who had imprisoned me.

Among the matters which the Convention had in view was one, to call the Royal attention to a promise held out to the Militia during war, that grants of land should be made to them in recompense for their extraordinary exertions. It had been the policy of the United States to hold out offers of land to their troops who invaded Canada, – offers, without which they could not have raised an army for that purpose, and these offers had been punctually and liberally fulfilled, the moment that peace was restored. On the British side, three years had passed away without attention to a promise which the Canadian militia kept in mind, not only as it concerned their interest, but their honour. While the Convention trusted the consideration of inquiry to the Lieutenant-Governor and Assembly, they ordered an address to be sent home to his Royal Highness the Prince Regent, as a matter of courtesy and respect, having annexed to it the rough sketch of an address originally intended to be borne home by a commission, in which sketch the neglect of giving land to the Militia was, among other matters, pointed out. This sketch, too, having been printed in America, found its way into British newspapers.

In June, 1819, the Lieutenant-Governor of Upper Canada, summoned the Assembly to meet a second time, and in his speech, notified that he had received an order form his Royal Highness the Prince Regent, to grant land to the Militia, but that he himself should think it proper to withhold such grant from those persons who had been members of Convention. The injustice of this measure was instantly in the mouth of every one, and the very Sheriff who held me in charge scrupled not to signify how it would go, should the province again be invaded, while at that very moment it was thought by many that a war with the United States would grow out of the affair of Ambristier.

The members of Convention had met at York, prior to any law to prevent the meeting of delegates: they had met in compliance with the desire of many thousands of their fellow-subjects, and were wholly unconscious of evil: they were men of tried loyalty: they had held militia commissions during the war: some had been wounded, some had been taken prisoners, and all had behaved well. Most of them owned more land than they could dispose of, and any gift of land could be to them, a mere pledge of approbation for duty performed to their sovereign and country. Several weeks passed away, while it was anxiously hoped that the Assembly would mark its disapprobation of the opening speech; but approval was at last carried by the speaker's vote, and the Legislative Council concurred in language the most direct and submissive.

To me, such conduct seemed subversive of every hope that Upper Canada could be retained to Britain in the event of war, and to startle those who so thoughtlessly put it in jeopardy into a consideration of consequences, I seized my pen, and called on God to assist my endeavours. My writing, when published, was voted by the Assembly to be libel, and the Lieutenant-Governor was solicited to order prosecutions. The editor of the newspaper, who had had the assurance of a magistrate, that he should not be molested while he had the manuscripts of authors to produce, and who was on this occasion wholly ignorant of what was printed in his office, being 150 miles from home, was seized in his bed during the middle of the night, hurried to Niagara jail, and thence, next morning, to that of York, where he was detained many days out of the reach of friends to bail him. After this he was led round the country nearly a hundred miles, exposed to view as a malefactor of the worst kind, all clearly for the purpose of working unfavourable impressions against him; and, to be sure, he was finally convicted on a charge, which, from its nature, the author alone was competent to repel.

My treatment was still more wantonly cruel. After two months close confinement in one of the cells of the jail, my health had begun to suffer, and, on complaint of this, the liberty of walking through the passages and sitting at the door was granted. This liberty prevented my getting worse the four succeeding months, although I never enjoyed a day's health, but by the power of medicine. At the end of this period, I was again locked up in the cell, cut off from all conversation with my friends, but through a hole in the door, while the jailor or under sheriff watched what was said, and for some time both my attorney and magistrates of my acquaintance were denied admission to me. The quarter sessions were held soon after this severe and unconstitutional treatment commenced, and, on these occasions, it was the custom and duty of the grand jury to perambulate the jail, and see that all was right with the prisoners. I prepared a memorial for their consideration, but, on this occasion, was not visited. I complained to a magistrate through the door, who promised to mention my case to the chairman of the session; but the chairman happened to be brother of one of those who had signed my commitment, and the court broke up without my obtaining the smallest relief.

Exasperation of mind now joined to the heat of the weather, which was excessive, rapidly wasted my health and impaired my faculties. I felt my memory sensibly affected, and could not connect my ideas through any length of reasoning, but by writing, which many days I was wholly unfitted for by the violence of continual head-ache. Immmediately before the sitting of the assizes, the weather became cool, so that I was able to apply constantly for three days, and finish a written defence, on every point likely to be questioned on the score of seditious libel. I also prepared a formal protest against any verdict which might pass against me, as subject to the statute, under colour of which I was confined.

It was again reported, that I should be tried only as to the fact of refusing to leave the province. A state of nervous irritability, of which I was not then sufficiently aware, deprived my mind of the power of reflection on the subject: I was seized with a fit of convulsive laughter, resolved not to defend such a suit, and was perhaps rejoiced that I might be even thus set at liberty from my horrible situation. On being called up for trial, the action of the fresh air, after six weeks close confinement, produced the effect of intoxication. I had no control over my conduct, no sense of consequence, nor little other feeling but of ridicule and disgust for the court which countenanced such a trial. At one moment I had a desire to protest against the whole proceeding; but, forgetting that I had a written protest in my pocket, I struggled in vain to call to mind the word *protest*, and in another moment the whole train of ideas which led to the wish had vanished from my mind. When the verdict was returned, that I was guilty of having refused to leave the province, I had forgot for what I was tried, and affronted a juryman by asking if it was for sedition.

Gentlemen, these are melancholy particulars, and so far as they concern myself only, I certainly should be inclined to conceal them. As they concern the legislation and spirit of governing in a British province, I have thought it my duty to offer the consideration of them to the public, prior to submitting the same to the Prince and Parliament of this country, for which purpose I more especially came home. It is my wish to return to Upper Canada, and to stand any fair trial for alleged crime: it is my wish to promote the settlement of that province with British subjects; but what British subject of spirit would settle in a country, where, in a moment, he may have to bow to arbitrary power, or be turned adrift into a foreign land, the sport of calumny, injured in health, and ruined in the fair expectation of doing well for his family?

... I shall ask the public to consider whether there is not reason for INSTANT PARLIAMENTARY INQUIRY, and if such inquiry is instituted, I PLEDGE MYSELF TO SHEW THAT UPPER CANADA; INSTEAD OF COSTING THIS COUNTRY A LARGE SUM OF MONEY TO MAINTAIN IT; COULD YIELD ANNUALLY A HANDSOME REVENUE TO THE BRITISH GOVERNMENT: THAT INSTEAD OF REMAINING THE POOREST, IT MAY SPEEDILY BECOME THE RICHEST PART OF NORTH AMERICA: THAT IT MAY THIS VERY YEAR GIVE EMPLOYMENT AND BREAD TO 50,000 OF THE POOR INHABITANTS OF BRITAIN; AND, FOR MANY YEARS TO COME, AFFORD ANNUALLY A SIMILAR DRAIN FOR REDUNDANT POPULATION: LASTLY, THAT IT MAY BE MADE A PERMANENT AND SECURE BULWARK TO THE BRITISH EMPIRE, INSTEAD OF BEING A LURE TO ITS INVASION AND DOWNFALL.

These, Gentlemen, are bold assertions: but they are not only bold, they are rational and sincere; and they proceed from a mind which has been devoted for two years to reflections on the subject – a mind which has sustained itself under every reasonable trial, and which has not yet entirely sunk beneath the most odious persecution.

ROBERT GOURLAY.

Sketch of a Petition

To the Honourable the Commons of the United Kingdom of Great Britain and Ireland, IN PARLIAMENT ASSEMBLED*.

The Petition of Robert Gourlay.

Humbly Sheweth,

That your Petitioner is a native of the parish of Ceres, (and) IN THE county of Fife (North Britain), IN SCOTLAND, and thence conceives himself entitled to all the constitutional privileges of a British subject.

That your Petitioner was born to the inheritance of considerable landed estates, and did entertain, till the year 1815, fair hopes of independent fortune: – that then, in the 38th year of his

---

* The words printed in capitals were added, those in small type, and enclosed in a circumflex, were omitted in the real petition.

age, being married, and having five children, he found himself, by causes which he could neither foresee nor prevent, sunk into a state of precarious dependence: – that, after more than a year's reflection, he resolved to visit Upper Canada, where he had some landed property and many friends, to ascertain whether he might not, with propriety, remove his family thither:—that, after a few months residence in that country, he (became enamoured of) WAS PLEASED WITH the natural excellence of its soil and climate, – saw prospects of providing comfortably for his family, and cherished schemes for rendering Upper Canada a comfortable refuge for the redundant population of England: – that, to qualify himself the better to represent at home the true state of the province, he resolved to prolong his stay, and by extended inquiry did greatly increase his knowledge of the actual state of its affairs.

That he then discovered political restraints on the prosperity of Upper Canada, which rendered it altogether inferior to the United States as a place of settlement, and such mismanagement on the part of the executive GOVERNMENT with regard to emigrants from Britain, as blasted every hope, unless (great) CONSIDERABLE changes could be effected.

That his first intention, after being fully apprized of these restraints and this mismanagement, was to proceed home and state the truth to the ministers of this country; but, doubtful of his individual representation being listened to, he recommended the inhabitants to petition their parliament for inquiry into the state of the province, and for a commission to go home with the result to the Prince and Parliament of Britain: – that this measure was actually moved and carried in the Assembly, but a quarrel presently afterwards arising between the different branches of the legislature, parliament was hastily prorogued.

That, on this juncture, your Petitioner being more and more convinced of the great necessity of examination, addressed the inhabitants of the province, and recommended them to raise a fund by subscription, for the purpose of sending home a petition to his Royal Highness the Prince Regent, to solicit the appointment of a commission from England for that purpose.

That this proposal giving great offence to certain persons in office, called down this resentment upon your Petitioner, whom they caused to be twice arrested, and tried upon charges of seditious libel.

That your Petitioner, being twice honourably acquitted, had then the fullest hope of succeeding in his purpose, by offering to lay before the Lieutenant-Governor, just arrived from England, his view of what was essential to the prosperity of the province, when, to his astonishment, a party in power not only succeeded in exciting prejudices in the mind of the Lieutenant-Governor against your Petitioner, but wantonly libelled a great portion of the inhabitants, and had a law enacted, abridging public liberty, equally uncalled for, and odious to the great body of the people.

That your Petitioner was after this on the point of setting off for England when a conspiracy was formed between three of his most notorious political enemies to ruin his character, and prevent his ever returning to Upper Canada. For this purpose they pretended that your Petitioner was subject to a provincial statute, [A COPY OF WHICH IS HEREUNTO ANNEXED,] which can only apply to aliens and outlaws, and one of them scrupling not to perjure himself to afford grounds for procedure, they presented him with an order to quit the province, upon his disobeying which they had him arrested and committed to jail, [THE ORDER BEING HEREUNTO ANNEXED.]

That your Petitioner, being thus situated, applied for liberation by writ of HABEAS CORPUS [THE WHOLE PROCESS BEING HEREUNTO ANNEXED]; but, being remanded to jail by the Chief Justice of the province, was detained there for nearly eight months.

That your Petitioner in this melancholy predicament, had still the hope of clearing his character from the base imputations of his enemies by a fair submission of their charges to the sense and feeling of a jury; and in the mean time having taken the advice of Sir Arthur Piggott, and other lawyers of eminence, as to the legality of his imprisonment, had their decided opinions that it was not legal – that the Chief Justice of Upper Canada was wrong in not having granted liberation, and that those who had caused the arrest, were subject to an action of damages for false imprisonment.

That, nevertheless, the hopes of your Petitioner were completely blasted. Before the day of trial, his body and mind were so weakened by confinement and exasperation from cruel, unnecessary, and unconstitutional treatment in jail, that, on being brought into the fresh air of the court, his whole ideas ran into confusion, and he lost all control over his conduct. A trial was brought on, not for any crime, but merely to determine the fact, that your Petitioner had refused to leave the province. To such a trial, under ordinary circumstances, your Petitioner would, undoubtedly, have demurred. As it happened, he, altogether insensible of consequences, suffered the trial to proceed till a sentence of banishment was pronounced against him by the same judge who detained him in prison.

(Your Petitioner desires to make no appeal to feeling on this occasion: neither is there any need for investigation into conduct. He desires that no consideration may rest on the palpable and vile pretence that your Petitioner had not been an inhabitant of Upper Canada for six months, when it was notorious, that he had resided there for more than double that period; or, that he had not taken the oath of allegiance, while at any moment of time he would willingly have gone through that ceremony, had he considered it essential to constitutional protection. Your Petitioner appeals to your Honourable House solely on the abstract question of right, inherent in a native born Briton, to that protection within his Majesty's dominions, which the British people bargained for in the claim of Rights, prior to the accession of the present family to the throne.

Your Honourable House, in conjunction with the other branches of the Legislature, passed an Act, in the year 1791, empowering his Majesty by and with the consent of a Legislative Council and Assembly to make laws for the government of Upper Canada, "during the continuance of this Act;" but your Petitioner has no belief that it was the intention of this *temporary* Act to confer a power on the Canadian Parliament of expatriating British subjects or, in any way to encroach on the fundamental principles of the British Constitution.

Your Petitioner begs leave to refer your Honourable House to the Act of the Canadian Parliament, under colour of which he was imprisoned and banished. Your Honourable House, by perusal of this Act, will see that its application to an untainted British subject is by mere implication, and he trusts your Honourable House will determine, that constitutional right is not to be overturned by such a breath. – Your Honourable House will see that to make this Act applicable to an untainted British subject, not only must the sacred bond of natural allegiance, with all its mutual obligations between the sovereign and subject, be considered null and void, in Upper Canada, but, that a mere inference must determine as to the ceremony of taking the oath of allegiance within the province. Your Honourable House will see that even a *reductio ad absurdum* flies in the face of such construction, for, were this act really applicable to British subjects, no individual could, with safety, proceed from the mother country to the colony: that even a newly appointed governor might be arrested and disgraced the moment he set his foot in Upper Canada, or a whole army of British soldiers, destined for its defence, be legally captured and imprisoned by a few perjured and unblushing villains.

Your Petitioner trusts that your Honourable House will not only mark such monstrous absurdity, and set aside all question as to ridiculous inference trenching on the boast and birthright of Britons, but loudly declare, that, though, by express terms, an untainted British subject had been made liable to this Act, yet that no such Act could be held as constitutional and valid any more than a Provincial Act, to make sale of Upper Canada to a foreign power. Your Petitioner, therefore, intreats that your Honourable House will take this subject into serious consideration; and shall ever pray.)*

---

* The above, printed in small type, stood in the original CIRCULAR as the continuation and conclusion of the first sketch Petition. A second draught was made out with additions; and what was struck out

Your Petitioner has recounted these facts and circumstances, not from any desire that your Honourable House should interfere in matters of judicial process, or correct the rigour of executive tyranny towards an individual. Your Petitioner is now in the course of applying to his Majesty in council, to take into consideration his particular case, – to consult the law officers of the crown thereupon, – to make inquiry into the cruel treatment he received, and into the fact of his being in that state which rendered him unfit to stand up in a court of justice as his own advocate, so that he may again be suffered to return to Upper Canada, there to support, fairly and manfully, his character, his principles, and opinions: – Your Petitioner comes before your Honourable House on public grounds alone, and pleads that the mere abstract consideration of the annexed provincial statute, taking it as intended to apply to unattainted British subjects, and as it has in your Petitioner's case been applied, affords sufficient cause for inquiry on the part of your Honourable House into the state of Upper Canada.

Your Honourable House, in conjunction with the other branches of the legislature, passed an Act, in the year 1791, empowering his Majesty, by and with the consent of a legislative council and assembly, to make laws for the government of Upper Canada, during the continuance of this Act; but your Petitioner has no belief that it was the intention of this temporary act, to confer a power on the Canadian Parliament, of expatriating British subjects, or, in any way to encroach on the fundamental principles of the British constitution. It was the clear intention of that act to convey to the people of Upper Canada, as near as circumstances would permit, the constitution of Britain both in form and spirit. The recorded debates of Parliament, on passing the Quebec Bill, bear ample testimony of this; and General Simcoe, when he opened the first Parliament of Upper Canada, in his capacity of Lieutenant-Governor of that province, expressly declared, that *the constitution then granted, was the very image and transcript of the British constitution.*

(Let it be supposed for a moment that a Bill was brought into your Honourable House, to enact a law by which on mere allegation any subject of his Majesty might be deprived of his right of *habeas corpus*, imprisoned, and ultimately banished from his native country, without a tinge of crime, what would be said? or, were it really enacted, what might not be done? Surely there would be an end to the constitution, and the

of that draught, is printed in small type, so that the real Petition presented by Sir James Mackintosh to the House of Commons 12th July, 1820, reads from beginning to end in large type.

social compact might be broken up. But if the Imperial Parliament could not go so far: – if by such an attempt the mass of the people would be entitled to interfere, and reorganize the constitution, there can be no doubt that a subordinate legislature could not do so; or, if doing so, ought immediately to be checked by the superior power.

Your Petitioner is aware that in some parts of his Majesty's dominions very arbitrary measures are resorted to by the executive, in thrusting out even British subjects without even alleged or convicted crime; but these dominions have no free and settled constitution, and they are held for very different purposes than the Canadian provinces. They have been dedicated to special purposes – to the use and benefit of trading companies, and to the ensuring of monopolies deemed necessary for increasing the store of national wealth. In these dominions the power permitted and used may be compared to that which individuals possess of excluding others from their dwelling-houses and workshops; but in his Majesty's Canadian dominions, neither necessity nor policy demand such licence; nay, it is the very reverse; there, population is the stable of the land: the settlement of British subjects, there, constitutes the strength and value of dominion, and their free ingress and egress must alone insure to his Majesty the sovereignty of that quarter of the world.)

At the present moment, when emigration from this country is at all hands allowed to be essential to relieve distress, how mischievous must be even the report that a native born British subject may be arrested, detained long in prison, and banished from Upper Canada without the shadow of crime, the moment he sets foot on its soil; surely your Honourable House will see the propriety of counteracting the effect of such report, to which the undue triumph of erring power, over an individual, has given credit and strength.

(Surely, for the public good, your Honourable House may declare by resolution and address, that British emigrants are not subject to the provincial statute in question; – that it can affect only aliens and outlaws; and, in its tenor regards local, not natural allegiance. Such declared construction of the statute would free the provincial legislature from the reproach of having encroached on constitutional principle, and give confidence to people of this country, who are contemplating a removal to the province of Upper Canada, of all His Majesty's foreign possessions the most capable of receiving an increase of inhabitants with comfort to the individuals, and advantage to the nation. Your Petitioner further pleads that there is urgent cause for inquiry into the state of Upper Canada, on other grounds than those above set forth.)

The Chancellor of the Exchequer has this session told your Honourable House, that, "the North American Provinces of Great Britain had been so overloaded with emigrants, that the government of Canada had made the strongest remonstrances to this government on the subject." Your Petitioner, residing and travelling in Upper Canada for two years, had sufficient opportunities of observing how the country came to be *overloaded* with emigrants, and how many of the emigrants suffered misery. It arose from mismanagement, want of contrivance, and, perhaps, want of knowledge on the part of those who had the direction of affairs. Your Petitioner states this freely and firmly, as he feels it his duty to do; and he is willing, at the bar of your Honourable House, or elsewhere, to set forth practicable plans, by which ten times the number of people who have ever, in one year, emigrated to Canada, may be annually transported thither, and comfortably settled.

Your Petitioner therefore humbly entreats that the state of Upper Canada, as it concerns emigration, may be taken into the serious consideration of your Honourable House.

And, as in duty bound, will ever pray,

ROBERT GOURLAY.

.... I shall now proceed to develop the principal design of this work, and must entreat the reader's indulgence, while I recount some circumstances of my own history, which led to the conception of it.

Through life, I have been enthusiastic in my pursuits; and for the last twenty years my mind has had a leading regard to the greatest evil which overshadows the fate of England – the system of the poor laws. When a young man, having time and money at command, I travelled over England for fifteen months together as an agriculturist, and during that time became acquainted with the late secretary to the Board of Agriculture, Mr. Arthur Young. One day, in conversation with him, we hit upon a subject to which each of us had devoted peculiar attention. My father, and indeed my grandfather, had been in the habit of letting out small portions of land on a kind of perpetual lease, called in Scotland a *feu*, to labouring people, whereon each man might build a dwelling-house, and enjoy the convenience of a garden. I had marked the wonderful influence which the possession of such a little property had upon the characters of the people, giving them a superior degree of consideration among their neighbours, more steady habits, and more persevering industry. I had noticed with what serene delight a labourer, especially of the sedentary class, would occupy himself in his garden at hours not devoted to his trade, and I had calculated what an addition, as well to individual as to national wealth and happiness, such economical arrangements, generally adopted, might produce. Speaking of this to Mr. Young, he mentioned to me a scheme he had in view, to provide the people at large with a little land, and descanted on the great advantages which the poor in some parts of England derived from the occupation of such a portion as enabled them to keep cows. A general inclosure bill was then in contemplation, and Mr. Young was anxious to have his views so far realized, by introducing into the bill a clause by which a portion of land sufficient to keep a cow should be secured to each man in lieu of his ancient common right of pasturage, &c. To establish the fact that labourers really derived benefit from keeping cows, and that those who had the benefit, required little or no assistance from parish funds, he asked me to make a journey into the counties of Rutland and Lincoln, where the practice prevailed of letting the poor have land and cows. I went, but after a little inquiry and reflection, being ashamed of plodding about merely to prove a truism, retraced my steps, and expressed a desire to relinquish the undertaking. Mr. Young, however, was now more keen than ever that I should complete his design. Nothing else, he said, was wanted to make good his point but the authority of names, and certain simple facts well authenticated. I complied, and spent two months much to my own satisfaction, having access, by a general introduction, to all, from the pauper to the peer; but obtained nothing for the Board of Agriculture which could do me credit, or strengthen any hope of success for the grand and benevolent purpose of the secretary.

As to the claim of poor people to a suitable portion of land, or other equivalent on the inclosure of a common, whereon they or their fathers had enjoyed rights of pasturage, &c. time out of mind, it was positive and clear, independent of any special benefit which they derived from these; and to have passed a general inclosure bill without a provision in lieu of such ancient rights, would have been a dangerous experiment.

With respect to the introduction generally through the kingdom of Mr. Young's scheme, there were obstacles which I was assured would never be overcome by the nerveless faculties of the Board of Agriculture, even though the scheme were of itself unobjectionable, which it was not.

Although I collected for Mr. Young abundant evidence to substantiate his simple position, and so arranged it, as, at one glance, to exhibit satisfactory results, my anticipations of what would be done were too truly verified. The general inclosure bill was indeed brought before parliament by Lord Carrington, the president, but this bill speedily went down to rise no more; and perhaps the dread of bringing into public discussion any question as to the common rights of the poor had no small weight in sinking it. Since that period the process of inclosure has gone on by bills for individual parishes and commons. Year after year, multitudes of these have been inclosed, without regard to the claims and complaints of the poor, who have been robbed of their rights, and who, from various causes, have been sinking gradually into a state of abject dependence on parish aid, deprived of property, and finally careless of its enjoyment. Year after year, and at this place and that, the poor, seeing themselves unjustly deprived of advantages which they had inherited from time immemorial, grumbled, rioted, and were put down. The process stealing gradually on, the strength of the mass was subdued piece-meal; and, finally, a change was effected, in the condition of English labourers, through a variety and succession of causes, but little reflected on or noticed by political economists and writers on the poor laws.

While I despaired of seeing any thing effectual accomplished by the Board of Agriculture, and was justified in my opinion by results, impressions as to the necessity of changing somehow the system of the poor laws became more and more riveted in my mind. My experience in Lincolnshire and Rutland – my conversations with the poor themselves – with the farmers and land-owners every where throughout England: my inspection of parish records; and observations made on the habits and manners of the people, altogether considered and put in contrast with what I knew of these in Scotland, induced reflections, which though they could then reach no satisfactory conclusion, determined me to follow out a study of such infinite importance; and I actually resolved to shape the course of my life for this express end. I resolved, after a few years' residence as a practical farmer in Scotland, to remove into England for a term of years, deliberately to study the causes of difference so very great and manifest between the lower orders in the one, and the other country. In the one, labourers were independent and improving their condition, even in the face of growing taxation: in the other they were verging to extreme poverty and degradation, while all was flourishing around them. In Scotland it was more generally the custom to accommodate farm labourers with cows than in England, but this was very far from constituting the difference which existed between the people of the sister kingdoms. It had, in fact, little to do with the matter, and was rather a consequence than a cause.

Untoward circumstances disturbed the order and harmony of my plans, but still I followed them out. I settled in Scotland for six years, occupying one of my father's farms, then removed into England, and never lost sight of the great object on which I had fixed my eye.

The year after I returned from my tour in the South (1802), and after the general inclosure bill was laid aside, Mr. Young, still musing on his scheme of providing land for the poor, published, in his Annals of Agriculture, some undigested notes, which I had furnished him with: introduced them with a narrative, and attached my name, as if the whole had been written and prepared by me for publication. After doing this, he despatched to me, in Scotland, a manuscript sent him by a third party, controverting the validity of my proofs; and I, resenting alike the sophistry of my opponent and the unfair liberty which Mr. Young had taken with my name, made reply, sparing neither him, his correspondent, nor the Board of Agriculture; and, to make the matter worse, this was also published in the Annals, with words altered, and sentences withheld. It was every way provoking to me, and much as I admired Mr. Young in many respects, obliged me to drop his acquaintance.

I had hoped that the awkward display in the Annals would be little noticed; but here again I was disappointed. Mr. Malthus soon after published that edition of his Essay on Population, which attracted such general notice, and in this he referred to the publication in the Annals of Agriculture, to which Mr. Young had set my name; and which, as it stood, made me appear as an advocate of his system of providing for the poor, which I never was.

Mr. Malthus has very properly pointed out the insufficiency of Mr. Young's proposal as a general remedy for the evil of poor laws; and, besides this, it is palpably impracticable, as a scheme that could be legally enforced throughout. The quantity of land requisite to keep a cow varies, according to soil and situation, from two to twenty acres, or more. In some parts of the country adapted to pasturage, the practice could easily be adopted; and so it is in Lincolnshire and Rutland. In other parts it is very different. To afford every individual land sufficient to keep a cow is indeed out of the question. It would neither be economical for the nation, nor beneficial to individuals, in proportion to the waste. Milk is but one of many articles in housekeeping; and several others are equally necessary, and more essential. Were law to provide for each man an independence, as to the supply of milk, why not ensure the same of bread – of flesh – of raiment – of fuel? Why not introduce agrarian law, the most frightful of all political expedients? – But it is more than law can accomplish; and if law cannot prevail, it is needless to preach up advice to land-owners, to make gratuitous offerings of land and cows, when circumstances admit of it.

Clear as this may appear, it is a curious fact that Mr. Young, a man who at one time gave evidence of the soundest faculties, should have got lost in confused reverie. Till the day of his death, he seems to have brooded over the scheme of making public provision of land and cows for the poor, as practised in Lincolnshire and Rutland. In the book entitled, "AGRICULTURAL STATE OF THE KINGDOM," printed by the Board of Agriculture in 1816, suppressed, and then brought before the public by a surreptitious edition, of which, no doubt, Mr. Young was the compiler, a chapter is dedicated to the subject of land and cows, and the result of my inquiries in 1801 are brought forward by way of proof. . . .

Mr. Malthus, who so ably refutes all the silly objections to his theory of the principle of population, and shews the inconsistency of Mr. Young's writings on the question of giving land and cows to the poor, says, "I have indeed myself ventured to recommend a general improvement of cottages, and even the cow system on a limited scale; and perhaps with proper precautions a certain portion of land might be given to a considerable body of the labouring classes. If the law which entitles the poor to support were repealed, I should most highly approve of any plan which would tend to render such repeal more palatable on its first promulgation; and in this way some kind of compact with the poor might be desirable." See Appendix, vol. iii. p. 365, of the last (5th) Edition of the Essay on Population. To have thus much granted by Mr. Malthus, is no small matter, and should not be lost sight of. It opens a door of reconciliation with the man who too unguardedly asserted that there was no cure for the evil of the poor laws but to declare, and act upon the declaration, that the poor had no right to public relief in the maintenance of their children.

Nothing can be more clear than the *abstract* reasonings of Mr. Malthus, on the principle of population; and of all his disciples, no one, I believe, ever enjoyed greater satisfaction than I did on the first perusal of his book. I had for years been embarrassed in my studies, on the subject of perfectibility, and could not reconcile results in nature with the attribute of perfect goodness in the Divinity. The theory of Mr. Malthus dissipated all my doubts; and though a few pages made clear what had puzzled me, such is the nature of truth, that I can, again and again, read over the illustrations of the important one, established by the Essay on Population, with renewed pleasure. I can go back with Mr. Malthus into ancient times: I can accompany him over the globe, from Britain to China, or from the frozen north to the torrid zone, delighted to find that the law of nature is just and invariable; requiring of man only virtue to reach the highest degree of sublunary bliss, and making misery as surely the concomitant of vice. Balmy, indeed, are such truths; but how strangely have some been led astray into reflections of the most opposite kind, from the perusal of the Essay on Population! How strange, that the man who has earned the immortal honour of having happily illustrated a principle so essential to individual peace, and so admirably fitted to be a corner-stone for the erection of a sound and liberal system of political economy, should have become the butt of acrimonious censure – should have been accused of designs utterly at variance with the whole scope and tendency of his reasoning! Can we suppose that Mr. Young, Mr. Godwin, and a swarm of inferior note, who have been the virulent and blind opposers of Mr. Malthus, were urged on by mere petulance or spite, – were wanting in liberality? Certainly not. Both Young and Godwin were benevolent men; but they caught up a wrong scent, and gave tongue to an erring pursuit.

Looking dispassionately to the controversy which the doctrine of Mr. Malthus started, I think we may discern whence has arisen the phelgm of opposition. Mr. Malthus pushes home his abstract reasoning too stoically. He dwells too much on gloomy results: he attributes these results too much to the innate weakness of humanity: he regards too little the consequences of vicious institutions: he almost seems to doat on the idea that the condition of man is hopeless: he cheers us too little with the view of improvement; and he is too rash, in asserting that the poor should be deprived of their *right* of maintenance for children, – a right which circumstances have created and time confirmed, – without due preparation and fair equivalent. When Mr. Malthus speaks of denying to the poor their right to public support, he reflects not a moment on rights, both natural and acquired, which have been gradually filched from them, and in lieu of which the *right* which they now enjoy is the wretched substitute. If Mr. Malthus will make a fair bargain with the poor, not only for what has been stolen from them, but which the progress of civilization has shewn to be necessary and proper for them to possess, I, for one, shall admit the sternest adoption of his proposal. I would cut off their claim of right to public support, both root and branch: I would not only do this, but enact a law, by which charitable foundations should be erased, and erring benevolence kept in check: I would suffer no societies to be formed for relieving distress; nay, were the streets stewed with the victims of vice and misery, I would say, "let the dead bury the dead."

There are two grand principles which rouse men to action, necessity and ambition; and in a truly civilized age, when all men shall have fair advantages, these will be found sufficient of themselves to admit of all public charities, and of every thing like poor-laws, being set aside. The public charities and poor-laws of England have, indeed, been its greatest curse. They have weakened the efforts of nature: they have blunted the spur of necessity, and taken from ambition its lure.

It is impossible for any man fully to conceive the mischief which has arisen from the poor-laws of England, without having put in comparison the condition of the labourers in that country with that of those in the sister kingdom. It was from ample practical experience in both countries that I made up my mind as to the causes of difference, – the causes which have brought on England a worse than useless expenditure of eight millions a year; – causes which must be removed before any great advance can be made in the improvement, moral or physical, of this country. The expenditure of eight millions annually by no means indicates the amount of evil generated by the system of the poor-laws. While that sum is squandered, double that is lost by its degrading the people, and lessening their exertions. Having travelled far and wide, both in England and Scotland, since my return from America, I have had occasion to notice a striking difference in the respective countries under the present agricultural distress. In England this is felt far beyond what it is in Scotland. Petitions for relief pour into Parliament from all parts of England, while few or none have appeared from Scotland. This greater urgency in a great measure springs from the growing evil of the poor-laws. Markets are equally bad every where; but in Scotland the exertions of labourers increase with the pressure. There, the labourers share with the farmer his distress. They become more obedient to his will: they enable him to do more with smaller means; and their wages fall. In England it is all the reverse. Here there is no spring for industry. In hard times the poor have no increased stimulus to toil; but fall heavier and heavier as a load on their employers, while their employers become less and less able to support them.

Farming in England, from 1809 till 1817, I could hire an English ploughman for £12 and his victuals, while the current rate in Scotland was from £18 to £20; and such was the superiority of the Scotch in point of sobriety, steadiness, and fidelity, that I could afford to bring them from the north, and pay them even upwards of £20 per annum; nor would I have limited my number of imported labourers, but for the necessity of employing parish poor, who, whether employed or not, I was bound to maintain. This difference clearly arose from the different circumstances in which the labourers of the respective countries had been trained up. In the one country they received education, were inspired with feelings of independence, and cherished hope of getting on in the world. In the other, without education or laudable ambition, they had no inclination to exert themselves either for character or gain. To better their condition, one only shift was left them – to marry, and procreate children, in proportion to the number of whom their proportion of parish-pay was increased. While I marked the real difference in point of economy, which sprung from the mere training of labourers: while I observed the effects of this better training in improving the moral qualities, the enjoyment, and respectability of the Scotch, I had the fullest conviction from experience, that the natural dispositions of the English were superior to those of my countrymen; and I more and more deprecated the infernal system of perversion and debasement. What such a damning system would ultimately come to, has been long evident; but only now begins to be impressive, from its consequences; and well will it be, if present consequences force on a remedy, while worse have not ensured.

The grand question is, How can the system of the poor-laws be changed? Mr. Malthus having made good his abstract position, – having allowed that *"the system of the poor-laws is an evil, in comparison of which the national debt, with all its terrors, is of little moment,"* and being alarmed with *"the prospect of a monstrous deformity in society,"* proposes a law, by which the children of the poor should cease to be relieved; and that to render this law palatable, a sermon should be preached on the subject at the solemnization of marriages. How strange, that a man should have a head so clear for abstract reasoning, and eyes so dim to the consequences which would certainly ensue upon the very first attempt to put such a law in execution! As well might Mr. Malthus, after a train of abstract deductions, propose to do away, by mere law and ceremony, with kings, whom the madness of the people, superstition, tyranny, habits, and prejudices, have confirmed on their thrones. Most certainly, civil war and bloodshed would be the consequence of any such attempt, as well in the one case as in the other. The poor of England might not have had an inherent right to maintenance for children; and if a clear understanding had been held in bar of such right, undoubtedly it would have been well to have maintained it; but now, that both law and practice have made good this right; – now, that circumstances have rendered it necessary, the case is entirely changed. The right of the poor for maintenance can no longer be done away with by mere words. Substantials have been taken from the poor, and substantials must be returned, if further sacrifices are to be required of them; nor can even this change be effected without cautious preparation and liberal treatment.

Though my main pursuit in removing from Scotland to England, was to examine into the causes, and contrive remedies for the evils of the poor-law system, it was several years before I could make up my mind on any point. For two years I interfered little in parochial management; keeping, however, a watchful eye over those who did interfere. The third year I became one of the overseers, and gave minute attention to every particular. In Wiltshire, and some counties round, a system of regulating the wages of labour, was completely matured and acted upon. Nine shillings per week was declared to be the pay of a labourer in Wiltshire, though in Fifshire, from whence I had come, twelve shillings per week, and often more, was the customary rate. As nine shillings per week could not maintain a man with a family, the rule was to allow him to apply to the overseer, when he had more than two children, for additional pay, which was thus regulated. First, the man's wages were set down, viz.: . . . . 9s. 0d.

Then a value was put on the labour of his wife, say   3   0

                                              Carried over 12s. 0d.

Brought over   12s. 0d.

Then an inquiry was made, as to how much each child, above seven years of age, earned, and that was set down; say 3s. for one, 2s. for another, and 1s. per week, for a third – in all   6   0

                                                             18   0

Then the whole family was numbered; say man, wife, three children above seven years old, and three under that age, – in all eight persons; for each of whom the selling price of a gallon loaf, with 3d. in addition, was allowed. If the gallon loaf was 3s. then there was to be reckoned 24s. for loaves, and the 3d. to each of eight persons, 2s. making in all   26   0

From which sum the earnings of the family were deducted, leaving a balance to be paid by the Overseer,   8   0

The glaring error in this part of the system was setting the wages of the labourer too low. In England the habits of labourers were not so economical as in Scotland: in England, labourers really required more money to maintain them; but here in England they had greatly less: here a *nominal* price was set upon labour, 3s. per week below what it was naturally worth in Scotland.

There was no difficulty in correcting this error. As soon as I got to be overseer of the poor, I reckoned the labour of every able-bodied man at 12s.; and thus, at a single stroke, not only lessened parish pay and poor-rates, but did infinite good otherwise. The poor themselves were quite pleased with this change: not so the farmers; who as soon as I was out of office reduced wages to 9s. per week. The farmers had a reason for this; but it was founded on ignorance; and to ignorance and bad reasoning we may safely ascribe a full half of all this world's misery. By holding down the nominal wages of married men with more than two children, the farmers had chiefly in view to hold down the real wages of single men, and those who had less than three children; and they really made good their point, to the great injury both of themselves and labourers. Thus, while statute-laws have been framed to prevent manufacturing labourers from combining to raise their pay, a most powerful combination, ratified by the magistracy of England, was at work to keep down husbandry labour below its proper level; and thus it was that I could hire an English ploughman for £12 per annum, while I could not hire a Scotch ploughman of the same appearance at less than £18. It will naturally be asked, why should an unincumbered English ploughman submit to this? And the question must be solved by looking to a variety of points; and gathering causes from all of them. The whole of the south of England was subjected to the cursed, artificial system of which a part now appears. A spirited young man might travel a hundred miles before he could get beyond the limit of the agricultural combination; and there were few spirited young men in a country where the mass of the people could not read and write. The want of mental energy, consequent on the want of education, aided by attachment to the place of birth, relations, friends, and still more to habits of indolence, caught from what they saw around them, all conspired to enslave labourers, and to enable farmers to triumph over them in a most pernicious victory. With a few sensible people I could prevail by reasoning, and obtain confession, that keeping down wages by artifice, was wrong and unthrifty; but there was no getting any body of farmers to act in the face of established practice.

While in Scotland, I was in the habit of advertising for labourers when pushed by extraordinary need. By the simple means of a dozen or two printed notices, stuck up at public places, I have had a hundred reapers come immediately to my aid; and, by such timely aid, I have repeatedly saved my crop from destruction, and harvested it at the very best moment of time. In England, being in want of an extraordinary number of haymakers, after a tract of wet weather, I wrote out a few advertisements, and had them stuck up in the neighbouring villages; but what ensued? – My advertisements were pulled down by the farmers: they were exhibited next market-day, in order to disgrace me; and some men, whose ignorance was backed by bad temper, were actually sulky. Here is scope for useful reflection. English labourers, I have said, have, naturally, better dispositions than my countrymen. I found the same of English farmers, where not immured in the mud of bad practices, or accustomed to lord it over the poor. Just in proportion, indeed, as men of all sorts are independent of each other, so much more will they be well disposed and kindly to each other. In Wiltshire, the farmers, in many respects, were excellent men. I remember them with the warmest regard, and have the felicity to know, that I am not forgotten as a friend in that county; but I must say that, to the poor, some, even of the best of them, were totally without feeling. . . .

Shortly before my departure for Canada, I had a second petition presented to the House of Commons, to record what was farther required for the relief of the poor from oppression; and to give them practice in the only peaceable mode of proceeding for that end. The following is a copy of the second Petition.

To the Honourable the Commons of the United Kingdom of Great Britain and Ireland, in Parliament assembled, The humble Petition of the undersigned Inhabitants of the Parish of Wily, in the County of Wilts, (the 5th of February, 1817.)

SHEWETH,
THAT on the 31st of May, *1815*, a Petition from this parish to your honourable House, was presented by Paul Methuen, Esq. member for this county, on the subject of the poor laws, to which your Petitioners beg leave again to call the attention of your honourable House.

That your Petitioners understood, that, at the close of the last Session of Parliament, your honourable House had appointed a committee, to take into consideration this most important subject, and your Petitioners would have looked with confidence towards the result of such consideration, had not a proposal been set forth, by the mover of this measure, not only subversive of hope, but indicative of an intention and spirit absolutely abhorrent to the minds of your Petitioners.

It was proposed in your honourable House, – not to better the condition of the poor, – not to lighten the overburthened wheels of industry, – not to rekindle the spirit of independence, nor to recruit the wasted strength of the labourers of England: – it was proposed to oblige them to pay four-pence out of every ten shillings of their earnings, that they who have hitherto paid poor rates, may be eased of their burden! When such a proposal has been made in the British Senate, under such circumstances as the present, it must be high time for every one, even the lowest, to think for himself, – to doubt if selfishness has left, in the human breast, one spark of benevolence, or, if any thing like reason is to dictate in the arrangements of civil society.

Your Petitioners were taught to believe, that after the struggle of war was at an end, plenty would come hand in hand with peace, to refresh the people, who had, with unparalleled fortitude and submission, for upwards of twenty years of war, supported the measures of their Government: your Petitioners have been disappointed, – most grievously disappointed. War had its horrors, but the present peace is more horrible than war: – the people in thousands stand every where idle, famished, dejected, and desperate.

At such a period of disappointment and gloom, your Petitioners would bridle in every inclination to reproach those who have been the more immediate instruments of bringing down upon the country its load of calamity. Looking backward they recognise the people at every step, identifying their will with that of the Government; fostering its ambition; cheering its victories; sharing its plunder. Your Petitioners wish to bury in oblivion the follies and the crimes that are passed: they wish, now, that most urgent necessity proclaims that something must be done, that that may be done, which may not only be safe and honourable for the British Government, but efficient to the comfort and prosperity of the people.

Your Petitioners conceive that there exists no mystery, as to the grand cause of the present distress. Excessive taxation, for a long period of years, has not only wasted the productions of industry, but the funding system has registered the price of a debt to be discharged by industry, while industry, deprived of the excitements which extraordinary circumstances afforded, has ceased to be able for such a discharge. Under these changed circumstances, your Petitioners have marked, for the last three years, a fatal blindness to consequences, and have beheld with sorrow, principles assumed and acted upon, with a design to remedy impending evils, not only of a narrow and selfish character, but palpably inadequate to the end in view. Your Petitioners conceive that the first step which should have been taken, after peace deprived this country of its monopoly of trade, and the peculiar incitements to industry, created by war and extraordinary circumstances, was, to have withdrawn those taxes which most directly bear upon the necessaries and comforts of life, and to have substituted in their place, taxes upon idle property and great incomes accruing from the same. Such measures would not only have been politic and just among individuals, but their adoption would at once have enabled our industry to cope with that of other nations, and would have upheld that due degree of confidence in substantial stock, which was clearly wanted to maintain a balance against the dangerous influence of funded property, whose immediate security does not rest on the success of trade and industry, but in the power of taxation, and whose pressure increases as the strength to bear it is diminished.

Your Petitioners hoped that time and approaching ruin would not only have opened the eyes of all to the real situation of affairs, but have made it the first duty of ministers, to have declared the truth, and to have quieted the public mind, by an assurance of instantly altering the scheme of taxation. With utmost dread, however, have they now heard the Royal speech proclaiming, that the evils, which assail the country, spring from temporary causes, and from the transition from war to peace. Your Petitioners deem it their most sacred duty to oppose such sentiments, to deprecate such advice to Royalty, and to declare it to be the very extreme of infatuation to rest under such impressions for a moment. Your Petitioners, being mostly labourers and poor men, have comparatively little interest in the fate of property; but as sincere friends to peace and good order, they wish to see that which regulates all the commercial transactions of men, and which is necessary to give excitement to industry, kept in its proper place: – they wish no longer to see real property swallowed up and endangered by a bubble, whose increase, under existing circumstances, must rapidly tend to explosion, and whose explosion can leave nothing behind, but wretchedness and woe. With a change in the scheme of taxation, your Petitioners have persuaded themselves, that certain proposals, if adopted, would co-operate *immediately* to revive the industry of the country, and, in a short time, do away all necessity, both for poor laws and poor rates.

These proposals are:

1st. That in every parish not comprehended in, nor containing a town of more than one thousand inhabitants, Government shall take possession of one hundred acres of land, being the nearest clear land to the respective parish churches, and otherwise best suiting the purposes in view.

2d. That Government shall pay to the owners of such land its fair estimated value, raising one half of the whole means for this purpose, by a rate similar to a poor rate, only that owners of property shall be assessed instead of tenants, these latter being obliged to pay legal interest to the former, during the currency of existing leases, upon the amount of assessment raised from their respective holdings: the other half of the whole means to be obtained by loan, so calculated, as to be liquidated by rents and purchase-money, mentioned below.

3d. That each hundred acres shall be divided into two equal parts, as to extent and in such a manner, as shall best suit purposes in view.

4th. That one of these parts, in each parish, shall be enclosed, and otherwise in the best manner improved, for the purpose of a common pasture, to remain so for ever.

5th. That the other half shall be divided into half-acre allotments, making one hundred allotments in each parish.

6th. That the present inhabitants, male parishioners, of such parishes, shall be allowed immediately to occupy the allotments, one each; the choice of allotments to proceed by seniority.

7th. That where the present inhabitants of parishes are not suffi-ciently numerous to occupy all the allotments of their respective parishes, other persons shall have a choice, seniority and proximity giving a prefer-ence, while any allotment remains unoccupied.

8th. That each person, when he takes possession of an allotment, shall thereby bind himself to pay forty shillings a year, as rent for the same; and at all times to keep it in good garden culture. A person, thus paying rent, shall be styled a parish-holder.

9th. That as long as these conditions are fulfilled, no parish-holder shall be disturbed in, nor turned out of his allotment; and at his death, his son may occupy in his stead, if twenty-one years of age: an elder son having a priority of choice to a younger son; and failing sons, the choice of occupancy shall proceed to the nearest male relation, before it falls to the public.

10th. That as soon as any parish-holder shall have paid into a savings bank, to be for that purpose established by Government, the sum of one hundred poujnds, he shall have a cottage built on his allotment to that value; he having the choice of a variety of plans for the construction of the said cottage.

11th. That neither the money deposited in the bank for the above purpose, nor the property of the cottage when built, shall be attachable for debt; nor shall they affect any claim of parochial relief, due by existing laws. A person when possessed of a cottage in this manner, shall be styled a cottage-holder. At his death, his cottage-hold shall go to the nearest heir-male, as in the case of the parish-hold, with this difference, that the heir who takes possession shall pay to relations, equally near of kin with himself to the deceased, male and female, or to the nearest of kin female relation or relations, if such there be, nearer than himself, to the exclusion of others, a certain value for the cottage; and in case no heir takes possession to fulfil these terms, then they may be fulfilled by other persons who may desire possession, and whose claim to possess, shall be regulated by proximity and seniority: but if neither relations nor others shall claim possession, then the cottage-hold shall revert to Govern-ment, from whom heirs shall receive the value of the cottage, and the cottage-hold shall be open to public purchase or exchange.

12th. That as soon as a cottage-holder shall have had no relief from the parish, for the space of two years, he shall be entitled to a vote in the parish, and have a right to pasture a cow on the common. He shall be styled a freeman.

13th. That if a freeman shall throw himself for relief on the parish, he shall lose that designation, his right to vote, and pasture; nor shall he recover these, till he has lived five years without parochial aid.

14th. That as soon as a freeman has paid into the bank the sum of sixty pounds, the same shall be received by Government as purchase-money for his allotment, shall free him from the yearly payment of rent, and make him eligible into parish offices. He shall be styled a parish freeholder. Succession to be regulated as above.

15th. That all sales and exchanges shall be made through public medium; and at once to facilitate and regulate these, there shall be corresponding registries; parochial, district, county, and national.

16th.   That no person whatever shall possess either in one or more parishes, more than one holding, and no person shall have a choice, nor be allowed to purchase, under twenty-one years of age;but an heir male shall be allowed, while a minor, to hold possession, although he shall have no vote, nor be eligible to offices, till he come of age: provided always, that none of the relations, entitled as above to a share of the valued property, become chargeable to the parish, while their share is unpaid, nor the heir himself, for in such cases the holding shall revert to public possession, and the residue only, if any, of the value of the cottage and freehold, be paid to the heir or heirs, after the parish charges for maintenance have been deducted.

Although your Petitioners frankly submit these Proposals to the consideration of your honourable House, they do not press their adoption in the letter. Your honourable House may see fit to modify the scheme. The common pasture may be dispensed with, and the number of allotments may be increased, diminished, or regulated, as circumstances may require. Your Petitioners chiefly insist that it is essential to the abolition of Pauperism in England, that an opportunity be afforded, for the labouring people to acquire property and personal freedom; both which they have lost through the operation of the poor laws, and which they can never regain under existing circumstances. To afford half an acre of land to all who would require it, would not occupy a hundredth part of the national territory: and when it is considered that the poor once possessed many houses and gardens in every parish, and enjoyed over all England extensive common rights, of which, in many cases, they have been unjustly deprived, such restitution must seem far from extravagant or unreasonable.

Your Petitioners would desire your honourable House to consider, what universal contentment would instantly ensue from the adoption of these proposals, or even of a modification of them: what a fund of employment would be created: how universally this would be diffused; and how long it would continue. Even the early production of provisions to eke out the supply, before next harvest, would be no small advantage, in the present year of scarcity, and would certainly be obtained by affording to the poor, garden allotments of land, for individual cultivation and convenience. Your Petitioners deny what has been asserted by some, that such arrangements in rural economy, would stir up in the minds of the people a desire for any thing like a general Agrarian law, or that their obtaining votes, would in any way endanger property. Your Petitioners refer to America, where, in many parts, the right of vote is equally shared among the rich and the poor, without having caused the least encroachment on property.

Your Petitioners, though they most earnestly desire to see a wise reform of Parliament, do not wish the parish vote to qualify directly for parliamentary election, and they positively disclaim and renounce what is commonly understood by universal suffrage. They feel that the mass of the people never could be competent, sufficiently to estimate the comparative merits of persons aspring to a seat in parliament; although they could well judge, which of their fellow parishioners were most worthy of offices and trust within their respective parishes, and which of them might be best qualified to act as parish deputies, at district or county meetings, whether assembled for parliamentary election or other business.

Your Petitioners therefore most earnestly entreat that your honourable House will immediately withdraw all taxes on malt, salt, soap, candles, leather, bricks, and tiles; contract no more debt; pay all national charges unprovided for, by an assessment on rents and interest of money, increasing the ratio of assessment upon great incomes derived from the same: — That, having done this, your honourable House will take into most serious consideration the above proposals; and particularly that you will so enact, that every British subject, grown to man's estate, shall have an opportunity of occupying half an acre of land for its value, whereon he may establish his freehold: and your petitioners shall ever pray.

(Subscribed by Robert Gourlay, and ninety-seven others, of Wily parish.)

.... It will be observed, from the Petition, that I was not rigid as to the quantity of land,* and that I admitted of modification as circumstances should require. I wished to set forth the greatest quantum required, to shew that even that was nothing before the mighty object aimed at; the rooting out of poor-laws, and improving the character and condition of the people. The half acre of land is condescended upon as being such a quantity as any poor man could make the most of at his spare hours, and from which he could raise sufficient food for a cow, along with his liberty of pasturage on the common; but there are reasons which would make it politic and right to diminish both the extent of the common and the garden plot. A quarter of an acre is the proper size for a garden, and 25 instead of 50 acres of common would be quite sufficient.

A rood of land, under good garden culture, will yield great abundance of every kind of vegetable for a family, besides a little for a cow and pig. If there is a ground on which a cow can range for part of a day, she can be kept in high condition for milk, upon articles of food, which can always be purchased; straw, hay, grains, &c.; and, on introducing a general system, the less bounds in which that can be accomplished, so much the better. It is not the intention to make labourers professional gardeners or farmers! it is intended to confine them to bare convenience. The bad effects of giving too much land to labourers was discovered more than thirty years ago, in the lowlands of Scotland. What were called the *Cotter rigs* (Cottager's ridges) are now every where

---

* There are in Great Britain . . . . 54,603,360 acres.
  Then, 50 acres set aside in each of 10,000 parishes, gives . . 500,000
  The quotient is *not* a hundredth part 109

done away with, and to the benefit of both masters and servants. The bad effects of the little potatoe farms in Ireland, are well known; and nothing but dirt and misery is witnessed among the *Crofters* of the highlands of Scotland. A tidy garden, with the right of turning out a cow in a small well-improved and well-fenced field, would produce effects of a very different kind indeed: would, at once, insure contentment, comfort, and a world of convenience. Independent of the advantage which would accrue to the inhabitants of a village, in the way of cow-keeping, from a small common or park, there is need of such a spot for various other purposes: the bleaching of linen; the gambols of the young; and the sober sauntering of the old; exercise and air; the feeling of independence and social union.

Objection has been started to the scheme, that its benefits could not be extended to people in towns; but it may as properly be said, that, because we cannot reach the North pole, we should not venture so far as Greenland. Were ten thousand country parishes accommodated with fifty acres each, no inhabitant of a town need be in want: and if inhabitants of towns were tempted out of them, to have the enjoyment of a garden and common right in the country, so much the better. Great towns, in many respects, are bad. They are unfavourable to morals, to health, to national economy. In villages of from fifty to one hundred families every good of combination can be obtained. In such villages every species of manufactory could find sufficient hands for supplying labour in all its divisions.

I am at a loss to understand what Mr. Malthus means, by the "improvement of cottages." If he means the improvement of dwelling-houses, there is a rule to be attended to, and it is this; that, every house, to contain a family with decency and comfort, should have a kitchen, parlour, and three sleeping apartments; one for the parent pair: one for male; and one for female children. . . . Such a one, finished plainly, and furnished with every wooden convenience, could be afforded in the wilds of Canada for £30. In England, a cottage, built of brick or stone, and finished as I would wish to see it, substantially and elegantly, would cost £80 now; and four years ago would have cost £100. Requiring such a cottage to be erected by an individual, before he could claim the rights of the cottage-holder, is proper, on various accounts. The difficulty of acquiring privileges would make these privileges be more esteemed, and would bring into the possession of them, superior merit; while the after-enjoyment of a handsome place of residence would, in no small degree, assist in upholding laudable pride and self-respect. It may be thought, that a common labourer could never accumulate, out of his wages, the sum requisite for the erection of such cottage; but he certainly could, if the rate of wages was fair. It has already been stated, that before the peace, a Scotch ploughman had £20 and his victuals: the half of this could, with economy, keep him in clothes, and the other half, regularly deposited in a savings bank, might amount to £100 by his 25th year.

Although I have an absolute abhorrence of the spade husbandry, as proposed by the benevolent Mr. Owen, I perfectly agree with him, that moral training may greatly improve the human character. Before Mr. Owen came before the public as an author, I had published my opinion, that "*circumstances and situation*," could mould this; and in America I have seen it so far verified. Man, indeed, is a ductile animal, and a good one, when not crossed with tyranny, or ruined from bad example. He is more hopeful than Mr. Malthus would have us believe; but his training must commence before the wedding-day, – it must commence from the cradle.

As to the "*Cow system,*" there is no possibility of introducing it, generally; but so far as a common adjoining every village would admit; and I trust that my plan is at once economical, safe, and practicable. I am perfectly aware of the difficulty of getting our rulers, and, indeed, the great body of the wealthy classes, to give a liberal hearing to such a proposal. They have a dread that any admission of the people to the enjoyment of civil rights would lead to unreasonable demands: but it is groundless and unchristian. As to the land required, the poor have a positive right to it, looking back to these last 30 years of spoil, under acts of enclosure. The land, unjustly taken from them, under these acts, has amounted to more than would be required to establish the Village system all over the island. Yes! much more than 500,000 acres have been thus unfairly taken from the poor; and, in another way, they have also been gradually and ruinously deprived of their property. By prevailing regulations, no person is entitled to parish-relief while he has any real property. If he is put to it, he must swear that *he is poor*; – that he has neither cottage nor garden, cow nor calf; that he has nothing but household furniture and wearing apparel. What has ensued from this law? Why, that not one in a hundred of English labourers has now a sheltering place which he can call his own. Almost universally the poor have been obliged to part with their cottages and gardens. The infernal poor-law system forced them to make this sacrifice. The stoutest, most active, and most willing labourer, could not maintain his family, after the combination to keep down wages was formed. There was a positive necessity for his applying to the parish for relief, and this relief he could not have till cottage, garden, and all was surrendered. For many years sore struggles were made to maintain independence, and keep possession of the little spots which, since England was, had descended by inheritance from father to son; but it would not do: indeed, it was foolishness to hold out; and it became a common saying, that "*a cottage and garden was the worst thing a poor man could have.*" Let the reader pause, and reflect upon this: let him think of consequences, – heart-sickening, appalling, ruinous consequences. What is property good for? for what has God created it? what, but a desire to possess property, can spur on the mass of mankind to exertion? what would we be but for this desire? yet here are millions of the English people in whom that desire has become extinct, – who must pass through life, and never enjoy the delight of having a home which they can call their own.

What does Mr. Malthus say to this? Is there a single word on the subject in his whole book on population? When we look to the index of that book, and run over the many heads, under which the poor and poor-laws are spoken of, do we find a single word regarding this? Do we find any thing of this in the chapter which treats of "*the only effectual mode of improving the condition of the poor?*" No: not a word – not a syllable: yet, in this, is the grand secret; in this is the germ of hope; in this is the *one thing needful.* Let but the poor have a little property to begin with – a little stock in trade; let them have a home, which they can call their own, with the hope of independence, and all will go well. God instituted property, and clearly tells us that, by the proper use of it, we can rise to excellence; but without property or, the chance of acquiring it, no good can be expected of us.

I have rapturously expressed my joy in accompanying Mr. Malthus from earlier to later times: from north to south, and from west to east; anon, musing on the abstract truth, that, in proportion as men are virtuous, so are they happy: but am I to dream only of this abstract truth? When I have obtained full information as to "*the checks to population*, in the lowest stage of society," – "among American Indians," – "in the islands of the South Sea," – "among the ancient inhabitants of the North of Europe," – "among modern pastoral nations," – "in different parts of Africa," – "in Siberia, north and south," – "in the Turkish dominions and Persia," – "in Indostan and Tibet," – "in China and Japan," – "among the Greeks," – "among the Romans," – "in Norway," – "in Sweden," – "in Russia," – "in the middle parts of Europe," – "in Switzerland," – "in France," –

"in England," – "in Scotland and Ireland," – when I have obtained full information as to the checks to population, in all these countries, ancient and modern, and in every stage of society, am I to fall asleep, and give up all inquiry as to the *means* by which moral restraint may be braced? Am I to make a jumble of crude ideas, and satisfy myself only of this bare abstract proposition, that all checks to population are "resolvable into moral restraint, vice, and misery?" Am I to rest satisfied with the belief, that the paupers of England may be exalted in character and conduct by a mere sermon; and that, too, on their wedding day? What! lecture a young couple on that day, against intemperance during the honey-moon!! Really, Mr. Malthus, there is no wonder that you have stirred up indignation. Nature should not be so provoked – so wantonly outraged. With all my admiration of the theory of population, I must hold your practice in derision. You make me think of an astronomer fixing his eye so intently on the milky-way, to discover its specks, that he forgets that there are stars of the first magnitude in the firmament.

That "population must always be kept down to the level of subsistence," – that "when unchecked," it may "increase in a geometrical ratio," that "population, could it be supplied with food, would go on with unexhausted vigour;" and that "the increase of one period would furnish a greater increase to the next, and this without any limit," &c. are all truisms, which any child may understand. I am convinced, with Mr. Malthus, that a nation's strength does not consist in the mere multitude of its people; but in the moral and physical strength of the individuals who compose the multitude; and, most assuredly, there is great room for improvement in this way. Bred to farming, I clearly comprehend Mr. Malthus, when he speaks of having good stock, instead of bad stock, on a farm; but the example which I have given, from experience, of the difference between Scotch and English labourers, one earning £20, while another earned but £12, renders all resort to figurative comparison unnecessary: it is direct to the point. And when it clearly appears by what *means* an English pauper may be made as good a man as any Scotchman whatever, why should he hesitate in resorting to the means for delivering one-half of the nation from misery, and another from the burden of poor-rates? The simple means is to give the English poor a chance of acquiring property, a hope of independence; and see the effects. Do but this: educate the young, and free the old from vassalage. Only 150 years ago the Scotch were very brutes – the basest rabble on earth; but the institution of parish schools wrought a miracle: I may, indeed, quote my own words on this subject, written, in 1815: "The Scotch, in one century, were the most unprincipled and desperate marauders; in the next, they were examples of sobriety and peace." As soon as the poor rascally Scotch got the rudiments of education, they began to work their way to independence; and they sought for it all the world over. Let the English have the same advantage, and they, in like manner, will profit by it. But I have said, that "substantials have been taken from the poor (of England), and that substantials must be returned." Even with education, the poor of England cannot have such a chance as the Scotch had; and that, because of the existing state of property. I do not know if there is a single parish in Scotland, where the labouring classes do not possess considerable property in houses and land; or, where they cannot find plenty of cottages and gardens to purchase, or take on lease. In England, it is all otherwise. I question if the poor of Wiltshire, were they emancipated to-morrow from parish bondage, and in the way of making money, could, in one parish out of ten, get land to purchase in small lots, or even have cottages for rent; and that ready accommodation, in this way, should be furnished them, is of the first importance. I have said that at least 500,000 acres have been unjustly taken from the poor within the last thirty years; and that in this time, too, they have been obliged to surrender their cottages and gardens. However unjustly and impolitically all this has come about, no restitution can be made of the very commons, – the very cottages and gardens, that have been taken from the poor; nor is it desirable that this should be attempted. Assuredly, however, the general right – the abstract right, to restitution, is good. Will Mr. Malthus deny it? Will he deny the propriety, justice, and good policy of restitution? or can he find fault with my mode of restitution – my plan for execution? Landed property is often seized upon, paid for, and applied to public purposes, under acts of parliament; and, if a hundredth part of each parish was so taken for the accommodation of the poor, it would be no great encroachment on the rights of private property. Some seven or eight years ago, the Bath Society gave a gold medal to the writer of an essay for proposing to purchase up land all over the kingdom, to be given to the clergy in lieu of tithes. This proposal was monstrous in a variety of views, but still it shows that people can bear with such a proposal. On the enclosure of commons, it has been customary to set aside one-seventh for the tithe-claimant, and, if we suppose tithe-claimants, throughout, to be entitled to half as much, here would be *a fourteenth* of the whole kingdom to be purchased up, and appropriated, for the maintenance of 15,000 parsons; not more than a thousand of whom are effective in the vineyard: – if we can listen to such a proposal with patience, how readily may my proposal be entertained of purchasing up *a hundredth* part of the kingdom, for the accommodation of a million of families; and for the removal of "*an evil, in comparison of which, the national debt, with all its terrors, is of little moment.*" It is of no avail for Mr. Malthus to be sending into the world edition after edition of his Essay on the Principle of Population, and gradually entrenching himself for more than twenty years within fastnesses of logic, if he does not come to some point: it is of no avail to be arguing nice points in political economy, or registering truisms, if no practical issue is reached: it is of no avail to be *venturing* "to recommend a general improvement of cottages, and even the cow-system, on a limited scale," if nothing is done. Mr. Malthus has said, that he "should most highly approve of any plan which would tend to render such repeal (the repeal of the law for public maintenance to the poor) more palatable on its first promulgation." Well then, I submit my plan, and challenge Mr. Malthus to find fault with it. My plan was laid on the table of the House of Commons, before Mr. Malthus published the 5th edition of his Essay on Population; and I do not suppose he was ignorant of it; yet not a word is said of it. Now it will be better known; and now I challenge not only Mr. Malthus, but the whole world, to say in what it is wrong; or to state what difficulty lies in the way of its adoption. Mr. Malthus hints at building cottages and *letting* them to the poor; but this would be a mighty expensive and compli- cated matter, while it would produce no grand effect. He also speaks of Mr. Estcourt's plan of providing for the poor, – of *letting* land to the poor, at Long Newton, in Gloucestershire, (North Wiltshire); but this is all trifling. I have repeatedly been at Long Newton, seen Mr. Estcourt's provision for the poor, and inquired into his plan. It is nothing more than a second edition of the *cotter-rigs* of old Scotland; and its continuance rests with Mr. Estcourt's will and pleasure. Mr. Estcourt can deprive his poor tenants of the ridges now let to them; on which they grow a little grain, beans, potatoes, and so forth. The poor must be made *independent* of all caprice: they must have something which they can call their own. They must have the power of loco-motion: they must have a chance of acquiring a freehold, – an opportunity of rising from out the mud in which they are now stuck. The poor of Lincolnshire are placed beyond the caprice of their imme- diate masters, the farmers. They rent their cottages and cow pastures from the chief landlords, (see page xciv) and as they never disturb them in possession, it is so far well; but it would be so much better if these cottagers could call their cottages their castles, as all Englishmen should be enabled to do. The little feuers of Ceres parish can do this. There, after they have obtained a *feu*, they are as independent as he that has granted it. The feuer can build to any extent on his land with safety: he can keep, sell, or divide at pleasure; and the foregoing Table shews how things go. The practice of thus accommodating the labouring class with land is infinite. There is no want of homes in Scotland; whether for sale, taking by lease, or exchange. In the parish of Ceres there are, perhaps, four times as many small properties as those exhibited in the table; and all over Scotland there are abundance. How was it in Wily parish and the country round? There, nothing of the kind was to be seen. In every parish there were a few cottages, generally in most ruinous condition, which had, formerly, had their little independent occupiers, but now were held by parish officers as public property. There were a few also attached to the farms; but not a place of refuge remained for the poor man who had spirit to wish for a home of his own; and what said a parish-officer of Wily, when he wanted to get quit of some of the poor. He said, " *he would put them so close that they would be obliged to swarm*;" meaning, that he would drive them from the parish, where they had a legal right of maintenance, by discomfort.

Whoever bestows serious reflection on this speech, cannot be longer insensible to the necessity which exists for a thorough change being made in favour of the poor of England, – the necessity of restoring to them some landed property in every parish, to ensure independence and the power of locomotion.

The ancient commons, though in many respects nuisances, were, in this way, of vast importance. Almost every parish in England used to have its common or cow-down; and every highway was skirted with waste land, on which the people could at will erect freeholds. There was not then in England a man to whom such a speech as the above could be appalling. Till within the last thirty years, that commons and wastes have been so generally enclosed, without regard to the rights of the poor, and till all the cottages and gardens were taken out of their hands, they could not be made to "*swarm*," from over-crowding in almshouses, or parish hovels. The moment that a poor man was oppressed, by farmer, priest, or 'squire, under whom he lived, he could find for himself a place of refuge. He had only to ask the assistance of a few friends. In a single night they could erect a hut, on the common or waste, and before day-light the boiling pot proclaimed him a freeholder; nor could the king himself drive out the poorest of his subjects from such a tenement. This, I say, was a mighty affair for the poor – a mighty stay for independence.

By the enclosure of commons, England has become greatly more productive: many millions a year have been added to rent-rolls; but by the regardless manner in which the change has been effected, millions of the poor have been deprived of their most valuable rights – have been enslaved.

Surely, I have said enough; nor must I forget that I am not writing a book, but an introduction to a book. To the theory of Mr. Malthus I shall most faithfully adhere; and most happy should I be to see so able a writer seconding my plans. If Mr. Young flattered me twenty years ago, by saying, that I "knew more of the poor of England than any man in it," it may not be taken amiss if I merely state what has happened since. At no moment, since then, have I lost sight of the cause for which, twenty years ago, I shaped the course of my life; – neither in Scotland, nor England, nor Canada, – neither by land nor by sea, – neither in prosperity nor in adversity, – neither free nor in jail, – neither supported by friends nor deserted by all: – surely, then, I must be a fool indeed, if this cause is worthless, or my schemes to advance it, are good for nothing.

Colonial Government.

On this subject I shall address myself

To the People of England.

SINCE the United States made good their independence by the sword, North American Colonies must have cost us little less than fifty millions of pounds sterling; and I question if they have returned so many farthings for our governmental care. Till of late the annual charge could not be much less than half a million; and this fact I shall maintain, that instead of throwing away money on these colonies, we may draw from them a considerable revenue, merely by the economical disposal of waste lands. At the present time, when the bonds of society are ready to burst with over-strained taxation, surely, such a consideration ought not to be thought a trifling one.

Our North American colonies are not yet ripe for independence, or that should be granted them; – not independence of the crown, but of ministers. The colonies stand in need of kind nursing for ten years to come; at the end of which period they might be allowed to meet in Convention, and choose a government for themselves. It is their interest to remain for ever connected with this country, and there is not the slightest reason to suppose that they would ever harbour a wish to throw off its sovereignty, or deny us the right of disposing of waste lands to the best advantage. Set free from the wretched controul of haughty, ignorant, and capricious governors, they would most assuredly cherish a pride in their affinity to the parent state: they would remain for ever our friends, and fellow-subjects. Were a liberal system of government established in the Colonies, liberal minded men would spring up there; and, thither, liberal-minded men would emigrate from Britain. It is from liberality alone, that Britain can retain and derive benefit from her colonies. Let us then at once have liberality.

Looking back to the history of America, how simple do the means appear by which we might have retained the United States. Good heavens! what madness was it to drive free-born Americans to rebellion, by denying them the rights of men! What folly to imagine that we, islanders, could coerce the people of a continent, 3,000 miles removed! Had Americans been permitted, in due time, to govern themselves, they never would have denied to this country the right of disposing of waste land; and by the judicious disposal of that we could not only have drawn home a considerable revenue, but have planted the new world with a superior race of men. Surely we may now be taught by experience; – surely, in this more enlightened age, we may learn how to turn to profit the immense territory which we yet possess on the continent of America. Let the eye only glance over the map, from the Atlantic to the Pacific, and from the St. Lawrence to the Pole; and, then let me ask, if it may not be for the honour of England, holding profit apart, to consider by what means so vast a region may be tenanted with civilized men – with happy souls and loyal subjects. Four years ago the charming possibility of this being realized dawned upon my mind; and I said that "England could spare 50,000 people annually, and be refreshed with the discharge." The truth has grown more and more obvious, and I now repeat it with perfect confidence. The vision of quickly and thickly peopling the earth with our species, brightens in my imagination day after day; and most earnestly would I intreat every benevolent mind to give serious attention to the subject. The idea may be easily realized. It requires but systematic arrangement, and the judicious application of capital which we have in abundance. It will pay: it may be resorted to, not only for the performance of the first great command to multiply and replenish; but for our individual advantage and our national aggrandizement: it may be looked forward to as the peaceful means of establishing a new and a better order of things in the world. Hitherto men's chief employment has been to butcher their kind. They have gone on from age to age, destroying and depopulating: they have striven to give aid to vice and misery. Why should it be so? Merciful God! What cause have we to quarrel with the people of the United States; or these people with their neighbours in Canada? Is there not room for us all, and should we not first consider how that room may be filled up? One and all of us may, for centuries to come, have positive and great advantage in settling the wastes of nature to their remotest verge. England *alone* could, in prosperity, *easily* supply 50,000 recruits annually, for emigration and settlement; and the United Kingdom 100,000. Yes! by the simplest arithmetic it can be proved, if proof is called for.

Our North American Provinces should be confederated. They should hold congress in the month of June, at Quebec. Lower Canada: Upper Canada: New Brunswick, having Gaspé and Prince Edward's Island laid to it; and Newfoundland, might constitute five independent, but confederated provinces. Labrador: East, South, West, and North Hudson, might fall into the confederacy as they became civilized and sufficiently populous; and, in the course of time, those parts of the United States, whose waters issue by Quebec, (never to be gained over by conquest), would, I doubt not, join the Northern Confederacy, and swell the Government of the St. Lawrence to its natural size.

The best Constitution for a North American Province, while at nurse, would, in my opinion, be this: to consist of an Assembly chosen by the people, as in Canada; a Governor and Council. The Governor might be a military man, and have the commissioning of militia officers, while he and the Council appointed judges, magistrates, &c., who should be subject to removal on the application of a certain large portion, say four-fifths of the people, among whom they were appointed to act. The Council might consist of ten members or more; one half to be chosen by the people eligible to sit in Assembly; the other half to be real men of business, sent from England on salaries for service. These men, besides doing duty in the Council, as advisers and legislators, might form a land-board, altogether independent of the Provincial Governors or Government, and be subservient, in that capacity, to a grand land-board at home. The grand national land-board, with its branches in the several Provinces, might dispose of waste lands on strict business principles; and by system, every way defined and adjusted, manage in the best possible manner for public good. Accurate surveys and maps might be made, and exhibited both at home and abroad, for the expediting of business, either in purchase or exchange; and under the auspices of the land-board and its branches, a grand system of emigration might be organized and maintained in constant operation. There is nothing in mere magnitude which should frighten us. Magnitude in general may be made to contribute to success; and with systematic arrangement, and adequate means, may be turned to its utmost account, without difficulty, confusion, of failure. I avoid particulars. The subject of profitable emigration and settlement, is one to which I have devoted part of my third volume, and should the public happily conceive favourable opinions of schemes now hinted at, it shall be my utmost ambition to go on to practical illustration and detail. A few words on the fundamental principle may not be thrown away: they may assist in arresting attention. Land is valuable, according to the degree of convenience attached to it; and other things being equal, increases in value as the density of population increases. A single family planted down on a square mile, as is the case in Upper Canada, can have no convenience – no sufficient strength to make head against obstacles to improvement; and while the settler is held in misery, little value is added to the land he occupies. Plant down two families, twelve, twenty, or more, on the same extent of ground, and each addition, up to a certain proportion, insures greater and greater comfort and convenience to the whole, while an instant and great value is given to the soil. One solitary family, settled on a square mile, must pine for years, become poor, dispirited, beggarly, and brutal, while twenty families will not only retain their strength, their spirit, and their manners, but instantly flourish, feel contented, feel happy, and be more and more ambitious to excel in activity and skill. England has thousands of people to spare; and for her thousands of people she has millions of acres to settle and improve. She is the greatest land-owner on the globe, and she has the greatest command of capital. That capital is now running to waste; or worse than waste, it is running on to increase pauperism and idleness; idleness both among the rich and the poor. While this capital is yet at command, England may do wonders, by setting in motion a vast machinery at home and abroad; but let this capital waste itself, as it is now doing, and a little time only will see its end, – a woful end!

Newfoundland now contains 70,000 permanent inhabitants. They are sending home petitions, to obtain a free and regular constitution of government. Let experiment be made there.

Before the chartered constitutions of Nova Scotia and New Brunswick, or those of Canada, framed by Act of Parliament, are pulled to pieces, let Newfoundland have one framed without delay; and when that is found perfect, the older constitutions may be new-modelled, to correspond with it. An immediate experiment may also be made in rightly laying out and disposing of land in Newfoundland. In general, that country is unfavourable to cultivation; but still it contains immense tracts, which, under good management, may be brought to value, and be occupied at once to the advantage of individuals, and the nation. At present, the people of Newfoundland are not allowed sufficient land, even for potatoe gardens. How monstrous! And this too, because of an absurd, antiquated notion, that the cultivation of the soil there, would injure the fisheries. It would assist the fisheries: it would enable us to cope with the people of the United States, in that trade, along the North American shores, where they are striving to rival, and, by all accounts, only require time to go beyond us, notwithstanding that our natural advantages are superior. But colonial policy is every where at war with nature. The people of Newfoundland would, no doubt, be willing to give a fair price for land, to suit their convenience; and a judicious mode of laying out, and disposing of land, as it came to be wanted, is of the utmost consequence to insure that convenience, and make it valuable. The North American Provinces might choose three or more members each, to attend congress at Quebec; and one of these for each Province, might be allowed to come home, and have a seat in the British Parliament, with liberty to speak, but not to vote. These members might, from the Congress being held in June, annually visit England, and return to perform their duties at Quebec; and thus a direct, social, lively, and watchful intelligence might be maintained between the home and the colonial governments: all would be simple and efficacious; friendly and independent; active and harmonious. If desired by the provincials, one of our Princes might reside at Quebec, as Viceroy, to be directed by ministers, subject to impeachment; and to the Viceroy might be given a power, much wanted abroad, to pardon offences of every kind: indeed, saving acknowledgment to the Sovereign of England, the Viceroy might be clothed with every royal prerogative. At Quebec, too, a supreme judicial tribunal might be established, to supersede the necessity of appealing to the King in Council at home; – a palpable bar to justice. The mere skeleton of provincial government is sufficient now to have exhibited. It is now only meant to attract notice to the subject, and to lay the foundation for mature discussion. Never did necessity call more loudly for investigation into colonial policy, than now. We cannot, indeed, *afford* longer to trifle with this most important subject. Our colonial policy over the whole world is abominable; but in North America it ought most speedily to be seen to; for there it cannot be much longer endured, even though our Ministers had still means to riot in folly and extravagance, in holding colonies only for the portioning of their friends and relations. Bickerings between provincial assemblies and their governors are now continually heard of; and even the little island of Bermuda has for years been in a state of distraction and discontent, from arbitrary proceedings. The cause is obvious. Colonial Governors are all of them armed with too much power, which, almost to a man, they abuse. They are blinded by the sycophants who surround them; and invariably become either stupid or mad. Our North American colonies afford, in their history, not a single trace of common sense, discretion, or economy. Mismanagement and misrule have prevailed, and are prevailing. Not only do they yield no revenue, but, as consumers of British manufactures, the inhabitants are not half so advantageous to us as any like number of people in the United States; for this clear reason, that colonial policy has kept them spiritless and poverty-stricken. By the simplest and safest measures, all may be changed for the better. We may speedily lessen our expenditure, and, from improved management alone, we may at once have a direct revenue and flourishing people to deal with in trade.

My pen must not be laid down without noticing the opposite sentiments of politicians in and out of power. Ministers seem to have no idea of holding Canada, but by enfeebling the people; ruling over them by a wretched system of patronage and favouritism; and guarding certain points by ships, and fortifications. Most expensive works have, within the last two years, been commenced at Quebec and Isle-au-Noix, for military defence, while neither the one nor the other post could have a thousandth share in maintaining the provinces to Britain, in the event of invasion. In fact, all that is wanted for this, is the good will of the people to defend themselves, and with liberal treatment, that would never be wanting.

Our Opposition men run to another extreme. They are for abandoning Canada, or selling it to the United States. This is worse and worse. I can answer for the loyalty of the Canadians: it abounds; and their desire to be independent of the United States is strong, from one end of the country to the other. All that they want to continue and ensure this for ever is, the promise of independence now, and the reality after a given period of years.

To attract notice to this most essential point, I have twice repeated the word in my engraved title-pages; and, by accident, the sun has been made to shine from the north, to emblazon it. The moment that the promise of independence is granted, that moment all chance of discord and war between the United States and British America will cease, and England may forthwith begin to reduce her military and naval establishments in that quarter of the world. At Kingston and Sackett's harbour immense ships of war are upheld, reproaching at once humanity and common sense. In a very few years these ships will be rotten, and why should not each nation, while the materials are yet fresh, have them disposed of for useful purposes? These and the Government stores, at Kingston and elsewhere, would go far to make good the navigation of the St. Lawrence; and nothing more can be required to have these safely disposed of, but a plain agreement with the United States, that the breaking up shall be mutual and simultaneous.

The late invasion of Canada by the people of the United States, was a burst of madness, of which these people are now ashamed, and which never would be repeated, were Canada independent of British Ministry. All of us rejoice in the independence of South America, now secured by years of civil war; and with that country there is now every reason to believe we shall cultivate a most friendly and profitable intercourse. How glorious would it be for Britain, while opportunity yet remains, to grant independence to North American colonies! how glorious for her to enjoy the immortal honour of being the first nation upon earth to do justice to her progeny, – the first truly entitled to the endearing appellation of *parent State*!

Niagara Spectator, June 10, 1819.

Niagara Jail, 7th June, 1819.

To The Parliamentary Representatives of the People of Upper Canada.

GENTLEMEN,
It is a lamentable fact, that men will sometimes continue to hate those whom they have injured, for no other reason, but because they themselves have already done so much wrong. Having made this remark, I shall not apply it to any particular case, but wish that all of us, for the future, may be guarded against a propensity so very detestable, and ruinous to human felicity.

You are this day meeting together, to legislate for your country; and I, driving from my memory all past occurrences, looking anxiously to the eventful moment, and keeping only one object in view, viz. the general good, have considered by what means, and to what end, your labours may be most beneficially directed. With a mind thus abstracted and serious, knowing that you are not prepared to go so far as could be wished, it seems prudent to confine myself to that which is most likely of being accomplished.

In my earliest reflections upon the political condition of this province, I saw restraints which greatly retarded its improvement, and which seemed so obvious, that I could not doubt they would be speedily removed. The greatest immediate restraint seemed to arise out of the state of property, to which there appeared a simple and effectual remedy in the adoption of a new system of taxation. To this subject my attention has been very often directed; and to this I would now beg leave to call particular notice.

It is not vanity to say that I have, for many years, devoted much reflection to the subject of taxation, generally. It is merely stating a fact; and liberal minds will admit of my frankly communicating some of the results, without being moved by this or any other passion.

My reflections have led me to believe, that the chief perfection of Government is to be looked for in the adoption of a correct and just system of taxation. This, I am convinced, may be so regulated, as not only to contribute sufficiently to every public enterprise, but to command the destinies of power and property, every way to good.

Mankind have looked with astonishment to the mighty achievements of England. They have seen her, single-handed, contending with Europe, – nay, almost with the world besides; and they have seen her rising in strength as effort was required; – they have seen her unexpectedly preva'l over innumerable difficulties. Whence has she derived her strength? From her system of taxation.

In former ages, the energies of our species have been called forth to war, as furiously as we in our day have witnessed. In former ages, we have seen those energies sometimes elicited by superior genius, and sometimes impelled by the influence of accumulated treasure; but, till this age, never did the evanescent skill of the financier fully display its powers; never did human policy so completely excite and control human exertion; never did waste, to such a degree, induce excitement; nor excitement so completely supply the devouring jaws of waste.

Often have I wandered in my fields at home, ruminating on the principle which upheld our national greatness: often have I indulged the blissful reverie, that it was possible to make the same principle operate in time of peace, to the increase and enjoyment of our kind, as, in war, it had been bent on destruction and misery. But where – where, I would say, is there room for action? This little island already overflows with people: every spot is cultivated – every art driven to perfection. Arrived in Canada, surveying its boundless forests and its noble river, there were at once before me scenes of action, objects of employment, and incitements to exertion. What more is wanted here, but to give the first impetus to motion? And what may not motion effect – what may not be its wonderful increase? – But before coming to the point of action for Canada, let me glance at some of those circumstances which have enabled England to display such mighty power. Her system of taxation is not one which could primarily have been brought into full play; neither could it at all have been practicable in every country. England, happy in her local situation, contains within herself more natural advantages than any other spot of equal extent; and her population, sufficiently great and dense, is pent up and secure by the surrounding ocean. In England, honour and shame are made to toil together. There ambition has the highest range, and necessity the direst spur: – there, from poverty to extreme wealth, we behold a highway, but it is crowded, and only he who labours hard can get on. He looks behind, and is terrified with want: he casts his eye before him, and longs for the glittering prize. Competitors pant by his side: there is health, there is vigour, there is joy in the race. Where, in the wide world, do we see mankind so busy, by night and by day, as in England? In England, at all events, there must be action, and in action there is gain. It was from the extraordinary increase of this action, arising from a variety of causes, that the means were created which sustained the late war. The Government sent abroad its armies, and tens of thousands were annually slain; yet the waste of life was inferior to the supply, and population continued to increase. The Government squandered its hundreds of millions, but the monied means became more and more ready at command. In all this, there was no miracle. A full inspection of the materials and machinery, is sufficient to account for the wonderful results.

Mere population, however great, will do nothing without excitement; nor will wealth alone continually sustain exertion. China swarms with human beings; but they are things without passion, – feeble, and tame – loiterers in the paths of improvement. Spain had her treasury long replenished from Mexico and Peru; but her wealth served, ultimately, only to enervate; and her body politic, as well as her people, became plethoric and dull. England has wealth, directly poured into her from the West and East Indies, besides the general profits of trade; but this wealth flows not immediately into the Treasury. Its course is better directed. It first spreads out among the people; gives pleasure to the rich, an aim to the ambitious, and employment to the poor. An inward flow of wealth so very great, would be ruinous to society, had it no vent: it would tend to repletion, and repletion would induce disease. The war afforded vent to the vast surplus of English wealth, as well as for her spare population. In one sense, it created health and vigour. The cessation of war has, in some respects, already produced languor and disease: it has diminished consumption, and stopped up the ducts of beneficial waste. War and waste were, of themselves, to be deplored; but so far their effects were good. The *desideratum* now is, seeing that such agents have promoted beneficial action and production, to draw forth activity, and thence have production by peaceful means, and for peaceful ends.

I have not lauded, and shall not laud, the English system of taxation, as one which I approve, or should wish to see imitated. It has rested on oppression, and has begotten oppressors. I have spoken of it only as it has displayed the wonderful efforts which mankind can make, with sufficient excitement. The English system of taxation would never have been made so productive, but by a corrupt representation of the people. With the people, Boroughmongers have no common feeling: nay, their interests run counter; and, as tools of the Minister, they are altogether perfect. They are the handspikes which squeeze from the grape the wine which itself would not yield. No system of this kind can be established here. The people, fairly represented, will not endure that degree of pressure which is required, to put industry to its full stretch; and while there is not sufficient necessity to goad, there is a want of ambition to lead on. Still, however, nature presents here most inviting objects for exertion, and when the course is fairly opened, the race may not be slack.

In contriving the system of taxation which now has place in this province, no thought, I am convinced, was bestowed on the *effects* which might be produced from one system more than another. It was only considered how the required means, for Government purposes, could be most directly procured. At first, money was only seen in shops and taverns; and a licence upon these was adequate, for a time, to afford the little wanted. By and by, the farmers' stock increased, and the principle of taxing property, according to its value, was adopted. As a burden, taxes are here trifling; and it is a saying that without challenge, all is well. The wild lands of absentees being untaxed, first gave rise to complaint. To tax the lands of absentees, has been the object of repeated motions in Parliament; and a Bill, for this purpose, got so far as to be printed. The order of the day now is, that they must, at least, be made to contribute to the improvement of roads. I am to propose that they shall do more. In fact, I mean to strike at the root of the present system of taxation, and exhibit an entire new one for adoption. I shall first briefly sketch out my scheme, then pull down the old one; and, lastly, set forth what effects may be produced by the other, when substituted in its place.

My proposal then is to have but one tax for the collection of revenue in this province – a general land tax, making no distinction whatever between wild and cultivated land, public or private property, that of residents or absentees; the rule of estimating value to be governed by one consideration, the rate of population of the township in which the land is situated, taken in conjunction with that of the neighbourhood. A few examples will best illustrate what I mean.

Let us take it for granted that the average value of land throughout the province is 20s. per acre, and the average rate of population, 1,000 souls to a township of 60,000 acres. Say that township A has this precise population and extent, is bounded nine miles by the lake or river, of which no account shall be taken, nine miles by Township B, containing 1,500 souls, nine miles by Township C, containing 1,500 souls, and nine miles by Township D, uninhabited, or, by unsurveyed land. Township A being within itself at par, and, thus bounded, remains at par, viz. 20s. per acre.

Say again, that Township E, of equal extent as Township A, contains 1,500 souls, is bounded nine miles by F, containing 1,000 souls, nine miles by G, containing 800 souls, nine miles by H, containing 1,800 souls, and nine miles by I, containing 2,000 souls. Thus situated, the land of E shall be reckoned worth 28s. 4⁸⁄₁₀d.

Again, say that Township R, of equal extent as the above, contains no inhabitants, and is bounded by Townships S, T, W, and X, containing, respectively, 500, 400, 300, and 200 souls. This will make the land of R worth 5s. 7⅕d.

Again, say that Township W contains 500 souls; and is bounded by Y for nine miles, containing 1,000 souls, and on the other three sides by uninhabited land. This will make the land of W worth 6s. per acre.

These examples sufficiently shew the principle upon which I would have the value of land estimated. A Township may contain more or less than 60,000 acres, or it may be bounded by more than four townships, and perhaps irregularly. In such cases a little more calculation only is wanted to give an equally fair result. The idea of raising all taxes from land, is not new. It has often been the subject of political discussion; and often have I mused upon it before my acquaintance with this country. In an old country, many objections start up against its adoption; here I know of none. Throughout the whole province nature has wonderfully equalized the value of land. What is better in point of quality, is generally worse in point of local situation; and, at this early state of settlement, minute differences in this respect are of very little consequence. The simplicity of such a scheme – the economy and ease of management are highly to be prized. If the owner of land is out of the country, or tardy in paying his assessment, an entry of debt can forthwith be made against him, his account to become chargeable with compound interest, a half per cent, above the ordinary rate; the law declaring this debt inseparable from the land, and preferable to every other, while it gave a power of sale for recovery, at the termination of a given number of years, say 10, 15, or 20. The perfection of a land tax, in a new country, is obvious, so far as speculators must either settle, sell, or pay for their profits.

Having said thus much of what I propose for adoption, let me briefly state wherein the present system of taxation is erroneous and impolitic.

In the first place, rating all wild land at the same value of 4s. per acre, is glaringly wrong. Some wild land in remote situations being worth less than even 4s., while other wild land is worth ten times as much. In the second place, it is very unfair to rate a lot of wild land one farthing less than a lot of cultivated land, to which it is immediately adjoining. The wild land rises in value merely from the labour bestowed on that which is cultivated, and, in strict justice, ought rather to be rated higher, from the consideration of its being a nuisance. The revenue from Town lots is a bagatelle, which should be left to the control of the inhabitants of the towns respectively, for their immediate comfort and convenience. Taxing houses, and their fire-places, in a new country, is a sin against nature: good houses should rather have a premium. Taxing mills is damnable: taxing shops and storehouses is nearly as bad; but, when we get among the taxed horses, the taxed milch cows, and the taxed horned cattle, what can we do but laugh at the monstrous absurdity, and think that the whole scheme was contrived by an ass? Suppose a mechanic, whose daily bread is earned by his ten fingers, has a certain weight continually to bear about with him, I should should think that, if he could not distribute the burden equally over his body, that somewhere between the shoulders might be an appropriate situation for the mass of it; but certainly, not a single grain should be allowed to entangle the fingers, or even the parts adjoining. Husbandry stock, shops, and mills, are the very fingers of industry, and ought, at all events, to go clear of incumbrance.

When we see any thing very far wrong, and but feeble efforts employed for amendment, we may with some reason suspect that there is a snake in the grass. To excuse the ass above-mentioned, I have occasionally thought that the present system of taxation had been introduced by some law-beleagured judge from England, partly perhaps under instructions from the landed oligarchy, or partly besotted with the notion that Mr. Pitt's practice was correct, of running into every corner to tax the middling and poorer classes of society, while his friends of the higher order went comparatively free; but then looking across Niagara river, and finding that a system somewhat of the same kind obtains among our neighbours, my investigation into the cause is still restless – I am still disposed to make further conjecture. The majority of those who legislate in all countries, rank with the wealthier class of society, and selfishness will invariably have its bias. Let us first consider the private circumstances of our legislative councillors of Upper Canada. Say that one holds 100,000 acres of land; another 80,000; a third 60,000; a fourth 40,000; and the remaining five so much as to bring the average of each councillor's landed estate to 20,000 acres. This being the case, we cannot wonder much that these gentlemen have hitherto stood in the way of fairly taxing wild lands. Now, further, among yourselves, most honourable representatives of the people of Upper Canada, we shall say that there is one who possesses 50,000 acres of land; another 25,000; a third 15,000; and the rest of you such extent, as to make out, on the whole, an average possession of 5,000 acres of land, which possession, though it will not operate so powerfully as a selfish bias against the due taxation of wild land, as the greater average possession of legislative councillors, will still make you tardy, as you really have been; it will still make you in some degree not so frank as in duty you ought to be, for promoting the interests of your constituents, who on an average do not possess above 400 acres of land, of which a fifth part is under tillage; while out of your 5,000 acres, not more than a 25th is cultivated, nor, out of the average possession of legislative councillors, not a 50th. Being myself a holder of little more than 400 acres of land, I, of course, sympathize most purely with my brother farmers; but, Gentlemen, were I a holder of 40,000 acres of land, such is my assurance that the principle of taxation now proposed by me, would be infinitely for the advantage of all, that I would push the adoption of it with so much the greater zeal. Land in America is the very lubber-fiend which checks its own improvement. Could nine-tenths of it be sunk in the sea, and afterwards emerge by tenths, gradually, as it became absolutely necessary for the wants of mankind, there would be infinite gain in every way. The people of the States are wasting their strength by spreading too rapidly over their wide domains: nor is the dropsical condition of that country likely to have a speedy cure. Here, in

Canada, circumscribed by narrower bounds, the disease may be easier checked, and the fullest advantage obtained from compact settlement.

Before proceeding to consider the use and effect to be made and produced by condensing all taxes into one upon land, let me sweep down the remaining lumber of the old system. There are all the trashy duties upon importations from the United States, which should fall by the lump, not excepting that upon salt, imposed by the wisdom of your very last session. To go to the cheapest market, wherever it may be, is economy: to punish ourselves, that others may suffer, is wretched policy: to give scope to free trade is noble: to beggar custom-houses is delightful; and, looking to moral improvement, there is more hope in the end of smuggling than in the beginning of preaching. The tax upon whiskey stills is merely a premium upon rum, a less wholesome beverage, and a drawback from the profits of the Canadian farmer, in favour of the West India planter. To tax billiard tables, which might give exercise in bad weather to idle gentlemen, and perhaps draw them off from drinking "One bottle more," is a foolish conceit, especially when dice may be rattled at will, and a dirty pack of cards makes part of the furniture of every cobbler's stool. Lastly, and here I shall have opposition from every bench of worshipful magistrates, there should not even be a tax upon taverns. All – all should be free of taxation but land. To tax taverns as a palliative against debauchery is delusive: to tax them in order to make advantage of travellers is ungenerous and unwise: to tax them at the discretion of magistrates, is giving an inlet to favouritism and arbitrary power: to tax them merely as a source of revenue, is altogether unnecessary. Off – off, with all taxes but one upon land; and then, the heavier that is made by large and judicious expenditure on public works, so much the better: – then, indeed, Canada shall flourish.

Let us take it for granted that the province contains one hundred townships of 60,000 acres each, on an average, valued at 20s. per acre, thus giving a total value of £6,000,000: one per cent on which, viz. £60,000, we shall assume as the first required annual revenue. How simple and fair becomes the business of voting the yearly supply in future. An estimate is made out of what is required; and whatever it is, double, treble, a half, a fourth, or a sixteenth, more or less, becomes the sole consideration. Out of this supply I should propose to defray every public charge whatever: the charges of the civil list – of making and repairing roads, canals, &c. As to roads, they should rank under three descriptions. Provincial, being those great leading roads which connect together the remotest points, and which should draw from the public fund an absolute sufficiency for their being made and kept perfect. Secondly, district roads, being those connecting less distant points, and which should have support proportionate to the assessed value of the districts through which they pass; and lastly, township roads, which should have their proportion afforded on the same principle.

It ought to be allowed, at all hands, that good roads are of the first consequence in the improvement of any country; and it is clear that if a fair principle is once fixed upon for the making and support of these, the hand to extort means to such ends may be at once relentless and just; for, the greater the expenditure, the greater, certainly, will be the gain. But, Gentlemen, I now proceed to the grand purposes which taxation, on the proposed plan, when once adopted, and put in spirited action, may accomplish – I mean its application to the improvement of the St. Lawrence navigation; and its being made a bond of connexion between Canada and England – a bond by which both countries may reap infinite advantage. Let me first, however, rid myself of a little latent contempt, by laughing outright at the grave resolutions of your last session, to apply to His Royal Highness the Prince Regent for *a hundred thousand acres of land*, to be intrusted to a committee for executing this great work out of the sales thereof. God help us! what will the sale of such a quantity of land fetch, as things are now managed? Truly, perhaps as much as, added to the pittance (£2,000) voted out of the taxes of the province for defraying the expenses of a survey, might complete that object respectably with plans and estimates. Very truly, my clodhopping brothers – most august legislators, I am ashamed of you: so do be so good as wipe off this nonsensical concern along with the gagging act, that we may all be friends again; and, in the issue, recover some little claim to the possession of common sense. You cannot think how anxious I am to get home to England, and report you all in a sane state of mind, after the damnable alarm you have given to John Bull. – Well, hoping the best, let us proceed.

Gentlemen, the St. Lawrence navigation should be looked to as a great national object; this province affording security for the repayment of all charges, and Britain promoting the work with a loan of money, and the supply of hands. Was the affair properly represented to the imperial parliament, there would neither be difficulty nor delay in the accomplishment. Permit me to give you a slight sketch of ways and means, for the sake of illustration. Now that there is peace, Britain could spare out of her population, annually, 100,000 souls with advantage; but they who would willingly emigrate, have not the means of transport. My very first fancy towards Upper Canada, burned forth from a desire to effect the vast object of finding a vent for these poor people, with whose circumstances I have been peculiarly well acquainted for near twenty years; but, *here* I am, for my zeal in the cause. Under the wing of wealthy farmers, many thousands of them might before now have been comfortably lodged in the province, had all gone well; and by next summer many thousands may still be at work on the St. Lawrence navigation. I have taken the present value of the settled part of the province to be 6,000,000*l.* Suppose a navigation for vessels of 200 tons could be opened from Montreal to Lake Ontario, in the course of five years from the present time, and that during the same time there was an influx of 20,000 souls annually into the province, pray, may we not fairly calculate that from 6,000,000*l.* value, the territory settled by the end of that period, would be fully worth three times as much; and that an expenditure of 2,000,000*l.* might very easily be repaid out of the taxation of the province before the end of ten years?

Let us exhibit a jotting of how things might go on; 5,000 able-bodied men could be transported from Britain, at the rate of 10*l*. each*, and be at work on the canal by the 1st of June, 1820   £ 50,000

Transport of 10,000 women and children, supposed to accompany the men	50,000
Pay of 5,000 men at work, from 1st June, till 1st December, 1820 – six months	100,000
Ditto, till 1st April, 1821, four months	30,000
Ditto, till 1st December, 1821, eight months	130,000
Transport of 5,000 men, with 10,000 women and children, 1821	100,000
Pay of these second year's men, from 1st June, till 1st December, 1821	100,000
Interest and contingencies	40,000
	600,000
At this period discharge the first year's men, who refund their transport, and have in pocket 10l. per man	100,000
Total expenditure up to 1st December, 1821	500,000
Brought forward	500,000
Pay of second year's men, from 1st December, 1821, till 1st April, 1822	30,000
Ditto, till 1st December, 1822, eight months	130,000
Transport of third year's men, with women and children	100,000
Pay of these men from 1st June, till 1st December, 1822, six months	100,000
Interest and contingencies	40,000
	900,000
Deduct, refunded by the second year's men, now discharged	100,000
Total expenditure up to 1st December, 1822	800,000

It would serve no purpose to go farther with such a sketch. My meaning is already clear; and the practicability of the proceeding is obvious. I suppose the men to contract at home only for the labour of two seasons; and they are above represented as entirely quit of the work at the end of the second season. One half however may be supposed to return, and make engagements for labour, the third, or even fourth summer, so as to give any required acceleration to the business. To employ the hands during the four months of their first winter, would require a little arrangement; but with this, jobs sufficient could be found while so great an undertaking was on foot. It will be observed, that there are never more than 5,000 men to be thus provided for; and being free by the commencement of the second winter, with a sufficiency of cash for present wants, they might either spread themselves over the country, in the service of others, or they might make a beginning in clearing land

---

* By personal inquiries made at the ports of Glasgow, Leith, and Aberdeen, spring, 1820, I found £ 7. was the common charge for a man. On contract, and after a grand system of emigration was set on foot, the charge would be greatly lowered.

for themselves. By this time, not only reconciled to the novelty of their situation, but pretty well informed as to the various modes of management, and taught to handle the axe, they would be free of all that gloom and awkwardness, which is so heartbreaking to old country people, when they have to go directly into the woods after their first arrival in this country.

Gentlemen, could I be assured that there was to be a speedy end to all illiberal and trifling proceedings, how joyfully should I continue to write on this glorious theme.

ROBERT GOURLAY.

Conclusion

To The People of Upper Canada

February 11, 1822.

CANADIANS,

It is this day two months since the date of my last Address to you. I was then feeble; and had shortly after to abandon part of my plan; to throw aside my pen, and fly to the country. That movement set afloat new ideas; and my Address to the People of Wiltshire led me first to produce some extracts from Salisbury newspapers, and then to exhibit others out of the Niagara Spectator, which you will find link well together, and manifest at least consistency in opinion and principle.

During these two months most eventful occurrences have taken place; and up to this hour the landed and farming interests have been getting into greater and greater trepidation: have been holding meetings in every direction; and coming forth with speeches altogether radical, led on by noble Lords. Parliament is now met; and we are all upon tip-toe to learn what is to be done. Ministers, it is said, are about to borrow five millions to lend to landlords and farmers, to keep peace in this island; while penal laws and military force is applied for to cure disturbances in Ireland!!! Mr. Cobbett having raised a cry about Peel's bill, (a most excellent bill) thinks, I presume, that he may trust to that for a while with more hope than to "Cobbett's parliament," which is put off, *sine die*: so, after all, our fate is left "to the force of events," and we know not what a day may bring forth.

Newspapers have informed us that your provincial parliament met on the 30th of November: that it was expected that the session would be short and tranquil; also, that the question of your farfamed sedition law was agitated. I am sorry for this. It has lessened my expectation of a commission coming home immediately; but I shall not yet despair. The sole duty of your representatives should rest in refusing supplies till a commission is appointed: but the silliness of last session makes me suspect that silliness may still prevail. It is reported that the Governor-in-Chief has asked the parliament of Lower Canada to grant the civil list during the life of the sovereign. Surely they will not be fools enough to comply.

Though I am a friend to free trade with all the world, and wish to see that brought about as speedily as possible, had your representatives sent home a commission last year, instead of trifling away time, by appointing a select committee (see page 666, Vol. II.) only to exhibit ignorance and vanity, I should have been happy to have seen the timber trade continued for a few years in favour of Canada, with notice that the favour should be gradually withdrawn. This would have given opportunity to people in the trade to have wound up their business economically, and to have disposed of or worn out their machinery (saw-mills, &c.) to some profit. Should a commission come home this session, I should on the same principle be happy to see our North American provinces favoured for a few years in the corn trade. I should wish to see your corn and flour admitted for sale here at all times on a certain duty, to be diminished year after year, till the trade was free to you; and, after being free to you, for some time, to be made free to all the world. An *ad valorem* duty would be the thing; but for illustration, say that your wheat should this year be admitted to sale, on paying a duty of 3*s.* per bushel, next year 2*s.* 6*d.*, and so on, diminishing 6*d.* every year till the duty was extinct. The Halton petition, and your parliamentary proceedings of last year, plainly manifest your wish to bar out your neighbours in the United States from trading through Quebec with England on equal terms with yourselves. This is a selfish and narrow-minded notion, on your part, and it would not suit England, even though you were to be gainers. It is besides impracticable. Whenever provincial duties are imposed to any great amount on produce of the United States, and vent is found for it at Quebec, the extent of unguarded boundary line between the Canadas and the States will afford such opportunities to smuggling, as effectually to blast your illiberal policy, and I rejoice in this truth. In the event of the St. Lawrence navigation being effected on my plan, I had a scheme to propose for making American produce pay towards that; but at present there is no occasion for enlarging on the subject. It is the interest of Britain to trade with Americans through the port of Quebec, as freely as with you, Canadians, though her shipping interest only was taken into consideration; and were an act immediately passed, admitting corn and flour to be imported from our North American colonies, and sold here at all times on a duty, as above proposed, the benefit would be instant and great both to England and the colonies. If your commission would come home, and propose this simple measure, without any invidious, grasping, and illiberal view towards your neighbours, I doubt not but it would be admitted; and perhaps you might yet get to rights without becoming bankrupt. Half the farmers of Halton probably have their names standing on the books of James Crooks, Esq. M.P. for goods furnished to them when prices were high. He again is perhaps indebted to merchants in Montreal; and they to merchants in London. In the course of time, trade might assist in adjusting these accounts. I spoke lightly of a general bankruptcy among you, keeping my eye bent on the infinitely greater distress which general bankruptcy among British farmers would produce. Your distress would be comparatively nothing to their's; and their's would not only be to themselves ruinous, but it would spread death and destruction around to millions: yes, were the public credit of England once vitally touched, and a general breaking down among the farmers would certainly so touch it, not less than two millions of human beings would be swept from existence – paupers, annuitants, and fundholders; young, old, and infirm! I have said above, and I say again, that no nation on earth was ever situated as we are, from the factitious state into which we have been brought by the Pitt system of finance, as it is called, in conjunction with the greatest of all evils – the evil of the poor-laws.

I have already said, and this too I repeat, that were reason to regulate our affairs, all danger could be avoided: even the Pitt system could with discretion be followed up in time of peace to infinite advantage; and taxation itself could be turned to profit. Reason, however, I am afraid, will never be consulted while we are ruled by boroughmongers: while ministers study only their own interest, and are totally regardless of public good. How mad are all their measures! Let us look for an example of it to Ireland, at the present moment. That unhappy country could be cheaply redeemed from distress. Emancipate the catholics: let not one-fifth of the nation lord it over four-fifths. If clergy are to be paid by government, let catholic clergy be paid as well as protestant clergy, on condition of their allowing the people to be educated: let tithes be commuted; and let emigration be assisted. All this would be reasonable; but ministers are equipping an army to make war against the poor, ignorant, distracted, starving Irish; and Lord Roden has just told us in parliament, that the great evil is to be traced to "the non-residence of gentry and landowners"!!!

In England we have much to gain by mere legislation. Tithes could be commuted by an act of the simplest kind, merely to make them payable at a fixed rate, depending on the price of grain. This would instantly ensure peace and harmony between tithe-holders and farmers: it would instantly give the rein to the spirit of improvement; and it would free the clergy from a world of reproach. But the clergy, who, of all others, would be most benefited, who would indeed secure to themselves, as a body, a chance of lengthened possession of church property; – the clergy set their faces against this!!!

In five years, five millions of annual expenditure on the poor could be saved to England by reforming the poor-laws; and at least five millions more would be added to national wealth by greater industry and better conduct on the part of the poor themselves; but, will the poor-laws be reformed? This session they could be reformed, as well as in any other session; but the last Edinburgh Review is for delaying that most necessary of all reforms for several years!!!

Since autumn, 1813, farming has been unprofitable (since then I calculate that 200 millions of money have been lost to the farming interest); and though the present low prices could have been guarded against, it was clear that war prices could not be kept up: it was clear that something should have been done to give farmers relief from contracts formed when prices were high, which could not possibly be fulfilled when prices were low: it was clear that an act of parliament, to allow them to pay rents according to the price of grain, would have protected them from ruin better than a cornbill; but their landlords could not think in time of lowering rents; and they now do it partially, only to increase mischief!!!

Had landlords, who rule this nation, – the landed oligarchy, seen, and they might have seen, had they opened their eyes; – had they seen that rents could not be paid in peace which were contracted for in war; – had they seen that even the Pitt system, *judiciously acted upon* in time of peace, could not uphold war prices, after our monopoly of trade was at an end, after other nations enjoyed domestic peace, and could supply themselves; after they were freed from ancient encumbrances; and, with "cheap labour and removed absurdity, could afford the productions of the soil at one-third of our price:" had our oligarchy seen all this, and it was quite visible; – had they seen this, and liberally proposed lowering their rents according to the fall of corn prices; – had they thus lowered rents, and insisted at the same time, which in the omnipotence of their power they could have done, that fundholders should be paid in the same portion; that all government officers should be paid in the same proportion, &c. &c.: – then, indeed, with peace we should have had plenty and prosperity. What is to prevent this to be done now? What is to prevent a general arrangement throughout his Majesty's dominions, that all contracts may be paid on a certain scale of reduction? Suppose you *august* parliament, Canadians, was to enact that all contracts were to be compounded for at a certain low rate, which would save you from universal bankruptcy among yourselves; which would enable the inhabitants of Halton to get out of the books of James Crooks, Esq. M.P. Your provincial law could not let him out of the books of the merchant in Montreal; nor could an enactment of the Lower Province let the Montreal merchant out of the books of the London merchant; but if the British Parliament were to set about the work; – if the supreme government were to admit of debts being extinguished at 30, or 40, or 50 per cent. discount at home, and our governments abroad were to act in unison, we should be all able to start afresh, hale, sound, and unincumbered; and with the dire experience of what has happened, avoid in future such scrapes as those in which we are involved. All this could be easily effected, had reason the controul; but I must confess, that my hope of reason guiding our destinies is not very sanguine. Again, adieu.

Introduction to Sketches and Township Reports of Upper Canada.

THE Sketches were prepared for publication in 1811, but laid aside in consequence of the war which broke out in 1812.

On the re-establishment of peace, the writer revised his Sketches, and inserted accounts of battles, &c. of which he had the best opportunities of being correctly informed, again intending to publish, but, for reasons not communicated to me, that intention was relinquished. In 1818 the manuscript was offered to me, as a fund of materials for my Statistical Account, and I had a written order to receive it from a printer in the United States on my way to England.

When shut up in Niagara jail, it occured to me, that I might beguile some dreary hours by publishing in Upper Canada the Township Reports, with a general Account of the Province, from my own knowledge, so as to have the whole improved on the spot, by additions and observations of the inhabitants, for rendering the publication in England more complete. I took steps towards this, and had the Sketches sent to me; but they did not arrive till after I had found it impossible to accomplish my purpose, and I did not give them an attentive reading till my return home. Here I found the work so perfect, the style so good, and the statements so candid and impartial, that I judged it wrong to pull it to pieces. I conceived that as a whole, it was better than any general account I could draw up, and would be more peculiarly interesting, as coming from the pen of a native American, and one who had been long resident in the province of Upper Canada.

The TOWNSHIP REPORTS need no other introduction than the following Address, which called them forth.

TO

The Resident Land-Owners of Upper Canada.
                                    Queenston, October, 1817.

GENTLEMEN,
I am a British farmer, and have visited this province to ascertain what advantages it possesses in an agricultural point of view. After three months residence I am convinced that these are great, – far superior indeed to what the mother country has ever held out, either as they concern speculative purchase, or the profits of present occupation.

Under such impressions, it is my purpose, as soon as circumstances will permit, to become a settler; and in the meantime, would willingly do what lies in my power to benefit the country of my choice.

When I speak in this sanguine manner of the capabilities of Canada, I take it for granted that certain political restraints to improvement will be speedily removed. Growing necessity, and the opinion of every sensible man with whom I have conversed on the subject, gives assurance of this. My present Address, therefore, waves all regard to political arrangements: it has in view, simply to open a correspondence between you and your fellow-subjects at home, where the utmost ignorance prevails with respect to the natural resources of this fine country.

Travellers have published passing remarks, – they have told wonderful stories, and amused the idle of England with descriptions of the beautiful and grand scenery which nature has here displayed; but no authentic account has yet been afforded to men of capital, to men of enterprise and skill, of those important facts which are essential to be known, before such men will launch into foreign speculation, or venture with their families, in quest of better fortune across the Atlantic.

In this state of ignorance, you have hitherto had for settlers chiefly poor men driven from home by despair. These men, ill-informed and lost in the novelties which surround them, make at first but a feeble commencement, and ultimately, form a society, crude, unambitious, and weak. In your newspapers I have frequently observed hints towards bettering the condition of those poor settlers, and for ensuring their residence in the provinces. Such hints evidently spring from benevolent feelings: they are well meant, and may tend to alleviate individual distress, but can produce no important good to the country. Canada is worthy of something better than a mere guidance to it of the blind and the lame: it has attractions to stimulate desire and place its colonization above the aids of necessity.

Hands no doubt are necessary, but, next to good laws, the grand requisite for the improvement of any country is capital. Could a flow of capital be once directed into this quarter, hands would not be wanting, nor would these hands be so chilled with poverty as to need the patronage of charitable institutions.

At this moment British capital is overflowing; trade is yielding it up: the funds cannot profitably absorb it: land mortgages are gorged; and it is streaming to waste in the six per cents. of America. Why should not this stream be diverted into the woods of Canada, where it would find a still higher rate of interest, with the most substantial security?

Gentlemen! The moment is most auspicious to your interests, and you should take advantage of it. You should make known the state of this country; you should advertise the excellence of the raw material which Nature has lavishly spread before you; you should inspire confidence, and tempt able adventurers from home. At this time there are thousands of British farmers sickened with disappointed hopes, who would readily come to Canada, did they but know the truth: many of these could still command a few thousand pounds to begin with here; while others, less able in means, have yet preserved their character for skill and probity, to entitle them to the confidence of capitalists at home, for whom they could act as agents in adventure. Under the wing of such men, the redundant population of Britain would emigrate with cheerfulness, and be planted here with hearts unbroken.

We hear of four or five thousand settlers arrived from home this season: and it is talked of as a great accession to the population of the provinces. It is a mere drop from the bucket. England alone could spare fifty thousand people annually, while she would be refreshed and strengthened by the discharge. In war, England sent abroad annually more than twenty thousand of her youthful sons to be slain, and more than twenty thousand of her daughters shot after them the last hope of honourable love. In these twenty-five years of war the population of England rapidly increased: what is it to do now, when war is at an end, when love and opportunity are no longer to be foiled, and the poor-laws have provided sustenance for children independent of the parent's care?

Under existing circumstances, it is absolutely necessary even for the domestic comfort of England, that a vent should be immediately opened for her increasing population, and the colonization of Canada, if once begun, upon a liberal footing, would afford this vent.

The present emigration from England affords no relief whatever to the calamity occasioned by the poor-laws. Thousands and tens of thousands of paupers could be spared, who cannot possibly now get off for want of means, but who would be brought over by men of capital, were confidence for adventure here once established.

The extent of calamity already occasioned by the system of the poor-laws, cannot be even imagined by strangers. They may form some idea, however, when I tell them, that last winter I saw in one parish (Blackwall, within five miles of London), several hundreds of able-bodied men, harnessed and yoked, fourteen together, in carts, hauling gravel for the repair of the highways; each fourteen men performing just about as much work as an old horse led by a boy could accomplish. We have heard since that £ 1,500,000 has been voted to keep the poor at work; and perhaps the most melancholy consideration of the whole is, that there are people who trust to such means as a cure for the evil.

While all this is true; when the money and labour of England is thus wasted; when thousands of our fellow-subjects are emigrating into the States of America; when we even hear of them being led off to mix with the boors of Poland, in the cultivation of a country where the nature of the government must counteract the utmost efforts towards improvement, – is it not provoking that all this should go on merely from a reigning ignorance of the superior advantages which Canada has in store, and a thoughtlessness as to the grand policy which might be adopted for the general aggrandizement of the British nation?

Some have thought the exclusion of American citizens a great bar to the speedy settlement of Canada; but a liberal system of colonization from Europe, would render this of small importance. Before coming to a decided opinion on this important subject, I took much pains to inform myself of facts. A minute inquiry on the spot where government has endeavoured to force a settlement, satisfied me as to the causes of the too notorious failure there. It convinced me that the fault by no means rested with the incapacity of the settlers, but resulted from the system pursued. I have since spent a month perambulating the Genesee country, for the express purpose of forming a comparison between British and American management. That country lies parallel to this: it possesses no superior advantages: its settlement began ten years later; yet I am ashamed to say, it is already ten years before Canada, in improvement. This has been ascribed to the superior dexterity of the American people, but most erroneously. The art of clearing land is as well understood here as in the States: men direct from Britain are as energetic, and after a little practice, sufficiently expert with the axe, while they are more regular in their habits and more persevering in their plans than the Americans.

No improvement has taken place in the Genesee country, which could not be far exceeded here, under a proper system. It was indeed British capital and enterprise which gave the first grand impetus to the improvement of that country: much of its improvement is still proceeding under British agency; and one of its most flourishing townships is wholly occupied by men, who came, with slender means, from the Highlands of Scotland. In the Genesee country, the government pocketed much, but *forced* nothing, and charity, there, has been left without an object.

GENTLEMEN, – The inquiries and observations which I have recently made on the subject of settlement, assure me, that neither in these Provinces nor in the United States, has a proper system been pursued. The mere filling of the world with men, should not be the sole object of political wisdom. This should regard the filling of it with beings of superior intellect and feeling, without which the desert had better remain occupied by the beaver and the bear. That society of a superior kind may be nursed up in Canada, by an enlarged and liberal connexion with the mother country, I am very confident; and its being realized is the fond hope which induces me to come forward with my present proposals, and which, if these proposals meet with support, will continue the spur of my exertions to complete the work which I have now in view.

Many of you, Gentlemen, have been bred up at home, and well know how superior, in many respects, are the arrangements and habits of society there, to what they are on this side the Atlantic. Such never can be hoped for here under the present system of colonization, which brings out only a part, and that the weakest part of society – which places poor and destitute individuals in remote situations, with no object before them but groveling selfishness – no aid – no example – no fear either of God or man. Is it not possible to create such a tide of commerce as would not only bring with it *part* of society, but society complete, with all the strength and order and refinement which it has now attained in Britain, beyond all precedent? Surely government would afford every facility to a commerce which would not only enrich, but eternally bind together Britain and her Provinces, by the most powerful sympathies of manners and taste and affection.

Government never can too much encourage the growth of this colony, by a liberal system of emigration. When we come from home, we are not expatriated: our feelings as British subjects grow more warm with distance, and our greater experience teaches us the more to venerate the principles of our native land–the country wherein the sciences have made the greatest progress, and where alone are cultivated to perfection the arts of social life. At home, we have experienced evils: we know that influences are there, which war against the principles of the constitution, and counteract its most benevolent designs. Here, we are free of such influences, we are perfectly contented, and a fine field lies open to us for cultivating the best fruits of civil and religous liberty.

An enlarged and liberal connexion between Canada and Britain, appears to me to promise the happiest results to the cause of civilization. It promises a new aera in the history of our species: it promises the growth of manners with manly spirit, modesty with acquirements, and a love of truth superior to the boasting of dispicable vanity.

The late war furnished the strongest proof of the rising spirit of this colony, even under every disadvantage; and pity it would be, were no noble a spirit ever again exposed to risk. The late war showed at once the affection which Britain bears to Canada, and the desire which Canada has to continue under the wing of Britain. When a connexion is established between the two countries worthy of such manifestations, all risk will cease. Britain will no longer have to expend her millions here. This country will not only be equal to its own defence, but the last hope of invasion will wither before its strength. While Canada remains poor and neglected she can only be a burthen to Britain: when improved and wealthy she will amply repay every debt, and become the powerful friend of the parent state.

What I conceive to be the first requisite for opening a suitable communication with the mother country, is the drawing out and publishing a well-authenticated statistical account of Upper Canada. This cannot be effected by a single hand: it must be the work, and have the authority of many. To give it commencement, I submit for your consideration the annexed queries; and could these be replied to, from every township in the Province, the work would be far advanced. These queries have been shewn to many of the most respectable individuals in the province, and the scheme of collecting materials in this way, for a statistical account, has, by every one, been approved. Some have doubted whether there exists sufficient energy and public spirit in the remote townships to reply to them. I hope there is; and certainly no organized township is destitute of individuals qualified for the task, *if they will but take so much trouble.*

Some gentlemen have met my ideas so cordially as to offer to collect information, not only for their own, but, for other townships. Correct information, however, is not the only requisite: authority is also wanted of that species which will not only carry weight with it to a distance, but remain answerable on the spot for what is advanced. The desirable point, therefore, is to obtain replies *separately from each township*, and to have these attested by the signature of as many of the respectable inhabitants as possible. To accomplish this in the speediest and most effectual manner, a meeting might be held in each township, and in the space of an hour or two the business might be perfected.

The Queries have been drawn out as simply as possible, with a view to the practicability of having them answered in this general way. They embrace only such matters as it must be in the power of every intelligent farmer to speak to, and the information to be obtained by them will be sufficient to assure farmers and others at home who have money to engage in adventure, that adventure here, will not only be rational and safe, but that they themselves may sit down in Canada with comfort and independence.

Although, to prevent confusion in the general fulfilment of the scheme, I have confined the range of Queries, it would still be very desirable if intelligent individuals would communicate their sentiments with regard to any measure of improvement which occurs to them, or any remarkable fact or observation they may have made concerning the climate, soil, or cultivation of the province.

Should any correspondent dislike my using his name publicly, he need only give a caution, and it shall be observed*.

---

* These lines were thrown in at the suggestion of the printer at York, who thought few people would choose to give their names, as authority. So very different was the issue, that I have received only

If the Queries obtain notice, and sufficient documents are forwarded to me, I shall arrange and publish them in England, whither I am soon to return. Had this task required superior ability, such an offer would be presumption. I think it requires industry alone, and that I shall contribute most willingly.

Whoever thinks well of the scheme, and feels a desire to promote it, let him not hesitate or delay: prompt assistance will be every thing; and, as to trouble, let individuals compare their's to mine.

Though I gratuitously make offer of my time, I must be relieved of expense as much as possible, and shall expect all communications to be post paid: No person, I think, who interests himself at all in the matter, will grudge his item in this way. Divided amongst many, such charges will be trifling, but accumulated upon one, they would be serious.

Should the work succeed to my wish, I would propose not only publishing it in the English, but German language. It is well known that the people of that nation are most desirable settlers, and it is a fact that many of them have not the means of communicating to their friends the very superior advantages of this country. One of them, who has been in Canada 13 years, lately told me, that "tousands and tousands would come over, did they but know how good a country it is for poor peoples."

ROBERT GOURLAY

N.B. *Address all communications for me, to the Post Office, Queenston.*
R. G.

The Upper Canada Gazette, in which the above was first published, having a very limited circulation, and the President, Colonel Smith, having approved of the Address, 700 copies were thrown off as a Circular, and sent by post to the public officers of each township, with the following note:

"Sir,
"The within Address, &c. appeared in the Upper Canada Gazette of the 30th October, but lest that paper should not fall into your hands, this is sent to you; and it is earnestly requested that you will endeavour to procure a meeting of your respectable neighbours, as soon as possible, and otherwise forward the object in view, which would be of the greatest service to the Province.

R. G."

---

one communication out of nearly a hundred, with a feigned signature. I mention this to the honour of the people of Upper Canada, while I express my regret for admitting of a supposition that any one would hesitate or withhold his name in support of the information required.

SKETCHES OF UPPER CANADA

Sketch V.

Civil Divisions.

BY the constitutional act the governor was authorized to divide the province into districts, counties, or circles, and towns or townships, and to establish the limits thereof; subject, however, to alteration by the provincial legislature.

Lord Dorchester had, three years before, formed that part of the province of Quebec, which now composes Upper Canada, into four districts; Lunenburgh, Mecklenburgh, Nassau, and Hesse.

At the first provincial parliament in 1792, those names were abolished, and the *Eastern,* the *Midland,* the *Home* and the *Western* substituted as the names of the respective districts; but their limits were not altered.

Soon after Lieutenant-Governor Simcoe undertook the administration of the province, he issued a proclamation, dated July 16, 1792, dividing it into 19 counties.

In 1798, the parliament revised the civil divisions of the province; and, making several alterations and additions, established eight Districts, 23 Counties, and 158 Townships.

The Eastern District

Was composed of five counties:
1st. *The County of Glengary*, containing the townships of Lancaster, Charlottenburgh, and Kenyon, with the tract of land claimed by the St. Regis Indians.
2d. *The County of Stormont*, containing the townships of Cornwall, Osnaburgh, Finch and Roxburg.
3d. *The County of Dundas*, containing the townships of Williamsburgh, Matilda, Mountain, and Winchester.
4th. *The County of Prescott*, containing the townships of Hawksbury, Longueil, with the tract of land in its rear, Alfred and Plantagenet.

5th. *The County of Russell*, containing the townships of Clarence, Cumberland, Gloucester, Osgood, Russell, and Cambridge.

The District of Johnstown

Was composed of three counties:

1st. *The County of Grenville*, containing the townships of Edwardsburgh, Augusta, Wolford, Oxford on the Rideau, Marlborough, Montague, North Gower, and South Gower.

2d. *The County of Leeds*, containing the townships of Elizabethtown, Yonge (including what was formerly called Escot), Lansdown, Leeds, Crosby, Bastard, Burgess, Elmsly, and Kitly.

3d. *The County of Carlton*, containing the township of Nepean, with the tract of land to be thereafter laid out into townships, between Nepean and a line drawn north, 16 degrees west from the north west angle of Crosby, until it intersects the Ottawa river.

The Midland District

Was composed of four counties, with the land in their rear, to the northern limits of the province.

1st. *The County of Frontinac*, containing the townships of Pittsburgh, Kingston, Loughborough, Portland, Hinchenbroke, Bedford, and Wolfe Island.

2d. *The incorporated Counties of Lenox and Addington*, containing the townships of Ernest Town, Fredericksburg, Adolphus Town, Richmond, Camden (east), Amherst Island, and Sheffield.

3d. *The County of Hastings*, containing the townships of Sidney, Thurlow, the tract of land occupied by the Mohawks, Hungerford, Huntingdon, and Rawdon.

4th. *The County of Prince Edward*, containing the townships of Marysburg, Hallowell, Sophiasburg, and Ameliasburg.

The District of Newcastle,

The organization of which was postponed until the number of its inhabitants amounted to a thousand, was composed of two counties, with the land in their rear, to the northern limits of the province.

1st. *The County of Northumberland*, containing the township of Murray, Cramahe, Haldimand, Hamilton, Alnwick, Percy, and Seymour.

2d. *The County of Durham*, containing the townships of Hope, Clarke, and Darlington, with some adjoining lands.

The Home District

Was composed of two counties.

1st. *The County of York*, containing, in its East Riding, the townships of Whitby, Pickering, Scarborough, York, Etobicoke, Markham, Vaughan, King, Whitchurch, Uxbridge, Guillembury, and a tract of land, thereafter to be laid out into townships, between the County of Durham and lake Simcoe; in the West Riding, the townships of Beverly, Hamborough (east and west), and several tracts of land, not then laid out into townships.

2d. *The County of Simcoe*, containing Matchedash, Gloucester, or Penetangueshine, with Prince William Henry's island, and a tract of unlocated land, extending to the northern limits of the province.

The District of Niagara

Was composed of two counties, together with the beach between the head of lake Ontario, and Burlington bay, and the promontory between that bay and Coot's Paradise.

1st. *The County of Lincoln*, containing, in its first riding, the townships of Clinton, Grimsby, Saltfleet, Barton, Ancaster, Glandford, Binbrook, Gainsborough, and Caistor: in the second riding, Niagara, Grantham, and Louth; in the third riding, Stamford, Thorold, and Pelham; in the fourth riding, Bertie, Willoughby, Crowland, Humberstone, and Wainfleet.

2d. *The County of Haldimand*, containing the tract of land on each side of the Grand river, then in the occupation of the Six Nation Indians, and lying to the southward and south west of Dundas Street.

The District of London

Was composed of three counties, with a tract of land extending back to lake Huron.

1st. *The County of Norfolk*, containing the townships of Rainham, Walpole, Woodhouse, Charlotteville, Walsingham, Houghton, Middleton, Windham, and Townsend, with Turkey Point, and the promontory of Long Point.

2d. *The County of Oxford*, containing the townships of Burford, Norwich, Dereham, Oxford upon the Thames, Blandford, and Blenheim.

3d. *The County of Middlesex*, containing the townships of London, Westminster, Dorchester, Yarmouth, Southwold, Malahide, Bayham, Dunwich, Aldborough, and Delaware.

The Western District

Was composed of two counties, with all the north western region of the province not included in any other district.

1st. *The County of Kent*, containing the townships of Dover, Chatham, Camden (west), the Moravian tract of land, called Orford (north and south), Howard, Harwich, Raleigh, Romney, Tilbury (east and west), and the Shawney Indians' town.

2d. *The County of Essex*, containing the townships of Rochester, Mersea, Gosfield, Maidstone, Sandwich, Colchester, Malden, and the lands of the Hurons, and other Indians upon the strait.

The adjacent islands, in the rivers and lakes, were generally annexed to the townships in front of which they were situated.

A number of other townships have been since laid out; and others still will doubtless be added as fast as the population and settlement of the province shall require them.

In a few of the townships there is a plat of a mile square, distinguished as a town, but without any distinct corporate privileges. In some instances, the name of the town is different from that of the township, as Brockville, in the township of Elizabeth town.

Several applications have been made to the provincial legislature for the incorporation of other districts; but they have not yet been granted.

As civil divisions, these districts are peculiar to this province, and have almost annihilated the importance of counties. There are district courts, but no county courts. The court house and gaol belong to the district. The sheriff's authority is commensurate with the district. The commission of the peace extends through the whole district, and of course, the jurisdiction of the court of sessions is equally extensive. So is that of the surrogate court, and the court of assize, &c. The locality of juries, of real and other local actions, and of crimes, has reference to the district. In short there are only two or three respects, in which counties are regarded by law: one is the registry of land titles; another the organization of the battalions of militia*.

The townships extend nine miles in front, and twelve miles back. This is a general rule, from which there have been exceptions, occasioned by the shape and quantity of land remaining to be laid out after preceding locations.

The townships were laid out into Concessions and lots, in this manner. A front line was first adjusted to the shore, so as to leave as little as possible of head land between it and the water, and of back water between it and the land. A second line was then drawn parallel with the first, and at the distance of a hundred chains, or a mile and a quarter, besides the allowance for a road. The intervening range of land was called the first or front Concession. In the same manner a second Concession was laid out, then a third, fourth, &c. In the front and between the Concessions, a strip of land was allowed for a road. The allowance for the front road was generally 60 feet, and for the other Concession roads 40 feet. Each Concession was divided into lots of 200 acres, by parallel lines at right angles with the Concession lines, and 20 chains, or a quarter of a mile distant from each other. At intervals of two or three miles, a strip of 40 feet, between two lots, was left for a cross road.

In several of the first townships the lots were laid only nineteen chains wide, and consequently the Concessions were proportionally wider, to give each lot, by an addition of length, its complement of 200 acres. And in some of the later townships, I believe the Concession lines have been drawn so as to make the 200 acre lots shorter and wider.

In the townships bordering upon the lakes and great rivers, the Concessions were fronted on the water. The ranges of townships laid out on each side of Yonge street and Dundas street, were fronted on those streets respectively.

The Concessions being numbered from the front to the rear of the townships, the lots in each Concession were distinguished by their appropriate numbers, and are commonly described in that manner; as lot No. – in the – Concession of the township of – .

---

* Members of parliament are generally chosen by counties. In Niagara district by ridings, which are equivalent to counties. The district of Ottawa is still joined to the eastern district, as it concerns assize courts. – R. G.

This description, by the number of the lot and of the Concession, with the name of the township, is simple, familiar, and uniform, and at the same time so definite, that it has been adjudged by the Court of King's Bench to be sufficient, not only in a deed of conveyance, but even in a writ of ejectment.

The inhabitants of these townships hold annual meetings, appoint certain officers, and regulate some matters of police agreeably to the provisions of law, but have not such various corporate powers and duties, as those little republics, the towns of New England.

Sketch VI.

Settlements.

The whole north eastern Limits settled – Cornwall – Charlottenburg – Williamsburg – Battle of Chrysler's Field – Johnstown – Prescott – Elizabeth Town – Brockville – Kingston – Ernest Town – Townships around the Bay of Quinte – Newcastle District – Yonge Street – York – Niagara District – Indian Lands – London District – Western District – Shores of Lakes Erie and Ontario – Lord Selkirk's Plantation – Situation of London on the Thames.

It has been stated that Upper Canada began to be settled in 1784. A brief sketch of the progress and present state of the settlements will be added.

From the north eastern line to Elizabeth town, about 70 miles, the whole width of the province, between the two boundary rivers St. Lawrence and Ottawa, was early laid out into townships, in two, three, and four ranges. These townships are all settled, and many of them well cultivated. Some of them have improvements on almost every lot.

Cornwall is a flourishing town, watered by a rivulet running through it, and situated on a commodious bay of the river below the *Longe Sault*. It is the seat of the courts for the eastern district, has a very respectable literary institution, a church and rectory, and considerable trade.

Charlottenburg next below, has more agriculture, and a larger number of inhabitants. It is well watered by the river Aux Raisins; but is not conveniently situated for trade. The first settlers were chiefly Catholics from Scotland. They have a Catholic chapel in the township.

The front of *Williamsburg* is a beautiful situation on the bank of the river. In this township there is a Lutheran church. Chrysler's farm, in this township, has acquired celebrity from a battle fought there, November 11th, 1814, between a part of General Wilkinson's army on their way down the St. Lawrence, and a body of British troops, collected and commanded by Lieutenant-Colonel Morrison, pursuing and harassing the Americans on their march. The latter, led by Brigadier-General Boyd, in the absence of Generals Wilkinson and Lewis, who were in the boats, faced about, and commenced the action, in the early part of which they were successful. But Colonel Morrison, by his judicious movements, and the discipline and firmness of his troops, maintained a well chosen position, and turned the fortune of the day. General Boyd being forced to retreat, formed his troops again, with a view to a further engagement; but was ordered to embark, and proceed down the river. The loss in killed and wounded was severe on both sides. General Covington, of the American army, died of his wounds a few days afterwards. This short but severe action is called by the British officers the battle of Chrysler's field, and by the Americans the battle of Williamsburg.

Johnstown, in the township of Edwardsburg, is calculated for a mercantile depot, at the head of the Rapids, being the lowest port to and from which lake vessels sail. It was the court town of the eastern district; and since the division of the original district, the courts for the district of Johnstown have been attended here, as well as at Elizabeth town. Johnstown has experienced a comparative decline.

Prescott, a village in Augusta, opposite to Ogdensburgh, is beginning to vie with that place in exertions to obtain the forwarding business of the Montreal boats, and the vessels of the lake. Although it is not so low down as Johnstown, it has a bolder shore.

Elizabeth is a populous and wealthy township, situated near the centre of the district, has a good agricultural country around it, and is increasing in commercial business.

The village at the front of this township has received the name of Brockville. Although not regularly fortified, it was the station of a few troops, and the scene of some military operations. On the 7th of February, 1813, Captain Forsyth, with 200 volunteers from Ogdensburgh, landed in this village, surprised the guard, and took about 40 prisoners, with some arms, ammunition, and other public stores.

From the townships adjoining the Ottawa, and the rivers Rideau and Petite Nation, which empty into the Ottawa, the produce is transported in boats down that river to Montreal, and goods are remitted through the same channel. The head waters of these streams communicate by short portages with those which fall into the St. Lawrence; and by means of locks and canals, an inland navigation might be easily effected between the St. Lawrence and the Ottawa, to the benefit of commercial intercourse, and the security of the province in time of war. The forks of the Rideau, around which the townships of Oxford, Marlborough, and Gower, are situated, are expected to become an emporium of interior commerce. They afford advantageous situations for water works, especially for the manufacture of iron, and it is said there is a good supply of ore in the vicinity.

From Elizabeth town upward, the settlements are of the depth of three townships, or between 30 or 40 miles throughout the district of Johnstown.

In Frontinac, the eastern county of the midland district, two ranges of townships are settled, besides the settlements on the islands.

The harbour of *Kingston* has already been described. The town fronts the harbour in full view of the water and shipping. Streets are laid out parallel with the harbour, at convenient distances from each other, and are intersected at right angles, by cross streets dividing the town into squares. One square is an open public area in front of the court house, and gaol, and episcopal church. – In this area is the market. Besides these public buildings there are a new Catholic church, barracks for the troops of the garrison, an hospital, and a house for the commanding officer, about 300 other dwelling houses, a number of warehouses and stores, about 50 shops of goods, several public offices, a respectable district school, a valuable library, besides mechanic shops, &c. Though the war destroyed Niagara, checked the progress of York, and made Ernest town "a deserted village," it doubled the population, the buildings, and business of Kingston.

The court house and gaol, Catholic church, many of the principal dwelling houses, and some stores, are built of a bluish limestone, dug out of the ground, in large quantities, in the midst of the town. This species of stone is common in the country, and will be more particularly noticed in a sketch of the soil. The quarries of it here are convenient and valuable for purposes of building; but the style of building is not tasty and elegant.

Kingston is not well supplied with water. – Wells are difficult to be obtained, and their water is not very good. The water of the bay is less pure than that of the open lake. Some springs in the rear of the town, yield a partial supply of clear water, very slightly affected by its passage through strata of limestone.

The township of Kingston is in some places stony, and contains a number of lots still unsettled, probably because they are owned by gentlemen engaged in other employments than the cultivation of land.

Kingston is subject to one local disadvantage, the want of a populous back country.

Loughborough situated north, and *Portland* north west, have made some progress in settlement, but are yet thinly inhabited.

The next township on the lake is *Ernest Town*, vulgarly called *Second Town*. It is level, and has a rich soil, with but little waste ground. There is more arable land than meadow or pasture. It is watered by two rivers and various smaller streams, running into the lake, and furnishing convenient mill seats. Nearly all the lots are settled, and generally under good improvement. The settlers are most of them practical husbandmen. Their farms are well fenced, well tilled, and accommodated with barns. There are now (1811) above 2,300 inhabitants, a greater number than are found in any other township in the province. They have three houses of public worship, one Episcopalian, one Presbyterian, and one Methodist, attended by clergymen of these respective denominations. In the front of the township, adjoining the harbour, 18 miles above Kingston, at the division of the great road into branches, passing up on the inside and outside of the bay of Quinte, a village is begun, which promises to be a place of considerable business. Its harbour has been noticed in the description of the lake. From the lake shore, the ground ascends about seventy rods, and thence slopes off in a gentle northern descent. The ascent is divided into regular squares by five streets, laid parallel with the shore; one of them being the lower branch of the main road, and all of them crossed at right angles, by streets running northerly. One of these cross streets is continued through the Concession, and forms that branch of the main road which passes round the bay of Quinte. On the east side of this street at the most elevated point stands the church; and on the opposite side is the academy, overlooking the village, and commanding a variegated prospect of the harbour, the sound, the adjacent island, the outlets into the open lake, and the shores stretching eastward and westward, with a fine landscape view of the country all around. The situation is healthy and delightful, not surpassed perhaps in natural advantages by any in America.

The village contains a valuable social Library; is increasing in buildings, accommodations, inhabitants, and business, and seems calculated to be the central point of a populous and productive tract of country around it.

Amherst island in front, has between one and two hundred inhabitants, and is a distinct township, although for some public purposes it is annexed to Ernest Town.

Camden lies north, and is settled to the distance of about twenty miles from the lake.

Although Ernest town is entirely east of the bay of Quinte, it is commonly considered, especially by people residing at a distance, to belong to the bay.

Fredericksburg, the next township, is not so uniformly settled and improved; but has a large population, and many excellent farms, an episcopal church*, and a Lutheran meeting house. The Appanee separates it from Richmond on the north.

Adolphus Town is surrounded on the south west, and north, by the bay, and is indented with several fine coves, furnishing convenient landing places. It is not large, but is well cultivated, and has a town, or village, with a court house, where the court of general quarter sessions for the Midland District sits semi-annually; the other two alternate terms being holden at Kingston. A society of friends have their meetings in Adolphus Town. Travelling the main road to the seat of government, you cross the bay from this town to the peninsula of Prince Edward, by a ferry of about a mile.

In *Marysburg, Hallowell, Sophiasburg, and Ameliasburg,* the four townships of Prince Edward, the peninsula south of the bay of Quinte, there is some rough and waste land; but a large proportion of noble farms under good cultivation. Hallowell is a flourishing village, advantageously situated on the bay. The road over the isthmus, from the head of the bay to the lake, has Ameliasburg in the midland district, on one side, and on the other, Murray, a township of the district of Newcastle. It appears to be a place of increasing activity; but the soil is not of the first quality.

In Marysburg, opposite to Adolphus Town, there is a lake or pond of several hundred acres on the top of a hill, two hundred feet higher than the surface of lake Ontario. There is no stream entering this small lake; but one issuing from it sufficient to carry a mill, called Van Alstine's mill, standing by the shore of the bay of Quinte.

North of the bay there are two ranges of townships. West of Richmond, is the Mohawk land, a fertile tract, nine miles in front, and twelve miles deep, assigned to a portion of the

Mohawks, who chose to separate from the Six Nations on the Grand river. It is inhabited by the Indians only, according to their mode of habitation, and of course is little improved, and the roads are bad. In the front of the village is a church built by the Society for propagating the Gospel in Foreign Parts, who have, for a number of years, maintained a reader of service, and a schoolmaster for these Indians.

Thurlow, adjoining westward, is well settled in front, and near its south western angle, Myers river has good improvements, extending five or six miles up the river. At the mouth there is a handsome collection of houses and shops, with a pleasant public square or common. This village is built on low ground, and is subject to inundation when the river is choked with ice.

The improvements continue pretty uniform throughout Sidney, and to the river Trent, in the township of Murray. Thence through the fertile well watered townships of the district of Newcastle, generally, the settlements appear new; but they are beginning to flourish. Their natural advantages are of a superior order. Cramahe, Haldimand, Hamilton, and Hope, are making good progress in population. Hamilton is the seat of justice for the district of Newcastle.

From that district to York, the country, notwithstanding its fertility, is thinly settled; and, consequently, the roads are unfinished and out of repair, the land having been granted in large blocks to non-resident proprietors.

The government, as well as travellers, appear to be convinced of the ill policy of such grants upon a great public road. For, in later instances, the lots located on such a road have been granted upon condition of actual settlement, the clearing of a certain quantity of the land, the erection of a house, and the making of the road across each lot.

Upon these principles, the two ranges of townships butting upon Yonge street were granted, except that the troops under General Simcoe were employed in opening the way at first. Thus a noble chain of agricultural improvements has, in a short time, been extended from York to Guillemburg, near lake Simcoe. A new region is peopled, and the public are accommodated with a good road. In consequence of which, the country is enriched, and the town of York highly benefited, notwithstanding some non-resident lands in its immediate vicinity.

York has other advantages, natural and adventitious. It is situated on a beautiful plain, in a rich soil, and temperate climate. Its harbour and connexion with the lake have been already sketched. The town plat, more than a mile and a half in length, is laid out in regular streets, lots, and squares, having the Garrison, and the site of the parliament house on its two wings, and a market near the center.

There is a public square open to the water. Many neat, and some elegant houses are erected, and the town has a mixed appearance of city and country. It is the seat of government, the place of the residence of his excellency the Lieutenant Governor, and of the annual session of parliament. Here the provincial offices are kept, the public officers reside, and the business of the province is transacted. It is the resort of persons applying for land, or making any other applications to government, and of travellers visiting the country. It is likewise the seat of the courts and offices of the home district, and has an episcopal church, a district school, a printing office, and much professional and mercantile business. In summer the beach of the peninsula is a healthy and delightful ride; and the bay, covered with level ice, forms an extensive plain for the winter amusement of sleighing.

York increased but little in its buildings during the war, except some military erections at the west end of the town, and a naval store-house and wharf in front of it.

Since the general establishment of civil divisions in 1798, several new townships have been surveyed, granted, and partially settled, among which are three in the new Indian purchase, west of York, between Etobicoke and the head of the lake: viz. *Toronto, Trafalgar*, and *Nelson*.

The district of Niagara was originally settled in 1784, by the disbanded rangers of Col. Butler's regiment. In 1785, and the succeeding years, many emigrants arrived there from the states of New York, Pennsylvania, and New Jersey, particularly the county of Sussex, in the latter state. Other settlers have been annually coming in from various quarters. The whole district, about seventy miles (since the formation of Gore much less) by forty, is now generally cleared, inhabited, and cultivated. In the cultivation of fruit, the inhabitants of Niagara district have been peculiarly successful.

Many of the settlers of the district of London also, particularly of the county of Norfolk, emigrated from the same states as the settlers of Niagara, and are pursuing similar modes of cultivation. The land being thinly timbered, settlements were easily effected, and good roads soon formed. Colonel Talbot has a flourishing new settlement called Port Talbot, on the lake shore, west of Long Point, in the township of Dunwich, and the townships in this section of the country generally are rapidly progressing in population and improvement. In August, 1814, a party of

Indians and Americans, painted like Indians, surprised the settlement of Port Talbot, took a number of the inhabitants, and plundered about fifty of them of their horses, and other property.

An extensive and valuable territory on the Grand river was assigned by Governor Haldimand, in the name of the crown, to the Six Nations of Indians, to compensate them for their services in the revolutionary war, and supply the loss of their lands in the province, now state of New York.

This confederacy of Indians was originally composed of five tribes only, who were called the Five Nations, or Iroquois. They afterwards received into their national union the Tuscaroras, a tribe that migrated from North Carolina; and thereafter they were generally denominated the Six Nations. In the revolution they divided, some of them sided with the colonies, and remained in possession of their lands. The others took up the hatchet on the side of the king; and being obliged to abandon their possessions, removed into Canada, and were liberally rewarded by the sovereign they had served with land on both sides of the Grand river, purchased for that purpose, of the Missassaga Indians.

Under the auspices of the late Captain Brandt, they sold several blocks, or townships of land, and took bonds for the payment of the stipulated price, upon condition that the sales should be confirmed by the crown; and they have accordingly been confirmed on certain terms, respecting the investment of the principal of the money arising from the sales.

The Indians have, according to their mode of proceeding, since given long leases of other blocks of their land; and the lessees, to the number of several hundreds, have entered and are now in possession of the land thus leased; but not having obtained confirmations, they are embarrassed for want of a legal title. They are formed into a county by the name of Haldimand.

Oxford, on the upper fork of the river Thames, in 42 miles from Burlington Bay, by the route of Dundas street. Blenheim and Blandford lie north. Dorchester is situated on the middle fork, and London on the lower or main fork, with Westminster adjoining it; Chatham and Harwich are lower down the river, in the county of Kent.

The country along this fine river, and between it and the shore of lake Erie, including the peninsula formed by that lake, the Detroit and lake Sinclair, is surveyed into townships, most of which are settled, is surveyed into townships, most of which are settled, or in a course of rapid settlement, with a prospect of becoming one of the most delightful regions in the world.

A line of settlements is thus marked out along the lakes

Ontario and Erie. Should population continue to advance with its usual ratio of increase, the shores of these lakes all around, as well on the side of the United States, as that of Canada, will in a few years be an extensive range of villages and cultivated fields. The produce of this fertile interior must be great, in whatever proportion it may eventually go to market, through the St. Lawrence or the Ohio and Mississippi. Or whether any of the gigantic projects of lock and canal communication with Hudson's river, the Delaware, the Susquehannah, or the Potowmac, shall be carried into effect or not. By an inspection of the map, it may be seen that the Canadian shore is all laid out into townships, from the lower province up to lake Sinclair.

Lord Selkirk, of Scotland, has commenced a plantation on that lake, but was not very fortunate in his location. The land in general is low and wet, and although it is exceedingly rich, proved at first to be unhealthy. Some of it, however, is adapted to the breeding of sheep, in which he was successful. His settlement is said to have suffered by the war.

General Simcoe, in his administration, is thought to have contemplated *London* as the future capital of the province. The natural advantages on which his expectation is alleged to have been founded, were the centrality of its position between the lakes Ontario, Erie, and Huron, its fortunate situation on the Thames; the fertility of the country; the mildness and salubrity of its climate; the abundance and purity of its water; its means of military and naval protection, and the facility of communication with lake Sinclair through the outlet of the Thames; with lake Huron by the northern branch of that noble river; with the Grand river by a short portage; and with lake Ontario, by the military way called Dundas street. With a view to this expected state of things, the names of the river, the contemplated metropolis, the adjacent towns, &c. were taken from those of corresponding objects in the mother country.

This project however of General Simcoe, if he ever entertained it, appears to have been a visionary one. Before London can become a seat of provincial government the province must be divided. If the government should be removed from York, the removal will probably be to Kingston.

Sketch VII.

Population.

I HAVE not been able to obtain accurate official returns of the number of inhabitants in the various townships and districts throughout the province, but have formed an estimate in the following manner.

In the statements of district taxes for the year ending March, 1811, returned to the Provincial Parliament by the clerks of the peace in the respective districts, the number of persons taxed is in most instances expressed; and where it is omitted, the omission being supplied by a calculation founded upon the relative numbers of persons, and amounts of taxes, the result is *nine thousand six hundred and twenty-three persons taxed*.

Then having the number of persons taxed in the most populous township, as returned by the assessors, and also the whole number of inhabitants in the same township, including men, women, and children, as taken by the clerk, I find upon comparing them, that rejecting a small fraction, the proportion is as one to eight. Applying that proportion to the province, it gives, for the whole population, *seventy-six thousand nine hundred and eighty-four*.

Although this calculation is not to be relied on for absolute exactness, it is sufficiently certain to answer the purposes of general information*.

I have no data for estimating the proportions of persons of different ages and sexes, or the exact ratio of increase. The latter being affected by accessions from Europe and the lower province, and still more from the United States, had depended, and must hereafter depend in a considerable degree upon the encouragement holden out to settlers. A fair understanding of the real state of the country in respect to climate and soil, the cheapness of land, the security of titles, the value of labour, the lightness of taxes, and the protection of property, will, under the continuance of a wise and liberal policy towards settlers, promote emigrations, and accelerate the progress of population.

---

* Mr. Heriot has estimated the population of Upper Canada at 80,000. This was in 1806.

Sketch XI.

I SHALL not attempt a classification or botanical description of the trees, shrubs, and plants of Upper Canada.

In 1784, the whole country was one continued forest. Some plains on the borders of lake Erie, at the head of lake Ontario, and in a few other places, were thinly wooded: but, in general, the land in its natural state was heavily loaded with trees; and after the clearings of more than 30 years, many wide spread forests still defy the settler's axe.

The forest trees most common are, beech, maple, birch, elm, bass, ash, oak, pine, hickory, butternut, balsam, hazel, hemlock, cherry, cedar, cypress, fir, poplar, sycamore (vulgarly called button wood, from its balls resembling buttons), whitewod, willow spruce. Of several of these kinds there are various species; and there are other trees less common. Chestnut, black walnut, and sassafras, although frequent at the head of lake Ontario, and thence westward and southward, are scarcely to be seen on the north side of that lake and the St. Lawrence. Near the line between Kingston and Ernest town, a black walnut has been planted, and flourishes, and bears nuts.

The sumach, whose leaves and berries are used for a black dye by the curriers here, and by the dyers of Manchester, and other manufacturing towns in England, grows plentifully in all parts of the country.

Elder, wild cherries, plums, thorns, gooseberries, blackberries, rasberries, grapes, and many other bushes, shrubs, and vines, abound. Whortleberries and cranberries (both the tall and the low or viny) grow in some places, but not generally through the province.

The sugar maple is common in every district. Its sap, which is extracted in the spring, and from which molasses and sugar are made, is useful to the inhabitants in the early stages of their settlement; and might be rendered of more extensive and permanent use, by proper attention to the preservation of the trees, the manner of tapping them, and some practical improvements in the process of reducing the sap to sugar. The wood, also, being beautifully veined and curled, is valuable for cabinet work.

The butternut tree is useful for various purposes. The kernel of its nut is nutritious and agreeable to the taste. If gathered when young and tender, about the first of July, the nut makes an excellent pickle. The bark dyes a durable brown colour; and an extract from it is a mild and safe cathartic.

A healthy beer is made of the essence of spruce, and also of a decoction of its boughs.

The juniper is an evergreen, the berries of which are used here, as in Holland, in the manufacture of gin, and give to that liquor its diuretic quality.

The prickly ash is considered to possess medical virtues. A decoction of its berries, bark, or roots, is taken for rheumatic complaints.

Red cedar, being the most durable of all known woods, when exposed to the weather, is highly valued for fence posts and other similar uses. It is also a beautiful material for cabinet work.

For a number of years past, large quantities of oak and pine timber have been annually cut on the banks of the St. Lawrence and lake Ontario, and its bays and creeks, and floated down on rafts to the Montreal and Quebec markets, for foreign exportaion.

The principal fruit of Upper Canada is the apple. The various species of this most useful of fruits grow in all the districts; but most plentifully around Niagara, and thence westward to the Detroit, where they have been cultivated with emulation and success. No country in the world exceeds those parts of the province in this particular. In the north eastern townships, orcharding has not been so much attended to, and perhaps the soil, although good for fruit, is not so peculiarly adapted to it. But there are many considerable orchards, most of them young, and some valuable nurseries of trees, not yet transplanted. A general taste for apples and for cider, a beverage most suitable to this climate, begins to prevail.

Peaches flourish at Niagara, and at the head of lake Ontario; but not on the northern shore of that lake. Cherries, plums, pears, and currants, suceed in every part of the country. Strawberries grow freely in the meadow, and are cultivated with success in gardens.

Sarsaparilla, spikenard, gold thread, elecampane, lobelia, bloodroot, and ginseng, are native plants. The latter root, when dried, has a sweetish taste, similar to that of liquorice, but mixed with a degree of bitterness, and some aromatic warmth. The Chinese esteem it very highly; and it might therefore be a valuable article of exportation to China; but it seems to be neglected.

Snake root also is a native of this province. It is of a pungent taste, and is stimulant and sudorific. The Indians are said to apply it as a remedy for the bite of rattlesnakes, and hence its name is derived.

Spearmint, hyssop, wormwood, winter-green, water-cresses, penny-royal, catnip, plantain, burdock, horehound, motherwort, mallows, and many other aromatic and medicinal plants are indigenous.

White clover springs up spontaneously as soon as the ground is cleared. Greensward also is spontaneous. There are several other native grasses. But red clover, and most of the useful species of grass must be sown, and then they grow very well. The most common are Timothy, herdsgrass, foul meadow, and red clover. Lucerne is cultivated in some places.

The soil, however, is not so favourable to grass as to grain.

Wheat is the staple of the province. When the land was first opened, the crops of this precious grain were luxuriant. They are still plentiful, although they become less abundant, as the land grows older.

Wheat, that is sown as early as the 1st of September, is found to be less liable to be winter killed, as it is termed, than that which is later sown, the former being more firmly rooted in the ground. As this injury from the frosts of winter, or more commonly of spring, is one of the principal causes of a failure of crops, it is an object of importance to the husbandman to seed his wheat fields in good season. Some years ago, when the country was infested by that destructive insect, erroneously named the Hessian fly, it was dangerous to sow this grain early, because it was then more exposed to the ravages of the insect. But, happily, that scourge of agriculture is no longer felt here*.

Other grains, such as rye, maize (here called Indian corn), pease, barley, oats, buck-wheat, &c. are successfully cultivated. The townships round the bay of Quinte, produce large harvests of pease, and generally furnish supplies of that article of provisions for the troops of the various garrisons.

Wild rice grows in marshes, and on the margin of lakes. It has even given a name to the Rice lake, a small lake about 25 miles long, from south west to north east, and four or five miles wide, in the district of Newcastle, north of Hamilton and Haldimand.

Wild fowls feed and fatten on this spontaneous grain. The Indians also gather it, by thrusting their canoes into the midst of it, and then beating it into the canoes with sticks. They eat it

---

* This paragraph was written in 1811, since which time the insect has reappeared, and almost destroyed many fields of wheat.

themselves, and sell it to the white inhabitants, who use it in puddings and other modes of cookery. It is rather larger than the Carolina rice, and its shell is of a dark brown colour.

The soil in all districts of the province is adapted to flax, and in some of them to hemp. Legislative encouragement has been given to the latter. Seed has been purchased and distributed gratis; a bounty has been granted to the growers of it, in addition to the price they could obtain for it in the market; and at last a liberal price, above that of the market, has been paid by government, for the purchase of the hemp, on public account.

The gardens produce, in abundance, melons, cucumbers, squashes, and all the esculent vegetables and roots, that are planted in them. The potatoe, that most valuable of all roots, for the use both of man and beast, finds a congenial and productive soil.

The country is not free from noxious weeds. Among others there are two species of thistles; one of them indigenous, which is prevalent in the United States also; the other, not a native of this province, but brought up from Lower Canada, among seed oats and pease, or some other grain. It has already spread very generally, except in the western districts. It has, likewise, passed from Canada into the United States, where it has received the name of the Canadian thistle, and is now known by that name even here. It is of a smaller leaf and stalk than the common thistle, and is not so easily eradicated. It is very troublesome, especially in grain; but grass overpowers it, and gradually roots it out.

An English gentleman of science, who has resided here twenty years, is of opinion that it is the proper thistle of Europe, brought over in seed from France, first into Lower Canada, and thence into the Upper Province.

Sketch XIII.

Domestic Animals.

OF all the domestic animals the noblest is the Horse. The horses of Upper Canada are of the American, the English, and Canadian French stocks. The first are the predominant species. The last are generally short, thick, and dull, not adapted to the saddle, but hardy and serviceable as drudges in the collar on a farm. They were never very numerous in this province, compared with Lower Canada, and their proportion is diminished. There are few full blooded English horses; but considerable portions of English as well as French blood are intermixed with the American breed.

The horses of the country have been improved in their appearance, and a taste for further improvement is gaining ground; although the unfinished state of the roads, and the moderate circumstances and simple manners of the inhabitants, have precluded that passion for equipage and elegant horses, which prevails in more populous and luxurious places.

I am not singular in the opinion that the farmers keep too many horses, in proportion to their oxen, considering the difference in their expences, the greater liability of the former to diseases and accidents, and the value of the latter for beef. The assessment lists for 1810 contained 9982, almost 10,000 horses, three years old, and upwards, and but 5991 oxen, four years old, and upwards.

The oxen, however, are of a good stock, and so are the cows; but large dairies are not frequent, although there were, in 1810, according to the assessment returns, 18,445 cows in the province.

Sheep would be more numerous were they not exposed to the ravages of wolves. As the country becomes more settled, that evil decreases. The spirit lately diffused through the United States for improving the breed of sheep, with a view to the quality of their wool for domestic manufactures, has already begun to find its way into this province. Lord Selkirk's sheep are a mixture of several valuable European stocks. His wool is not manufactured in the province, but exported to Scotland.

The Canadian hogs are of a good size and quality. In fattening them the inhabitants make considerable use of pease, which are produced in greater plenty than Indian corn. When the market for grain is high, pork cannot be afforded for exportation.

The poultry of the country consists of turkeys, geese, hens, ducks, and pigeons.

Sketch XXI.

Money.

BEFORE we consider the subjects of revenue and taxes, it will be proper to attend to the currency of the province.

The value of gold and silver coins here current, is established by law at the following rates:

	Dwt.	Gr.	£.	s.	d.
The British Guinea, weighing	5	6	1	3	4
The Portuguese Johannes	18	0	4	0	0
Ditto Moidore	6	18	1	10	0
Spanish milled Doubloon, or four Pistole pieces	17	0	3	14	6
French Louis d'or, coined before 1793	5	4	1	2	8
French Pistole piece	4	4	0	18	3
American Eagle	11	6	2	10	0
British Crown	—		0	5	6
French do. coined before 1793	—		0	5	6
Spanish Dollar	—		0	5	0
American do.	—		0	5	0
French piece of four Livres, ten Sols Tournois	—		0	4	2
Do. Thirty-six Sols	—		0	1	3
French piece of Twenty-four Sols	—		0	1	1
English Shilling	—		0	1	1
Spanish Pistareen	—		0	1	0

And all the higher and lower denominations of the said gold and silver coins in the same proportion, two pence and one farthing to be added or deducted for every grain of British, Portuguese, or American gold; and two pence and one-fifth of a penny for every grain of French or Spanish gold over or under the standard weight.

Upon a payment of more than £20. in gold, at the request of either party, it is to be weighed in bulk, the coins of Great Britain, Portugal, and America together, at the rate of eighty-nine shillings for each ounce troy; and those of France and Spain together, at the rate of eighty-seven shillings and eight-pence halfpenny for each ounce; after deducting one half of a grain for each piece so weighed, on account of the loss which may accrue, by paying it away in detail.

Before 1809, several of the gold coins were differently valued; but this standard was then established in conformity to that of the Lower Province. The currency of Halifax and the Two Canadas is the same.

American eagles and half eagles commonly pass without being weighed; all other gold coin by weight.

The value of copper coins is not regulated by statute; yet coppers pass two of them for a penny, without much discrimination; but no person is obliged by law to receive, at one payment, more than a shilling in copper money.

From the foregoing rates of the value of coins established by law, it will be perceived, that one pound of the lawful money of this province is equal to four dollars, or eighteen shillings sterling, that is nine-tenths of a pound sterling.

From a little east of York, the currency of the state of New York is in general popular use through all the southern and western parts of this province.

Sketch XXII.

Revenue and Taxes.

THE engagement of the British parliament not to tax the provinces is understood to be prospective, and not retrospective, renouncing future taxation, but not repealing taxes already laid.

There was then in force, an act of parliament entitled, "an Act to establish a fund towards further defraying the charges of the administration of justice and support of the civil government, within the province of Quebec in America," laying certain duties on brandies, rum, spirits, molasses, and sirups imported into the said province, and also a duty of one pound and sixteen shillings sterling on each annual licence, to keep a tavern or retail wines and spirituous liquors, and appropriating the proceeds of said impost duties to the objects expressed in the title of the act.

These duties continue to be collected, the imposts at Quebec, and the licence duties in each province, to his Majesty's use.

After the division of the province of Quebec into Upper and Lower Canada, the legislature of the Lower Province laid impost duties, for provincial uses, in addition to those laid by the British parliament. As the goods thus dutied were in part consumed in the Uppper Province, and as the consumer ultimately pays the duty, this additional impost, although collected by that province, operated as a tax upon this. To prevent the injustice of such operation, an agreement has been entered into between the two provinces, that the dutied goods passing from the Lower to the Upper Province, shall be entered at *Coteau-du-Lac*, and the net proceeds of the duties on such a proportion of the imported goods, shall be paid over to the latter.

The legislature of Upper Canada, in the 41st year of the present king (1801), enacted that there should be raised, levied, collected, and paid into the hands of the receiver general, as treasurer of the province, to and for the use of his Majesty, and to and for the uses of the province, the like duties on all goods imported into the province from the United States, as are laid, levied, and collected under and by virtue of any act of the parliament of Great Britain, or of any provincial act of Lower Canada, on goods imported from Great Britain, or parts beyond the seas; establishing in this province ports of entry and clearance, providing for the appointment of collectors, and directing them to collect and pay over, report and account for all duties thus levied "under and by virtue of any act or acts of the parliament of Great Britain, or under and by virtue of this act."

The duties thus collected, to the amount of the sums specified in the above stated act of the British parliament, being distinguished from the residue, are considered as belonging to his Majesty, and not to the province, and are accounted for accordingly, upon the principle that they are levied under and by virtue of that act, although their collection is provided for by a provincial act. But some gentlemen in the province are of a different opinion, and have contended that they ought to be considered as levied by provincial authority, and belonging to the province.

Since the division of the old province into Upper and Lower Canada, the chief officers of government have been paid by the crown. It is understood that the fund collected for the purpose is not equal to the whole amount of the civil list, a part of which is consequently supplied from some other source. Whether the grants and leases of crown lands in this province, furnish such supply, I know not, though there is very little doubt that the rents of the reserved lands of the crown, if applied to that use, will eventually be sufficient*.

As the principal expenses of the civil list are thus defrayed by the crown, the expenditures of the province are moderate, and the provincial revenue is proportionally small. It arises first from the duties collected in the Lower Province, on good entered at *Coteau-du-Lac*, on their passage up to this province, the amount of which, for the year 1810, according to the annexed statement, was £4848 12 11

2d. The duties on goods imported from the United States, supposed to amount annually to about   1500 0 0

3d. Duties on tavern and shop licences, in addition to those laid by the British parliament, and on still licences, the net amount of all which for 1810, was   1304 0 0

4th. Duties on licences to hawkers, pedlars, and petty chapmen, amounting in 1810 to   420 0 0

£8072 12 11

The number of hawkers, pedlars, and petty chapmen, licensed in 1810, was seventy-six. The duties on their Licences, after deducting the inspector's 10 per cent., amounted to £420.

There is no provincial direct tax. The only tax of that nature is a district tax for defraying the expences of the several districts. The court of sessions in each district, determine the amount of it, under certain limitations of law, and apportion it according to an assessment List returned by the assessors of each township, containing the name of every person possessed of property, subject to taxation, with a statement of his taxable articles, viz. lands cultivated and uncultivated, houses of various specified descriptions, mills, stores, shops, horses and cattle. The rateable value of these several articles is not estimated by the assessors, but fixed by law; and a person possessing no such property is not assessed at all.

The direct taxes of the several districts, for one year, ending March 1, 1811, were as follows:

Eastern District	£627	8	2
Johnstown	451	8	1½
Midland	690	14	8
Newcastle	180	2	3¼

* Lower Canada, since 1816, has discharged its own civil list. The vote of the Imperial Parliament for the Upper Province was this year, 1820, £10,800. – R.G.

Home	479	11	7½
Niagara	1060	4	5
London	279	17	2½
Western	364	10	1¼
Total *	4,133	16	7

There is no pauper tax, no capitation, no tithes or ecclesiastical rates, the clergy of the established church being provided for by government, from a fund growing out of the lands reserved for that purpose, and by the Society for propagating the Gospel; and those of the dissenting denominations being supported by voluntary contracts with their societies.

Instead of highway taxes, every person included in the district assessment, is required to perform not less than three, nor more than twelve days labour annually on the highways, according to the list of his rateable estate. The apportionment of this statute labour, I perceive, is a subject of some popular complaint; but the amount of it is light, compared with the value of public roads.

No country in the world, perhaps, is less burdened with taxes. In no other country is the produce of labour left to the labourer's own use and benefit, more undiminished by public exactions or deductions in favour of landlords and other private persons; and it may, with great truth and propriety be added, that the objects of labour, especially of agricultural labour, the most useful of all, are no where more abundant, in proportion to the quantum of labour expended upon them.

Sketch XXIII.

Commerce.

MANY circumstances relating to the commercial situation of the country, have been incidentally mentioned under different heads, and need not be recapitulated.

---

* Some additional duties have been laid, and the amount of the revenue as well as the expenditures of the province, are increased since the late war.

Although agriculture is the first interest of Upper Canada, as it employs the greatest number of hands, and produces most of the articles of prime necessity, it is inseparably connected with commerce, without which the cultivators of the soil could not be supplied with many of the comforts and conveniences of life, in exchange for the surplus produce of their farms.

Such an exchange constitutes the natural trade of the province. It is negociated by the merchants who receive and market the productions of the country, and introduce and sell such goods, wares, and merchandise, as the inhabitants want for their consumption.

These are principally British manufacturers, and products, imported from Liverpool, Bristol, and Glasgow, by the way of Montreal. Some of them, however, in times of ordinary intercourse, have heretofore come through New York, and other ports of the United States*. But the statements in the last Sketch, will not satisfactorily shew the relative amounts or proportions even of dutied goods introduced through these respective channels of importation. For some of the articles brought from the United States into Lower Canada, are forwarded from thence to the Upper Province, and form a part of the entries at Coteau-du-Lac. The tobacco, for instance, entered there is most of it of American growth.

The ports of entry and clearance, opened in the province for communication with the United States, are Cornwall, Johnstown, Kingston, Newcastle, York, Niagara, Queenston, Fort Erie, Turkey Point, Amherstburgh and Sandwich. In such an extended line of water communication there are places of landing, where, it is supposed, duticd goods are sometimes smuggled into the province.

No considerable factories of cloth are established; but the farmers by their household manufactures, supply their families with most of their ordinary clothing.

The principal exports from the province are lumber, wheat (which is generally manufactured into flour before it is sent to market), peas, pot and pearl ashes, furs and peltries, pork, beef, and butter. Of the two last articles but small quantities are yet furnished for exportation.

Provision is made by law for the inspection of pot and pearl ashes, flour, beef, and pork; but as these exports pass through Lower Canada, on their way to market, they are subject to reinspection there, by the laws of that province.

* By an act of the British parliament, no goods, wares, or merchandise, except of the growth, produce, or manufacture of the United States, can now be imported thence into the province.

By a statement in the preceding Sketch of Revenue and Taxes, it may be seen that there were, in 1810, 132 licensed retailers. At the same time there were no less than 76 licensed pedlars. These travelling traders supply the interior of the country with light, cheap goods. The duty, however, on their licences is now raised, with a view to suppress their employment, as less beneficial than that of regular, stationary traders.

Much of the trade of the country is a species of indirect barter. The merchant trusts his customers with goods, and, at the proper season, receives their produce in payment, and forwards it by way of remittance to the importer. In this manner farmers frequently anticipate their crops, and if these are cut short, too often remain in debt to the merchant, whose occasion for punctual payment compels him, in such cases, to complain of the difficulty of collecting debts, while interest is accumulating against him and them. At present the inhabitants are generally less indebted than they were before the war. The public expenditures threw into circulation an unusual quantity of money, or what passed for money, and thereby facilitated the collection and payment of debts.

The lawful rate of interest is six per cent. This regulation of interest, different from that of the mother country, and the neighbouring state of New York, the former of which is five per cent. and the latter seven, depended upon an ordinance of the old province of Quebec, until 1811, when a statute was passed by the legislature of Upper Canada on the subject.

The same act has established the damages upon protested bills of exchange drawn in this province on Europe or the West Indies, at ten per cent. in addition to the interest, besides the cost of noting, protesting, and postage; and four per cent. on such bills drawn here on any part of North America, except the West Indies.

Sterling bills, drawn by persons entitled to full or half pay from government, are negociated and remitted by merchants; and, in many instances, prevent the necessity of transmitting money across the Atlantic.

There is no bank in the province, or indeed in any of the British provinces in America. Some efforts were lately made to procure the establishment of one at Kingston*; but the current of public opinion was perceived to set so strongly against the measure, that although supported by advocates of intelligence and

---

* There is now a bank established at Kingston, and two at Montreal, which have agents throughout Upper Canada. – R. G.

respectability, it was abandoned, without even presenting the petitions for incorporation to the legislature.

Bills of the bank of England are rarely seen here. Those of the banks in the United States, although discounted by a few individuals, who have remittances to make to the States, are not in circulation. Besides the distrust arising from the foreign situation of those banks, the number of counterfeits among the bills brought them into discredit. They were, indeed, counterfeited in Canada with impunity, there being no law to prohibit or punish the counterfeiting of foreign bills, until 1810, when an act was passed for that purpose by the legislature of Upper Canada. It has been followed by a similar act in the Lower Province.

Most of the circulating specie is gold. Its plenty or scarcity is affected by the fluctuations of crops and markets, and the varying state of commercial intercourse with the United States.

Army bills, as a medium of circulation, grew out of the war. They were substituted for specie, of which there was such a scarcity, that many private individuals issued their own notes, which passed for some time instead of cash.

Sketch XXV.

Religion and Ecclesiastic Institutions.

THE episcopal form of religion, according to the establishment of the Church of England, is supported by the government of this province. The constitutional act provided for a reservation of lands equal to one seventh part of all the lands then granted, and to be granted. These reserves, altogether distinct and different from those of another seventh, called the crown reserves, were required to be specified in the patents, and are appropriated exclusively to the maintenance of a Protestant clergy in the province.

Under instructions from the crown, the lieutenant-governor is empowered to erect parsonages or rectories in the several townships; to endow them with any proportion of the lands reserved in respect of such townships, and to present incumbents, subject to the bishop's right of institution.

At present, these reserved lands are leased by government, as lessees apply for them, for twenty-one years, at moderate rents, which go into the funds destined to support the clergy, and will eventually furnish a very ample support. The clergy reserves, and crown reserves, are leased on the same terms. The rent of a lot of 200 acres, taken in its uncultivated state, has been ten shillings a year for the first seven years, twenty shillings a year for the second seven years, and one pound ten shillings a year for the last seven years of the lease. Orders, I believe have lately been issued for doubling the sums to be reserved on lots hereafter leased. Whether the raising of the rents will proportionably increase the income, or prevent applications for leases, is a question on which theoretic reasoners differ, but which will be determined by the experiment.

There is only one bishop for the two provinces of Upper and Lower Canada, and he resides at Quebec.

In Upper Canada there are six ministers of the church of England, situated at Cornwall, Kingston, Ernest Town, and Fredericksburgh*, York, Niagara, and Sandwich. They severally receive £100 per annum from government, and £50 from the Society for Propagating the Gospel in Foreign Parts. They solemnize marriages; but there is no ecclesiastical court in the province.

Dissenters of all denominations are tolerated and protected by law. They are not subject to tithes, or civil disabilities, nor disqualified for offices, or a seat in the legislature. Their contracts respecting the support of public worship are legally enforceable. Ordained ministers of the Scotch, Lutheran, and Calvinist churches, upon producing satisfactory credentials in a court of sessions, are authorized to perform marriages, where one of the parties to be married is a member of their respective societies. Any denomination, holding the distinguishing Calvinistic doctrines, are included under the term *Calvinist*. As such, Presbyterian, Congregational, and Baptist clergymen, exercise the power of marriage.

The dissenting denominations are, Presbyterians, Lutherans, Methodists, Congregationalists, Moravians, Anabaptists, Roman Catholics, Quakers, Menonists, and Tunkers. Several of them are more numerous than the Episcopalians. The most numerous of all

---

* The rectory of Ernest Town and Fredericksburgh has become vacant by the return of the Rev. John Langhorn to his native place in England.

are the Methodists, who are spread over the whole province. They are followers of Wesley as to doctrines, and acknowledge the episcopal authority of the Wesleyan bishops. Next in number are the Presbyterians, who are of the Dutch Reformed Church, the Church of Scotland, and Scotch Seceders, or the Associate Reformed Synod. The Presbyterians appear to be increasing in numbers and respectability.

The Roman Catholics, who are comparatively few, are attached to the government, and grateful for the religious freedom which they enjoy, and by which they are distinguished from their brethren in Ireland.

Quakers, Menonists, and Tunkers, being conscientiously scrupulous of bearing arms, are conditionally exempted from militia duties.

Sketch XXVI.

Profession and Practice of Law.

In the early stages of the province, gentlemen were admitted to the bar by licence from the lieutenant-governor, specially provided for by two successive acts of the legislature. But in 1797, those who were then in practice were authorized to form themselves into a society, by the name of *The Law Society of Upper Canada*, and to establish rules and regulations, under the inspection of the judges; and it was enacted, that no other person, except licensed practitioners from some other British province or dominion, shall be permitted to practise at the bar of any of his Majesty's courts in this province, unless he shall have been previously entered of, and admitted into, the said society, as a student of law, and shall have been standing in their books for five years, and have conformed himself to their rules and regulations, and been duly called and admitted as a barrister.

The society was accordingly organized, and the act still remains in force. Every barrister is now allowed to have four apprentices or clerks.

Sketch XXVII.

Physic and Surgery.

ONE of the ordinances of the province of Quebec prohibited the practice of physic or surgery by any person not licensed in the manner therein prescribed.

In 1795, an act of the legislature of Upper Canada, repealing, in general terms, all former laws on the subject, established a board for examining and licensing medical candidates. From the state of the province it became impossible to form such a board of examiners, and the act was repealed. Many physicians and surgeons have gone into practice without any provincial license, supposing there was no prohibition, and not suspecting that an old ordinance of the former province of Quebec, which was not executed and had not been published among the laws of this province, was revived by a repeal of the provincial act, so as to be in force here. An act passed in 1815 has established a new licensing board, to consist of the senior army physician or surgeon, with one other practitioner, regularly licensed in some of the British dominions. It subjects to a penalty of £100 every person practising, after the date of the act, as a physician, surgeon, or male-midwife, without a licence, excepting, however, any one who has had a warrant as a surgeon or surgeon's mate in the army or navy.

Sketch XXVIII.

Trades and Apprenticeships.

THE statute of Elizabeth, requiring seven years apprenticeship before the exercise of a trade, being local in its application, is not considered to be applicable to this province; and no provincial act has been passed on the subject. Any mechanic, therefore, is at liberty to set up his trade, whether he has served a stated term of apprenticeship or not. But as the same liberty is common to others, and customers left to their own choice will employ the best workmen, he cannot expect employment and success without skill in his trade; and that is not ordinarily acquired without an apprenticeship, or regular education for the business. In this view apprenticeships are useful and necessary; and contracts for them, in the usual form of indentures, are respected and enforced by law.

Sketch XXIX.

Imprisonment For Debt, Insolvent Laws, and Liability of Land for Debt.

PERSONAL liberty is so highly respected by the laws of the province, that, in civil actions, the body is not subject to arrest or imprisonment, except in a case of debt certain, and above 40 shillings, where there has been an attempt, or is an apparent intention to avoid payment. Before a capias can be sued out as mesne process or execution, the creditor, his agent, or servant, must make affidavit that he believes the debtor is about leaving the province, with an intent to defraud his creditors, or has secreted or conveyed his effects, to prevent their being taken in execution.

An insolvent debtor, detained in prison on execution, upon applying to the court, and making oath that he is not worth five pounds, is entitled to a discharge of his person, or a dollar a week for his support, to be paid by the creditor in advance every Monday, unless the creditor prove, to the satisfaction of the court, that the debtor has fraudulently secreted or conveyed away his effects.

Where the debt does not exceed £10 sterling, and the debtor has been imprisoned a month, if he makes oath that he is not worth more than the amount of the debt, and has not fraudulently disposed of any property, his person is discharged; but any estate which he then has, or may thereafter acquire, remains liable for the debt.

A debtor's land is liable to be taken and sold on execution, after a writ of execution against his goods and chattels is returned unsatisfied; and though upon a person's decease his land descends to his heir or heirs, according to the rules of the common law, and is not subject to administration, as assets for the payment of debts; yet it is questioned whether the same British statute which subjects the land of a living debtor in the provinces to the payment of debts, be not applicable to the land of a deceased debtor. If this be the true construction of the law, the jurisdiction of the court of probate, and of executors and administrators, should be extended to the administration of lands in such cases.

There is no bankrupt law in the province. In the general adoption of English laws, those respecting bankrupts were expressly excepted; and the provincial legislature have made no provision on the subject.

In cases of failure and insolvency, traders stand on the same ground with other debtors.

Sketch XXX.

Gradual Abolition of Slavery.

THE common law of England does not admit of slavery. But an act of parliament authorized the governor of the province of Quebec, to license the importation of slaves. Under that authority a few negro slaves were introduced before the division of the province. At the second session of the legislature of Upper Canada, in 1793, the further importation of them was prohibited; and voluntary contracts for personal service were limited to a term not exceeding nine years. As to slaves theretofore imported under authorized licences, the property of their masters was confirmed; but provision was made, that the children of such slaves, born after the passing of the act, should be free at the age of 25 years; and that their births should be registered, to furnish evidence of their age. It was further declared, that if such minors, during their term of servitude, should have children born, those children should be entitled to all the rights and privileges of freemen. Of course they cannot be holden to service after the age of 21 years.

The principle of this gradual abolition of slavery, is similar to that of some of the American States.

The number of slaves in the province is very small.

Sketch XXXIII.

Character, Manners, and Customs of the Inhabitants.

IF the people of Upper Canada have any predominant national character, it is the Anglo-American. Among the first settlers there were natives of Great Britain and Ireland, and a few of some other European countries; but the mass of them were Americans, born in New England, New York, New Jersey, and Pennsylvania. They retain a strong attachment to their sovereign, who remunerated them for their revolutionary losses, made them liberal grants of land to settle on, with farming tools, building materials and provisions, to facilitate their settlement, and is still granting lands to their children as fast as they become of age.

Those who have since joined the province are of a similar national mixture. A considerable number of emigrants from Scotland, settled together in the eastern districts, and others have, at a later period, been planted in the western district, under the auspices of Lord Selkirk. One township on Yonge Street has been chiefly taken up by Germans. British, Irish, and a few French gentlemen of business have located themselves in various situations. Some inhabitants have removed from Lower Canada, Nova Scotia, and New Brunswick. Still greater numbers have come from the United States, because of their adjacency, and in consequence of the original American settlers, who left behind them in the States, their fathers, their brothers, and other relatives, neighbours, and friends, from whom they had been separated by the revolution. As their revolutionary passions mutually subsided, the natural feelings of consanguinity, amnity, and personal friendship revived. They were still interesting objects to each other. Friendly inquiries, correspondencies, exchanges of visits, and renewals of attachment ensued. The tide of emigration naturally flows from old to new settlements. These causes, combined with the fertility of the Canadian soil, the relative cheapness of land and lightness of public burdens, have induced many Americans, from year to year, to move into the province. Here they have generally acquired farms and engaged in business, not as a distinct people, like the French population in Lower Canada, but blended and intermixed with the former inhabitants.

This intermixture produces no effervescence, personal or political. Politics, indeed, are scarcely named or known among them. They have very little agency in the affairs of government, except that the freeholders once in four years elect their representatives. The people are not agitated by parties, as they are in the United States, where all branches of government depend, directly or indirectly, upon frequent popular elections.

They are here distinguished rather by their occupations, than by their political connexions, or the places of their birth. A due proportion of them are in professional, mercantile, and mechanic employments; but the most numerous class are engaged in agriculture, and have the appropriate views, manners, and sentiments of agriculturists.

There is here, as well as every where else, a certain portion of idle and vicious persons, who hang loose upon society, and, instead of adding, by their labour, to the general sum of wealth and prosperity, diminish it by their consumption and waste. Their number, however, is not peculiar. The main body of the inhabitants may be characterised as industrious.

Their diversions are similar to those of the interior of New England. Dancing is a favourite amusement of the youth. Athletic sports are common. Family visits and tea parties are the most frequent scenes of sociability.

The country is too young for regular theatric entertainments, and those delicacies and refinements of luxury, which are the usual attendants of wealth. Dissipation, with her fascinating train of expences and vices, has made but little progress on the shores of the lakes.

There are no splendid equipages, and few common carriages; but the face of the country being level, they will doubtless be multiplied, as the roads become well fitted for wheels.

In winter great use is made of sleighs; and sleighing parties are fashionable; but taverns and provisions for travellers are, in many parts of the country, quite indifferent. The improvement of travelling accommodations has been retarded by the preference given to passages by water, during the summer months. Yet travel by land increases, and the roads are advancing towards a more perfect state, by the annual application of statute labour, and the aids granted, from time to time, by the legislature out of the provincial funds.

So many Townships are situated upon waters filled with fish, that fishing is a common amusement, easily connected with occasional supplies of provisions.

Fashions of dress and modes of living are common to the inhabitants of the province and their neighbours in the States. The style of building, however, on the Canadian side of the line is less elegant; and, in general, there are less ambition, enterprise, and exertion. This difference is the natural consequence of the different circumstances, under which the original settlements were commenced.

The habit of smoking is very common among all classes of people throughout the province. By the statements of dutiable imports, inserted in the sketch of revenue and taxes, it appears that the duty was paid upon almost 100,000 pounds of manufactured tobacco, imported in the year 1810, besides all that was smuggled in, all that was produced in the province, and all the cigars, which, not being subject to the duty, are not entered in those statements.

In new countries people generally make too free use of ardent spirits, for their health or their morals. To this fault the early settlers here were peculiarly exposed, from the manner of life they had followed several years in the army, their want of cider, that common drink to which they had been accustomed before the revolution, and the facility with which distilled liquors could be procured as a substitute. With a decrease of these causes, the pernicious effects are decreasing. Instances of occasional excess and habitual intemperance are becoming less frequent. The rising generation, it is to be hoped, will complete the reformation thus begun.

Another bad custom, once considerably prevalent in some parts of the province, appears to be declining. I mean the vulgar practice of pugilism.

Wherever this prevails, it marks a low stage of civilization. It is indeed a relic of the savage state, in which the avenging of private wrongs, by personal violence, under the immediate impulse of excited passions, is a ruling principle. Whereas the object of civil society and government is to protect the weak against the strong, and the peaceable against the quarrelsome, and to establish reason and law, under the administration of disinterested judges, as substitutes for personal vengeance inflicted by every man, judging, or rather feeling, in his own cause. Upon this ground assaults and batteries are condemned by law. The practice of personal combats, therefore, is a departure from the first principle of civilization; and, so far as it obtains, is a return to the barbarous, savage state of life.

It is also a direct violation of the known law of the land. Men of honour ought to view it in this light, and reflect well upon the tendency of countenancing it by example or indulgence. If one plain law is violated with impunity, or with only nominal or very slight punishment, the respect due to laws in general is thereby diminished, and the arm of government proportionally weakened. This tendency to insubordination and contempt of authority is strengthened, when the violation of law is rendered fashionable and popular, either by the passions of our nature, or the contagion of influential examples.

Men of conscience should contemplate the subject in a still more serious light. The practice under consideration is a transgression of the law of God. Its indulgence promotes other sins. It increases the venom of hatred, resentment, and all the angry passions, from which the parties probably suffer more than from the pain occasioned by blows and wounds. It sometimes ends in homicide, and frequently produces loss of labour and health, and plants the seeds of lameness, disability, and disease. It involves families and friends in quarrels, and spreads animosities through whole neighbourhoods and townships. It degrades a national or provincial character, injures public morals and manners, vulgarizes public taste, and checks the progress of social refinement.

Popular customs, deriving their force from habit, are not easily changed; especially those which are prompted by the strong passions of human nature. Such is that we are speaking of, which is stimulated by anger and revenge, and not less by pride; for vulgar fashion has made it an object of a false kind of heroism. It is not, however, too inveterate to be restrained by public sentiment, which may always be directed by the enlightened part of a community.

The decline of so degrading a practice indicates a state of improvement. Its extinction would be a subject of additional congratulation.

I have observed no essential peculiarity in the funerals or weddings of this country; but there is a singular custom of *chereverreeing*, as it is called, a newly married couple, where the match is thought to be unequal or unseasonable; as, between an old man and a young girl, or within a short period after the death of a former husband or wife. Sometimes it is in consequence of the offence so frequently caused by a neglect of invitation to the wedding. It is a kind of riotous frolic derived from the French of Lower Canada. Young men, disguised in masks, assemble in the evening before the house of the bride and bridegroom, bearing some significant emblem, accompanied with horns, bells, pans, and other instruments, with which they perform a discordant serenade. It is often in vain for the parties, who are the objects of such a visit, to resist or resent it. Their wisest course is to treat it with good humour, as a joke unworthy of serious notice.

This custom being discountenanced by people of consideration, as rude and injurious, seems to be going into disrepute and disuse. It has lately been a subject of prosecution; and, as practised in many instances, is undoubtedly indictable as a riot. In Lower Canada, it is said to have been suppressed by the interposition of the police.

Public days are not so frequent here as they are in some countries.

The fourth of June, being the anniversary of his Majesty's birth, is noticed throughout the province, as a national holyday; but not with such orations, processions, and parade, as are displayed in the United States, on the fourth of July.

Freemasons attend their festivals as in other places.

The Christmas holydays are observed in the usual manner.

The churches and dissenting meeting houses are generally plain. The worshipping assemblies appear grave and devout, except that in some of them it is customary for certain persons to go out and come in frequently in time of service, to the disturbance of others, and the interruption of that silence and solemnity which are enjoined by politeness, no less than a sense of religion. This indecorous practice prevails among several different denominations; but it is local in its prevalence, and scarcely deserves to be mentioned in a description of provincial customs.

The observance of the sabbath, instituted by religion, and required by law, is most strict in those places, where public worship is regularly maintained. Such places are not so numerous as might be wished, although their number is increasing. In a country recently settled, and thinly peopled; where various creeds are professed, and religious freedom is enjoyed, a regular maintenance of the public worship of God is a matter of difficulty; but its salutary influence on civil society, renders it an important object; and, when viewed in the light of that eternal state of retributions, to which this life is only a probationary introduction, it rises in importance, beyond the reach of description. In this point of view, every believer of the Christian system, whether connected or not by national ties, must wish success to the means of propagating the gospel of salvation, in any land where human beings dwell.

Appendix

To Sketches

AFTER the foregoing Sketches were finished, the Provincial Legislature, at their Session in 1816, enacted several laws, which will be summarily sketched in this Appendix.

Two new Districts were formed; the District of Gore, at the head of Lake Ontario, taken from the Niagara and Home Districts; and the District of Ottawa, composed of the northern part of the Eastern District. The principal Settlements in this new District, are situated on or near the river Ottawa. This north-easterly Section of the Province has hitherto attracted little attention, but is rising in importance. Many Settlers, who have recently emigrated from the British European dominions, under the auspices of government, and a considerable number of the officers and soldiers of the regiments lately disbanded, are located or to be located there, and a new route of inland navigation, between Montreal and Kingston, is to be opened in that direction. The country has been explored, and the reports of it are favourable. It is expected to pass up the Ottawa to the mouth of the Rideau, and up that river near to its head waters, thence by a short portage to Kingston Mill river, and down that stream to Kingston. The distance will be greater than down the St. Lawrence. But the difficult and dangerous rapids will be avoided; and, in the event of another war, this interior communication between the two Provinces, will be more safe than the old one along the frontier.

The two new Districts are organized, and their respective officers appointed and sworn into office.

An act was passed for the establishment and encouragement of common schools. It provides for a board of education, to be appointed by the Governor in Council, in each District, and authorizes the inhabitants of any town, township, village or place, to associate by subscription for a school, and to choose three trustees of such school, who have power to appoint a teacher, designate the school books to be used, and direct the course of education, subject to the superintendance of the District Board of Education. These trustees are annually to certify the number of scholars instructed in their respective schools, and report the state of the schools to the District Board, who are to make a similar report to the Governor, to be laid before the Legislature. The act grants 6,000 pounds (24,000 dollars) a year, from the provincial fund, and apportions it to the ten Districts. The District Boards are to apportion it among the schools in their several Districts, according to the number of their scholars, with these limitations, that none be given to a school of less than 20 scholars, and no school have less than a hundred dollars; and the money is to be paid to the teachers upon their producing certificates of qualification and good conduct from their trustees.

This law, however incomplete as a system, indicates a favourable progress of public sentiment on the subject of education.

Commercial intercourse between the province and the states not having been regulated by treaty, an act was passed for that purpose. . . .

SCHEDULE OF DUTIES *to be received on Articles of Manufacture, being of the Growth and Produce of the United States of America, under the Order in Council, of the 18th of April, 1816.*

	Ad valorem per cent	£	s.	d.
Anchors	22	0	0	0
Brass, iron, or steel locks, hinges, hoes, anvils and vices	22	0	0	0
Beer, ale, or porter, in casks, per gallon	0	0	0	6
Do. in bottles, do.	0	0	1	0
Books, blank, &c.	35	0	0	0
Broaches	35	0	0	0
Cables and tarred cordage, per lib.		0	0	3½
Carriages or parts of carriages	35	0	0	0
Cards, playing, per pack		0	1	6
Wool and Cotton, per dozen		0	5	3
Candles of tallow, per lib.		0	0	2½
Candles, Spermaceti or wax		0	0	7½
Canes, walking sticks, and whips	35	0	0	0
Cotton goods	25	0	0	0
Cabinet wares, chairs, and manufactures of wood	35	0	0	0
Cordage tarred, per lib.		0	0	3½
_____untarred, do.		0	0	3
Cotton wool, do.		0	0	2

	Ad valorem per cent	£	s	d
Clothing, ready made	35	0	0	0
Fish dried, per quintal		0	5	0
Mackerel, per barrel		0	6	0
Salmon, do.		0	10	0
All other pickled fish, do.		0	5	0
Furs of all kinds, undressed	free	0	0	0
Glass, window, not above 8 by 10, per 100 square feet		0	12	6
Do. do. 10 by 12		0	13	9
Do. do. above 10 by 12		0	16	3
All other manufactures thereof	30	0	0	0
Glauber salts, per cwt.		1	0	0
Glue, per lib.		0	0	5
Gunpowder		0	0	4
Hairpowder		0	0	4
Hemp, per cwt.		0	7	6
Indigo, per lib.		0	0	9
Iron hoop, and slit, per cwt.		0	7	6
_____ sheet, do.		0	7	6
Lead and musket ball	22	0	0	0
All other manufactures in which lead is the chief article	22	0	0	0
Looking glasses	40	0	0	0
Malt, per bushel		0	1	0
Nails, per lib.		0	0	2½
Paper of all descriptions	35	0	0	0
Packthread and twine, per cwt.		2	0	0
Pasteboard, parchment, and vellum	35	0	0	0
Pictures and prints	35	0	0	0
Salt, per bushel, of 59lb.	0	0	1	0
Starch, per lib.	0	0	0	3½
Steel, per cwt.	0	0	10	0
Spirits, distilled from grain, First proof, per gallon	0	0	2	1½
Second ditto ditto	0	0	2	3
Third ditto ditto	0	0	2	5
Fourth ditto ditto	0	0	2	7
Fifth ditto ditto	0	0	3	0
Sixth ditto ditto	0	0	3	9

	Ad valorem per cent	£	s	d
Spirits, from molasses, do.	0	0	3	9
Men's and women's shoes of all descriptions, made of leather, per pair	0	0	1	3
Children's do. do.	0	0	0	9
Soap, per lib.	0	0	0	2
Snuff, ditto	0	0	0	7½
Tobacco, unmanufactured, ditto	0	0	0	4
_____, manufactured, do.	0	0	0	7
Tallow	free	0	0	0
Types for printing	20	0	0	0
Wearing apparel, and personal baggage	free	0	0	0
Wood, manufactured	25	0	0	0
All other manufactures and goods of the growth and produce of the United States of America, not otherwise enumerated	30	0	0	0
Except wheat, barley, rye, oats, pease, beans, pot and pearl ashes, staves, heading, oak and pine timber, and other lumber; beef, pork, and live cattle, cheese, butter, and all other provisions, which may be admitted free.				
12 per cent. upon the above duties to be paid on such articles, as are imported in foreign vessels				
Every ship's boat, or vessel, exceeding five tons burden, belonging to the subjects of the United States of America, entering any port or harbour within this province, to pay a duty, per ton, of	0	0	12	6

JOHN SMALL,
Clerk of the Executive Council.

The tonnage duty laid by this order, although intended to correspond with that of the United States upon British vessels, was found to be higher. Its effects were to exclude the American packets and small vessels, or to cause them to be covered with names of British owners, by real or fictitious sales; and at the same time to turn the forwarding business from ports on the British side of the lakes and rivers to those on the other side.

The duty was soon reduced by the following

ORDER

OF THE LIEUTENANT-GOVERNOR, IN COUNCIL

Province of At a Council for the affairs of the Province, held at *Upper Canada.* York in the said Province, on the 22d day of May, in the 56th year of his Majesty's reign, and in the year of our Lord 1816,

PRESENT,
HIS EXCELLENCY THE LIEUTENANT-GOVERNOR

WHEREAS it has been represented that the tonnage duty of 12s. 6d. per ton, imposed on all vessels exceeding five tons, belonging to the subjects of the United States of America, entering any port or harbour in this province, is higher than is imposed in the ports of the United States, on the tonnage of vessels belonging to his Majesty's subjects; it is ordered that so much of the Order in Council of the 18th of April, 1816, as imposes a tonnage duty on vessels belonging to the subjects of the United States, be cancelled, and that the following tonnage duty be imposed in lieu thereof.

On all vessels above five tons to fifty tons, the tonnage duty to be three-pence halfpenny per ton.

From fifty to a hundred tons, five shillings, or one dollar per ton. On all vessels above a hundred tons, twelve shillings and sixpence per ton.

JOHN SMALL, Clerk of the Executive Council.

The reasons here alleged for annulling the former rates of tonnage duty, and substituting these in conformity to the American standard, manifests a disposition for friendly intercourse; a disposition which it is to be hoped will be obviated on both sides as well by the governments as their respective subjects. A war of legislation, although not so destructive as a war of arms, would occasion serious inconveniences. On the other hand a free commercial intercourse, on liberal terms, is not only pleasant, but mutually beneficial.

Instances of national civility have been witnessed with much satisfaction. Of that character was the act passed by Congress, to exempt from impost duty, Governor Gore's carriage, which was landed at New York, on its way to Upper Canada. Such civilities have a conciliatory tendency, and are far more gratifying to a benevolent mind than acts of retaliation or reciprocal irritation.

At the session of the Provincial parliament in 1816, the annual labour required by law to be expended upon roads was extended, and some other alterations made in the statute. The important object of improving the public roads continues to occupy the attention of the legislature.

In addition to the statute labour annually required of the inhabitants, liberal grants have, from time to time, been made from the provincial funds, and applied under the direction of road commissioners, appointed for that purpose in the several districts.

The provincial revenue has increased to such a degree as to enable the legislature at their session this year (1816) to make liberal grants. The view of this subject, contained in a preceding Sketch, as taken from the statements of the year 1810, gives no adequate idea of its present state. An authentic abstract of the amount of the several sources of revenue for the last year could not be obtained in season to be inserted in this appendix.

At the same session, the jurisdiction of the courts of requests was enlarged to five pounds, in cases of liquidated debts; but their process was declared to be confined within the limits of their respective justiciary divisions, instead of extending through the whole district.

Provision was also made for regulating the police of the town of Kingston. This town is now progressing rapidly in population and buildings, as well as business. From 1811 to 1816, the number of dwelling houses only increased from 130 to 300; but it is estimated that a hundred more will have been erected at the close of this year. A regular market is established; though the country immediately around is not yet cultivated enough to furnish sufficient supplies of vegetables and other provisions. Improvements in many respects are taking place throughout the town; but further regulations had become necessary, and are provided for by the act. These regulations respect the repairing, paving, and cleaning of the streets, removing nuisances, regulating slaughter-houses, restraining cattle, providing fire engines and buckets, and forming companies of enginemen, and promoting in general the health, comfort, and security of the inhabitants. For these valuable objects, the magistrates are authorized to lay a town tax of a limited amount.

Here closes a very fair and impartial account of Upper Canada, up to the year 1817. A destructive war seems to have had little effect in repressing the prosperity of the Province. Kingston continues to increase rapidly: Queenston "is in a flourishing state," &c.

In 1817 great changes took place; partly from external circumstances, which affected the world at large; partly from the internal policy of the executive government, or rather its impolitic haste, in running counter to established law and confirmed good practice.

The change alluded to will little appear from the perusal of the following Reports; for the world does not contain a more contented people than those of Upper Canada: indeed a cow in clover takes little heed of the scythe which does not scratch its hoof; but if the clover is yet made into good hay, the cow may have no reason to complain of a temporary stint. – R.G.

Queries.

1st. *Name, Situation, and Extent of your Township?*
2d. DATE OF THE FIRST SETTLEMENT OF YOUR TOWNSHIP, NUMBER OF PEOPLE AND INHABITED HOUSES?
3d. NUMBER OF CHURCHES OR MEETING HOUSES; NUMBER OF PROFESSIONAL PREACHERS, AND OF WHAT SECTS?
4th. NUMBER OF MEDICAL PRACTITIONERS?
5th. NUMBER OF SCHOOLS, AND THE FEES PER QUARTER?
6th. NUMBER OF STORES?
7th. NUMBER OF TAVERNS?
8th. NUMBER OF MILLS, AND OF WHAT DESCRIPTION, WITH THE RATE OF *grinding*, SAWING AND CARDING WOOL?
9th. THE GENERAL CHARACTER OF THE SOIL AND SURFACE?
10th. THE KINDS OF TIMBER PRODUCED, NAMING THEM IN ORDER, AS THEY MOST ABOUND?

11th. WHAT MINERALS, IF ANY, HAVE BEEN DISCOVERED OR INDICATED; COAL LIMESTONE, IRON, STONE, PLAISTER OF PARIS, SALT ROCK, SALT OR OTHER REMARKABLE SPRINGS?

*12th. BUILDING STONES, IF ANY, OF WHAT QUALITY, AND HOW MUCH PER TOISE THEY CAN BE OBTAINED FOR AT THE QUARRY?

13th. IF BRICKS HAVE BEEN MADE, AND THEIR COST PER THOUSAND?

14th. IF LIME IS BURNED, AND THE PRICE PER BUSHEL, AT THE KILN?

15th. WAGES OF BLACKSMITHS, MASONS, AND CARPENTERS; AND THE RATE OF THEIR PIECE-WORK RESPECTIVELY?

16th. WAGES OF COMMON LABOURERS PER ANNUM, PER WINTER MONTH, PER SUMMER MONTH, PER DAY IN HARVEST; ALSO, WAGES OF WOMEN SERVANTS PER WEEK, FOR HOUSEWORK, AND FOR SPINNING?

17th. PRICE OF MOWING GRASS FOR HAY; PRICE OF REAPING AND CRADLING WHEAT; *saying in each case if board and lodging is included?*

18th. COST OF CLEARING AND FENCING A GIVEN QUANTITY OF WOOD LAND; SAY FIVE ACRES, BY CONTRACT?

19th. PRESENT PRICE OF A GOOD WORK HORSE FOUR YEARS OLD; ALSO, A GOOD COW, OX, SHEEP, OF THE SAME AGE?

20th. AVERAGE QUANTITY OF WOOL YIELDED BY SHEEP; AND WHAT PRICE THE WOOL NOW BRINGS PER POUND?

**21st. ORDINARY TIME OF TURNING OUT BEASTS TO PASTURE, AND OF TAKING THEM HOME INTO THE YARD OR STABLE?

22d. ORDINARY ENDURANCE OF THE SLEIGHING SEASON, AND OF COMMENCING PLOUGHING IN SPRING?

23d. ORDINARY SEASON OF SOWING AND REAPING WHEAT?

24th. QUANTITY OF WHEAT REQUIRED TO SOW AN ACRE, AND HOW MANY BUSHELS PER ACRE ARE CONSIDERED AN AVERAGE CROP?

---

* In many of the Reports, prices were given in DOLLARS: in some, NEW YORK CURRENCY, or 8s. to the dollar, was spoken of. To prevent confusion, I have converted these into the provincial currency of 5s. to a dollar, and four dollars to the pound, of 18s. sterling.

** To quote all the Replies to Queries 21st. 22nd. and 23d. would be unnecessarily tedious. I shall, therefore, only give them in two adjoining Reports of each District, which will be quite Sufficient for the reader's information.

25th.   QUALITY OF PASTURE: 1ST. AS IT RESPECTS FEEDING, AND
WHAT WEIGHT AN OX OF FOUR YEARS OLD WILL GAIN WITH
A SUMMER'S RUN; 2D. AS IT RESPECTS MILK, AND THE QUAL-
ITY OF DAIRY PRODUCE, NOTING THE PRICE WHICH BUTTER
AND CHEESE MADE IN THE TOWNSHIP WILL NOW FETCH?

26th.   ORDINARY COURSE OF CROPPING UPON NEW LANDS, AND
AFTERWARDS WHEN BROKEN UP FROM GRASS; STATING ALSO
WHEN AND FOR WHAT CROPS MANURE IS APPLIED?

27th.   IF ANY LAND IS LET ON SHARES; TO WHAT EXTENT THIS IS
PRACTISED; AND WHAT THE ORDINARY TERMS?

* 28th.   THE PRICE OF WILD LAND AT THE FIRST SETTLEMENT OF
THE TOWNSHIP; ITS PROGRESSIVE RISE AND PRESENT PRICE;
ALSO OF LAND SO FAR CLEARED; STATING CIRCUMSTANCES AS
TO BUILDINGS, PROPORTION CLEARED, OR PECULIARITY, IF
ANY, OF LOCAL SITUATION; REFERRING IN EVERY INSTANCE
TO ACTUAL SALES?

29th.   QUALITY OF LAND NOW FOR SALE?

30th.   STATE OF PUBLIC ROADS, AND IF CAPABLE OF MUCH
IMPROVEMENT AT A MODERATE EXPENCE; ALSO, IF ANY
WATER CONVEYANCE; OR, IF THIS COULD BE OBTAINED,
EXTENDED, OR IMPROVED, BY MEANS OF CANALS, LOCKS, &C.
&C.

31st.   WHAT, IN YOUR OPINION, RETARDS THE IMPROVEMENT OF
YOUR TOWNSHIP IN PARTICULAR, OR THE PROVINCE IN GEN-
ERAL; AND WHAT WOULD MOST CONTRIBUTE TO THE SAME?**

Township Reports of Upper Canada

Western District

Sandwich

*At a Meeting of the Resident Land Owners of the Township of
Sandwich, in the Western District of Upper Canada, this 18th
Day of December, 1817,*

RESOLVED,
THAT an answer be given to the Queries of Mr. Robert Gourlay,

---

* My 28th Query required a reference to ACTUAL SALES; which unfortunately has been to little attended to.

** For Gourlay's tabulation of the replies to the thirty-first of these queries, see p. 293. For his comments on the replies, see p. 312. [Ed.]

for the information of our fellow subjects in Britain, who apparently are ignorant of the advantages in this section of the empire, when they emigrate into the dominions of foreign potentates, incongenial to their habits and feelings, and where they become for ever lost to their country.

2d. The township of Sandwich began to settle under the French government about the year 1750, and perhaps earlier, and contains at present about 200 inhabited houses, and about 1000 souls. The front on the river only is settled, with the exception of a few houses in the interior, and notwithstanding its nearness to market, and natural advantages, we do not know of one additional settler for this number of years.

3d. One Roman Catholic church, and two priests, no Protestant church or chapel (the same having been destroyed by the enemy during the late war), and but one preacher of the church of England.

4th. Two medical practitioners.

5th. One school, with one master, who draws a salary from the provincial fund, of £100 per annum, besides tuition fees. There are also two inferior schools, the teachers of which receive from the same fund £25 per annum, besides moderate fees.

6th. Thirteen shops or stores. 7th. 8 taverns.

8th. Eight wind-mills and one water-mill for grinding wheat. No saw or carding-mills. Inch pine boards are at present 5l. per thousand feet; but they will soon be at half that price.

9th. The face of the township is level, and much ditching required; the general character of the soil is yellow and black loam, with a clay under stratum. The middle of the township is sandy; but a mixture of these renders the soil warm and grateful to vegetation. Wild hay in abundance. Cattle thrive well.

10th. A great part of the township is a plain, and the timber most abounding is, white, red, and black oak, ash, elm, hickory, poplar, maple, and chestnut.

11th. No minerals, lime-stone, salt rock or springs, coal, plaster, or remarkable springs have as yet been discovered.

12th. No stone of any kind but what is transported from Malden, the next township, and sold from 3l. to 3l. 15s. per toise, of 6 cubic feet. In the quarry they may be had for 2s. 6d. per toise, and quarried for 7s. 6d. one mile from the river.

13th. Bricks are made, but not in a sufficient quantity, and are from 2l. to 2l. 10s. per thousand at the kiln, though the soil is favourable for making them.

---

* This seems extremely high; but I give it as given to me . . . R.G.

14th. No lime but what is brought from Malden, and generally sold at 1s. 3d. per bushel; but it can be made for much less, and has been sold at 7½d. per bushel.

15th. Blacksmiths generally have shops of their own, and earn from 11. to 21. per day*. Carpenters and masons, 10s. per day, with board and lodging; and when they work by the piece, they calculate on more.

16th. Wages of common labourers, per annum, 25l. to 37l. 10s.; per winter month, 21. to 21. 10s.; per summer month, 31. to 31. 15s.; per day in harvest, 5s. to 6s. 3d.; women servants, 11. 5s. per month, but very few are to be hired; spinners none.

17th. Mowing, reaping, and cradling, 5s. to 6s. 3d.

18th. Cost of clearing and fencing five acres of land, about 121. 10s. on an average. Sometimes woodlands are given for a certain time, and then on shares to repay the person by whose labour it was cleared.

19th. The price of a work horse of four years, 121. 10s., a cow 51., an ox 71. 10s., and a sheep 11.

20th. Wool three to four pounds per fleece; some has had nine pounds and twenty pounds of tallow: common wool, 2s. 6d. per pound.

21st. About the 10th of April, and the 10th of December. Horned cattle are seldom housed; they do better under sheds, and if near the woods, they browse, and want but very little fodder; horses the same, except those kept for work.

22d. Sleighing season from the latter end of December, to the beginning of March; but commonly its duration is but two months, January and February; ploughing begins about the beginning of April.

23d. Sowing fall wheat in August and September, and reaping in July. Spring wheat is sown as early as the season will admit; in March, if the frost is out of the ground.

24th. One to one and a half bushels of wheat per acre, according to the richness of the ground: average crop about 10 bushels per arpent*, but when well cultivated it has been known to produce 20 bushels. The land is not as well cultivated here as in Britain; it has never more than one ploughing, and the sod has not sufficient time to rot and to pulverize.

25th. Blue grass and white clover, the natural production of the land; no made meadows to signify; yet an ox of four years in a summer's run, will gain about 120 lb. Milk is rich, and in the season overflows the pail. Butter excellent; cheese very little

---

* The arpent is to the acre as 180 to 200.

made; it is purchased from our neighbours over the straight, and is generally at 1*s*. 3*d*. per pound. Butter is from 1*s*. 3*d*. to 2*s*. 6*d*. per pound.

26th. Land is often cleared for the first crop, and sometimes three crops, according to the labour; and when taken, it is at for half the produce. Manure is seldom wanted but on old ground, for wheat; two or three crops of Indian corn is taken off new lands before wheat is sown.

27th. Land within fence, and fit for cultivation, is generally let for half the produce; but there are few tenants of this description, as every one that chooses can get land of his own.

28th. The price of wild land about twenty years ago was from 1*s*. 3*d*. to 2*s*. 6*d*. per acre, and its progressive rise about 2*s*. 6*d*. for every five years. The present price of land is from 10*s*. to 15*s*. except in particular situations, such as lie on the straight. No lands have been recently sold in the township; the settlement has been long at a *stand*. Improved farms on the border of the straight, with a common farm-house, barn, and out-houses, orchard, and about 50 acres, within fence, would rate from £2. 10*s*. to £6. 5*s*. per acre, and more, according to the situation and value of the improvements.

29th. Several tracts of woodland are for sale; but for cleared and improved lands, high price would be the only inducement.

30th. Only one road in front on the river, which is kept in tolerable repair. The back part of the township unsettled, except a few scattered houses; good roads might be made at a moderate expence. No water conveyance in the interior, and from the evenness of the ground, canals would add much to the value of the lands, and the encouragement of the settler.

31st. The want of some *incentive* to *emulation*, the reserve of two-sevenths of the lands for the crown and clergy, must for a long time keep the country a wilderness; a harbour for wolves; a hindrance to a compact and good neighbourhood; and as these reserves grow in value, they increase as a political inducement to an enemy. Other reasons may be added; a defect in the system of colonization, and too great a quantity of the lands in the hands of individuals, who do not reside in the province, and who are not assessed for those lands. All these circumstances considered, it must be evident that the present system is very prejudicial to the internal welfare of this township.

(Signed)
ANGUS MACKINTOSH, J. P. Chairman.
F. BABY, J. P.
G. JACOB, J. P.

JOHN MCGREGOR.
J. B. BABY, J. P.
JAMES MCINTOSH.
JAMES M'INTOSH.
RICHARD POLLARD, Rector of Sandwich.

Malden

At a Meeting of the principal Inhabitants of the Township of Malden, at William Searl's Hotel, William Caldwell, Esq. in the Chair, and Mr. Alexis Maisonville, Secretary. – Unanimously resolved, that the Queries made by Mr. Robert Gourlay, in his Circular Letter respecting the Agricultural State of the Township, be answered as follows:

2d.   The first improvement was made in the year 1784. At present there are 108 inhabited houses, and 675 persons.

3d.   One Catholic chapel, and a Roman Catholic clergyman.

4th.   Two medical practitioners.

5th.   Three schools, and rate per quarter, is 20s.

6th.   Twelve stores.

7th.   Five taverns.

8th.   Two wind-mills.

9th.   The country is level, with good soil.

10th.   Oak, hickory, walnut, ash, maple, beech, elm, and white wood.

12th.   Limestone in abundance, which sells at 12s. 6d. per toise at the quarry.

13th.   Bricks are made, and now sell at 40s. per thousand.

14th.   Lime is burnt and sold at 1s. 3d. per bushel.

15th.   Blacksmiths, masons, and carpenters, get 10s. per diem.

16th.   Common labourers get 30l. per annum; 50s. per winter month; 75s. per summer month; 5s. per day in harvest; 7s. 6d. per week is given to women servants, for house-work.

17th.   Mowing, 5s.; and cradling, 7s. 6d. per day.

18th.   £5. is the rate for clearing and fencing an acre of land.

19th.   The price of a good work horse of four years old, is £16. A good cow, four years old, £6. Ox £7. and sheep, 17s. 6d.

20th.   Small sheep yield from three to four lb. of wool; the larger breed about 8 lb.; the price of wool is from 2s. to 2s. 6d. per lb.

21st. Beasts are commonly turned out to pasture the 1st of April, and taken into stable 1st of December: those that are not used, can be left out all winter.

22d. Sleighing lasts from two to three months; ploughing begins about the 1st of April.

23d. The fall, or winter wheat, is sown about the 1st of September.

24th. Reaping is from the 20th of July to the 10th of August. From four to five pecks of wheat is sown per acre; and twenty-five to thirty bushels of wheat is considered an average crop.

25th. Pasture in general excellent, and improves much on the land being cleared. Butter and cheese 1s. 3d. per lb.

26th. New land, in the first instance, is planted with corn; the ensuing season, wheat or oats are sown.

27th. A very small quantity of wild land is let on halves at present, for want of inhabitants.

28th. At first settlement, the price of land was from 1s. to 3s. per acre; the present price is 25s. per acre; some land, partly cleared, has been lately sold at 40s. per acre.

29th. A quantity of land in this township, is in the hands of individuals, who, doubtless, would sell to actual settlers.

30th. The public roads in general are pretty good, and a water communication in front of the township.

31st. Within this township is the port and town of Amherstburgh, where a ready market is always found for every kind of produce. The chief reason that the township is not more settled, is that, independent of the extensive crown and clergy reserves, which are common throughout this province, there is a large tract of excellent land, (on which there are one or two mill seats,) reserved for the Huron Indians, in the upper part of this township; a great part of this last reserve, it is presumed, might be purchased by government, and settled. Another drawback on the improvement of this township, arises from a quantity of the lands being in the hands of individuals who are not inclined to sell, and also large tracts belonging to minors, who cannot convey.

(Signed) WM. CALDWELL, J. P. Chairman.
A. MAISONVILLE,
Secretary.

Raleigh.

MR. ROBERT GOURLAY,
Raleigh, 2d Dec. 1817.

SIR,

YOUR very interesting Address to the resident householders of Upper Canada having but lately come to our hands, we the undersigned inhabitants of the township of Raleigh, deeply impressed with the sense of the many and important advantages to be expected (not only to the inhabitants of this province, but to thousands of our fellow subjects in Great Britain) from the system you propose to adopt, for the encouragement of emigrants to Canada, have taken the earliest opportunity of assembling together to answer the Queries contained in your Address; in doing which, Sir, we have to observe that, as agriculture is not carried on so systematically in this country as in Europe, some of our answers may appear imperfect to an English farmer; however, in answering to the best of our skill and knowledge, we hope the ends you aim at will be obtained, particularly as we have adhered to facts; happy if any information or trouble on our part or power to bestow can in anywise conduce to ameliorate the unhappy situation of any part of our distressed fellow creatures, particularly those of our mother country; and at the same time add strength and increase the prosperity of this province.

We beg of you, Sir, to accept of our sincere thanks for the judicious and prompt manner you have commenced this humane and important object, and hope every success may attend your future endeavours to promote so desirable a measure as the colonization of this fine country. You will please to observe that the price affixed to any article or rate is in New York currency, which is the currency mostly used in this part of the province, namely, eight shillings to the dollar, or two and a half dollars to the pound. Provision, board, and lodging, is not included in prices stated for labour, but which may be fairly estimated at 1s. 10½d. per diem.

2d. The settlement of this township commenced as early as the year 1792; nevertheless there are but 28 inhabited houses on the bank of the Thames at present, containing 198 souls, and a settlement commenced on the banks of lake Erie last spring, inhabiting 25 houses, containing 75 souls.

3d. No churches: one methodist preacher.

4th. No medical practitioner.

5th. One common school, the teacher of which receives 15s. per quarter for each scholar, and the legislature, by a late act, grants the teacher of each common school in the province a further sum of 25l. yearly, provided there are taught in the said school at least twenty scholars.

6th and 7th. Five stores, and one tavern.

8th. Two mills wrought by horses or oxen, which grind merely for home consumption.

9th. The soil varies but little on the dry lands, being a rich black soil on the surface, underneath a strong loam several feet in depth, then stiff blue clay.

10th. Timber, white oak, red oak, lynn, elm, hard and soft maple, beech, ash, hickory, black and white walnut, poplar, iron wood, and cherry.

11th. No minerals, limestones, salt, or plaster of Paris, have been yet discovered; nor is there any building stone.

13th. Bricks are made in this township, and sold for 1l. 17s. 6d. per thousand at the kiln.

14th. No lime burnt.

15th. Wages of a mason, 10s. per diem; a carpenter, 5s. to 6s. 3d.; a blacksmith, 5s. We know of no rule that masons and carpenters have for piece-work. Blacksmiths sell their wrought iron for 1s. 10½d. per lb.

16th. Labourers, 2l. 10s. in winter, and 3l. 2s. 6d. in summer per month; 5s. per day in harvest, and hay. Wages for women servants, 6s. 3d. per week, for house-work and spinning.

17th. For mowing and putting in cocks, wild grass, 5s. per ton. Cradling wheat, and putting in shock, 7s. 6d. per acre.

18th. For clearing five acres of all timber, and fencing it, 25l. For clearing five acres of all under-bush and trees, under a foot diameter at the stump, and putting the same under fence, 15l. 12s. 6d.

19. A four-year old work horse, £15. A four-year old cow, 5l. 12s. 6d. A sheep, £1.

20th. Average quantity of wool from each country sheep, two pounds and a half: price 2s. 6d. per pound. Part Merino, three pounds, 3s. 9d. per pound.

21st. Cattle go to pasture about the middle of April, and are stabled or taken to the yard about the beginning of December.

22d. Sleighing commences about the last of December, or beginning of January, and generally lasts to the beginning of March. Ploughing commences the beginning of April.

23d. Wheat is usually sown in September, and reaping commences the latter end of July.

24th. If wheat is sown early in September, a bushel per acre is sufficient; but if late in September, one and a quarter bushel is usually taken. Twenty bushels of wheat per quarter is considered an average crop.

25th. The wild range is so extensive, that no one has tame pasture for their cattle, nor can we, with any degree of certainty, answer to the increase of an ox in a summer's run. Cheese and butter, 1s. 3d. per pound.

26th. New land is generally planted with Indian corn in the month of May, and in September following wheat is sown among the corn. After taking off the wheat, the ensuing year, if the land is a good quality, it is again sown with wheat; if not, it lays waste until May or June, then ploughed, and in September sown again with wheat. Manure is not used for any particular crops, and was it not for the quantities accumulating in barn yards, very little would be used. Many fields in the space of 25 years have produced 20 crops without a single shovel full of manure, and the last a good average crop.

27th. When arable land is let on shares, the tenant gives the proprietor one third what is raised; thus, wheat and oats (after being cut) in the shock; Indian corn, when pulled and husked; pease when threshed, the proprietor paying for threshing; potatoes and turnips, when dug or pulled, in the same proportion.

28th. At the commencement of the settlement, lots of 200 acres, situated on the banks of the Thames, were sold at £25. In 1804, they sold for £131. 5s. The same lands are now selling at £250 without improvements. Back lands of the best quality may be fairly estimated at one third of these prices.

29th. It is impossible for us to state what quantity of land is for sale in the township, the greatest part being deeded to non-residents, some of whom are in Lower Canada, and others in England; nor do we know what quantity government has granted to individuals.

30th. The lands being level, roads are good, and easily kept in repair. The Thames, which washes the north west bank of this township, affords those near it an excellent means of conveyance, there being from 18 to 20 feet water in the river, and from six to seven feet on the bar where it empties into lake St. Clair, which affords water enough for small vessels to enter or go out loaded. On the south west, lake Erie affords water communication, either upwards or downwards, for vessels of any size. The face of the township, generally speaking, is low, particularly that part joining Tilbury, it being overflowed part of the year; but from pretty correct information, a wide ditch, half a mile in length, leading into lake Erie, would drain great part of the wet lands, the banks of the lake being at least 80 feet high, and the descent in the rear not exceeding 10 to 12 feet. The lands adjoining Harwich are nearly all dry, and fit for cultivation. On the whole, about one half of the township, in its present state, is fit for cultivation. A plain, or meadow, about a mile wide, crosses the township from Tilbury to Harwich, within half a mile of the Thames, part of which is considered of the best quality of land in the township.

31st. The want of settlers, particularly men of sufficient means to purchase lands, we conceive to be the greatest cause of retarding the improvement of our township: situated at such a distance from the seaports of Canada, those who come from Europe either think the distance too great, or have not the means of transporting their families 600 or 700 miles after landing in Lower Canada. There are many thousand acres of excellent land now lying waste in this township, which might be bought or leased at very moderate terms, were there only purchasers or tenants to be found.

WM. M'CRAE, J. P.   JACOB DOLSON,
THOS. CROW,   DANIEL DOLSON,
JAMES FORSYTH,   GEO. JACOB, Jun.
HEECKIA WILLCOX,   WM. STIRLING,
JOHN LAIRD,   JOHN PECK,
FRANCIS DRAKE,   NINIAN HOLMES.
JOHN WILLIAMS,

NOTE.

In the following Report, page 139, a canal is mentioned as practicable between the townships of Raleigh and Tilbury east, from the Thames to lake Erie; and, no doubt, such may be executed, were the time come in which expences could be discharged. The reporters, I suspect, make a great mistake as to the fall of 30 feet, by which is meant the fall from the surface level of lake St. Claire to that of lake Erie. Mr. Dencke, the Moravian missionary, told me that he was at the meeting, and gave his opinion that the fall was not more than 15 feet. In my opinion it is not more than half of that. There is a considerable current in Detroit river; but a very few feet of fall will produce that appearance, even for miles.

In the heading of next Report, Dover, east and west, would make us think there were two townships; but neither the map, nor the record of civil divisions, justifies this. Lord Selkirk's purchase of upwards of 70,000 acres lies, I think, partly in Dover, partly in Chatham; but the reporters do not reckon in their statement of population his settlement at Baldoon.

Dover, East and West, Chatham, Camden, Orford, Howard, and Harwich, on the River Thames.

A Report of a Convention of the Inhabitants of the above Townships, in answer to certain Queries proposed by Mr. R. Gourlay.

2d.   In Dover, east and west, there are 45 (I suppose, inhabited houses); in Chatham 27; Camden 17; Harwich 19; Howard 25; Orford *(see Supplement)*. The said townships commenced settling in 1794.

3d.   (Referred to Rev. C. F. Denkey), *see Supplement.*

4th.   One practitioner of physic.

5th.   Four schools – rate 15*s.* per quarter.

6th.   Seven stores.

7th.   Four taverns.

8th.   Two grist mills. One saw mill – rate one quarter of the timber when sawed. *(See Supplement.)*

9th.   A level surface generally throughout the said townships; soil of the first quality, the surface of which is a black light loam, with a grey clay under, and void of stone of any description whatever.

10th.   Beech, black ash, white ash, red and white oak, hickory, black and white walnut, linden, bass wood, by some called white wood, maple, wild cherry, chestnut, tulip.

11th.   (Referred to the Rev. C. F. Denkey), *see Supplement.*

12th.   Brick is made, and sells at 35*s.* per thousand.

14th.   None.

15th.   Carpenters' and smiths' wages 7*s.* 6*d.* per day. – Mason's 10*s.* per day.

16th.   Men's wages average at £30 per annum: in the winter months 40*s.*; summer months 70*s.*; days in harvest 5*s.*; women's and girls' wages at from 5*s.* to 6*s.* 3*d.* per week.

17th.   Price for mowing an acre of grass, harvesting, cradling, and reaping wheat, 7*s.* 6*d.*

18th.   Clearing and fencing according to the custom of the country (say), leaving such timber as can be killed with the axe over one foot diameter, at £4 per acre.

19th.   A work horse of four years old from £13 to £15; a good ox £10; a good cow £6 5*s.*; a sheep from 15*s.* to 20*s.*

20th.   Average wool from a sheep from three to four pounds; price from 2*s.* 6*d.* to 3*s.* 9*d.* per pound.

21st.   Turning out to pasture about 15th April, and taken in 1st December.

22d.   Ordinary sleighing season, from 1st January to the 10th of March.

23d. Sowing season is from the 1st September until 10th October. – Reaping wheat commences 1st August.

24th. The quantity of wheat generally sown is five pecks per acre, and the increase from one acre is 25 bushels on an average; but when well cultivated, will produce from 35 to 40 bushels.

25th. An ox of four years old will gain on a summer run, 200 pounds: price of butter and cheese is 1s. 3d. per pound.

26th. Manure not particularly required, on ground that has been cultivated upwards of 10 years.

27th. Lands rent (particular spots) at 12s. 6d. per acre; and if on shares, at one third of the produce.

28th. Some farms in good local situations, with tolerable buildings and orchards thereon, well cultivated, containing 200 acres of land, sold for £690. The average price of lands from the first settlement of these townships, were from 2s. 6d. to 20s. per acre.

29th. Not known.

30th. One on each side of the river, and not in so good repair, on account of the facility of the water communication. One canal in particular is practicable of being cut between the townships of Raleigh and Tilbury East, form the river Thames across to lake Erie, a distance only of 15 miles in extent, and will admit of a fall of 30 feet, which canal, if made, will save a distance of 140 miles in the communication to Fort Erie, and will be the means of draining thousands of acres of land.

31st. From the great quantities of lands held by individuals and absentees, and the want of a population.

The quantity of wheat harvested in the summer of 1817, by the small number of 114 farmers residing in the townships above mentioned, was 40,000 bushels, and the lands in said townships will produce, in proportionable abundance, pease, oats, barley, Indian corn, hemp, and flax.

JOSHUA CORNWALL, *Chairman.*
JOHN DOLSON, *Assistant Chairman.*

By Order,
SAMUEL OSBORN, *Secretary.*

Supplement *to the Report of a Convention, &c. &c. on the River Thames.*

QUERY 3d. In all those named townships, there is at present but *one* pro tempore church at Orford township, in the Indian missionariot, having one stated, ordained missionary, and an assistant. Besides this, the Methodist connexion have regularly *one* itinerant missionary on the river.

The inhabitant Indians on Orford township, are in the town of New Fairfield, containing 29 houses and huts, and one church; say 30 buildings, inhabited by 120 houses and huts, and one church; say 30 buildings, inhabited by 120 Christian Indians belonging to the society. The Indians live in 27 houses and huts, then the missionary's and assistant's dwellings and a church; in all 30 buildings. Besides these, there are wintering upon the tract 47 persons, who attend Divine service, in all, 167 souls at present abiding here of the Delaware and Iroquois nation. An Indian school is kept in Indian and English. In regular seasons more than 4000 bushels of Indian corn was raised here. The cleared flats amount to about 350 acres of the best soil. Of this, some part, after yielding corn upwards of 20 years, is now sowed in wheat.

QUERY 8th. As an addition of one quarter is given to the sawyer, one quarter goes to the mill master, and the half belongs to the log owners.

QUERY 11th. Natural History in general, through its three kingdoms, has not yet been sufficiently investigated; therefore not much may be said. Respecting the mineral kingdom, the following may be answered in a cursory view. In the townships of Orford and Camden are salt springs; besides this, in the first there are several petrolinian springs, as the sulphur and naphtha, or oil spring; indicating, we think, coal in the bed. Besides this, several fossils, and a kind of red earth, and a softened ore slate, much resembling ochre, which, when burned, gives a kind of paint, near to Spanish brown. Pieces of petrification and ore found at the bank of the river at the rapids.

Potters' clay generally found throughout all the townships, and potters' ware well made.

CHRISTIAN FREDERICK DENKEY,
Missionary.

Additional Information by Mr. Dencke.

THE Indians under his charge have not increased by breeding since the first Moravian church establishment; but others come in among them, as will appear from the following table:

The war will account for the greater number of deaths these years: six were slain in battle.

Mr. D. wishes it to be known that no women or children of the

| Years. | Baptisms. | | Deaths. |
	Infants.	Adults come into Society.	
1800	6	2	5
1801	6	0	1
1802	7	1	5
1803	12	2	7
1804	13	1	11
1805	4	1	5
1806	7	1	6
1807	4	1	0
1808	5	0	5
1809	0	2	1
1810	10	0	8
1811	4	2	2
1812	1	1	3
1813	12	5	26
1814	9	0	20
1815	6	1	9
1816	3	2	11
1817	3	3	6
	114	25	131

Moravians were killed, all having arrived safe at Burlington after their village was burnt. Sister Eleonora, reported to be killed, was afterwards seen alive by Mr. D. There was one Chippawa woman killed and scalped.

The habit and desire of drinking is conquered in general among the Moravian Indians; but when tipsy, with few exceptions, or none, they still shew the savage. They have, of late years, hired out in harvest to neighbouring farmers, and have kept themselves more sober than the white people. From 1809, and up to the present time, more children have been taken off by diseases (not small pox, for Mr. D. vaccinates) but by epidemic and bilious fevers.

Indians in general make light of marriage. Mr. D. has got those under his charge to consider it sacred and binding. As to property, they do not hold all things in common. Town lots are laid out for buildings and gardens, while each Indian may clear and fence in as much land as he chooses, keeping the produce to himself.

The women do most of the agricultural work; cut and carry wood, plant, hoe, and gather in the corn, &c. The men are chiefly occupied in hunting. When they bring home the game it is offered to the women as their property, while the men claim the produce of agriculture as theirs. Prior to the war they had about 30 horses, and 50 horned cattle, besides a great many hogs and poultry. They have now from 15 to 20 horses, 10 cows, and about as many other horned cattle. They make brooms and baskets of swamp ash split down; also mats of the same material, and of flags and rushes. They stain these articles red with the bark of the alder; black with that of butter nut and black walnut; and blue with indigo, bought in the stores. Belt cords for carrying burdens are made of the wild hemp (asclapius). Belts and knee bands of woolen thread, the shreds of old blankets, &c. The men are expert at hewing wood, erecting houses, making furniture, & c. Corn is their principal vegetable food, prepared in many different ways; and of late years a few potatoes, turnips, and cabbage, have been raised.

Other Indians have vermilion from government to paint their bodies; but the Moravians are forbidden to practise this.

Western District.

Summary of Population, &c.

IN the above reported townships, there seem to be of white inhabitants, reckoning the inhabited houses of Dover, East and West, Chatham, Campden, Howard, and Harwich, to contain six persons each. 2728.

Besides these townships, there are, in the Western District, eight others, viz. Colchester, Gosfield, Mersea, Romney, Tilbury, East and West, Rochester, and Maidstone. The three first began setting in 1784, under the name of the New settlement, in contradistinction to the old French settlement; and we may suppose them to contain 1200.

The five remaining townships have no regular settlements, and I have reason to think they do not contain about 30 straggling houses, which, calculating six persons to each, will give 180.

Lord Selkirk began his settlement of Baldoon, 15 miles north of the mouth of the river Thames, in 1803, with 111 people, of whom 42 died the first season; and the settlement was laid waste during the war by a party of Americans under M'Arthur, who landed here and penetrated within a little way of the Grand river. There are now (1817) only nine or ten families – say 50.

Making the whole white population 4158.

The Indians of Orford are stated to be in number 167.

A little way up the Thames, and on the north side, there are two villages, in the tract called the Longwoods, of Indians, denominated

Munsies, originally from the States, but permitted to settle here by the Chippawa Indians. Their number about 200.

There are two regular reserves for Indians in the Western District, viz. that of the Hurons, between Sandwich and Malden; and the Shawnese tract lying north of Baldoon. The inhabitants of these, with parties which encamp in the woods at various places, do not, I presume, make the whole Indian population, in or within 20 miles of surveyed land, amount in whole to 1000.

To the reported population of 2728, there appear to be 3 Roman catholic, 1 episcopal, and 1 methodist, preachers, 5 medical practitioners, 11 schools, and 18 taverns.

Improvement is said to be retarded by crown and clergy reserves; lands of non-occupants; want of settlers and capital; want of incentive to emulation; and a defect in the system of colonization.

London District
Township Reports.

Delaware, Westminster, and Dorchester.

At a Meeting of all the Inhabitants of the Townships of Delaware, Westminster, and Dorchester, assembled at the House of Archibald M'Millan, at Westminster Plains, on the 15th December, 1817, for the purpose of considering the propriety of answering certain Queries submitted to the Resident Land Owners of Upper Canada, by Robert Gourlay, Esq. in his Address of October last, it was unanimously agreed, that the said Queries could not be so correctly answered by the People in their collective Capacity, as by certain discreet Persons, delegated by them for that Purpose. They, therefore, elected a Committee, consisting of Daniel Springer, Esq. Mr. Gideon Tiffaney, Mr. B. B. Brigam, Mr. Timothy Kilbourn, Mr. Joseph Webster, Mr. Archibald M'Millan, Mr. Aaron Kilbourn, Mr. Andrew Banghart, Mr. Jacobus Shenich, Mr. Joseph Idel, Mr. Joseph Flaningan, Mr. Seth Putman, Mr. Sylvanis Reynolds, Mr. James A. Mullet, to constitute and form a Committee to answer the said Queries, in such a Manner as to them might seem expedient, and to meet for that Purpose on the 17th Instant. The Meeting adjourned.

Westminster Plains, 17th December, 1817.

THE Committee met pursuant to adjournment, and elected Daniel Springer, Esq. Chairman, and Mr. Joseph Webster, Secretary, when the following were adopted, as answers to the said Queries:

3d. In Delaware, one church, but no Clergyman*. Westminster, no church; but visited by itinerant preachers. Dorchester the same.

9th. All, generally speaking, level and well watered, with a marly loamy soil, and extensive flats on the Thames.

10th. White pine, red and white oak, cherry, elm, black walnut, ash, beech, maple, and bass-wood.

11th. No minerals in Delaware; but there is iron ore in Westminster and Dorchester.

12th. Some building stones of good quality in each township.

14th. Farmers burn lime in log heaps, consequently no particular price per bushel.

25th. Not only the flats of the Thames, but woods in general are covered with grass, in a state of nature, which is good. An ox will gain one-fourth of his weight with a summer's run.

26th. First crop, wheat harrowed in and stocked with grass. When the sod is broken up, we summer fallow and sow with wheat. No manure has yet been applied.

27th. Very little land is rented or let on shares. The land, if let, draws one-third of the crop. Land is so plenty, that almost every person is the owner of some.

28th. The flats on the Thames have always sold high, and are now worth £3 per acre.

29th. There are lands for sale; but the quantity is not ascertained.

30th. The public roads are not in a very good state, but are gradually improving, by means of annual labour, which the law imposes on every individual inhabitant. Our townships are bounded on the river Thames, which affords a good water communication to Sandwich and Amherstburgh.

31st. The greater part of the lands which constitute the township of Delaware, were granted many years ago to persons not resident in this part of the province; or are crown and clergy reserves, which has been and still continues to be an unsurmountable obstacle to the formation of a compact settlement in it. In the township of Westminster, no lands have as yet been granted, but to actual settlers. And if that system is pursued by the

* This church was erected in a beautiful situation during Simcoe's government. It is now falling to wreck, a sad monument of an unprincipled departure from liberal measure. – R. G.

government, it will, no doubt, soon form a most delightful, populous, and wealthy settlement.

The principal part of the township of Dorchester, which is not composed of crown and clergy reserves, has been granted to persons not resident in this part of the province; and there does not appear at present to be any probability that it will be settled soon, unless men of capital should purchase.

If his Majesty's government should grant or dispose of the crown and clergy reserves to actual settlers, and the colonial legislature should lay a tax upon the lands of absentees, so as to induce them to sell or contribute to the improvement of roads, &c. we are of opinion that the province in general would be more prosperous and happy.

If granting the lands bounded on Dundas street to actual settlers only, had not been deviated from, the province would most unquestionably be in a much higher state of improvement, by the passage of so direct and well settled a road through it. And we esteem it as an object of the most primary importance to the welfare of the province, for the Colonial Executive Government to purchase from the natives, the tract of land on the west side of the Thames, between the township of Delaware and the Moravian grant, the road through which is now in a tolerable state, and lay out a continuation of Dundas street through the same, subject to actual settlement on the principle of Talbot road.

By order of the Committee,

(Signed) DANIEL SPRINGER,
Chairman.

(Signed)
JOSEPH WEBSTER, *Secretary.*

Oxford.

At a Meeting of the Resident Landholders of the Township of Oxford, held at the School-house on Wednesday the 24th day of December, 1817, for the Purpose of taking into Consideration the Propriety of answering certain Queries proposed in an Address to the Resident Landowners of Upper Canada, published in the Upper Canada Gazette in October last, and signed Robert Gourlay; Peter Teeple, Esq. in the Chair.

IT was resolved unanimously, That we conceive it proper to answer the same, and that the following answers to the Queries, as they come in order, be given.

9th. *Soil,* a dark loam surface; level, and extremely well watered.

10th. *Timber* – maple, beech, elm, pine, cedar, oak, cherry, ash, basswood, and butternut.

11th. Abundance of limestone: a sulphur spring.

12th. None.

21st. Ordinary time of turning out beasts to pasture, first of April; and taking them in, 1st December.

22d. Sleighing, two months; ploughing commences 1st of April.

23d. Wheat sown in September, and reaped in August.

25th. Pasture good; an ox will gain one fourth in a summer's run; quality of the dairy produce is good.

26th. First crop wheat: second Indian corn, or oats: land stocked with grass, with the oat crop, and with rye after the corn. When broken up from grass, wheat or peas: no manure has been applied.

27th. Land sometimes let on shares; the owner of the land receives one third of the crop in the field when harvested.

28th. A two hundred acre lot, with thirty acres cultivated land, a log house, and frame barn, 30 by 40 feet, is worth £500.

28th. Greatest part of the land in the township for sale.

30th. Roads tolerably good; can be much improved at a moderate expence; conveyance by water down the river Thames; the north-east branch of the river passing through the township. The navigation of the river is capable of improvement, by removing some obstructions, and deepening the channel in some places.

31st. We conceive that a want of persons of ability to purchase the lands in the township, and becoming actual settlers, is what principally retards the improvement of the same.

It is unanimously agreed, that the Chairman do sign the proceedings of this day, and transmit the same to Mr. Gourlay.

(Signed) PETER TEEPLE,
Chairman.

Blenheim and The First Concession of Burford.

9th. Sand and loam, with some good clay; a good soil.

10th. Beech, maple, oak, hickory, and good pine mixed

with other, as elm, bass, and white ash: of the maple, sugar is made, of which one man will make 5 cwt. in six weeks.

11th. Minerals none, except a few limestone on the surface.

12th. None discovered as yet.

18th. New land 3l. 15s. per acre; the first crop generally pays it.

21st. Middle of April, turn out; take into barn 1st of December.

22d. Sleighing two months; ploughing commences 20th of April.

23d. September, sowing; reaping in August.

25th. Quality good, suppose one-fifth or one-sixth; 2d. one cow will make three quarters of a pound of butter per day.

26th. To clear and fence, three years crop: from grass, one-third for land, manure applied for none; not being wanted.

27th. Some let for the half; the owner finding team.

28th. Drawn from government at first; price from 10s. to 15s. at this time – Farms at 3l. 15s. per acre; or, 2l. with log buildings.

29th. Not known; but we suppose all but what is now occupied; probably 50 lots not sold, except two-sevenths reserves.

30th. Roads good, for new; might be better by work; one small river for rafts.

31st. Not certainly known, but we suppose that land being not known where the owners are, and there not being any highway tax on non-resident lands to be paid in the town, or the land to be sold.

The above answers given by a general meeting, holden on Dundas Street, in Blenheim, and signed by us, being landholders in said places first mentioned, this 2d day of December, 1817, and by our Chairman,

SAMUEL BARTLETT.	HENRY DANIAD.
JOSIAL F. DEAN.	JOHN EACHENS.
STEPHEN GRAHAM.	ALEX. STARKEY.
JOHN GALBRAITH.	JAMES SMILEY.
SILAS MARTIN.	

Burford.

At a Meeting of the principal Inhabitants of Burford, and the Gore of Burford, assembled for the purpose of answering certain

Queries, proposed by Mr. Gourlay, respecting the general and particular State of the said Township.

LIEUT.-COL. WILLIAM D. BOWEN, *Chairman.*

8th.   One fulling mill, one carding machine, 6d. per lb. for carding.

9th.   The township of Burford and the Gore, has a level surface, interspersed with useful streams and springs, the water very fine. The soil a sandy loam, fertile and durable.

10th.   Timbered with sugar maple, beech, white pine, white, black, red, chesnut, &c. oak, white and red elm, basswood, butternut, white and black ash, hickory, chesnut, cedar, &c.

11th.   An indication of iron ore has lately been discovered, on a branch of the Grand river, that runs through the township: no other minerals have yet been discovered.

12th.   Stone scarce, and none fit for building.

15th.   Four blacksmiths, who charge for shoeing a horse 12s. 6d. for an axe 12s. 6d. for a scythe 8s. 9d. There are two tailors, who charge 27s. 6d. for making a coat, and 10s. for pantaloons: two shoemakers, who charge 3s. 9d. for making a pair of shoes: five carpenters, charge 10s. per day and found.

25th.   The pasture is capable of great improvement. A cow is estimated to give one lb. of butter and two of cheese per day.

26th.   Wheat is the first crop put on new lands, afterwards Indian corn, rye, oats, peas, flax, potatoes, &c. Plaster of Paris is used as a manure for clover, on the plains, one bushel of which is sown per acre, and the ordinary crop of clover is three tons per acre; little other manure is used.

27th.   Land is let out to no great extent, new land on the plains is let for the halves, the person who takes it, to be at half of the expense of clearing, fencing, ploughing, and harvesting. It (the crop) is divided in the sheaf. On improved lands, if the owner finds team, plough, board, and lodging, the workman has one third of the crop, divided in the sheaf.

29th.   The quantity of land for sale within the township unknown, and the owners of the soil generally unknown to the inhabitants.

30th.   The roads on the plains generally good, and made at a small expence. In the wood lands, they are capable of great improvement, which might be accomplished at no great expence.

31st.   The principal cause affecting the prosperity and growth of the township, is considered by the inhabitants at this meeting, as resulting from the quantities of land granted to non-residents, and the great number of reserved lots; these reserves being scattered all over the township, not only preclude the compact settlement of the same, but materially affects its settlement in general; as the purchaser of a lot, if he is not so fortunate as to procure one handy to the roads already made, is under the necessity of making them, through perhaps several reserves, and the lands belonging to people that reside in other parts of the world, thereby enhancing their value at a great individual expence.

We consider that good English farmers, mechanics, and labourers, if they could obtain lands in this township, and all the crown and a proportion of the clergy reserves, sold or given to actual settlers, would be an object of great importance to the further improvement and growth of this township.

Signed, in behalf of the Inhabitants, by

WILLIAM D. BOWEN,
Chairman.

BURFORD, 5TH DEC. 1817.

Windham.

MR. ROBERT GOURLAY.
Sir,
Having received a circular letter, with your signature, directed to the Collector and Town Clerk of the Township of Windham, requesting a reply to each query set forth in your address, we therefore subscribe to this our reply, and consider ourselves answerable for whatever is advanced.

3d. We have no church or chapel in the township, but most of the houses are open for preaching. There is one professional preacher of the Presbyterian order, and there are itinerant preachers of the Methodist order, that preach once in two weeks, in different parts of the township, and sometimes we have Baptist preaching.

4th. We have no medical practitioner in the township, but we can generally get one within eight or ten miles.

5th. We have two schools, we board the teachers, and give them 12l. 10s. per quarter.

6th. We have two small stores; but we can be supplied with goods from the neighbouring townships.

7th. We have no taverns; but we profess to be a hospitable people, and do entertain strangers.

8th. There are a number of good mill seats in the township, but the parts where they lay are unsettled, and those parts that are settled lay near the settled parts of other townships that have mills.

9th.   The general character of the soil is loam and sand, without gravel or stone, and the surface level in a general way, without high hills or bad swamps, except about 1000 acres near the middle of the township, which may in time become the best part of the township, by ditching and clearing off the timber; perhaps there is not over 200 acres that is not covered with timber in this swamp.

10th.   The timber on the high dry lands is mostly oak, pine, and chesnut; on the low moist lands, beech and maple, elm and ash, and almost every kind of timber that the country affords.

11th.   No minerals have as yet been discovered in the township; there is excellent iron ore in the adjoining township of Charlotteville.

12th.   There is but one place in the township where building stone has been discovered, but it is not settled near the place, so that it is not much used.

24th.   We sow one bushel of wheat per acre in the good season for sowing, in the late season we sow a few quarts more; and if the ground is in good order for sowing, it will average 15 bushels per acre, although there are many instances that the yield has been from 20 to 30 bushels per acre.

26th.   We have no regular mode of farming our land: as to particular kind of grain, very little manure has as yet been wanted; but we find that plaster has a good effect upon our land, of which there is plenty in our country, within a few miles of our township.

27th.   We frequently let out land to crop, on shares: the terms generally are for the cropper to find team and seed, and to give his landlord one-third; of the winter crop, in stock in the field; the summer crop, if Indian corn, in the ear; if buck wheat, ready for the granary; if oats, in the sheaf; if potatoes, in the half bushel; but if the landlord find team and seed, he takes two-thirds, and the croppers one-third.

28th.   At our first settlement, wild land sold for 5s. per acre; at present the wild land in the unsettled parts of the township will sell for 10s. per acre; but there is wild land in the settlement that cannot be bought for 1l. 5s. per acre; and some improved farms are held at 3l. 15s. per acre, where there is not above 60 acres improved; but there have been actual sales of farms, from 1l. 5s. to 3l. 15s. per acre, according to the improvement made on them.

29th.   There is not less than 57,000 acres of wild land now in the township for sale.

30th.   In laying out the township into 200 acre lots, government has reserved five public roads from north to south, and fourteen from east to west, each one chain in width, so that every 200 acre lot touches two of these roads, and every fifth lot touches three of them.

Statute labour is done on them as far as the settlement extends, and if it were settled, there soon would be good roads throughout the township, by statute labour alone.

31st. In our most candid opinion there is nothing wanting, but the filling up with industrious men, men of property, monied men, men of enterprise, speculative men with capital, to make our township, our county, our district, one of the best countries for farming in all British America; and, lastly, could a liberal system of emigration be set on foot, and men of enterprise, skill, and capital, be induced to come among us, they would find a high rate of interest and substantial security.

Windham, December 4th, 1817.

(Signed)

GABRIEL COLLOW,	JONATHAN AXFORD,
JOHN TISDALE,	JOSEPH AXFORD,
JOHN ROBINS,	BENJAMIN HOWELL,
A. COWELL,	ABRAHAM YOUNGS,
SAMUEL WOOD,	JOHN BRAY,
DAVID HUNTER,	SAMUEL HORTON,
BENJAMIN YOUNG,	ASA COLLVER,
SAMUEL FISHER,	WILLIAM DELL,
PHILIP FORCE, SEN.	PHILIP FORCE, JUN.
JABEZ COLLVER,	WILLIAM FORCE.
PHILIP BUTLER.	

Townsend.

Dec. 6, 1817.

A Meeting having been recommended by the Magistrates of this Division, to consider of Mr. Robert Gourlay's Address, published in the Upper Canada Gazette of the 30th of October last, and reply to his Queries:

WE, the inhabitants (freeholders of the township of Townsend), have this day assembled at the house of Job Lodor, of the aforesaid township, and Morris Sovereene has been unanimously called to the chair, and the following answers to the queries have been adopted; the Chairman is requested to sign the same in the name of the meeting, and transmit it to the above magistrates, to be forwarded to Mr. Robert Gourlay.

9th. 'The soil is of a good quality, producing wheat, rye, Indian corn, oats, buckwheat, peas, and potatoes in abundance. The surface of the earth is level and well watered.

10th.   The timber is sugar maple, beech, oak, pine, bass wood, elm, butternut, white ash, hickory, and chestnut.

11th.   Limestone abounds here, and is the principle stone made use of. There is one medicinal spring of considerable note. There has not been any quarries of free stone discovered as yet.

15th.   The price of blacksmith's work is 7½d. per lb. for making all kinds of farming utensils, spikes, &c.

17th.   The price of mowing grass for hay is 5s. an acre, for cradling and binding wheat, 6s. 3d. an acre.

18th.   The cost of clearing and fencing an acre of timbered land is 61.5s.; of plains, 2l. 10s. an acre.

25th.   Pastures are good; an ox, of four years old, will weigh 700 lb. by having a summer's run; In timbered land, after the timber is cleared off, the seed is harrowed in; but on the plains it is first ploughed.

26th.   Manure is used for wheat and corn.

27th.   When land is let on shares, the owner receives one-third of the produce.

28th.   Farms, say one-fourth cleared, with a log house and barn, will fetch 1l. 5s. an acre.

29th.   There are about 20,000 acres of land now for sale.

30th.   The roads are good.

31st. One great reason why this township is not more settled, is that a great part of the unsettled land was granted in large quantities to gentlemen, many of them residing in England and elsewhere, who do not wish to dispose of it. Another is the vast number of crown and clergy reserves, many of them situated in the very place, where, if they would be exchanged or sold, there might be a handsome village erected in a short time; and another is the want of cash, to make improvements with.

(Signed)

MORRIS SOVEREENE, *Chairman.*

Walpole and Rainham.

Dec. 19, 1817.

A Meeting having been recommended by the Magistrates of this

Division to consider of Mr. Robert Gourlay's Address, published in the Upper Canada Gazette, of the 30th of October last, and to reply to his Queries:

WE, the inhabitant householders of the townships of Walpole and Rainham, have this day assembled at the house of Abraham Hoover, of the aforesaid township, Mr. Abraham Hoover being unanimously called to the chair, the following Answers to the Queries have been adopted, and the chairman is requested to sign the same in the name of the meeting, and transmit to the above Magistrates to be forwarded to Mr. Robert Gourlay.

9th.   The soil is chiefly clay, with a rich surface.

10th.   It abounds with most kinds of timber. The most abounding is oak.

11th.   No ore has as yet been discovered. There are three sulphur springs.

12th.   Plenty of limestone can be had at the quarry for 10s. per toise.

17th.   Three shillings and ninepence per day is allowed for cutting grass for hay; and the price of reaping and cradling wheat per day is equal to the price of a bushel of wheat.

25th.   Here the pasture is a mixture of clover and Timothy. Seven pounds of butter can be made per week with one cow, and ten of cheese.

26th.   The usual course of crops are, first, wheat, then Indian corn, or any other grain: and manure is chiefly used for Indian corn, and potatoes.

27th.   Considerable quantities of land are let on shares, for which the landlord receives one-third.

29th.   Upwards of thirty thousand acres of land may now be purchased.

30th.   Roads generally bad – can be made good with a reasonable expence. The principal water conveyance is lake Erie.

31st.   It is the opinion of this meeting, that the improvement of their township is much retarded by large tracts of land having been granted to persons not residing in the country, and which still remain unsettled, and that if such tracts of land were placed in a situation to be settled, the taxes regularly paid, and the roads properly worked, it would contribute materially to the improvement of the townships and province in general.

(Signed)

ABRAHAM HOOVER, *Chairman.*

Woodhouse

December 9th, 1817.

A Meeting having been recommended by the Magistrates of this Division, to consider of and reply to certain Queries contained in Mr. Robert Gourlay's Address, published in the Upper Canada Gazette of the 30th October last,

WE, the inhabitant freeholders of the aforesaid township of Woodhouse, have this day assembled at the house of Mr. Wm. Culver, and after having unanimously chosen the said William Culver chairman, and John Tinbroock secretary, to this meeting, and taken the said Queries into consideration, have formed and adopted the following Replies, to be signed by the chairman, and transmitted to the magistrates, to be forwarded to Mr. Gourlay.

8th.   There are two carding machines, and wool is carded at 7½*d.* per pound.

9th.   The surface is level; the soil varies in different parts of the township: part is clay and part a mixture of clay and sand.

10th.   It abounds with almost all kinds of timber. That part which is plains is generally white oak.

11th.   Discoveries have been made of iron ore; but no thorough search has been made, to ascertain the quantity. There is one medicinal or sulphur spring.

12th.   Plenty of lime-stone can be had at 25*s.* by the toise at the quarry.

25th.   The pastures are clover and Timothy. Seven pounds of butter can be made in a week with one cow, and 10 pounds of cheese.

26th.   The ordinary course of cropping is, first, wheat, then Indian corn, or any other grain; and manure is used for Indian corn and potatoes.

27th.   Land is let on shares, for which the landlord receives one-third.

29th.   Upwards of 10,000 acres of land may be now purchased.

30th.   The roads are generally good, but can be much improved at a moderate expense. The principal water conveyance is lake Erie.

31st.   It is the opinion of this meeting, that the improvement of this township is much retarded by large tracts of land having been granted to persons not residing in the country, and which still remain unsettled; and that, if such tracts of land were placed in a situation to be settled, the taxes regularly paid, and the roads properly worked or improved, it would contribute most materially to the improvement not only of the township, but of the province in general.

(Signed)

WM. CULVER,
Chairman to the Meeting.

Charlotteville

December 13th, 1817.
Pursuant to Notice from the Magistrates of the Division, a Number of the Farmers and other Resident Land Owners of the Township, have this day met at the Court-House, to consider of and reply to the Queries, put by Mr. Gourlay, relative to the Agricultural State of the Province, published in the Upper Canada Gazette of the 30th of October last. The Rev. Daniel Freeman in the Chair.

THE queries being regularly put by the chairman, the following answers may be considered as the sense of the meeting, on the points to which they refer.

5th. The district public school, and four common schools; the medium rate of tuition about 12*s.* 6*d.*

9th. Sand and loam intermixed with clay, the surface level.

10th. Timber in the order most abounding; oak, pine, chestnut, maple, walnut, hickory, ash, beech, and white wood.

11th. Iron ore in abundance (observations on the ore, &c. will be made by the enterprising individual, who is now erecting a forge in the township*); some limestone; no plaster of Paris, one

---

* This individual being applied to, wrote me the following letter.

Potter's Creek, Dec. 4th, 1817.
"SIR,

"You desired me to give you every information in my power, of the probability, or certainty, of making iron in this part of the Province, so as to be beneficial to the manufacturer and the public. I will state to you what is for, and what against. In favour of Iron Works, is the high price of iron, and plenty of timber for coal: every thing but these is against the first beginner. The bog ore is scattered over the whole country; but, I do not know any one bed of ore that will exceed 120 tons. I spent three months in examining the country for ore, and I calculate that it will take all the ore I found, within 20 miles of this place, to supply a small furnace for seven years; but I believe considerable quantities, within that space, are not yet found. No rock ore has yet been found in this part of the Province; and if

remarkable spring near Big creek, resembling in taste the Harrowgate waters.

12th.   Few building stone   no quarries.

14th.   No lime has been burnt for sale.

15th. Journeymen blacksmiths are hired at 6l. 5s. per month; masons 10s. and carpenters 7s. 6d. per day: the ploughs in common use will cost from 5l. to 6l.; a good axe 12s. 6d.; shoeing a horse, (four shoes) 10s.; for working iron into implements of husbandry, 7½d. per pound.

18th.   Five acres of heavy timbered land, may be cleared and fenced for about 25l. The same quantity of light timbered or plain land, may be cleared for about 12l. and occasionally for less.

25th.   The increase of weight, &c. cannot be determined with precision.

26th.   No regular rotation of cropping has hitherto been observed. Manure is seldom used, except for Indian corn and potatoes.

27th.   Land is frequently let on shares, the owner of the land receiving one-third of the crop, for the use of the land.

28th.   About the first settlement of the township, land sold for 5s. per acre; but will now average about 1l. A farm of 200 acres of land, with a log house and barn, with 50 acres cleared and fenced, and a small orchard of bearing trees, might be purchased for about 700l. and occasionally less.

---

there is any, it must be at a considerable depth from the surface of the ground, and will be difficult to find, as the strata lie horizontal. Another thing against iron works, is that it will require many experiments before we can know the best method of working the ore; and there is not any stone in this part of the Province, that will stand the fire, and, I believe, it will be best if it comes from three different places in the United States. I want five or six pieces of cast iron, each 30 cwt.; these will come to an enormous expence. I intended to ask government to give or lend me five or six disabled cannon for this. I asked government to pay the passage of five or six families, from England, to work in the furnace. This could not be granted, and therefore I would not ask for the cannon. Another thing against me is, that there is not a man in the country, that I know of, capable of working in the furnace. But the greatest difficulty I have to overcome is, ironmen, as we call them, are the very worst sort of men to manage, colliers not excepted. Not one of a hundred of them but will take every advantage of his master, in his power. If I have just the number of hands for the work, every one of them will know that I cannot do without every one of them; therefore, every one of them will be my master: anxiety and trouble will be the consequence: and if I keep more hands than are necessary, so as to have it in my

29th. The quantity for sale, several thousand acres.

30th. Public roads, good and improvable at small expence.

31st. It is the opinion of this meeting, that large tracts of land, owned by non-residents, retard the settlement of the township, and that wholesome settlers, artificers, labourers, and *capital*, would contribute most effectually to improve this township, and the province generally.

Signed, in name of the meeting, by

DANIEL FREEMAN, *Chairman.*

Walsingham

TO MR. ROBERT GOURLAY.

Dec. 5th, 1817.

SIR,

IN compliance with your request, we, the inhabitant householders of the township of Walsingham, have convened ourselves, for the purpose of answering certain queries, which appeared in your Address of October last, which are as follows:

3d. No churches; but make use occasionally of our school houses for that purpose. No professional preachers; but are frequently visited by different dissenting ministers.

9th. The three or four front Concessions, of superior quality, equal to any in the province. The remainder of a lighter soil. The township tolerably well watered.

---

power to turn those away who will not do right, this will be expensive. But, after all, if the ore is as good as I expect, I hope to reduce the price of iron very considerably. The place where I am is a reserved lot. Governor Gore has promised encouragement to the works, when government is satisfied that they will answer a good purpose. If Governor Gore does not return to this country, and what he promised should be refused me, iron works will be at an end with me, and at this place; but, I shall not ask for the promise, until the inhabitants of the country will be my bondsmen, for the benefits arising from the iron works. When I saw you, I offered a considerable sum of money to take them off my hands: this I repeat; not but I believe they will answer, but the trouble will be more than equal to any profit from them. Those who begin iron works after me, in this country, will start many thousand dollars a-head of me: every thing they want, except stone, will be had here; the best method of working the ore will be known, and men will be learned to work it.

"I am, Sir, your obedient servant,
"John Mason."

10th.   Pine, oak, ash, beech, sugar maple, basswood, black walnut, hickory, butternut, elm, with different other sorts.

11th.   No minerals of any description have as yet been discovered.

12th.   None.

18th.   Five acres of wood land may be cleared and fenced from 151. to 201.; all expence accruing, to be borne by the party performing the labour.

25th.   Pasture excellent; butter and cheese sells from 7½d. to 1s. 3d.

26th.   Cropping on new land not practised; manure necessary for Indian corn and potatoes.

27th.   Land is usually let on shares for one half, provided the proprietor furnish seed and team.

29th.   Half of the township supposed to be for sale.

30th.   Public roads in a very bad state, and capable of great improvement, at a moderate expence: only one stream capable of boat navigation.

31st.   What, in our opinion, retards the improvement of our township, is that large bodies of land are owned by different gentlemen who do not occupy it. As to the province in general, we are of opinion that it is owing to our remoteness from a foreign market, and the great expence of transportation, occasioned in a great measure from the difficulty of the water communication with the Lower Province.

(Signed)

H. WEBSTER, *Collector,*	HENRY SMITH,
MICHAEL TROYER,	PAUL DRESTIN, SEN.
Assessor,	JOHN KILLMASTER,
JAMES MC.CALL,	ANTHONY PIKE,
JOHN BECKER,	JEREMIAH WOLFEN,
JOHN DUTCH,	FRED. BAUMWART,
SAMUEL BROWN,	TOBIAS LAMAN,
ABRAHAM SMITH,	JACOB COPE,
CORNWALL ELLIS,	HENRY BECKER.
PAUL DRESTIN, JUN.	

Middleton

SIR,

Dec. 8th, 1817.

HAVING seen your Address in the Upper Canada Gazette of the

30th October, 1817 – We, the undersigned, unanimously agree with you in sentiment, that the local situation of this province has never been fully made known either to government or the British farmer; we likewise are of opinion, that your Queries annexed to your Address, being answered in a simple, but correct manner, will, when published in England, give a fair opportunity to every individual to judge for himself. We, the inhabitant landholders for the township of Middleton, having, at a general meeting held at the house of John Coltman, Esq. unanimously called John Coltman, Esq. to the chair, and cordially agreed to the following answers:

9th. The soil is of a rich loam, and the surface generally level.

10th. The timber, ash, maple, basswood, beech, black walnut, butternut, hickory, cherry, white pine, oak of different kinds, chestnut. The above timber generally stands in equal proportions.

11th. Iron ore in abundance.

12th. None.

14th. No lime burnt for sale.

15th. Blacksmith, being found with shop tools, and coal, wages at 10s. per day.

26th. First sown with wheat, and laid down to grass for three years, then summer fallowed, and sown with wheat, without manure.

27th. If the landlord furnish team and seed, the tenant receives half the crop. If the tenant furnish team and seed, the landlord receives one third.

28th. No wild lands for sale, as the whole of the township of Middleton and Howton is reserved by government, except Talbot street.

29th. A log-house built, and ten acres cleared on a 200 acre lot, is now selling at 250l.

30th. Talbot street leads through the township, running nearly east and west, about 12 miles from lake Erie.

31st. We think that the townships of Houghton and Middleton, being reserved, hinders the improvement of this part of the country, as there is but one road through the said towns, and one bypath.

(Signed)

JOHN COLTMAN, *Chairman.*

JAMES BROWN,
Town Clerk.

GEORGE COLTMAN,

JAMES COLTMAN,
JOSEPH WOOD,
JOHN YOUNG,
ELIJAH HARRIS,

HEZEKIAH CART-	BRENTEN BROWN,
WRIGHT,	ESEKIAH OVERBAUG,
MICHAEL CULP,	JOSEPH ADAIR,
DAVID ADAIR,	PETER NEWKIRK,
JAMES MOREHOUSE,	MOSES BROWN,
JOSHUA BROWN,	AB. BROWN.
SAMUEL BROWN,	

Norwich

At a Town Meeting, held in the Township of Norwich the 5th of the 1st Month, 1818, according to Law, for choosing Town Officers. The Proposals by R. Gourlay for publishing a Statistical Account of the Province of Upper Canada, in order to exhibit correct Ideas respecting the Encouragement this fine Country holds out to such Europeans as have a mind to emigrate in quest of a Country rich in natural Resources, but poor in point of Population, in order to occupy and improve the natural advantages thereof, to their individual interest and happiness of their Families.

HIS proposals being read, the meeting made choice of Peter Lossing, to draft a schedule of the beginning and progress of several of the first adventurers into the wilderness*, about 12 miles from any settlements, and also appointed John Throckmorton, William Curtis, Elias Moore, and Peter M'Lees, to assist the afore-mentioned Peter Lossing in preparing correct answers to the several Queries suggested by the said R. Gourlay, affording materials for giving an accurate description of Norwich in an agricultural point of view, and to affix their signatures to the statement forwarded to the said R. Gourlay.

    2d. A few families arrived in 1808, but very little progress till 1811.

    3d. Two houses appropriated for public worship of the society of Friends, three approved ministers of that society.

    4th. One regular bred practitioner of physic and surgery.

    5th. Three schools; common fees per quarter 151.† board and lodging found.

    6th. No lack of houses of entertainment.

    7th. No licensed taverns, dramshops, nor distilleries.

---

   * See Supplement to this Report. [That is, the statistical table on Norwich Township, p. 162 – Ed.]

   † This must mean the schoolmaster's salary. – R.G.

8th.   One store, one grist mill, two others building, three saw mills; price of boards at the saw mill, pine 11. 11s. 3d. per thousand square feet; no carding machine, but one wanted.

9th.   Soil generally a sandy loam, interspersed with small intervals of clay; in its wild state covered with a rich body of black vegetable mould.

10th.   Timber – pine, beech, maple, bass, elm, oak, ash, chestnut, butternut, hickory, poplar, iron wood, plum, thorn, hazle, grape, crab apple, &c. A large proportion of rock maple, from which the inhabitants supply themselves with sugar, molasses, and vinegar, and the pine generally much in a body by itself.

11th.   Some indications of iron ore of the bog kind; salt licks, as they are here called; plaster of Paris or gypsum, chalybeate and sulphurous springs, the springs generally clear, wholesome water, somewhat impregnated with lime.

12th.   Building stones scarce; some indications of plenty of limestone in the bottoms of small brooks, but not much opened.

13th.   Bricks of a good quality have been made and sold at 11. 5s. per thousand; indications of clay suitable for pottery and stone ware, and paints.

14th.   Lime has been burnt on log heaps; sells for about 8d. per bushel.

15th.   Carpenter's wages by the day, about 6s. 3d.; mason's 7s. 6d.; blacksmith's work about 1s. 3d. per lb. iron included.

25th.   Timothy and clover is most common and grows luxuriantly: an ox four years old gains about one-third in a summer's run; they become excellent beef in a summer's run in the woods; a good cow gives, per day, four gallons of milk, producing good butter and cheese: price of butter 9d. and cheese 7½d. per pound.

26th.   First crop has generally been wheat, though excellent Indian corn: oats and potatoes have been raised on new land by harrowing only: a crop of wheat has been succeeded by corn, oats and potatoes, and vice versa, and done well.

27th.   Very little done on cropping, on shares.

28th.   About 6s. 3d. was at our commencement the price of land, and has progressively risen to 13s. per acre: one sale lately made of an improvement 100 acres, 35 cleared, frame barn, log house, good fence, price 3751.

29th.   About 25,000 acres of wild land yet for sale.

30th.   Roads still bad, but capable of much improvement, at a moderate expence: water conveyance contemplated as attainable, by cutting and clearing drift wood out of the bed waters of the Otter creek, from near the centre of Norwich, into lake Erie, which is about 30 miles; it is clothed with pine timber, and many good mill seats.

STATISTICAL
Shewing the Progress of Improvement

Names of Residents.	Of what Place Natives.	Date of commencing Improvement.	Family, consisting of	Number of Acres owned.	Extent of Crop put in first Season.	Do. second Season.	Do. third Season.	Do. fourth Season.	Do. fifth Season.	Do. sixth Season.	No. of Horses, first Season.
Peter Lossing.	Dutchess County, State of N. York	Spring of 1811	Wife and 5 childr.	300	14	20	23	25	28	30	3
Michael Stover.	Ditto	late in the season.	Do. and 9 children	1000	4	11	13	16	13	15	1
Fred. Stover.	Ditto	Ditto	Do. and 6 children	1000	4	10	10	10	18	18	3
Adam Stover.	Ditto	Ditto	Do. and 5 children	1000	0	5	9	18	18	14	0
Sears Mold.	Ditto	1811	Do. and 6 reserve children	100	8	12	14	16	18	20	0
Sam. Cornwell.	Ditto	Ditto	Do. and 9 children	200	0	16	20	22	23	25	1
Elias Moore.	Nova Scotia	Ditto	Do. and 5 children	400	0	24	24	28	30	44	2
John Syple.	Albany Street, N. York	Ditto	Do. and 5 children	200	0	18	18	20	22	30	0
Sol. Sackrider.	Dutchess County, State of N. York	Ditto	Do. and 5 children	200	0	20	25	26	26	27	2
Peter De Long.	Ditto	Ditto	Do. and 5 children	400	7	25	24	28	28	30	3
Peter M'Lees.	Ditto	Ditto	Do. and 7 children	400	0	4	5	5	6	8	1
11 Farmers	89 Persons.		11 wives, 67 children.	5,200	37	165	185	214	230	261	16

31st.   Land held in fee by distant owners in large quantities, not responsible for defraying any charges for opening roads, while the whole burden falls on actual settlers, is a hinderance to the growth of the settlement.

An increase of population, with an adequate capital, the improvement of morals, the reduction of distilleries and dram shops, to the encouragement of good inns, the improvement of roads and building of bridges, removing of obstructions in boatable waters, are prominent objects to promote the prosperity of this country.

(Signed)

PETER LOSSING.   ELIAS MOORE.

TABLE.
in Norwich Township, London District.

No. of Oxen, do.	No. of Cows, do.	No. of Horses now in possession.	No. of Oxen, do.	No. of Cows, do.	No. of young Cattle, do.	No. of Sheep.	Number of Acres now under Improvement, Plough and Meadow.	Bushels of Wheat, last Crop.	Bushels of Corn, Oats, and Pease.	Bushels of Potatoes.	Money expended.	The first work of all, on settling, is the erection of a temporary log house. New Buildings.
0	3	2	2	8	18	25	80	300	300	1000	£200	Frame Barn and Timber House.
2	2	2	2	7	24	39	60	400	350	100	120	Frame Barn.
2	4	3	2	7	11	18	70	250	300	200	350	Frame Barn and House.
2	2	3	0	6	15	26	80	100	120	60	24	Log House and Barn.
0	2	2	2	4	6	16	50	200	80	100	0	Frame Barn.
2	2	2	4	4	6	25	55	200	220	300	62	Log House and Barn.
2	1	4	6	9	14	20	100	500	150	200	300	Two Frame Barns.
2	2	3	0	6	14	13	40	200	200	200	0	Frame Barn.
4	4	2	4	7	7	20	60	200	200	200	50	Log House and Barn.
2	4	2	3	7	8	24	100	150	300	150	100	Frame Barn.
2	2	1	2	8	11	19	40	250	100	320	36	Frame Barn.
20	28	26	27	73	134	245	735	2750	2320	2830	1242	12 barns and 5 houses.

JOHN THROCKMORTON.   PETER M'LEES.
WILLIAM CURTIS.

SUPPLEMENT.

The following Schedule may serve as a sample of the general body of settlers, according to the time they have become residents of this township. Several thousand bushels of wheat to spare this season, beyond a supply of bread for the inhabitants. There has been no disease of an epidemic nature since the settlement commenced: three deaths of adults and three children only. Diseases of an inflammatory, pulmonic and rheumatic nature are the most frequent, and the instances rare even of these. The inhabitants consist of the Society of Friends, some Methodists, a few Baptists, and some, as to profession, Nothingarians, but, generally speaking, encouragers of good moral, sober, and industrious habits.

Bayham

SIR,

HAVING seen your Address in the Upper Canada Gazette, of the 30th of October last, we, the undersigned landholders of the township of Bayham, agree with you in sentiment, that the situation of this province has not been fully made known to the British farmer. We are likewise of opinion, that the Queries annexed to your Address, being answered in a correct manner, when published in England, will give a fair opportunity to every individual to judge for himself. We have held a general meeting at the house of John Lodor, in Bayham, having called Joseph Bowes to the chair, unanimously agreed to the following answers:

3d. No churches nor settled ministers, but frequently visited by the Methodist and Baptist.

9th. The soil is of a rich loam, and the surface generally level.

10th. The timber, maple, ash, basswood, butternut, black walnut, hickory, cherry, white pine of a superior quality, and oak of different kinds, chestnut; the above timber generally stands in equal proportions.

11th. Limestone and iron ore in abundance.

12th. None.

14th. No lime burnt for sale.

15th. Blacksmiths, being found with shop tools and coal, wages 10s. per day.

19th. Price of sheep, ewes, 15s.; and wethers, 1l. weighing, when fatted, from 20 to 25lb. per quarter.

25th. Artificial grasses are little known here; small quantities of red clover have been sown, cut twice a season; two tons the first, and one ton the second cutting; the pasture, the small white clover, with Timothy and spear grass, which comes naturally after the first crop. An ox, turned in poor condition, the first of May, to grass, will, with a summer's run, by the first of December, be good beef, and have 100lb. of rough tallow. Cows in this country do not afford as much milk as in some parts of England, but more butter and cheese in proportion; one cow will make 10lb. of butter per week; and a dairy of 20 cows will make 40lb. of cheese per day, from the first of May, to the last of September.

26th. First sown with wheat, and laid down to grass for three years; then ploughed and sown again, without manure.

27th. If the landlord furnish team and seed, he receives one-half the crop. If the tenant furnishes the above, the landlord receives one-third.

29th. A log house built, and 10 acres cleared on a two hundred acre lot, is now selling for 250l. Some small quantities of land for sale, at 12s. 6d. per acre, and large quantities not located.

30th. Talbot street leads through the township, about 7 miles from the lake. Ottawa river, leading through the centre of the township, and is navigable for boats of 20 tons, for forty miles from the mouth.

31st. We think that the very great number of reserve lots, retard the settlement or improvement of the township more than any thing else.

(Signed)

JOSEPH BOWES, *Chairman.*
WILLIAM HAZEN, *Town Clerk.*

JOHN HAZEN.	JAMES RUSSELL.
SAMUEL EDISON.	WILLIAM RAYMOND.
SAMUEL SHWARTS.	THOMAS EDISON.
WILLIAM HATT.	JOSEPH MERILL.
EZEKIEL FORSYTH.	JOHN EDISON.
JOHN LODOR.	M. EDISON.
JOHN SAXTON, SEN.	JAMES WILSON.
WILLIAM SAXTON.	DENNIS DAWLIR.
JOHN SAXTON, JUN.	ALEXANDER SAXTON.
MOSES EDISON.	PETER WEAVER.

Malahide.

At a Meeting of all the Inhabitants of the Township of Malahide, assembled at the House of Mr. William Summers, on Talbot Road, on the 10th of December, 1817, for the Purpose of examining the Queries proposed by Robert Gourlay, Esq. to the Resident Land Owners of Upper Canada, in his Address of October last. William Summers was chosen Chairman, and Simeon Dav-

ies, Secretary, upon which Occasion the following were adopted as Answers to the said Queries.

9th. Soil excellent, and very well watered. The surface nearly level.

10th. Maple, beech, elm, white and red oak, white and black ash, basswood and ironwood.

11th. No minerals discovered; some quarries of limestone.

12th. Few building stones have been found.

13th. No bricks have been made in this township.

14th. No lime has been burnt; but there are some quarries of limestone.

15th. Blacksmiths generally charge as much for their work as the iron costs; carpenters and masons have done but little good work as yet. The inhabitants as yet live mostly in round log houses.

26th. First crop wheat; second ditto, rye and grass seed: when the sod is broken up, we summer fallow and sow with wheat again.

27th. Land has not been let on shares to any extent, almost every inhabitant being owner of the tract he occupies.

29th. Little for sale; quantity not ascertained.

30th. The roads are not very good; but the annual labour required from the settlers by law, improves them fast. No canals are necessary, lake Erie being contiguously situated.

31st. The lots reserved for the crown and clergy, constitute two-sevenths of the township, and prevent the settlement from becoming compact. – Their being disposed of by sale to actual settlers, and applied to provincial purposes, might be the means of increasing the wealth and respectability of the province; and would doubtless, in its operation, contribute largely to the wealth and improvement of every individual township.

By order of the Meeting,
(Signed) WILLIAM SUMMERS, *Chairman.*
SIMEON DAVIES, *Secretary.*

Yarmouth.

At a Meeting of the Settlers of the Township of Yarmouth, assembled at the Inn of Justice Wilcox, on Talbot Road, on the 10th Day of December, 1817, for the purpose of considering the Address of Robert Gourlay, Esq. of October last, to the Land Owners of Upper Canada, Captain Daniel Rapelje was chosen

Chairman, and Adjutant James Nevills Secretary, when the following Answers to his Queries were adopted.

8th.   Rate for sawing 3s. 6d. per 100 feet.

9th.   Soil black sandy loam; surface level; remarkably well watered with living springs, rivulets, &c.

10th.   Timber, generally beech and maple, interspersed with black walnut, white walnut, oak, ash, cherry, and many other kinds of timber peculiar to the climate.

11th.   Limestone in many places. Many mineral springs; their qualities not ascertained.

12th.   No quarries discovered.

14th.   No lime burned.

15th.   Blacksmith's wages at the same rate per pound as the cost of the iron: making an axe, smith find the materials, 12s. 6d.; and other piece work in proportion. Carpenter's wages 10s. per day: mason's 10s. per day, or 1l. 5s. per thousand for laying brick.

25th.   Common pasture, Timothy, red and white clover. A four year old steer taken from the yard in the spring, is allowed to gain one-fifth in the summer's run, either in the meadow or forest; the forest pasture excellent for causing cows to produce large quantities of milk.

26th.   Ordinary course of cropping upon new land – the first crop wheat; second crop rye: manure not required.

27th.   Lands let upon shares draw one-third.

29th.   Lands for sale supposed 30,000 acres.

30th.   Public roads very good, considering the infancy of the settlement; capable of much improvement, with a moderate expence.

31st.   The lands granted to persons not resident at present in the province, or living at the seat of government, or in other towns of the province, and the crown and clergy reserves intervening so often amongst our farms, have a tendency to retard the improvement of our settlement very materially. What, in our opinion also, that further retards the growth of our settlement, is an improper system of emigration; and we are confident that the introduction of men of capital would much tend to the improvement of the same.

By order of the Meeting,

(Signed)   DANIEL RAPELJE, *Chairman.*
JAMES NEVILLS, *Secretary.*

Southwold.

*At a Meeting of all the Inhabitants of the Township of South-
wold, assembled at the House of Mr. Alexander Ross, of Talbot
Road, in the said Township, on the 10th Day of December, in the
Year of our Lord, 1817, for the Purpose of considering of the
Address of Robert Gourlay, Esq. of October last, to the resident
Land Owners of Upper Canada, Mahlon Burwell, of Southwold
aforesaid, Esq. was chosen Chairman, and Mr. Alexander Ross,
of the same Place aforesaid, Farmer, was chosen Secretary, and
the following were adopted as Answers to his Queries.*

9th.   The soil is excellent. Marly in places, and diversified
with sandy loam and clay alternately. The surface in general level;
and there are some ancient fortifications still to be seen.

10th.   Maple, elm, beech, walnut, butternut, red and white
oak, hickory, black and white ash, cherry, basswood, and iron
wood.

11th.   No minerals have been discovered.

12th.   No building stones; but several quarries of limestone
have been discovered.

13th.   Very few bricks have been made.

14th.   No lime has been burned; but several quarries of
limestone have been discovered.

15th.   There are but two blacksmiths, who charge high. But
little carpenters' and masons' work has been done; the inhabitants
as yet living principally in round log-houses, which they construct
themselves.

25th.   We as yet have only made use of pasture in the
woods, in a state of nature, which is very good. Milk very good,
as also the quality of dairy produce.

26th.   The first crop is wheat harrowed in, the second rye,
mixed with hay seed; when the grass is broken up, the ground is
summer fallowed, and sown with wheat again. No manure has
been strewed on the ground yet.

27th.   No land has been let amongst us, every man being
himself a landlord.

28th.   We have good timber for building; but for want of
saw mills it is difficult to get lumber; nearly one tenth part of the
settled land in the township is cleared.

29th.   We know of but little offered for sale, almost every
man being content with his situation.

30th.   Roads are tolerable, and the statute labour improves
them fast. Our settlement is near the borders of lake Erie, which
is a good water communication toward Montreal.

31st. Nothing retards our settlement more than the lands of absentees, and the crown and clergy reserves being interspersed amongst our farms; and nothing could contribute more to the improvement of our settlement than their being sold to active and industrious persons. We are confident that the province in general would be much benefited by the sale of the lands of absentees, and the crown and clergy reserves to actual settlers.

By order of the meeting,

(Signed)

M. BURWELL, *Chairman.*

ALEXANDER ROSS,
  Secretary.

Dunwich.

At a Meeting of all the Inhabitants of the Township of Dunwich, assembled at the House of Mr. Singleton Gardiner, on Talbot Road, in the said Township, the 11th day of December, 1817, to deliberate upon the Propriety of answering sundry Queries, proposed in an Address of October last, to the Resident Landowners of Upper Canada, by Robert Gourlay, Esq. Captain Gilman Wilson of said Township, was chosen Chairman, and Mr. Singleton Gardiner, of the same Place, was chosen Secretary.

UPON which occasion, the following Answers to his Queries, were unanimously adopted.

2d. The first settlement was made by the Hon. Thomas Talbot, of Port Talbot, Esq. in the year 1803, at which time there was not a white inhabitant within sixty miles on the east, and seventy-five miles on the west. Colonel Talbot encountered many difficulties, with a zeal which will for ever do honour to his memory; by his unremitting solicitations and exertions, he at length prevailed on the provincial executive government, to lay the country between Port Talbot and Long Point, open for actual settlement, which they only did partially, in the year 1809 and 10. There are supposed to be about 500 souls in the township, and about 100 inhabited houses.

8th. One mill only. Colonel Talbot's mills, which were excellent, were burnt by the enemy in time of the late war, and are not rebuilt.

9th. Soil in general excellent and marly, and the surface level and well watered.

10th. Maple, beech, black walnut, butternut, cherry, white

and black ash, white and red oak, white pine, elm, basswood, and iron wood.

11th. No minerals have been discovered; there are some quarries of limestone.

12th. But few building stones have been discovered.

13th. But few bricks have been made; the earth however is good for that purpose.

14th. Very little lime has been burnt.

15th. No blacksmith.

16th. Few women servants and but little spinning as yet; good ground for flax.

23d. First crop wheat, harrowed in; 2d do. rye and Timothy, with clover; when the sod is broken up, we summer fallow and sow with wheat again; no manure has as yet been applied.

25th. Our only pasture is in a state of nature, and is good. An ox will gain 200 pounds by a summer's run; milk and dairy produce good; butter, 1s.: no cheese.

27th. No land is let; the most humble individuals here are proprietors of the soil.

29th. But little for sale; the quantity not ascertained.

30th. Roads are indifferent; but the statute labour is fast improving them. Our township is bounded on the north shore of lake Erie, which affords a good water communication towards Montreal.

31st. The crown and clergy reserves intervening so frequently amongst our farms, impedes the improvement of our township; and we are of opinion, that the growth and prosperity of the province in general is impeded by them. These being removed, or disposed of to active and industrious settlers, would, in our opinion, be a blessing to the province.

By order of the Meeting,
(Signed)

GILMAN WILSON, *Chairman.*
SINGLETON GARDINER, *Secretary.*

Aldborough.

At a Meeting of sundry Inhabitants of the Township of Aldborough, assembled at the House of Mr. Archibald Gillies, of Talbot Road, in said Township, on the 11th Day of December, 1817, for the Purpose of agreeing upon Answers to certain Queries, pro-

posed to the Resident Land Owners of Upper Canada, in an Address of Robert Gourlay, Esq. of October last, Captain Leslie Paterson was chosen Chairman, and Mr. Archibald Gillies, Secretary, when the following were adopted as Answers to the said Queries.

2d.   Some time after Colonel Talbot settled at Port Talbot.

9th.   Soil excellent, marly and sandy alternately, and generally level and well watered.

10th.   Maple, beech, elm, basswood, black walnut, chestnut, hickory, white and black ash.

11th.   No minerals have been discovered. Some limestone about the creeks and shore of the lake.

12th.   No building stone; but famous rocks for millstones are discovered in many places.

13th.   No bricks have been made.

14th.   No lime has yet been burnt.

15th.   No blacksmiths, masons, or carpenters, who work at their professions.

25th.   Natural pasture good. Not ascertained what an ox will gain by a summer's run. Milk and butter excellent, but none for sale.

26th.   The first crop is wheat, the second rye or grass. When the grass is ploughed up, the common course is to summer fallow the ground and sow it with wheat.

27th.   No land has been let upon shares.

29th.   Not much for sale; we do not know the quantity.

30th.   The public roads are tolerable, and are improving; the labour required by law to be performed annually by each settler tends to improve the roads fast. We live contiguous to the Thames and lake Erie.

31st.   The lands owned by non-residents in the Concessions, near the river Thames, and the reserved lots, seem to retard the growth of our township, as well as the province at large. A tax upon the lands of absentees might induce them to sell to persons who would become actual settlers, which would facilitate the improvement of our settlement; and if his Majesty's government would dispose of the reserved lands throughout the province, we are of opinion, it would much contribute to improve the same.

By order of the Meeting,

(Signed) LESLIE PATERSON, *Chairman.*
ARCHIBALD GILLIES, *Secretary.*

STATISTICAL

Shewing the commencement of improvement in

Names of Settlers.	To what Profession bred.	Native of	How long in Canada.	Family at Home.
Henry Crook	Farmer and lime burner.	Armagh, Ireland.	Arrived this year, 1817.	A wife.
Wm. Orr	Farmer and weaver.	Ditto.	Ditto.	Wife, 2 children, and sister.
John Smith	Farmer and shoemaker.	United States.	30 years.	Wife and 6 children.
James Tomlinson ...	Distiller.	Ditto.	20 ditto.	Wife and 3 chil.
Joseph Lyons	Farmer.	Ditto.	8 ditto.	Wife and 1 child
Thomas Orr	Weaver and farmer.	Armagh, Ireland.	Arrived this year.	————
Isaac Riley	Carpenter and farmer.	Ditto.	Ditto.	Wife not arrived.
Joseph Tomlinson ...	Farmer.	United States.	20 years.	Wife and 3 children.
Lawrence Renney ...	Ditto.	Canada.	Lifetime.	Wife.
Samuel Renney	Ditto.	Ditto.	Ditto.	————
Andrew Nevells ...	Ditto.	Ditto.	Ditto.	Wife and 1 child.
Daniel McPherson...	Ditto.	United States.	25 years.	Wife and 4 children.
Gurden Chapel	Ditto.	Ditto.	19 ditto.	Wife.
Charles Pettys	Ditto.	Ditto.	30 ditto.	Wife and 2 children.
John Cummons	Ditto.	Ditto.	6 ditto.	Ditto.
Samuel Hunt	Farmer and Currier.	Ditto.	6 ditto.	Wife and 3 children.
John Vansickel	Farmer.	Ditto.	11 ditto.	Wife and 5 children.
Aaron Kilburn	Millwright.	Ditto.	21 ditto.	Wife and 7 chil.
Andrew Banghart ...	Carpenter.	Ditto.	9 ditto.	Wife and 5 chil.
Abraham Sloot... ...	Carpenter and Farmer.	Canada.	Lifetime.	Wife and 3 children, father and mother.
Vernum Mathews ...	Farmer.	United States.	23 years.	Wife and 5 children.

21 Farmers, 19 Wives, 51 Children,— in all 94 Persons.

The above Table was made out by me when travelling through the country, and I left schedules to be filled up in Norwich, and on the Talbot Road, which will be found in their proper places. This table exhibits a settlement just beginning. They mark the progress of some years of improvement.—R. G.

TABLE.

Westminster New Settlement, London District.

Date of commencing improvement.	Cows.	Oxen.	Horses.	?	Number of Acres put in crop and reaped.	Total chopt acres.	Dimension of house erected.	Size of farm.	Original cost.
17th August, 1817.	2	2	0	0	0	3	20 by 18	200	41 Dollars and 1s.
Ditto.	1	2	0	0	0	4½	27 by 19	Do.	Do.
1st June, 1817.	2	Bull & 4 yo.cattle	0	0	0	7	18 by 18	Do.	Free, being a U. E. loyalist.
July, 1816.	2	2	0	0	0	15	30 by 14	Do.	41 Dollars & 1s
Nov. 1816.	2	0	0	0	10 mo. unwell.	½	20 by 18	Do.	Do.
1st Oct 1817.	0	0	0	0	0	2½	0	Do.	Do.
17th August, 1817.	0	0	0	0	0	7	0	Do.	Do.
June, 1816.	0	0	0	0	0	7	22 by 17	Do.	Do.
1st March, 1817.	2	2	0	0	4½	1½	0	Do.	Do.
Ditto.	1	2	0	0	3	5	20 by 16	Do.	Do.
Ditto.	0	2	0	0	6	6	26 by 18	Do.	Do.
Began 1816, Settled Sept. 1817.	3	2	2	0	0	5	28 by 20	Do.	Do.
March, 1817.	1	2	0	0	2	5	21 by 18	Do.	Do.
Ditto.	2	0	1	7	4½	11	24 by 16	Do.	Do.
Ditto.	1	2	0	7	3	13	20 by 20	Do.	Do.
Ditto.	2	2	0	0	13	17	22 by 22	Do.	Do.
10th June, Ditto.	2	2	0	0	4	10	20 by 20	Do.	Do.
April, Ditto.	3	2	2	12	15	15	18 by 16	Do.	Do.
March, Ditto.	2	0	2	0	10	22	20 by 14	Do.	Do.
February, Ditto.	1	0	0	0	4	5½	20 by 20	Do.	Free, being a U. E. loyalist.
June, Ditto.	3	0	1	0	4	10	22 by 22	Do.	41 Dollars and 1s.*
Totals.	32	29	8	26	73	175½			

* The fees were lately raised from 9l. 7s. 6d. to this sum.

STATISTICAL

Shewing the Progress of Improvement on

Names of Settlers in order as they took Possession, and commenced Improvement.	Original Profession in Business	Wife or none with Number of Children at home under fourteen Years.	Of what Country a Native.	Date of taking Possession.	Stock, first Year of Settlement.	
					No. of Cows.	No. of Oxen.
John Barber.	Farmer.	Wife & 4 Children	U. States.	1811	2	2
Freeman Waters.	Ditto.	Do. & 1 Do.	Ditto.	1814	2	...
James Best.*	Ditto.	Do. & 4 Do.	Ditto.	1813	2	...
Chas. Wells Waters.	Ditto.	Do. & 2 Do.	Ditto.	1814	...	...
James Watson	Ditto.	Do. & 7 Do.	Ditto.	1812	2	2
David Watson.*	Ditto.	Do. & 4 Do.	Ditto.	1813	2	...
Richard Williams.	Weaver.	Do. & 7 Do.	England.	1815	...	...
Andrew Spring.	Farmer.	Do. & 6 Do.	U. States	1814	1	2
David Wallace.	Weaver.	Do. & 8 Do.	Scotland.	1813	...	...
Timothy Neal.	Sailor.	...	Ireland.	1811	...	...
Burges Swisher.	Farmer.	Wife & 5 Children.	U. States.	1811	...	...
George Clunes.	Brick maker.	...	L. Canad.	1816	...	...
Charles Benedict.	Farmer.	...	U. States.	1815	...	...
Joseph Vanlese.	Ditto.	Wife & 3 Children.	U. States.	1813	...	...
Richard Barret.	Brick maker.	...	Ireland.	1813	...	...
James Burwell, U. E.*	Farmer.	Wife & 9 Children.	Colonies.	1812	2	2
Neil M'Nair.	Ditto.	do. & 2 do.	Ireland.	1811	2	2
John Burwell, U. E.	Ditto.	...	U.Canad.	1813	...	...
Benjamin Johnson.	Ditto.	Wife & 5 Children.	U. States.	1812	...	...
John Robins.	Saddler.	do. & 3 do.	Ditto.	1815	...	...
Samuel M'Intyre.	Farmer.	Do. & 1 Do.	Nova Scotia.	1812	...	...
Daniel M'Intyre.	Ditto.	Do. & 3 Do.	Ditto.	1812	...	...
James M'Intyre.	Ditto.	Do. & 6 Do.	Ditto.	1815	...	...
John Philpot.	Ditto.	Do. & 5 Do.	Ditto.	1812	...	...
Samuel Harris.	Ditto.	Do. & 2 Do.	Ditto.	1816	...	...
			Total Stock at first, 3 horses		15	10

The above Table was filled up and attested by M. Burwell, Esq. M. P. 19th Dec. 1817, who remarked that all the persons, whose names are mentioned as in possession of their lands in the years 1812-1813, or early in 1814, had to perform a great deal of militia service in time of the late war with the United States, and were plundered by marauding parties of the enemy, who made several eruptions to Port Talbot and its vicinity, in the year 1814. The progress therefore which they have made in the improvement of their farms, and increase of their stock, is much less than it would have been had the war not existed. Each settler has 200 acres of land. Those marked U. E. got their land for nothing from government. Others paid fees amounting to £9. 7s. 6d. each.

TABLE,

Talbot Road, in the London District.

No. of Cows.	No. of Oxen.	No. Horses.*	No. of Sheep.	First Year.	Sec. Year.	Third Year.	Fourth Year.	Fifth Year.	Sixth Year.	Total Number of Acres cleared up to the present Time.	Estimated Worth of the Farm, with its Improvements at this Time.
5	3	2	20	5	14	2?	8	13	...	60	£550
3	4	2	...	8	12	10	10	...	...	40	450
3	2	1	...	2	3	7	8	...	...	20	340
2	...	...	...	1	4	5	...	...	...	10	300
5	2	2	12	4	5	5	4	14	...	32	410
4	2	1	...	3	4	5	7	3	...	22	355
2	...	1	...	4	5	...	...	...	...	9	295
6	2	...	...	4	7	6	...	...	...	17	335
2	2	...	...	1	2	3	4	...	...	10	290
4	2	...	...	5	4	6	6	12	8	40	450
3	2	...	...	1	3	3	3	5	8	23	365
1	...	...	...	4	..		...	...	...	4	270
2	2	...	...	3	7	...	...	...	...	10	300
2	2	...	...	1	2	3	2	...	...	8	290
4	2	...	...	2	4	5	11	...	...	22	360
4	2	2	...	5	5	5	7	8	...	30	400
4	2	...	16	7	8	6	6	10	11	43	465
2	...	1	...	1	2	3	4	...	...	10	300
4	2	...	...	1	2	4	5	...	...	12	310
4	...	...	...	6	6	...	...	...	...	12	310
2	...	1	3	4	7	5	4	10	...	30	400
4	2	1	9	9	7	10	6	8	...	40	450
3	...	...	...	7	8	...	...	...	...	15	325
4	2	...	15	4	10	8	9	9	...	40	450
2	2	...	...	15	...	...	...	...	...	15	325
81	39	14	75 Total Stock, 1817.								

* Those marked with an asterisk, had each a horse at first settlement. The original Table contained 25 more names; but the above are quite enough for the purpose of this publication.

STATISTICAL

Composed of Extracts from the Township

Names of Townships.	When Settled.	Inhabited Houses.	No. of People.	No. of Places of Worship.	No. of Preachers.	No. of Medical Practitioners.	No. of Schools.	Fees per Quarter.	No. of Stores.	No. of Tavern.	No. of Grist M. &c.	No. of Saw M. &c.	Prices of Bricks per 1000.	Prices of lime per bush.	Bark made per month and day.	WAGES OF		
																Carpenters p.day.	Mch ac per day.	Common Labourers per Annum.
								s. d.						s. d. s. d	Per M. £ s.	s. d. s. d	£. s.
Delaware	1795	18	90	1	0	0	1		1	1	1	2			Per M. £ s.			
Westminster....	1811	107	4 6	0	0	0	8		1	2	1	1	30 0	}	6 6	10 0 10 0	0 18 10
Dorchester	..	..	..	0	0	0	0		1	0	0	1	..		..	..	..
Oxford	1795	76	5 40	0	1 B.	0	4	16 0	3	3	8	8	30 0 1 3		6 3	7 6 10 0	40 0
Blenheim, &c.	1797	31	188	0	0	1	1	15 0	0	0	2	8	32 6 1 2		7 10	7 6 19 6	5 0
Burford & its Gore	1798	100	566	0	2 M.	1	2	12 6	2	2	3	4	25 0 1 2		Per Day. s. d.	10 0 ..	5 0
Windham	1794	48	295	0	1 P.	0	2	..	2	0	0	0	25 0 1 8		5 3	6 3 6 3	5 0
Townsend	1796	120	710	1 P.	1 B.	0	4	18 6	2	0	1	3	30 0 1		..	8 9 8 9	13 10
Walpole and Rainham	1795	47	347	0	1 Men.	0	0	..	0	0	1	1	25 0 1 0		5 0	5 0 5 0	25
Woodhouse ..	1795	100	715	1 M.	1 M.	1	3	12 6	3	3	3	7	25 0 1 3		7 6	7 6 7 6	25 0
Charlotteville ..	1795	137	900	1 B.	{ 3 M. 1 B. }	0	5	12 6	4	7	3	3	30 0		Per M. £ s. 6 5	7 6 10 0	27 10
Walsingham ..	1791	50	337	0	0	0	2	10 0	0	1	3	2	30 0		PrD. s. d. 6 3	6 3 6 3	..
Middleton	1815	30	..	0	0	0	0	..	0	1	0	0	30 0		10 0	6 3 ..	27 10
Norwich ..	1808	..	..	3 Q.	3 Q.	1	3	..	1	0	3	3	25 0	8	..	6 3 7 6	30 0
Bayham .	1813	60	..	0	0	0	2	10 0	2	1	1	1	25 0		10 0	7 6	30 0
Malahide.	1811	150	775	0	0	0	2	12 6	1	2	1	0	..		..	..	27 10
Yarmouth	1811	75	700	0	0	2	2	..	2	2	2	1	33 0		10 0 10 0	6 25	0
Southwold ..	1811	180	900	0	0	0	3	12 6	1	2	0	0	..		..	40 0
Dunwich .	1800	160	500	0	0	0	1	12 6	1	1	1	0	..		..	30 0
Aldborough ..	..	90	700	0	0	0	1	10 0	1	1	0	0	..		..	52 0
Totals.	..	1516	7917	6	14	6	40	42 6	28	29	28	33	397 6	9	4Sh. & 6L.3s	106 3 96 9	510 10
Averaged by	..	19	17	21	21	21	21	12	12	21	21	21	14	8	6 & 6	14 11	17
Averages	..	79	465	..	..	..	11 10		..	..	..	24 4	13	6 3 6 11 3	7 7 8 7	30 0 7

In the fifth and sixth columns B. stands for Baptist; M. for Methodist;

TABLE.

Reports of the London District.

WAGES O.				Cost of clearing and fencing per Acre of wild Land	PRICES OF LIVE STOCK.				Quantity of Wool per she p.	Price of Wool per lb.	Produce of wheat in bushels per acr.	An Ox, all eating in a Summer's run.	Price of Butter, per lb.	Price of Cheese, per lb.	Price of Land per Acre, at first	Price of Land per Acre now.
Common Labourers per month Winter	Common Labourers per Summer month.	Common Labourers per Day in Harvest.	Women's wages per week.		A Work-horse.	A Cow.	An Ox.	A Sheep.								
L. s.	L. s	s. d.	s. d.	L. s.	L. s.	L. s.	L. s.	L. s. s. d.	lb.	s. d.		lb.	s. d. s. d.	s. d.	s. d.
2 10	3 15	5 0 6	3	25 0	15 0	6 5	..	13 0	3½	3 0	22		½ 1 0 1 0	5 0	80 0
2 10	3 15	5 0 5	0	25 0	16 5	6 5	10	0 13 0	3	2 6	25		0 1 0 7½	6 13 6
2 10	3 15	5 0 6	3	18 15	15 0	5 0	5	15 13 6	3	2 6	27		.. 1 0 0 7½	.. 13 6
2 0	3 15	5 0 5	0	18 15	25 0	6 5	10	0 13 6	3	2 6	22	200	1 0 0 7½	5 0 13 3
2 5	3 7	5 0 5	0	18 15	15 0	5 3	5	2 13 6	3	2 6	..	145	 5	0 10 0
2 0	3 15	6 3 5	0	31 5	20 0	5 0	5	15 10 0	3	2 6	15		.. 1 0 0 7½	1 3 7 6
2 0	3 0	5 0 5	0	15 0	15 0	5 0	6	5 13 0	3	2 6	15	150	1 0 1 0	5 0 15 0
2 0	3 0	5 0 5	0	13 10	15 0	5 0	6	5 13 6	3	2 6	15	150	1 0 1 0	5 0 80 0
2 0	3 5	..	5 0	25 0	17 10	5 10	7	10 13 6	3	2 9	17		.. 1 3 1 3	5 0 80 0
2 0	3 2	5 0 5	0	17 10	13 15	5 12	6	13 13 6	3½	2 8	22		 5	0 17 6
1 18	3 7	5 0 5	0	18 2	16 5	5 12	9	8 15 0	4	2 6	30		.. 1 3 1 3	..
2 10	3 15	5 0 5	0	22 10	15 0	6 5	7	10 13 6	3½	2 0	25	..	0 9 0 7½	1 3 18 0
2 0	4 0	5 0 5	0	18 15	16 5	5 0	9	6 17 6	4	2 6	30	..	1 3 1 3	5 0 12 6
2 0	3 0	5 0	..	25 0	15 0	5 0	..	13 6	2½	3 0	27	150	..	5 0 27 6
2 0	3 0	5 0 5	0	25 0	15 0	5 0	..	13 6	3	3 6	25	½	1 3 1 3	5 0 20 0
2 5	3 0	..	..	25 0	15 0	5 0	10	0 13 6	2½	2 6	25	175	1 0 ..	5 0 25 0
2 0	3 10	5 0	..	30 0	15 0	5 0	9	0 12 6	3	2 6	27	200	1 0 ..	5 0 30 0
2 0	3 10	5 0	..	27 10	16 0	5 10	..	13 0	8½	..	30	..	.. ..	5 0 80 0
41 8	61 11	81 3 72 6	189 7	292 4	97 7	117 14	235	57	44 5 399	1160	14 6 11 1	75 0 360
18	18	16 14	18	18	18	14	18	18	17 17	7 14 12	16 17
2 6	3 8	4 5 1 5	2 21 12	7 16 4	5 8	8	6 13 0	3 ⅙	2 7½ 25½	165 1 0 1 1/12	4 6 21 6

London District:
Summary of Population, &c.

From the foregoing Table it appears that there are in 17 townships being 465 for each township. The houses inhabited by these people amount to 1514, which gives five and a little more than one-fourth* for each house or family.

7917 people;

Middleton and Bayham have 90 houses, and their people, not being reported, may be reckoned by the above average of five and a fourth to a house

472

Norwich, whereof neither the number of houses nor people are given, may be reckoned to contain the average number of people to a township

465

The only townships of the London district not regularly reported are Burford, London, Dereham, and Houghton. The first contained in 1817 only one family; the second two families; the third one family; and in the report of Middleton the settlers of Houghton are said to be six, say altogether 10 families, reckoned at five and a little more than a fourth

53

Total population of the London district

8907

There are no Indian settlements in this district, although parties of the Six Nations, Missasagas, &c. may be seen occasionally wandering about and pitching their wigwams as it suits their temporary convenience for hunting, &c.

It appears, that for the above population there are but six places of worship and 14 resident preachers: viz. three Baptists, six Methodists, one Presbyterian, one Menonist, and three Quakers. There are six medical practitioners, 40 schools, and 29 taverns.

What retards improvement is stated in 14 reports to be the great quantity of land granted to non-residents: in nine reports to be the crown, clergy, and other reserves: in three reports, the

---

* Five and a fourth to a family is too little for Upper Canada; but at the beginning of a settlement there are many families with men but lately married at their head. Seven will perhaps be near the true average in old settled districts: but the reader will see how it turns out in Niagara district.

want of settlers, with capital, enterprise, &c.; in one report, remoteness from market, and the difficulty of the water communication with the lower province.

Gore District
Township Reports

Trafalgar.

MR. ROBERT GOURLAY.

SIR,

AT a meeting of the inhabitants of our township, holden on the
27th November, 1817, at the house of Daniel Munn, innkeeper,
the following answers were framed in reply to your queries, as
they appeared to us in the Niagara Spectator.

9th.   The surface of the land is level; the top soil is clay,
mixed with loam and a little gravel; under that is clay, mostly of a
red colour.

10th.   Our timber consists of oak, two kinds, white and red;
pine, very large, of the white kind; beech; maple, two kinds; sugar maple, and soft maple; ash, two kinds, the black or swamp
ash, and white ash; basswood; hickory; elm; white and red; hemlock; ironwood; chestnut; some birch; quaking asp; some cedar;
some butternut, and a little tamarask: the timber mostly large,
and stands thick on the land.

11th.   Respecting minerals, there is a considerable quantity
of the mineral of iron, called bog ore; also a few salt springs of an
inferior kind.

12th.   Building stones, none, excepting a few, which may be
found over the land of a very indifferent kind.

15th.   Blacksmiths most generally work by the pound; that
is, 7½d. per lb. when the iron and steel are found, and 1s. 3d.
when the blacksmith finds the materials; to this there are some
exceptions, but not many.

18th.   The common custom of our township is to cut down
no more at first than the timber which is a foot in diameter, mea-
sured about two feet and a half from the root of the tree, and all
under that size; and the rest they girdle and kill with the axe. In
this state it will produce nearly as good a crop as if all were cut
down, and this only costs 1 lb. 10s. per acre; the rest of the timber is
cut down by degrees, for fencing and for fire wood, &c.

21st. Beasts are turned out about the first of May, and taken in about the first of December.

22d. Sleighing lasts about three months, that is, beginning about the first of January, and ends about the last of March. Ploughing begins about the 20th of April.

23d. Season of sowing wheat is from the 25th of August till the 1st of October; the time of harvesting of said grain is from the twentieth of July till the end of August.

25th. Respecting pasture, as the wild woods constitute our principal pasture lands, we have not yet made sufficient experiments to enable us to answer your query; but our meadow lands will generally produce one ton per acre.

26th. The ordinary course of cropping in new land, is wheat the first year, harrowed in, and sometimes a crop of oats are harrowed in, in the spring, on the stubble; then it is sown down with Timothy or clover, or both together, and is used for meadow for three or four years, till the roots rot in the ground, and then ploughed up, after which buckwheat or pease are generally sown first, and then wheat, perhaps the same season; and then pease or buckwheat, or oats, and then wheat, and so on alternately; little or no manure is used, but corn land and orchards require it most.

27th. Land is frequently let on shares on the following terms: if new, the leaser finds the leasee in team, in boarding, in farming utensils, and in half the seed, and then receives one half the produce. If old land, and the leasee finds every thing, the leaser has one third of the produce. If the leaser finds every thing, the leasee has only one third of the produce. Enough of land can be had on either of these ways.

28th. A farm of two hundred acres, with a log house and barn upon it, with 40 acres, cleared in the customary way, may be had for 375l. If frame buildings are upon it, a greater price; but seldom in proportion to the buildings.

29th. The quantity of land for sale we cannot justly describe, but we suppose 3 or 4000 acres; and there are but few farmers in our township, who would not even sell their improved farms, if they had the offer of a good price.

30th. The state of public roads at present is but indifferent; but they are capable of improvement at a very moderate expence. As the face of our country is generally level, great improvement might be made by means of canals and locks. Respecting our navigation, we are situated on the coast of lake Ontario, and thence we have the benefit of all the adjoining waters. Besides we have two very fine streams, called the Twelve and Sixteen Mile Creeks; these can be made navigable for boats, some part of the year, four miles from the mouth, to communicate with our mills on Dundas Street. The mouth of the Sixteen, where it empties into lake Ontario, is navigable for vessels of a considerable burden, and forms a safe and commodious harbour.

31st. The causes which retard the improvement of our township and the province at large are various. The first and principal cause you have already very justly observed, that is, the want of capital; this may perhaps be best illustrated by facts: know then, that the greater number of our farmers, when they first settled in the wild woods, have little more property than a cow, a yoke of oxen, a log chain, and an axe; and some have little or no property at all but their axe alone. The family generally consists of a man and his wife, and a number of young children, unable to hire hands; the whole of the labour naturally devolves upon the man, and hence it is, that for six or seven years, till such time as the roots of the timber begin to rot in the ground, so that he can use the plough, and until the eldest of his children grows up to help him, his toil is incessant; four or five acres are all that he is able to clear and sow in a season, and that is generally put in so late, that it produces but little; so that the whole of his crop will scarcely support him through the year; but many times he has to work out for a part of his bread. Clothes he must have for himself and his family, and these must be got out of the store; and merchant's goods are very dear in this province; and as he hath nothing to pay with, he is obliged to go on credit. These in a few years soon run up high, so that by the time he gets his farm in such a state of improvement, as might enable him to live comfortable, he is frequently obliged to sell it, in order to pay off his debts. Such is the consequence of beginning poor. But this, you will observe, is only the gloomy side of things; for those who are so fortunate as to weather out the storm the first ten years, without sinking their plantations, are generally enabled to spend the remainder of their days in comfort. The scarcity of labourers, and the very high price of labour, so that the produce will scarcely pay the hands, forms another hindrance to the improvement of our township, and the province at large. Another hindrance is, that in many places of this province, large tracts of land have been granted to certain individuals, and these being generally men of fortune, are under no necessity of selling their lands, but hold them at so high a price, that poor people are not able to buy them; again, there are many of these gentlemen gone out of the province, so that there is no opportunity to purchase from them; so it still remains a wilderness, and the poor people who are settled round such tracts, have roads to make, and every other public duty to perform, at their own expence, which greatly enhances the value of such land, to the great injury of the inhabitants.

Another hindrance respecting our township, is that a great number of lots are reserved for the crown and the clergy, and notwithstanding that these lots might be rented for 21 years, for a very small sum of money, yet the land, in this province, has hitherto been so plenty and cheap, that no one cares for renting land, who can have it in fee simple: hence it is, that the greater number of them still remain unsettled; but when settlers become numerous, this evil will soon be done away.

What, in our opinion, would most contribute to the improvement of our township and the province at large, would be to encourage men of property into the country, to purchase the waste lands of our province, which if sold even at a moderate price, would introduce such a flow of capital into our province, as would not only encourage a respectable race of settlers of every description, to come in and cultivate the face of the country, and turn the wilderness into fruitful fields, but it would also make trade and manufactures of all kinds flourish; then would our province no longer remain poor, neglected, and unknown to the rest of the world; but would become a respectable colony, not only able to support herself, but she would add a large revenue to the British Crown and her redundancies would contribute to feed the hungry, and clothe the poor of other nations.

Sir,
We have also seen your second address* with your additional query, which we answer as follows:

32d.   We know of none in Upper Canada, whom we would sooner trust to publish the statistics of our province than yourself.

We are willing therefore to trust the whole to your own veracity, and may the highest success crown your labours.

---

* Owing to an opposition set up immediately after the publication of my first address to the resident landholders, I conferred with some magistrates as to what should be done, and it was resolved to publish a letter, desiring the township reports to be sent in to one of these magistrates, to be made use of by him and the other magistrates as they thought proper; while, at the same time, I put a question to the people as to their confidence in me. The letter, after getting out of my hands, was altered, and caused the reports to be still directed to me. In many of the reports similar additions were added to the regular replies in the same way as here quoted, together with compliments and good wishes. These, however, I have withheld, allowing this report only to go in full, as a specimen. — R. G.

It is true, we have seen a parcel of heterogeneous stuff in the Niagara Spectator pointed against your plan, which, like the Palace of Vanity, appears to have no foundation, and like it too shall vanish into air; yes, into thin air, and leave not a trace behind.

Indeed, such ill timed jargon, quite unsupported by reason, will only serve to urge the business on more rapidly; and here, Sir, is a striking proof, for it has reminded us at the end of our work of what we should have done at the beginning, namely, to jointly offer you our warmest thanks for the strenuous efforts you have made, and the spirit of benevolence you have displayed in endeavouring to promote the prosperity of our province, and the happiness of our fellow subjects.

(Signed)

JAMES M'BRIDE, J.P.
DANIEL MUNN.
CHARLES BIGGER.
DUNCAN M'QUEEN.
ABSALOM SMITH.
JAMES BIGGER.
JAMES HOPPER.
LAWRENCE HAGER.

AMOS BIGGER.
MICHAEL BUCK.
TIMOTHY ROBINS.
JAMES THOMPSON.
BENJAMIN SMITH.
NATHANIEL CORNWAL.
HENRY LOUCKS.
JOSEPH SMITH.

Nelson.

To MR. ROBERT GOURLAY.
SIR,
HAVING observed in the public papers your address to the resident land owners of Upper Canada, we avail ourselves of the present opportunity, as a proof of our high approbation of your plan, to communicate, with a statistic of this township, our acknowledgment, for the interest you take in the colonial and agricultural improvement of this infant country. We flatter ourselves, from the nature of the subject, in which public and private interest are so nearly connected, that it will not fail producing the desired effect. If the annexed statement will be in any manner subservient to your purposes, you are at liberty to make use of the same.

3d.   Two itinerant professional Methodist preachers*.

---

* I presume these may be the same noticed in Trafalgar Report; but, having doubt, I enter one Methodist preacher in the Table for this Township. – R.G.

9th. The soil is generally clay, suitable for winter grain and grass, gradually descending to the south.

10th. The kinds of timber are, white oak, red oak, white pine, maple, hickory, basswood, black and white ash, and a small quantity of some other kinds.

12th. There are lime and freestone for building, which may be had for 5s. per toise at the quarry.

15th. Blacksmiths commonly charge 7½d per lb. for working iron, which sells also for 7½d. per lb.

21st. The ordinary time of turning out beasts to pasture, is the first of May, and of taking them home into the yard or stable, 1st of December.

22d. The ordinary endurance of the sleighing season, is from the 1st of January to the 15th of March, and the ordinary time to commence ploughing in the spring, is the 1st of May.

23d. The ordinary season for sowing wheat, is the first week in September, and of reaping it the first week in August.

25th. One cow will produce 4lb. of butter per week during pasturing.

26th. The ordinary course of cropping on new lands, is to sow wheat the first year; the second, seed it with grass; and the fourth year, plough it up for fallow: autumn is the time for manuring.

27th. Land is let on shares to a small extent, for which the owner receives one-third of the produce.

28th. The present price of a farm with 30 acres improvement, 2l. 10s. per acre.

29th. There are 1,500 acres of land for sale.

30th. Public roads are capable of much improvement, at a moderate expense; there can be no improvement of water conveyances by canals or locks.

31st. The impediments to the improvement of our township are two, many crown and clergy reserved lots, and the want of mechanics of all kinds. There is a large tract of wild land adjoining us, owned by the native Indians; if the assistance of government could be had in procuring this land*, and sending settlers of an enterprising disposition upon it, it would contribute much to the improvement of our situation. As it respects the province in general, we are induced to believe that men of capital with a

---

* It has since been purchased by government, and is now settling. Much of it is excellent land. – R.G.

sufficient proportion of hands would contribute to the improvement of the same.

We have the honour to be,

Sir,

Your most obedient humble servants,

THOMAS ATKINSON.   MOSES M'CAY.
GEORGE GRAME.   NATHANIEL BELL.
WILLIAM CHISHOLM.   HECTOR G. TAYLOR.
DANIEL O'REILLEY.

Wellington Square.

MR. ROBERT GOURLAY.

SIR,

WE, the inhabitants of Wellington Square, being settlers on a tract of land granted to the late Captain Brant, for his military services; and being also part of the township of Nelson, having met in order to answer the questions you have stated, the result of which we transmit to you, in hopes that it may be some assistance towards accomplishing the plan you have undertaken.

9th. The soil is variable; on the front, near the lake, it is sandy; on the rear it inclines more to a clay; for about two miles from the lake it is level, and then rises into ridges, and more uneven land.

10th. The timber consists of white pine, oak, hickory, ash, sugar maple, and most kinds of hard wood.

11th. There is no kind of mineral except limestone, which is in great plenty, and which is made use of for building. There is no price set, as every one gets what he likes by quarrying them.

16th. Women, for spinning, 7s. 6d. per week.

17th. The price of mowing grass for hay is 3s. 9d. per day.

19th. A fat sheep in the summer season will fetch 1l. 5s.

25th. A good milch cow, in the course of the summer, will produce 100lbs. of butter, and as much cheese.

30th. Roads in general are not in a good state of improvement, owing in part to the large proportion of reserved lands: this compels the inhabitants to do that much statute labour more than they would do if the whole was settled.

In many parts of the province large tracts are owned by private gentlemen, many of whom are non-residents in the country: in those townships there are but few settlers, and the roads in a bad state.

31st. The reason that the province has not improved more since the first settlement is in part owing to the inhabitants wanting the means of assisting themselves more than they were capable of doing by manual labour; and the damage they sustained during the late war, has added much to their disadvantage.

Wellington Square,
21st November, 1817.

(Signed)   JOHN BRANT,
AUGUSTUS BATES,
ASAHEL DAVIS,
THOMAS GHENT,
JAMES MORDEN,
RALPH MORDEN,
NICHOLAS KERN.

East Flamboro'.

At a Meeting of a few of the Inhabitants of the Township of East Flamboro', held in pursuance of a public Notice at the House of Mr. Alexander Brown, 22d November, 1817, for the Purpose of taking the Address of Mr. Robert Gourlay into Consideration, and answering the Queries by him proposed, at which Meeting, George Chisholm, Jun. was chosen Chairman, and Alexander Brown, Secretary.

9th.   The soil is generally good.

10th.   All kinds of timber, black walnut excepted.

11th.   None.   12th. Limestone in great plenty.

14th.   Lime is burnt only in small quantities.

15th.   Blacksmith's wages, 7½d. per lb. for iron.

16th.   Wages of common labourers, from 1l. 10s. to 4l. per month.

17th.   Mowing grass, and harvesting, from 3s. 6d. to 7s. 6d. per day.

26th.   On new land the first crop is wheat, and then grass. Fruit of almost all kinds common to this country grows here.

27th.   No land is rented on shares.

28th.   Cleared land sells from 2l. 10s. to 7l. 10s. per acre.

29th.   A great quantity of land now for sale.

30th.   Roads generally good: capable of improvement.

31st.   At the first settlement of this township, the land was chiefly granted to gentlemen for their military services.   The situation being eligible, they hold it at a high price, and for want of capital, few persons are able to purchase it, which is the reason of its remaining uncultivated.

We are, Sir, with due respect,

Your most obedient, humble Servants,

GEO. CHISHOLM, ESQ.
ALEXANDER BROWN,
GEO. CHISHOLM, JUN.
JOHN M'CARTEY.

West Flamboro' and Beverly.

At a numerous Meeting of the Inhabitants of West Flamboro' and Beverly, held in pursuance of a Public Notice, at Matthews's Tavern, in West Flamboro', on Monday the 1st of December, 1817, for the Purpose of taking the Address of Mr. Robert Gourlay into Consideration, and answering the Queries by him proposed. At which Richard Hatt, Esq. was chosen Chairman, and James Crooks, Esq. Secretary.

3d.   No Episcopal church or public place of worship in either township, or any resident minister, though we are sometimes visited by the resident clergyman of Ancaster, and by Methodist preachers regularly attended every Sunday at private houses. The Tunkers also have divine service regularly performed.

8th.   Two carding machines, charge 6d. per lb. One fulling mill. One oil mill.

9th.   The soil of Beverly, rich loam, and intervals; West Flamboro' the same; both very healthy and pleasantly diversified with hill and dale; are well watered with spring streams.

10th.   White oak, red oak, pine, chestnut, sugar maple, beech, basswood, elm, hickory, black walnut, butternut, cedar, cherry, mulberry, plums, and crab apple trees.

11th.   Salt springs, and indications of iron ore, as yet but little explored. Plaster of Paris and marl are found in these townships.

12th.   Limestone abounds, and some freestone, both of very good quality for building; the expence of labour in quarrying being the only one.

16th.   Wages of labourers from 1l. 10s. to 4l. 10s. per month.

24th. We generally sow one to one and a half bushel of wheat per acre, and get in return from 12 to 40 bushels per acre; average crop about 16 bushels per acre.

25th. Quality of pasture, clover, and Timothy; white clover springs up naturally after clearing. Our young cattle and cows generally run out till after harvest, then we put them into our folds.

26th. On new lands we generally harrow in wheat first, then seed down with grass, or plough, sow oats, or plant Indian corn, then pease and wheat again; or fallowing, sow wheat, then rye, and a succession of spring crops. Very little land has yet been manured, and that generally orchards, and ground for flax and Indian corn. Our orchards produce apples, pears, peaches, nectarines, apricots, plums, and cherries. Gooseberries and currants are the natural productions of this country. We generally cultivate our orchards in grain, which produces us large crops; such is the genial nature of our climate.

27th. The ordinary mode of renting land is on shares. Landlord furnishes lands fenced, team, utensils, and half the seed; for which the tenant returns half the produce in the bushel. Tenant feeds himself: or landlord furnishes only land fenced; gets one-third in the bushel; tenant finding team, seed, utensils, and feeds himself: lands are always to be obtained on these terms.

28th. Wild lands at first settling, sold for 10l. per lot of 200 acres; and now sells from 10s. to 1l. 10s. and 2l. per acre. Cleared land sells from 2l. to 12l. 10s. per acre, according to its situation and advantages. A farm house may be built of logs for 25l.; frame house, 75l. to 250l.; a good frame barn, 125l.

29th. Much land is for sale in these townships, and if a good price is offered, scarcely any farmer will refuse to sell his improved farm.

30th. Our roads are tolerably good, and are improving; they are yet capable of much improvement. We consider the water communication of these townships not much improvable by can-alling, the ground being too high. We have at present a very flourishing village, increasing fast, in West Flamboro', on the head waters of Lake Ontario.

31st. The remainder of these townships, that is, the uncultivated lots, are in the hands of persons not resident in the province, or in the hands of such residents in Canada, who keep them – asking high prices: depending on the industry of the inhabitant settlers for making roads, and improving their own lands, by which means the unsettled lots become valuable enough in time to bring the high prices demanded for them. With respect to the province in general, could some other mode be devised, to dispose of the vacant lands of the crown, or part of them, rather by selling them, than granting them in the present mode, it would, no doubt, not only bring capital into Canada, to make purchases, but it would also beget a further interest in the purchasers, to bring in useful settlers, as well those with property, as those wanted for clearing the lands, and handicraft tradesmen. It would settle the country with a yeomanry, who in times requiring soldiers, would no doubt be found such as were wanted; besides procuring a fund to the crown for its lands, which at present appear to produce little or nothing. Under such policy, we think Canada would immediately shew another face; and would, we presume, improve full as fast as we have seen the country opposite to us in the United States; our natural advantages being infinitely superior to those enjoyed by the citizens of that country.

RICHARD HATT, *Chairman.*

JAMES CROOKS, *Secretary.*

Names of persons present.

WILLIAM HARE, J. P.
JAMES DURAND,
JACOB COCHENOUR,
JAMES M'BRYDE, J. P.
CONRADT COPE,
HENRY COPE,
WM. NEVILLS,
ROSWELL MATHEWS,
ANDREW JONES,
JACOB NEVILLS,
JOHN KEAGY, Jun.
ANDW. VAN EVERY,
BARNARD EMERY,
MOSES CORNELL,
GAB. CORNELL,
WM. SHACKELTON,
BENJAMIN MARKLE,
SAMUEL CORNELL.
H. LYONS,
JOHN HEAGY.

Nichol.

TO ROBERT GOURLAY, ESQ.

Niagara Falls, Nov. 18th, 1817.

SIR,

HAVING seen in the Upper Canada Gazette your address to the resident land-owners of the province, and it appearing to us that should your views of publishing a Statistical Account of Upper Canada be carried into effect, it will be of much benefit not only to the province, but also to our mother country, we therefore take upon ourselves to answer your queries as far as relates to the township of Nichol, in the district of Gore, we being the proprietors of that township.

This township is a part of the tract of land given by Governor-General Sir Frederick Haldimand in 1784 to the Six Nation Indians who had adhered to the British standard in the former American war, as a residence, and in compensation for the lands they had left in the United States. This tract commences at the mouth of the Grand river, where it empties into lake Erie, and extends about ninety miles up stream, being twelve miles deep, that is six miles on each side of the river. This extensive tract of country was originally intended as a residence for the Indians and their posterity, as also to serve them for hunting ground – for which purposes it answered very well for many years; and until the advancement of the settlements of white people on both sides of this tract drove away and destroyed the game in such a measure, that the Indians could no longer subsist themselves by their usual mode of hunting; in consequence of which the government permitted the Indians to dispose of a certain part of this land to individuals at as good a price as could be got for it; the principal sum being placed in the hands of trustees, who annually pay the interest to the Indians. About 356,000 acres were accordingly sold in different parcels, the first part of which is at the east side of the mouth of the river, and is about 53,000 acres, called the township of Wedderburn and Canbury. The next part, a parcel of about 94,000 acres, about 60 miles from the mouth of the river, now called the township of Dumfries, which is 12 miles square, extending six miles of each side of the river. The next parcel is of about the same size, and immediately joining the last, now called the township of Waterloo; and adjoining this last, and immediately above, is a tract of about 86,000 acres, now called the township of Woolwich; adjoining to, and immediately above, is the township of Nichol, extending six miles on each side of the river by nearly four miles up stream, containing about 29,000 acres; is situated in about 34 miles in a north-west course from the west end of lake Ontario, and is about 44 miles distant from the west end of that lake by the road which is at present travelled. This township was granted to Thomas Clark, one of the subscribers by deed from government, under the great seal of the province, in April, 1807, in which no settlement has as yet been attempted, and this owing to the proprietors, from their other avocations, not having had time to attend to it. They are, however, now taking steps to have it laid out into 200 acre lots, in the course of the ensuing winter, the outside lines being only as yet marked out.

The soil of this township is of an excellent quality, as the size and growth of the trees indicate. It is a deep, black, sandy loam, with abundance of spring brooks in all directions. There are no hills or other very high land; the surface in general level, with a gentle declivity towards the river on both sides. The prevalent timber is maple, elm, beech, white ash, basswood, black ash, and cherry. The bottoms of the brooks are gravel; but no building stones have been noticed, excepting at the river, which in the whole of its course through this township is on a limestone rock. The land of this township originally cost 4s. per acre, and is expected, so soon as laid out into farm lots, to sell for from two to four dollars, according to situations. To this township there is now a good road from the head of lake Ontario through the townships of Flamboro' West, Dumfries, Waterloo, and part of Woolwich, to within seven miles of its lowest boundary, which seven miles of road is intended to be made this ensuing winter. At about half a mile above the lower boundary line of this township are the falls of the Grand river, of about 40 feet high, where the river is about 60 yards wide, and navigable for boats or rafts from below the falls to the mouth of the river. These falls are admirably situated for mills or any other machinery, to which purposes it is expected they will soon be applied.

Having already said what has hitherto retarded the improvement of this township, we come now to say what, in our opinion, retards the settlement of the province in general, and for which we see many reasons; the first of which is the want of emigration, which has hitherto been but small; and this, diminished by the difficulties which emigrants from the United Kingdom are in general subject to after their arrival at Quebec, a distance of 500 miles from hence, where, and at Montreal, and at other places on their way hither, there is no agent or person to whom they can apply for advice or assistance in getting to York in this province, where the land-granting department sits. The next reason is, that when such of the emigrants as get as far as York, where also there is no agent, there is much delay and difficulty in getting a grant of any land, owing to which causes many get dissatisfied even before they reach this province, and go off to the United States, where they purchase land, if able, at from five to ten dollars per acre, and get a good title without difficulty. Those emigrants who persevere and dance attendance at York for a length of time, at last get a grant of 100 acres, upon paying £   sterling, in some remote and insulated situation, many miles from any Christian inhabitant, where he is destitute of society, roads, mills, and every other comfort, which to a European is worse than Botany Bay: in consequence of which, many of them never settle upon their locations, which, by the bye, are too small for a farm, so much of the land having to remain uncultivated for supplying fuel, fencing, and building timber; and many cannot undergo the fatigue of finding them out. Most of those who hunt out their lots being too poor to purchase near a settlement, find themselves so immersed in woods and wilds, that they often get discouraged, and leave their habitations, if able, having little prospect of ever getting neighbours to assist them in making roads, bridges, mills and other public works, owing to so much of the adjoining lands being reserved for the crown, clergy, and other purposes, and by large tracts being given to non-residents for favour or past services, who have no idea of settling the land, but of disposing of it when the labour of a few adjoining individuals may have made it more valuable; and we have further to remark as our opinion, that this province even in its oldest settled townships is by far too thinly peopled, owing to these reserves and grants to non-residents; and this was severely felt during the late war, when provisions and transport could not be had for the king's troops; besides this, our neighbours the Americans were perfectly aware of the situation of the country, having furnished many of their regiments who invaded the province with maps of the different townships, specifying the reserved and vacant lots which were promised to the American soldiery as a bounty, if they conquered the country.

We next think that it would tend much to the improvement of this province, were all the townships already surveyed to be filled up with actual settlers previous to any more remote lands being laid out for location, which would form a compact and strong colony, at present there not being one-twentieth part of the land settled that is laid out into townships.

We have further to remark, that we think it would be of much benefit to the province, as also a relief to the mother country, were all the ungranted lands in the already surveyed townships sold at a moderate price per acre; when emigrants and others could select soil, situation, and neighbours, to their mind, for which they would far rather pay than go to the wilderness by lottery: the fund thereby raised could be well applied to the improvement of the internal navigation of the province and other public purposes, as also help to relieve many of the claimants who suffered losses during the late war.

It is a general idea, that a less sum than was expended in building ships of war on lake Ontario, during the late war, would have made a canal to have brought sloops of war and small frigates into that lake from the sea.

Many well-informed people of this province think that the door being shut at the end of the late war against emigration hither from the United States was of much injury to the improvement of the country. On this head we decline giving our opinion; but think that many valuable settlers would have been obtained from the United States, had these been admitted under proper restrictions.

This province, if properly peopled, under good laws well administered, will defend itself against any invasion, and its trade be of much benefit to Great Britain: if settled in its present thin and scattered state, its trade can be of little consequence, and the country must fall a prey to its first invader.

May your laudable exertions, in traversing this province to collect information, be the means of making this country better known in Britain, and of procuring from thence some of its redundant population, so much wanted in this colony.

We have the honour to be,

Sir,

Your very obedient Servants,

THOMAS CLARK,
ROBERT ADDISON,

For Self and Robert Nichol, Esq.

Waterloo.

By the undersigned Gentlemen, respectable Inhabitants of said Township, at a Meeting convened for that Purpose.

3d.   No churches, two Tunkers and Menonists preachers (the people are principally Germans).

8th.   Carding wool 6½d. per pound.

9th.   Sand, loam, and clay, good and productive; generally level and well watered.

10th.   Pine, oak, sugar maple, beech, cherry, cypress, &c.

11th.   None discovered, but many signs of iron; limestone in great quantities. Signs of plaster; indications of salt springs: no remarkable springs.

12th. Building stones in great plenty: no price.

20th. Township produces 3000 pounds of wool per annum; 2s. 6d. per pound.

26th. The general rule is, if a man clears wild land, he has the first year's produce. Cropping on cultivated land, a man gets half, and finds himself.

27th. The same as above; extent very great.

30th. Roads very bad, but capable of great improvement: will require great expence.

What hinders the improvement of the township, is, bad roads, want of men and money. Respecting water conveyance; the beautiful Grand river running nearly through the middle of the township, affords a most fascinating prospect to adventure. Capitalists might hereafter form a canal, the whole extent of the river.

JOSEPH LOCKWOOD.
JAMES VAN EVERY.
JACOB ERB.
ABRAHAM ERB,
And seven others.

Dumfries.

SIR,

INCLOSED I send you an account of the progress of the settlement of the township of Dumfries, with answers to a few of your queries. The remainder, no doubt, will be answered by persons longer resident in the country, who are more adequate to the task.

9th. The soil in general is loam; very little clay to be found in the township.

10th. The kinds of timber are, oak, hard maple, beech, basswood, elm, and cherry in some parts of the township. Others are chestnut, cedar, and pine, with considerable of the before mentioned kinds intermixed. Limestone in abundance.

11th. One bed of plaster has been discovered in Dumfries, and proves to be the best kind for cementing; also for manure, none is superior. One ton, when ground, will make from 26 to 28 bushels; one bushel is sufficient for an acre. It is known by experience, that on clover, wheat, oats, or potatoes, it will bring 1/3 more than the land without plaster; it can be had for 30s. per ton at the quarry.

31st. As respects the progress of the settlement of the country, in my opinion many things combine to retard it. In the first place, there is certain quantities of land in each township, called crown and clergy reserves, nearly one-fourth. Combined with that, there are many gentlemen owning large tracts of land unsettled. This causes the settlements in Canada to be very much scattered, in consequence of which, little work is done on the roads, and in some parts where a trifling labour would make it good. Could some plan be formed, to settle the country more compact, and also to make good roads through such lands as are the property of gentlemen at home, not wishing to sell them, would, in my opinion, add much to the progress of the settlements.

There also is a want of enterprise. The minds of the people want rousing up: they only want to be made sensible that their country possesses as many (if not more) natural advantages than any part of North America.

The soil is good, and the means of conveyance to market, connecting sleighing and water carriage, is easy. The only necessary requisite is industry and enterprise.

Your's truly,
ABSALOM SHADE.

MR. ROBERT GOURLAY,
    Queenston.

Haldimand.

At a Meeting of the principal Inhabitants of the Township of Haldimand, in the County of Wentworth, and District of Gore, in the Province of Upper Canada, including the Chiefs of the Five Nations of Indians, held at the House of Frederick Yeoward, Merchant, in Mount Pleasant, in said Township, on Thursday, the 11th of December, 1817, for the Purpose of taking into Consideration the Queries proposed by Robert Gourlay, Esq. and of giving Answers thereto, to enable him to prepare a Statistical Account of Upper Canada. – F. Yeoward being called to the Chair, the following were adopted as Answers to the Queries proposed, and were directed to be forwarded by the Chairman, to the said Robert Gourlay, Esq. viz.

1st. Haldimand – its length is estimated at about twenty miles, commencing at Dundas street, and its breadth twelve miles, that is, according to the original grant, extending six miles from each side of the Grand river, or river Ouse.

2d.   Settled in the year 1783, by Captain Joseph Brant, with the Five Nations of Indians, and a few volunteer white people. The population of the white inhabitants is supposed to be 430; people of colour 30, and the number of the whole of the Five Nations about 1800, residing on the Grand river; the number of inhabited houses supposed to be sixty, exclusive of Indian dwellings.

3d.   One established church, with a clergyman attending occasionally.

8th.   The price of boards, for 100 feet, one inch stuff, 3s. 9d.; one carding machine; rate of carding wool, 5d. per lb.; one fulling mill.

9th.   The land is composed of a variety of soil, generally of sandy loam, and much very fertile.

10th.   The kinds of timber are various, and consist of white oak, white pine, sugar maple, beech, black oak, red oak, elm, basswood, ash, butternut, or white walnut, hickory, wild cherry, black walnut, chestnut.

11th.   Plaster of Paris in abundance, and of a good quality; also salt springs, equal to those of Onandagua, and which, if worked, would supply the upper part of the province at about 17s. 6d. per barrel. Limestone in considerable quantities.

12th.   No building stones have as yet been discovered.

15th.   Wages of blacksmiths for the working of iron for husbandry uses, are 7½d. per lb.

18th.   The cost of clearing and fencing 5 acres of woodland, per contract, is estimated at 15l.; but great part of this township consists of plane lands, the expence of clearing and fencing which is trifling, and estimated at 7l. 10s.; board not included.

26th.   New lands are generally put in with winter wheat, and seeded down with Timothy and clover, in which they will continue from 3 to 5 years; and when broken up again, will produce either wheat, rye, or oats; but are usually put in with wheat. The usual way of putting in grain on the plains, is by ploughing and harrowing, and on timbered lands the first crops are only harrowed in.

27th.   Land cultivated on shares, is generally let for one-third of the produce of grain and hay. The grain for seed, and team, and all expences of management, are usually found and paid by the tenants. In this township, not much land let on shares.

28th.   The land within this township is granted by government to the Five Nations of Indians; some part of the same being leased by their late agent, Captain Joseph Brant, to the present white settlers, for the term of 999 years, at 7s. 6d. per acre, for the whole of that period.

29th.   No land for sale, but leases for 21 years may yet be obtained from the Indians, on very moderate terms.

TABLE,

Shewing the Beginning and Progress of Dumfries Settlement.

Names of Settlers.	Number in Family.	Date of taking Possession.	Bushels of Grain sown Autumn, 1817.	Total No. of Acres cleared and chopped up to the end of Nov., 1817.	No. of Horses.	Number of Cows.	Number of Oxen.
Wm. Vanevry.........	4	March, 1817.	8 W.	8	1	2	2
Michael Vanevry ...	3	March, 1817.	5 W.	6	0	1	2
L. Sichermerholm ...	3	March, 1817.	8 W.	9	0	1	0
Cornelius Conner ...	7	December, 1816.	5 W.	10	1	2	0
Samuel Muma	6	March, 1817.	11 W.	20	0	1	0
John Pettit............	9	June, 1817.	9 R.	2	2	3	0
R. Phillips ....••	8	August, 1816.	......	40	3	3	0
John Scott ....••	3	May, 1817.	1½ W. 1½ R.	12	0	1	0
Isaac Shaver	3	March, 1817.	12½ W.	15	1	2	0.
John Chambers	3	December, 1816.	6 W.	15	1	2	0
Thomas Laurison ...	1	May, 1817.	......	2	0	1	0
Miller Laurison......	9	May, 1817.	23¼ W.	25	2	3	2
John Laurison ...••	4	May, 1817.	15½ W.	20	0	4	2
Enos Griffeth	7	December, 1816.	13 W.	23	2	3	0
Ephraim Munson ...	7	May, 1817.	4 W.	9	2	3	2
Niel Mc Mullen......	6	July, 1817.	......	7	0	2	0
Gutlip Mort	5	May, 1817.	5 W.	6	0	2	2
William Rosebrugh .	7	December, 1816.	......	½	0	3	2
William Mc Kenkie .	1	June, 1817.	5 W.	6	0	0	0
John Buchannan ..	3	May, 1817.	5 W.	10	0	2	2
Totals, 20.	99	....	127¼ W. 10½ R.	245½	15	41	16

In column fourth of the above Table, W. stands for wheat, and R. for rye. In the same column the number of bushels may also be taken for the number of acres sown. The word chopped, used in column fifth, means when all the timber is cut down, and in pieces ready for burning. Some of this township is plain, which may account for some of the settlers having so large an extent chopped and cleared in so short a time. The original Table contained 16 more settlers; but those exhibited are sufficient for the purpose.

30th. State of roads is generally good, but capable of improvement, at a small expence. The Grand river, or Ouse, is at present navigable for rafts for a considerable distance above this township, down to its confluence with lake Erie, and a great part of this extent may be navigated with boats and vessels of considerable burden; which water conveyance might be much further obtained, extended and improved by widening and deepening the river in certain places.

31st. The Indians possessing the fee of the township, as tenants in-tail only (and not in fee simple) prevents them from alienating lands, and of consequence, retards its improvement.

Signed, in behalf of the Meeting, by
FREDERICK YEOWARD.

Ancaster.

29th November, 1817.

At a Meeting of the Inhabitants of the Township of Ancaster, convened by public Notice, at Newton's Hotel, in the Village of Ancaster, this Day, James Durand, Esq. Member for the County of Wentworth, was called to the Chair, and Mr. John Wilson, of Ancaster, chosen Secretary.

FIRST

Resolved, That this meeting do highly approve of the plan proposed by Mr. Robert Gourlay, of publishing a Statistical Account of this Province, and most cordially agree with him on the subject matter of his address to the resident land owners of Upper Canada; the remarks contained in which, as far as they respect the resources of the county, being, to their knowledge, from actual experience, correct, and capable of realization, by all who possess the qualification of industry, and the means for making the experiment.

SECONDLY.

Resolved, – That the inhabitants of this township would rejoice in the opportunity of receiving into their society, a respectable emigration of their fellow subjects from the mother country, and in furtherance of that object, and with a sincere desire of disseminating an accurate account of the country and its productions, do now proceed to reply to the queries of Mr. Gourlay, in the order they are proposed by him.

3d. No Episcopal church; one Methodist meeting house; one resident episcopal minister.

8th. One carding machine; charge 6d. per lb.; one fulling mill.

9th. The soil, a sandy loam, in part; rich interval in part, and some clay loam. The face of the township is pleasantly diversified with hill and dale, and some plains.

10th. Timber – White oak, white pine, red and black oak, chestnut, beech, sugar maple, black ash, white ash, elm, basswood or linden, hickory, butternut, birch, ironwood, sassafrass, dogwood, black walnut, cherry, swamp oak, aspin tree, soft maple, hemlock, tamarack, tamarisk, or turmerick, balm of Gilead, buttonwood, cedar, willow, black and white thorn, crabtree and wild plum; also various kinds of shrubs and vines, among which are black and spotted alder, boortree or elder, sumach, hazel, sloe, blackberry, dewberry, gooseberry, brown and red raspberry, wild current, whortleberry, mountainberry, tall cranberry, choke cherry, blue grape, bitter, sweet, strawberry, &c.

11th. Salt springs – One chalybeate spring: strong indications of iron, and some trifling indications of lead; but none of these have been explored.

12th. Limestone and freestone, both of excellent quality, and in great abundance; price 2½ dollars per toise at the quarry.

16th. Wages – Labourers, from 11.10s. to 4l.10s. per month.

24th. Sown on new land ¾ to 1¼, on old land 1 to 1½, and reap from 12 to 20 bushels per acre: – 16 bushels per acre considered an average crop.

26th. On new lands, generally harrow in wheat first, then seed down to grass, or plough and sow oats, or plant maize or Indian corn, then pease, then wheat, or fallow sowing wheat, then rye, then a succession of spring crops.

Very little land has as yet been manured, and when manure is used, it is chiefly for flax and Indian corn.

27th. The usual mode of letting land, is on shares. The landlord furnishes land fenced, team, and half the seed, and receives half the produce, tenant finding himself; or landlord furnishes land fenced, and receives one third, the tenant finding team, and every thing else; farms are almost always to be obtained at these lays.

28th. Wild lands, at the first settling of this township, sold at 6l. 5s. per lot of 200 acres; now sells at 12s. 6d. to 1l. 10s. and 5l. per acre. Cleared lands sell from 2l. 10s. to 12l. 10s. per acre, according to the situation and advantages. A tolerable farm house may be built at 125l. to 250l.; a good frame barn at 125l.

29th. Any lands, and in fact, all lands in this township, may be purchased; it consists of about 200 lots.

30th. State of public roads – middling; may be very much improved by the statute labour of the inhabitants as imposed by law, if honestly applied.

31st. Want of capital and enterprise, are doubtless the greatest causes that have contributed to retard the improvement of this township. The *former* has of late years made small efforts, accompanied by the *latter*, and the consequences may be seen in neat villages rising, where a few scattered cottages were before only to be found. Together with grist and saw mills, carding machines, fulling mills, merchants' stores, sadlers' shops, tin shops, hatters' shops, shoemakers' shops, tailors' shops, joiners' shops, and other mechanical branches, all of which find full employ, and buildings are continually erecting with the profits of the farmer's toils.

A reply to the latter part of the 31st query, as to *what in our opinion, retards the improvement of the province in general*, would be more lengthy than the nature of this meeting admits of, were the subject done justice to. Briefly, however, want of capital and enterprise may be again considered as having a large share in it; for what besides, you would say, with a climate and soil so fine, and laws so excellent, could intervene to check its progress? There are, however, other causes, and those causes out of our power to control, even with the aid of legislative interference. It is our gracious Sovereign, and the Parliament of the United Kingdom, that can alone lay the axe to the root of these obstructions; but without the slightest feeling of murmur, or idea of right to dictate, we think it our duty to point out the road to their removal.

A large portion of the province, equal in every respect, in point of quality, to the granted lands, still lays locked up in the shape of Crown and Clergy reserves, in almost every township, commonly two-sevenths of the township, and these interspersed as a *caput mortuum* amidst the settlements, tend largely to check the improvement of roads, added to the extensive tracts of land formerly granted to individuals, many of whom reside across the Atlantic, and contribute nothing to the means of the province. Besides these, there are whole townships shut up, as reserves for schools, and beautiful tracts of first rate lands, of almost immeasurable extent, immediately in rear of all the settlements, remain in a desert state.

Occasionally, a township is surveyed off, and given out. This important gift and patronage, is vested in the hands of the Administrator for the time being, and the Executive Council, – is acted upon with a slow motion, producing little manifest improvement to the province, – no visible invitation to men of capital, yielding no benefit to the mother country, or restitution of her great expences here: whereas, the reverse would be the undoubted result, were these tracts settled; whilst, at present, they operate as a dark and shady cloud, keeping off the genial rays of the sun, and now and then affording only a trifling emolument, as fees, to a few individuals, instead of the abundant harvests of the necessaries of life.

To remedy these obstructions (or shall we call them evils) to the improvement of the province, all that is wanting is, for the Crown to dispose of those lands, impartially, to the highest bidder, that they may be immediately settled, without waiting the tardy movements of a land-granting department: then, indeed, there would be room for the redundant population of Great Britain, an ample field for capitalists, and the exercise of enterprising spirits, and an opening to cement upon a large scale that connexion with the mother country, which (to use your own words) 'Would cause the idea of invasion to wither before its strength.' The munificent bounty of the Crown might still be employed in Canada, in making roads, improving the *navigation*, and other projects to which the geographical figure of Canada offers every invitation.

(Signed)

JAMES DURAND, *Chairman.*
JOHN WILSON, *Secretary.*
RICHARD HATT,
WM. RYMAL,
CHRIST, ALMOS,
JACOB RYMAL,
ELIJAH SECORD,
MATTHEW CROOKS,
PETER HOGEBOOM,

CONRADT FILMAN,
JOSEFH HOUSE,
JOHN AIKMAN,
DANIEL SHOWERS,
WILLIAM CLINTON,
PETER BAWTINHEYMER,
LOT TISDALE,
WM. TISDALE,
AND SIXTY-EIGHT OTHERS.

Barton.

At a Meeting of a Number of respectable Free-holders, convened at the House of Samuel Price, Innkeeper, in the Town of Hamilton, District of Gore, on Wednesday the 17th Day of December, 1817, for the Purpose of taking into Consideration the Queries offered to the Public by Robert Gourlay, Esq. relative to the Agricultural Interest of the Province, Richard Beasley, Esq. was chosen Chairman, and William B. Peters, Esq. Secretary to the said Meeting.

9th. Under the mountain from the front to the third concession almost altogether a sandy soil. On the mountain generally clay, with a slight mixture of loam.

10th. White oak, black oak, and pine, maple, hickory, beech, dry ash, black walnut, close under, and on the top of the mountain.

11th. Coal, none. What is called the mountain, composed of limestone, with a very little freestone, runs lengthways through the township; the breadth of limestone is 1¼ miles; one salt spring, yielding a trifling profit.

12th. Generally limestone, with a little freestone, at 10s. per toise.

24th. One bushel per acre, and 25 to 30 bushels on new land; and on old, cultivated land, from 16 to 20.

25th. About 100lb.

26th. Wheat first, then grass three years, then wheat to spring grain. Manure potatoes, Indian corn, pease.

27th. About 2000 acres. If landlord furnish every thing for the use of the farm, he receives two-thirds of the product. In 1792 land sold at 15d. per acre; in 1800, 5s.; in 1806, 15s.; in 1810, 1l. 10s.; in 1817, about 2l. 10s. On an average, about 5l. per acre for an improved farm of 200 acres, with small frame, or log-house and barn, and other outhouses. Improved farms have sold from 6l. 5s. to 7l. 10s. per acre.

30th. Tolerably good, and capable of much improvement at a moderate expence.

31st. The want of a cut through the beach to the lake Ontario. This concerns the district, and the upper part of the province materially, inasmuch as a safe and commodious harbour would then be found in the heart of the country, of much importance to the government in time of war, as it would lead to a safe communication across the peninsula to lake Erie. As to the causes which have retarded, and do retard, the improvement of the province in general, among the most prominent may be enumerated:

1st. The want of capital, which the establishment of a banking system would, it is conceived, in a great degree supply; and individual enterprise, which would be also much encouraged by such an establishment.

2d. Large quantities of wild land, the property of absentees, not subject to taxation.

3d. The want of a liberal and indiscriminate encouragement to emigration, by the government of the province, more particularly the exclusion of American settlers since the late war, which has deprived the country of much wealth, which numerous valuable settlers would have introduced, and still would continue to introduce, were such restraint removed.

4th. The wild lands of the crown intermixed with the settlements throughout the province, commonly called crown reserves, lying in the unimproved state they are, would, were they sold at auction by the government, not only produce large sums of money, which could be applied to useful purposes, but tend essentially to improve every part of the province.

RICHARD BEASLEY, *Chairman.*
W. B. PETERS, *Secretary.*

Saltfleet.

SIR,

10th Dec. 1817.

A MEETING of the inhabitants, householders of the aforesaid township, this day, for the purpose of taking into consideration your queries, as published in the Spectator, and the following are the answers, and are numbered agreeable to the number of queries.

There is attached to this township a long sandy beach, of at least 5½-miles, which divides between Burlington bay and the lake, of from one to four hundred yards in breadth, and has every appearance of being thrown up by the surf of the lake, and forming an excellent highway.

3d. There is one house for religious worship, built by the Methodist society, but almost ruined by the late war, and has not been repaired since. The people are of various denominations, but the Methodists are the most numerous, and are regularly supplied by itinerant and local preachers. The itinerant preachers are two in number; and here justice demands of us to say, that much is due to this succession of itinerant Methodist preachers, for the good morals, and steady habits that are observable, with so few exceptions, throughout this township; and there has never been one of any other denomination resident therein.

4th. There is not a doctor in the town, and generally but little for them to do.

9th. The soil is various; in some parts sandy; in others clay, and in others a sand and clay loam, which seems to abound most, and the whole is natural to grass; but produces excellent crops of wheat, rye, oats, and Indian corn, when well put in. The surface is generally level, from the lake to the mountain, which is from two to three miles.

10th. The whole of this township was covered with a heavy growth of pine, oak, maple, hickory, ash, linden, elm, and black walnut timber.

11th. There has no ore as yet been discovered, but in several places along the mountain, there are springs strongly impregnated with sulphur; and sulphur in entire lumps, as large as a pint measure, and in large quantities, and so pure as to answer various purposes, equal to the most refined roll brimstone. Two salt springs have also been discovered on the western side of the township, which have been worked for several years to considerable advantage, particularly during the late war; but being supplied at a cheaper rate from the United States, they are now neglected. Limestone in large quantities.

12th. Excellent building stone, and inexhaustible quantities; but from the liberality of the owners, we have not heard of any being sold.

15th. The piece work of a blacksmith, rates nearly as follows: for a good chopping axe, 12s. 6d.; for a corn or garden hoe, 5s.; for shoeing a horse, 8s. 9d.; for sharping plough irons, 1s.; for making ox, or log chains, 1s. per pound.

17th. Price of mowing grass for hay 3s. 9d. per day.

25th. The pasture is mostly white clover and Timothy grass, with considerable quantities of spear and blue grass, and some others of less note; but the former is the most esteemed for feeding cattle. Cows pastured on Timothy and clover grass, will yield the greatest quantity of milk, and is always rich and pleasant. Considerable quantities of butter are made for the market, and of a quality probably not exceeded in the province, and which now fetches 1s. 3d. per lb. Cheese is made, but in less quantities, and generally finds a ready market, at 10d. per pound.

26th. The common method of treating new land is to sow a crop of wheat in the autumn, without ploughing (which would be neither necessary nor practicable, as in a state of nature there is neither grass nor weeds to prevent the growth of grain, for the first season after clearing away the timber), and in the spring following sow Timothy or clover seed, which produces pasture after harvest, and for seven, eight, or ten succeeding years makes excellent meadow: after which time the roots of the timber being sufficiently rotted, it may be turned over with the plough; and many have raised large crops of wheat (and which seldom fails), by sowing and harrowing in the seed with one ploughing only; but the land may be worked five or six years successively to advantage, after breaking up the sod, and will need no manure; after which, to produce good crops of wheat, flax, Indian corn, or potatoes, it will require manure; but by laying the land down to grass for three or four years (it being so natural thereto), will recover its strength without any manure.

27th. But little land has hitherto been let on shares, as from the cheapness of land every industrious and prudent man can, and does, in a short time, become the proprietor of land. But in the instances where lands that are improved have been worked to the shares, the tenant, when finding all but the land, returns the landlord one-third of the products: and where the landlord finds team, wear and tear, and two-thirds of the seed, and gathers in one-half, he draws two-thirds of the products, and the tenant one-third.

28th. The price of land in this township, at the first settlement thereof, rated so low as to make it no object with many. A lot of 100 acres might be purchased for 5l. or 6l.5s., and large quantities were actually bought and sold at these prices; it has gradually rose from that time to the year 1812, since which time it seems stationary for want of purchasers. But the average price of wild land may be rated at 11.5s. per acre. A farm of about 300 acres of land, one-third of which cleared, and a comfortable house and good barn, with a bearing orchard of one or two hundred apple trees, the whole premises being in tolerable repair, may be purchased from 1000l. to 1,500l., according to the situation: A farm nearly answering to this description was actually sold for the highest sum here mentioned.

29th. It would be impossible to ascertain the quantity of lands in this township for sale; but from its extent, and the thinness of the population, and a considerable quantity being owned by non-residents, there is no doubt a great deal for sale.

30th. The roads are in a most deplorable situation, although some of the principal ones have been considerably repaired at the public expence. But should an increase of public expenditure, or diminution of revenue, prevent legislative aid, the statute labour will be insufficient to keep the best of them in repair. Much improvement might be made, and a handsome profit yielded, were companies authorized to make and keep public highways in repair; the making of which would be a most suitable employment for Europeans upon their first introduction into this province, they being better acquainted with that business than the Canadians. The grand mode of conveyance here, and through the whole province, is upon the great lakes; but were public spirit once roused, much might be effected to improve the water com-

STATISTICAL

Composed of Extracts from the Township

Names of Townships.	When Settled.	Inhabited Houses.	No. of People.	No. of Churches or Places of Worship.	No. of Preachers.	No. of Medical Practitioners.	No. of Schools.	Fees per Quarter.	No. of Stores.	No. of Taverns.	No. of Grist Mills.	No. of Saw Mills.	Prices of Bricks per 1000.	Prices of Lime per bushel.	Black-smiths per month and day.	WAGES OF		
																Carpenters p.day.	Masons per day.	Common Labourers per Annum.
								s. d.					*s. d. s. d.*			*s. d. s. d.*		*£ s.*
Trafalgar.....	1807	97	548	0	2 M.	0	3	10 10	0	4	1	4	30 0	0	..	..	5 0	25 0
Nelson ..	1807	68	476	0	1 M.	1	2	12 6	1	3	2	3	24 0	0 9	..	..	7 6	31 5
Wellington Square, part of Nelson	1802	16	..	0	0	1	1	15 0	1	1	0	0	..	0 7½	..	10 0	8 3	25 0
East Flamboro	..	38	..	0	0		2	..	0	0	1	2	30 0	0	.. Per M. £ s.	6 3	6 3	..
West Flamboro' and Beverly......	1794 / 1800	72 / 60	360 / 309	0	0		4 / 1	12 6	5 2 / 0 1		6 / 3 / 2		30 0	0 7½	6 5 Per Day. s. d.	10 0	10 0	..
Waterloo...	1800	138	850	0	2 T. & Men.	0	3	15 0	3	1	3 5		50 0	0	7 6	10 0	10 0	37 10
Dumfries	1816	32	163	0	0	0	0	0	1	0 ..		1	..	0 7½	..	..	..	..
Haldimand..	1783	60	439	1	..	0	5	12 6	3	5	2	3	25 0	1 3	.. Per M. £ s.	7 6	7 6	22 10
Ancaster	1790	162	1037	1 M.	1 E.	1	6	16 3	6	8	4	5	35 0	1 0	6 5	10 0	10 0	..
Barton ..	1787	130	800	1	..	0	5	13 6	5	4	1	4	40 0	0 7½	6 5	11 3	11 3	26 0
Saltfleet	1787	100	700	1	..	0	5	..	2	5	1	6	37 6	1 0	..	7 6	5 0	25 0
Totals.	..	973	5673	4	6	3	37	107 3	27	34	18	41	301 6	6	18 15	72 6	80 9	192 ..
Averaged by	..	11	10	..	..	.. ..	8	..	.. ..	.. ..		9	8	3	8	10	7
Average	..	88	567	..	..	..	13 5	.. ..	.. ..		33 6	0 9¾	5	0 9½	8 1	27 9

T. in column six stands for Tunker; Men. for Menonist;

TABLE 207

TABLE.

Reports of the District of Gore.

WAGES OF				Cost of clearing and fencing five Acres of wild Land.	PRICES OF LIVE STOCK.				Quantity of Wool per Sheep.	Price of Wool per lb.	Produce of wheat in bushels, per acre.	An Ox will gain in a Summer's run.	Price of Butter, per lb.	Price of Cheese, per lb.	Price of Land per Acre, at first.	Price of Land per Acre now.
Common Labourer per Winter month.	Common Labourer per Summer month.	Common Labourers per day in Harvest.	Women's wages, per week.		A Work-horse.	A Cow.	An Ox.	A Sheep.								
L. s.	L. s.	s. d.	s. d.	L. s.	L. s.	L. s.	L. s. s. d.	s. d.	lb.	s. d.		lb.	s. d.	s. d.	s. d.	s. d.
2 0	3 2	..	5 0	15 0	13 15	4 15	7 10 12 6		2¼	1 10	20	200	1 0	1 0	7 6	22 6
2 5	3 15	5 0	6 4	18 15	15 0	5 0	7 10 15 0		4	2 6	18	1 0 / 3	0 11	0 7½	10 0	..
2 0	3 7	5 0	6 3	15 0	15 0	6	5 8 15 12 6		3½	2 6	22½	..	1 3	0 7½	10 0	25 0
..	..	..	6 0	20 0	17 10	4 17	9 0 10 0		3	2 6	18½	100	..	..	7 6	20 0
..	..	..	..	..	..	..	..		..	..	..	..	..	..	..	..
..	..	6 3	6 3	20 0	15 0	4 7	9 7 11 3		3	2 6	16	100	0 10	0 7½	..	..
..	..	..	..	..	..	..	..		..	..	..	..	..	..	..	..
..	..	5 0	6 6	25 0	20 0	5 0	10 0 12 6		..	2 6	20	100	1 0	1 0	5 0	20 0
..	..	..	..	..	..	..	..		..	..	..	..	..	..	..	..
2 10	3 15	5 0	5 0	15 0	15 0	5 0	7 10 10 0		3½	2 6	20	200	0 10	7½	..	..
..	..	6 3	6 8	20 0	15 0	4 7	9 7 11 3		3	3 6	16	200	0 11	7½	..	..
2 0	3 0	6	3 5	12 10	16 5	4 10	10 0 10 0		3	2 6	25	100	0 11	7½	..	..
2 0	3 0	..	5 0	20 0	17 10	5 0	10 0 12 6		3	3 6	20	150	1 3	0 10	..	..
12 15	19 19	38 9	57 7	181 5	160 0	49 1	88 19 117 6		28½	24 4	196	1150	9 0	6 7	40 0	87 6
6	6	7	10	10	10	10	10	9	10	10	8	9	9	5	4	
2 2	3 6	5 6	6 5	18 2	16 0	4 18	8 18 11 9	3 $\frac{1}{7}$	2 5	19½	143	1 0 0	8½	8 0	21 10	

E. for Episcopal; M. for Methodist.

munication. But to confine the matter to Saltfleet, a canal might be easily cut through the long beach which separates Burlington bay from lake Ontario, (the present outlet only admitting small boats, and sometimes a canoe can scarcely pass), the distance not exceeding one-fourth of a mile, and the height above the water not more than eight or ten feet, composed wholly of a fine sand; with a bold shore in many places on both sides; and the bottom of both lakes indicating nothing more to resist than a clay; the accomplishment of which would be an object of no less importance to the government than the people; and here the benefit derived would not be confined to Saltfleet: this little work, of vast importance, would form one of the most secure and capacious harbours to be found; here the fleet might bid defiance to an enemy in time of war, or act in conjunction with an army; Burlington heights having once been the last resort of the army, and ultimately proved the saving of the country. It would also, by changing the route, shorten the distance of conveying the exports and imports of a large portion of the district of Gore in which it lies; and also a large portion of the London District, lying westward, and could not fail to add new life and energy to the whole.

(Signed)

HUGH WILLSON, *Chairman*.

Gore District

Summary of Population, &c.

The above Table directly exhibits and the average to each of nine townships, completely reckoned, is 577. The average number of persons to a house in these townships is 6⅙. Wellington Square

The above Table directly exhibits		5673 people;
has . . . . 16 houses		
East Flamboro' . . . . 38 ditto		
These multiplied by 6⅙ 54, give		330
Total population thus calculated		6003

The only organized township in the district of Gore, not reported, is Glandford: it is pretty well settled, and will equal in population at least the average of the reported townships, ... 577

Binbrook had in 1817 only 16 families,
which reckoned at 6⅛ gives 98
    Woolwich only one family 6

           — 681

Total white population   6684

The Indians on the Grand river are stated
in the Report of Haldimand, to be about 1800

People of colour, by whom are meant, I
presume, negroes and mulattoes 30

But I have seen an accurate government list of
the Grand river Indians, which made their
number   1829

           —1859

Total population, reported and estimated   8543

For the reported population of 6003, there appear to be four places
of worship, and six resident preachers; viz. three Methodists; two
Tunkers and Menonists; and one Episcopalian. There are three
medical practitioners; thirty-seven schools; and thirty-four taverns.

Improvement is said to be retarded, in seven reports, by
crown, clergy, and other reserves: in seven reports, by the great
extent of non-resident's land: in three reports, by want of capital:
in two reports, by shutting out American settlers: in one report,
by want of enterprise: in one report, by want of mechanics: in
one report, by the poverty of beginners: in one report, by the
effects of the late war: in one report, by the want of emigrants,
and the difficulties opposed to them: in one report, by bad roads:
in one report, by want of men: in one report, by lands held by
Indians, who cannot alienate: in one report, by want of liberal
and indiscriminate encouragement to emigration, by the government of the province: in one report, the people want rousing up.

Niagara District.
Township Reports.

Humberston

14th January, 1818.

MR. ROBERT GOURLAY,

SIR,

HAVING considered your queries, we now present you with answers to the same:

5th. There is one English and one Dutch school.

8th. The rate of sawing, 3*s.* 6*d.* per hundred feet, or one half of the timber.

9th. Much of the soil is a rich black loam; some of a yellowish cast and poorer, and a small proportion clay. There is a considerable extent of marsh. The surface throughout is flat and low, unless along the lake shore, where there is a narrow ridge of blown sand, occasionally elevated into little hills, the highest of which is called the Sugar Loaf. It may be 150 feet high, or upwards.

10th. Timber abounds in the following order; oak, pine, hickory, beech, maple, walnut, ash, elm, bass, tamarack, black spruce, hemlock, and cedar, red and white.

11th. There is abundance of limestone, and two sulphur springs.

12th. Limestone is used for building, and is got on the lake shore for the picking up.

18th. No land has been cleared by contract for many years.

21st. Beasts are turned out to pasture about the beginning of May, and taken home the beginning of November.

22d. Sleighing generally lasts two months, and ploughing commences the first of April.

23d. Wheat is sown in September, and reaped the beginning of August.

25th. The pasture is capital. Cheese is seldom taken to market.

26th. After clearing the land, wheat is the first crop, and is often sown the second year, when it is sown down with timothy and clover. When broken up from grass, wheat is sown, then oats, and then again laid down to grass. Sometimes the succession is wheat, Indian corn, wheat and grass. On the best spots, Indian corn is grown several years in succession. Manure is generally applied to meadows, and sometimes to wheat.

27th. Some land is let on shares, one-third of the crop being given to the landlord, and one-half if he furnishes team, and tackle; excepting always, potatoes, flax, and garden stuffs.

28th. At the first settlement, when much land was held on location tickets, lots of 200 acres could be bought for 20 dollars. The price has gradually increased, and of late years sales have been effected at 2½ dollars per acre.

29th. A considerable quantity of land is now for sale.

30th. The roads are not good, but could be much improved. Water conveyance is by lake Erie; and a canal could be very easily cut from this to Lyons' creek, to communicate with Chippawa.

31st. Increased population, and improved roads, are most to be desired.

(Signed)

CHRISTIAN ZAVITZ,
ALEXANDER GLEN,
JESSE ZAVITZ,
ISAAC MINER,
DAVID STEEL, (for self and father)
WILLIAM STEEL.

Bertie

3d. About once a fortnight a Methodist preacher holds a meeting here.

6th. There are eight merchant shops, and four store houses for receiving and storing merchandise in the township.

8th. One carding machine. Rate of carding wool, 6d. per pound.

9th. The soil, generally, is a mixture of clay and loam; the surface flat.

10th. This township is timbered with white and red oak, beech, sugar maple, pine, elm, basswood, black and white ash, whitewood, hickory, black and white walnut, and tamarack.

11th. The only mineral that has been discovered is what is here called bog ore, of which there is said to be plenty in the marshes. Limestone abounds in every part of the township.

12th. Limestone is the only building stone we have. It can be obtained for about 15s. per toise at the quarry.

15th. Blacksmiths have generally 7½d. for working iron brought to the shops, and 5s. for shoeing a horse; none of the iron found by the smith.

21st. Cattle are not generally put out to pasture fields in the spring, but are turned into the woods, about the 1st of May, at which time they thrive well on the tender growth, and are taken into the yard again about the 1st of December.

22d. Sleighing commences about the 1st of January, and ends about the 1st of March. Ploughing commerces the 1st of April.

23d. The season for sowing wheat, is from the 1st to the 20th of September. Wheat harvest generally commences about the 1st of August.

25th. Pasture is productive. An ox of four years old, will gain about one-third his weight in a summer's run; that is, if he weighs 400 lbs. in the spring, he will weigh 600 lbs. in the autumn. A milch cow, at pasture, gives from ten to fourteen quarts of milk per day.

26th. New lands are generally sown with wheat in the autumn, with grass seed in the spring; after which, they remain in meadow or pasture ground for three or four years; when the roots and stumps become decayed: they are then ploughed in the spring, and sown with wheat in the fall. Manure is more generally applied to the spring crop, that is, Indian corn, buck wheat, potatoes, and flax.

27th. Lands are frequently let on shares, and the custom here is, to allow the landlord one-third of the produce raised on the land.

29th. The quantity of land now for sale in this township, is about 2000 acres.

30th. Perhaps no township in the province has greater advantages on account of the water communication than this. Property of all kinds is conveyed in vessels of 130 tons burden, from hence nearly 100 miles westward. A canal is projected at Fort Erie rapids, which, when completed, will admit of boats passing through, of five tons burden. Public roads are rather in a bad state, but by a strict application of the statute labour, and a moderate expence, they might be made good.

31st. For the last two years this township has improved; but its improvement might be greatly advanced, and that in a very few years, had we but a few men of capital and enterprise from the mother country among us. Perhaps, no township in the district of Niagara, can boast of better lands than the township of Bertie, and we are certain that very few have greater advantages either for the mechanic or farmer.

We, Sir, are convinced that the plan you have undertaken for encouraging our fellow subjects to migrate to this province, and settle amongst us, is an excellent one, and we earnestly hope and trust it may and will succeed.

Township of Bertie, 1st January, 1818.

(Signed)

J WARREN, J. P.	JOHN APPL: ...RTH,
ANDREW MILLER,	THOMAS MOORE,
SAMUEL M'AFEE,	B. HARDISON,
CHARLES HILL,	JOHN MAXWELL,
HENRY WARREN,	MATTHIAS HAUN.
WILLIAM POWELL,	

Willoughby

2d. Surveyed and laid out by government in 1787, at which time it got its present name; previous to this, in 1784, there were about ten families settled upon some parts of the land, under the sanction of the then commanding officer at Niagara.

3d. There are frequently illiterate Methodist preachers, of whom there is no scarcity in the country, who occasionally hold forth; and such of the inhabitants who have not the benefit of these, attend divine worship in the neighbouring townships when an occasion offers.

9th. Surface is in general flat and low. Soil in general a black loam and clay; and very heavily timbered.

10th. The kinds of timber are red oak, elm, maple, beech, pine, hickory, basswood, black walnut, black spruce, white oak, and a variety of different descriptions.

11th. There are two sulphur springs in the interior of the township, very strongly impregnated.

16th. Wages of a labourer per day in harvest for cradling, the price of a bushel of wheat; the same for the person that rakes and binds, both being found in provision, and in as much grog as they choose to drink.

17th. Price for mowing grass per day, about 3s. 9d. and treated as above.

18th. Cost of clearing and fencing five acres of land, about 20l.; that is, cutting, burning up all the timber a foot diameter and under; the larger timber being killed by cutting the bark all round; in doing this, the person clearing the land, finds himself in provisions and every other expense.

21st. Beasts are commonly turned out to pasture in the

beginning of March, or so soon as the snow is off the ground; cattle finding food much earlier in heavy timbered land, than upon open land; working cattle are only housed when the snow begins to fall, which is about January; young cattle commonly run out all winter and get a little fodder in very severe weather.

24th. One bushel, and sometimes only three quarters to an acre, if sown early.

25th. The pasture throughout the township is excellent; the white clover growing so soon as ever the land is cleared. A good cow will give milk enough to make six or seven pounds of butter per week.

26th. New land, when first cleared, is commonly sowed with wheat in the month of September; timothy and red clover seeds are sown on the same ground early in the spring following, then lays in grass till the roots are rotted, so as to allow the plough to go through; this requires three or four years; then ploughed, and four or five crops of any kind of grain are taken off successively, without any manure whatever; then laid down in grass for two or three years, and again cropped as before.

27th. Very little land let upon shares; but when this is the case, the landlord gets one-third of the grain, and one-half of the hay, the tenant finding team and tackling; but if the landlord finds team, and tackling, and stock, he gets half of all the increase, both grain and stock.

28th. A farm of 200 acres, one-half under cultivation, with tolerable frame buildings, and orchard, sells now for 625l. to 700l. Farms, however, upon the Niagara or Chippawa rivers, will sell much higher according to their situation.

29th. From the best information there may be from eight to ten thousand acres of wild lands, and eight or ten improved farms for sale in this township.

30th. The roads in this township are principally upon the east, west, and north sides, and are in general good, there being little or no settlement in the interior and south side, owing to large tracts being owned there by non-residents; good roads can be made any where through the township, if ever settled; good water conveyance on the east and north sides by the Niagara and Chippawa rivers, and Lyons creek, on the north-west part of the township. Much might be done in the improvement of this township and the adjoining townships of Crowland and Wainfleet, by bringing the water of lake Erie into Lyons creek, which empties into the Chippawa river, about a mile from the mouth, the distance from the head of Lyons creek not being more than a mile from lake Erie, in digging which, eight feet would be the deepest to about three feet at the least; the soil of which, part sand and part clay; this improvement has been talked of, but from the want of means and inhabitants, has never been attempted. Did this improvement take place, it would be a great benefit to the transport between lakes Ontario and Erie, the distance from the mouth of Chippawa to the place where it is proposed to let the waters of lake Erie into Lyons creek, not being greater than from the mouth of the Chippawa to Fort Erie; besides, at the proposed place for this cut, there is a good harbour for vessels on lake Erie. In case of a war this line of transport would be of much use, it being quite removed from the division line between this country and the United States.

31st. What in our opinion retards the improvement of this township, is, that a great part of it is in large tracts, being owned by persons not resident on the land, and who cannot find purchasers; what retards the improvement of the province in general, is the want of good wholesome inhabitants to cultivate the soil. Emigration from the united kingdom of Great Britain and Ireland is much wished for, and at the same time it would be strengthening the province against our enemies; even a few inhabitants from the United States, under proper restrictions, would add much to the advantage of this, as also to the mother country in cultivating the wild lands.

We would earnestly recommend a large emigration from the mother country of industrious people, who, by obtaining one or two hundred acres of wild lands from government, might set themselves down with their families, and in the course of one or two years make a good living in the province.

(Signed)

THOMAS CUMMINGS, J. P.
JAMES CUMMINGS, J. P.
Willoughby, 4th Dec. 1817.

Stamford.

Nov. 17th, 1817.
ROBERT GOURLAY, ESQ.

SIR,

HAVING seen your address to the resident land owners of Upper Canada, and it appearing to me that if the views of which are carried into effect, much benefit, in my humble opinion, will result to this township, but more particularly to the province at large, I have, therefore, convened a few of our oldest and most respectable inhabitants, in conjunction with whom I now send the following answers to your queries for the township of Stamford, viz.

1st.   This township, at its first settlement, was called Mount Dorchester, or township No. 2, and got its present name from Lieutenant Governor Simcoe, in 1793.

2d.   It was first settled in 1784, by about 10 families, who had adhered to the British cause during the American war.

3d.   It has one Presbyterian church, built in 1791, by subscription; another church was also built by subscription in 1795, for the use of all persuasions. This last was destroyed during the late war. One other church is now building for the Methodists. We have one resident Presbyterian clergyman (supported by subscription); also itinerant Methodist preachers, who preach once a fortnight: and occasionally divine service is performed by the established episcopal clergymen of the neighbourhood, when they see convenient.

8th.   One fulling mill, and two carding mills. About 7d. sterling per yard for fulling and pressing cloth, and about 5½d. per pound for carding wool.

9th.   The soil is in general of a loamy clay, with some sandy and other soils, all of which have been found good for wheat and other grain, as also for hay and pasture.

10th.   The timber is chiefly oak, beech, maple, hickory, walnut, elm, chestnut, basswood, ash, and some pine, as also a small quantity of other sorts.

11th.   Of minerals there are none, except bog iron ore: limestone there is abundance; it being the general strata of the township, all the bank of the Niagara river being of this, as also the rock over which the Niagara Falls pour. No plaster of Paris has yet been found of a good quality; some marl; no salt rock; some salt licks on the banks of the Chippawa; no salt springs; several inflammable gas springs, which ooze out of the bank of the Niagara river, from the mouth of Chippawa river, and extend about 1½ miles down. The air, from some of these, when confined in a tube, will burn constantly.

12th.   There are building-stones plenty; the quality a bastard limestone, and cost about 25s. per toise at the quarry.

17th.   Hay, in a plentiful season, is frequently mowed and cured to the halves, either divided in stacks, or in cocks, as agreed upon. Price of mowing and making an acre of grass, 3s. 9d. to 5s.

18th.   The cost of clearing and fencing five acres of land fit for the harrow, is from 50 to 60 dollars: by clearing, is meant all the fallen timber, and the standing timber of a foot diameter under, being cut up and burnt; the larger standing timber to be girdled.

21st.   Young cattle and horses frequently stay out for two or three months in the winter, where the woods are contiguous, a little fodder being only given them in storms and severe weather.

25th.   The quality of the pasture is in general good; the white clover coming in naturally so soon as the land is cleared of timber. A good cow will yield from 5lb. to 6lb. of butter per week.

26th.   Wheat is generally the first crop after clearing the land; sometimes, but not generally, a second crop of wheat; then grass three or four years; then ploughed up for wheat, or any other grain, and continued in crop for three or four years. Manure seldom used for any other crop than that of Indian corn or potatoes. Wheat is commonly sown on fallow, that is, ground two or three times ploughed, in May, June, and July.

27th.   Several farms are let out on shares, say to the extent of 20.

28th.   A farm of 100 acres partly cleared, say half, and under cultivation, with tolerable farm buildings, including a good orchard (which almost every farm has), will sell for 500l. sterling, quick sale, and some places at a higher rate, according to situation.

29th.   The land being principally settled, and in general improved, there is none for sale, unless an offer is made which the owner thinks advantageous.

30th.   The great portage road from Queenston to the water communication above the falls goes through this township, and is in general good, as are also the other roads. The roads here, as in the other townships of the province, are made and repaired by statute labour, which is too generally but indifferently applied. Much improvement might be made in the roads, was this labour commuted. No water carriage, except on the Chippawa river, on the south of the township, which is navigable for boats of any description from the mouth for 40 miles. Locks may be made to pass the great falls, and connect lakes Ontario and Erie; but many years must elapse before the province is rich enough to meet the expence.

31st.   What retards the further improvement of the township is the scarcity of labourers, there being few not only in this township, but throughout the province in general. This scarcity is caused principally by the want of emigration, and by the ease with which industrious labourers can obtain lands in the interior of the country, where they can make farms of their own; this township, however, is much better improved in roads, and in every other respect than most townships of the province, owing to its being owned principally by actual settlers, with moderate quantities of land, and no reserves being made in it for 1/7th of the land for the crown, and another 1/7th for the clergy. Some few of the adjoining townships are in the same fortunate situation, these being surveyed and allotted to actual settlers before the reservation of the above 2/7ths of the land was thought of; other tracts have, however, suffered severely for this; in which are not only made reservations of their own 2/7ths, but reservations are also made in them for the townships granted without. Another great hindrance to the improvement of the province in general is, that in many of the townships large tracts are taken up by officers of government, and others non-resident in the country, for which lands non-residents pay no tax whatever towards opening and making roads and bridges, and other improvements, which subjects the inhabitants (who must of consequence be thinly settled) to many serious inconveniences, for which I see no remedy until a tax is laid upon all wild lands, which will be the means of bringing about sales, and actual settlement. It is an idea with me, and with most of my best informed acquaintance, that, were government, in place of giving away lands to actual settlers, in specific situations, it would be much better to sell them, which would raise a very large fund for public purposes, besides allowing settlers and emigrants to place themselves agreeable to their choice and means.

Should I have answered your queries in a satisfactory manner, I shall be gratified, and with every wish for success in your present undertaking,

I have the honour to be, Sir,

Your very obedient Servant,

(Signed) JOHN GARNER, SEN.

Collector for Stamford.

Grantham.

Pursuant to public Notice, a Number of the oldest Inhabitants assembled, to take into Consideration your Queries. A Commit-

tee being appointed, the following Answers were adopted, which, we presume, will be satisfactory.

3d.   One church; one Presbyterian (non-resident); two travelling preachers (Methodists).

8th.   Millers' wages, from 5l. to 7l. 10s. per month. Four saw mills; if logs delivered at the mill, they take one half the boards; sawyers' wages, from 5l. to 6l. 10s. a month. One carding machine; price of carding wool, 6d. per lb.; carders' wages, 5l. per month.

9th.   The soil in its natural state is covered with a black loam, from three to nine inches deep; is of two kinds; the northern part, a sandy loam; the other a brown clay, intermixed with marl, generally rich and productive.

10th.   The lands are heavily timbered with white and red oak; white pine; beech; sugar and white maple; red and white elm; black and white ash; white wood; chestnut; basswood; hickory, and black walnut; with some cherry, butternut, button wood, sassafras, iron wood, dog or box wood.

11th.   Very few minerals yet discovered. A saline spring near the village of St. Catherine's, of an excellent quality, has lately been discovered, and with improvement will be capable of supplying the district with the valuable article, salt. Iron bog ore in great plenty; it is found in low wet lands; is raised in large lumps, the size of common stone, and made use of for the backs of fire-places, in place of stone.

12th.   There is a ridge or mountain running along the southern boundary of this township, which is composed of an inexhaustible body of lime, fire and building stone, which can be obtained at 5s. per toise at the quarry.

15th.   Blacksmiths' work at the rate of 7½d. per lb.; shoeing a horse, 10s.; journeymen blacksmiths, 5l. per month.

18th.   Heavy timbered lands, 5l. to 6l. 5s. per acre. Light timbered, from 2l. to 5l. per acre.

25th.   White clover, red top, and spear grass, natural to the soil; but produces red clover and herds grass, if sown in good crops; white clover, best feeding pasture. A good four year old ox will gain, if attended, from 200 to 250 lb.; by running on the commons, or in the woods, will gain 150 to 170lb. A milch cow will produce, (well kept), 8lb. butter, or 14lb. cheese per week.

26th.   New land, in its natural state, given from 6 to 10 years; the owner receiving the improvement for his rent at the expiration of the stated time. Manure is applied for flax, potatoes, oats, Indian corn, wheat, and rye.

27th. Improved lands are let out upon shares, owner furnishing team and utensils, one half the seed, and receives half the produce. If the owner furnish land only, to cultivate, he receives one-third the produce. A single man gets one-third of what he raises, and found everything.

28th. Farms of 200 acres, situate on the most public roads, of a good quality, comfortable house, good barn, orchard, &c. from 100 to 150 acres improved, will sell for 6l. to 7l. 10s. per acre. Farms of 100 acres, small house and barn, 60 acres improved, will sell from 5l. to 6l. per acre. Lands sold in the township, in 1809, 10, and 11, for 6l. 5s. per acre, now sells from 30l. to 200l. for building lots.

29th. From 3000 to 5000 acres.

30th. Very bad. Capable of being made good at the rate of from 5s. to 7s. 6d. per rod; a water communication within a mile and a half of the village of St. Catherine's, for boats of 10 tons burden, say 4 miles, is capable of being extended and improved, by means of a canal of three miles distant, which will bring the Chippawa creek into the Twelve Mile Creek, by which means it will connect the waters of lake Erie and lake Ontario. The greatest expence, 10,000l.; the Twelve Mile Creek runs by the flourishing village of St. Catherine's, and is the best stream for mills and machinery in this district.

31st. The last of your queries is a question of the greatest importance, and we do not feel ourselves competent to answer it correctly. The province was in a most prosperous state at the commencement of the late war; that of course injured it in a most serious manner, a stop being put to all agriculture. It was drained of all its resources; money was left in the country, it is true, but it went but a short way to replace those necessaries each family stood in need of. Since then, we conceive the prosperity of the country has been materially retarded, for the want of its being correctly represented to his Majesty's ministers. In consequence of the stop put to emigration from abroad, hardly a family of wealth or respectability has become a settler among us; but swarms of mechanics and labourers overrun the country, and take to the United States most of the ready money we have, they finding no inducement to become settlers from the above restrictions.

We think the removal of the above evil, taxing non-residents for the lands they hold in the province, and the emigration of a few foreigners of capital, is all that we want at present, to make us a prosperous and happy people.

In the chair, MR. W. H. MERRITT.
Committee, MR. WM. CHISHOLM,
          CHARLES INGERSOLL,
          WM. MANN, SEN.
          AMOS M'KENNEY,
          PAUL SHIPMAN.

  (Signed)
SAMUEL WOOD, *Secretary.*
Grantham, St. Catherine's, November 29th, 1817.

Louth.

                                          Jan. 5, 1818.
*At a Meeting of the Inhabitants of the Township of Louth,
District of Niagara, and Province of Upper Canada, held this
Day at the House of Mr. Robert Runchey, Innkeeper – the Queries proposed in an Address of Robert Gourlay Esq. to the Resident Land-Owners, respecting the Agricultural State of this Province, were submitted; and after due Consideration, the following
Answers were resolved upon, approved of, ordered to be signed by
the Chairman, and forwarded to R. Gourlay, Esq.*

EBENEZER CULLVER, *Chairman,*
JOHN CLARK, *Secretary.*

  8th.   One carding machine. Wool is carded for 6½d. per lb.
  9th.   About one half of the township is a clay soil, the other
half a sandy loam, adapted to grass, wheat, rye, barley, oats,
Indian corn, buck wheat, beans, peas, and potatoes. The soil and
climate throughout the province is favourable to fruit, of which
we have the following – apples, pears, peaches, nectarines, apricots, plums, cherries, gooseberries, raspberries, and currants.
Grapes have succeeded well in the Niagara district.
  10th.   The timber is oak, pine, black walnut, butternut,
beech, maple, cherry, hickory, basswood, ash, and elm.
  11th.   Several salt springs have been discovered in this township. On the Fifteen and Twenty Mile Creeks works have been in
operation for some years past; at the Fifteen Mile Creek, for
want of proper attention, they yield but trifling, though we are of
opinion, if they were rightly managed, a sufficiency of salt might

be made for the use of the township from that spring alone. Salt, 7s. 6d. per bushel.

12th. Building stone, of an excellent quality, can be obtained at 5s. per toise, at the quarry, from a ledge of building, and lime, stone running along the south side of the township.

17th. Mowing 3s. 9d. per day; cradling wheat 5s.

25th. The average product of a cow per day is 10 to 12 quarts of milk, and about six pounds of butter per week from each cow.

26th. New land, when cleared, is never ploughed; the wheat is sowed, and harrowed in after the crop is taken off the following year; then pastured, and the next year ploughed and sowed: manure is seldom used until the land becomes somewhat exhausted.

27th. There are several farms in the township let upon shares, the land proprietor getting one-third of the produce.

29th. There is no land at present offered for sale; but should purchasers appear, no doubt sales would take place. A farm of 200 acres, with a house and barn, 60 acres cleared or improved, with a small orchard, will sell for £750.

30th. The roads principally travelled are capable of being made good at a small expence, and we do conceive that sufficient attention has not been paid to that particular. The manner in which the statute labour is performed on them is quite inadequate to the importance of the object.

We have three water communications with lake Ontario, say the Fifteen, Sixteen, and Twenty Mile Creeks, running through this township, and are navigable in their present state for boats of from five to 20 tons burden. The Twenty Mile Creek is quite navigable to the centre of the township for boats of 20 tons burden, and is capable of being improved by locks and canals, by which means a water communication may be carried on between lakes Erie and Ontario, at a trifling expence, considering the importance of the thing. This creek abounds with fine fish, say salmon, bass, pike, pickerel, eels, mullets, suckers, perch, and many other small fish.

Above the navigable waters of this creek are many excellent mill seats unoccupied.

31st. We conceive the improvement of this township and the province in general is much retarded, from large tracts of wild lands holden by persons residing in Europe. Lower Canada, and the United States, who do not in any way contribute towards the revenue or improvement of the country.

The statute labour is performed entirely by the people residing in the township, as also the revenue is raised from the same.

The evil just mentioned, and great want of capital in our township, is what most retards the improvement of it.

N.B. We know of but one instance of men of capital that have purchased lands to any extent in this province. A company of Dutchmen purchased a block of land on the Grand river, now called the township of Waterloo. The province, generally speaking, is composed of discharged soldiers, who served during the American revolution, and emigrants from the United States: most of the latter are what are termed U.E. loyalists, all of whom had but little to begin with.

Further. We have known men going into new lands, pay for the same, by manufacturing the ashes made from the timber burnt in clearing their farms.

(Signed) EBENEZER COLLVER,
Chairman.

By order, JOHN CLARK,
Secretary.

Grimsby.

Two carding machines; two fulling mills; carding wool, per pound, 6d. The soil very good for wheat, rye, oats, pease, buck wheat, flax, Indian corn, and grass. The timber is white pine, white and red oak, hickory, ash, elm, sugar and soft maple, chestnut, butternut, beech, and iron wood. Price of reaping and mowing, per day, 5s.; for cradling, 6s. Twenty-five bushels an acre from new land, 15 from old land. If let on shares, if new, give the first crop for clearing and fencing; if old land, give one-third of the crop: land improved, according to the situation, say from 1l. to 4l. per acre. Quantity of land for sale unknown, but a great deal. State of the roads at present is bad, but may be made good at a moderate expence.

As to what retards the improvement of our township is, that the whole of the township is located, and a great deal of land in the township for sale, but no buyers; and the province in general, is the small commerce, and the low prices of what we have to export, and the high prices of what we have imported.

(Signed) ANDREW PETTIT,
Town Clerk of Township of Grimsby.

A Second Report Was Sent to Me From Grimsby, of Which the Following are Extracts.

As to population, I may with propriety say that there would have been at least one-third or a half more, had the laws of the British Parliament, for the encouragement of the colonization of this fine province, been allowed to take their full scope; but for what reason or cause some of our rulers have, by a dash of the pen, endeavoured to abrogate some of the wisest statutes that ever emanated from the British senate; or whether, from political motives, or with a mistaken notion of the interests or security of the province, or by what other motives they have been actuated I know not, but it has been endeavoured, in the face of a British statute, to interdict the admission of people coming from the United States, avowedly with the intention of becoming subjects, by taking the oaths of allegiance, and settling in the country. These reasons, Sir, will go a great way in elucidating your query, of "What are the causes that retard the settlement of the country." Let these prohibitions be done away, and proclaim the high way from which this country can derive an efficacious population, open, and wealth and prosperity will again smile upon it. It has been said, but without foundation, that it is not safe to admit Americans amongst us; that their politics are dangerous to our monarchical institutions, and that if encouragement were given to them, they would ultimately become dangerous to the government; but I would beg leave to tell such, that if it had not been for Americans, or emigrants from thence, immediately after the rebellion, and long since, that this fine country, now so flourishing, would in all probability be yet a howling wilderness; and let me further tell, that such men, and their immediate descendants, behaved during the late war with the United States, with as much fidelity and loyalty to his Majesty's government as any natural born subject could do; and had it not been for their zeal and gallantry, we might perhaps at this time been a province of America, and enjoying all the blessings of republican fraternity. Thus debarred from getting a wealthy and industrious emigration from the United States, the country is in a great measure left to its own natural means of population. Another cause which may be named as powerfully operating against the settlement of the country generally, is the large and fine portions of it which are locked up as crown and clergy reserves. Large tracts are likewise held by the o_____rs of g_____t and absentees, who will not sell but at an exorbitant price, thus putting it out of the power of the industrious poor man to add his mite to the general advancement and prosperity of the colony.

Religion, I am sorry to say, has hitherto been but of second-ary consideration. This, however, is not to be ascribed to the general immoral character of the people, who are naturally of pious and orderly habits; but is to be attributed more to the seeming disregard of the head of the established church in the Canadas, under whose immediate care and protection it more especially belongs; and although this parish is one of the few which can boast of a church regularly dedicated to the form of the worship of the church of England, we have the mortification to say, that in twenty years we have had but one solitary visit from the lord bishop of the diocese. While such apathy prevailed for the advancement of the interest of the mother church, other sects and denominations were not idle, and the result has proved, that their labours have been but too successful; as our church congregation, which was once respectable, is now almost dwindled to nought. One good thing, however, has resulted to us from his lordship's visit. A representation was drawn up to him by the parishioners, requesting a clergyman; upon which one was sent us from England last spring; and although his efforts have not hith-erto added to the number of the congregation, yet he has served to keep the remnant of the flock from the jaws of the all-devouring wolf; and if proper perseverance is shewn, the good cause may yet ultimately prevail. Independent of the regular church there is one of the Methodist denomination, which is generally numerously attended. The Baptists are likewise a numerous body in the parish; but having as yet no public place of worship, their meetings are for the most part held in private houses; but the prevailing religion of this township may be classed under Presbyterians and Methodists.

The state of education is also at a very low ebb, not only in this township, but generally throughout the district; although the liberality of the legislature has been great in support of the district schools, (giving to the teachers of each 100l. per annum), yet they have been productive of little or no good hitherto, for this obvious cause, they are looked upon as seminaries exclusively instituted for the education of the children of the more wealthy classes of society, and to which the poor man's child is considered as unfit to be admitted. From such causes, instead of their being a benefit to the province, they are sunk into obscurity, and the heads of most of them are at this moment enjoying their situations as comfortable sinecures. Another class of schools has within a short time been likewise founded upon the liberality of the legislative purse, denominated common or parish schools, but like the preced-ing, the anxiety of the teacher employed, seems more alive to his stipend than the advancement of the education of those placed under his care: from the pecuniary advantages thus held out, we have been inundated with the worthless scum, under the character of schoolmasters, not only of this, but of every other country where the knowledge has been promulgated, of the easy means our laws afford of getting a living here, by obtaining a parish school, which is done upon the recommendation of some few freeholders, getting his salary from the public, and making his employers contribute handsomely besides.

It is true, rules are laid down for their government, and the proper books prescribed for their use; but scarcely in one case in ten are they adhered to, for in the same class you will frequently see one child with Noah Webster's spelling book in his hand, and the next with Lindley Murray's. However prone the teachers are to variety in their schools, much blame is to be attributed to the trustees, who are in many instances too careless, and I might almost add too ignorant to discriminate right from wrong, in the trust they have undertaken for the public benefit. It is therefore not to be wondered at why the parish school system should meet with almost universal reprobation from most discerning men.

Of these parish schools, we are burdened with a liberal share, having no less than three of them. If the establishment of this system was meant by the legislature to abbreviate the present enormous price of education, they have been miserably deceived; for I can see no alteration or reduction from the charge made before the passing of the act. The price then was 12s. 6d., and is now the same per quarter.

We have hitherto been blessed with so healthy a climate, as to require little or no aid from medical men, the consequence, therefore, is, that there is none in the parish, the nearest to us being six miles, whose practice is not too lucrative from the country 12 miles round.

Fulling is regulated by the quality of the dye, and description of work bestowed on the yard of cloth; but may be estimated at from 1s. 6d. to 3s. per yard when finished.

No minerals of any consequence have yet been discovered, although the face of the country indicates it as favourable to such productions. In many parts, salt springs have shewn themselves, and little doubt exists but the solid strata of this necessary article lays at no great depth below the surface. On the summit of the ridge numerous specimens of marine fossils, and petrifactions, are to be found, all which indicate that the country has, at some remote period, been covered with water.

With respect to the advantages possessed by this township for internal communication, or navigation, nature indeed has been lavish of her gifts, both in a commercial and political point of view.

It is washed by lake Ontario in front, which affords a good roadstead for the vessels that come to carry off the superabundant produce of the country. From the lake to the village, where the principal mills are established, is about a mile, and from here vessels carrying 6 or 800 barrels of flour, are generally loaded in a day; but this is of minor importance to what nature has done for its interior. After you ascend to the summit of the mountain, to where the creek makes a rumbling fall of about 25 feet, it immediately becomes, by the help of a small dam, a natural navigable canal, running in a southerly direction towards the Chippawa, which in a right line does not exceed a distance of nine miles from the fall just mentioned: through this tract there is no difficulty whatever in uniting the waters of the Chippawa with those of the Forty Mile Creek, there being no rising ground between them, and the make of the country has a gentle descent to facilitate the run of the water to lake Ontario. Indeed, were it necessary, I might have extended my views of its superior internal advantages from the Chippawa to the Grand river, a distance of only six miles more, which has already been surveyed, and a fall of between six and seven feet has been ascertained in this short distance.

So strongly are the inhabitants of this and the neighbouring townships convinced of the practicability of it, that measures have been taken at their own expence to have a survey made of the most advantageous ground between the nearest points of the Forty Mile Creek and Chippawa. Was this communication once opened, its political importance would immediately manifest itself in the event of a future war, as affording a safe and direct inland navigation from this part of lake Ontario to the naval establishment at the mouth of the Grand river. Its commercial advantages would be the opening a short and safe route for the produce of the country west of the Grand river and the upper parts of lake Erie into lake Ontario. Thus, in both cases, avoiding the dangerous coast navigation, and the circuitous route of the Niagara, subject at all times in case of war to the inroads and obstructions of the enemy. Before the late war with the United States, the roads generally throughout the country were very bad, during the existence of which, the public service very often suffered by it. The common way of opening, making, and keeping roads in repair, is by statute labour, apportioned to the assessments or rates paid by the householders in each township. Thus, if a person is assessed to the amount of £100, his proportion of labour for that year is six days, and so on in proportion as his rates advance, until it amounts to twelve days, which is the highest, and which seems altogether out of reason, compared with the poor man, whose smallest quantum is three days, and whose assessment is perhaps a cow, value 3*d*. tax. This system has long since been found rotten, and has been often attempted to be regenerated by the legislature at different times; but hitherto, with little advantage to the public; and the reason is in some degree evident, for when a man is ordered to do his statute labour on the highways, he considers it as so much of his time lost, or of no profit to him: hence arises the indifference with which he does his day's labour, and it often happens that the most rigid overseer (who is elected annually from the parish), cannot get even the most willing of his party to do justice to his task. It is true that the laws provides for a commutation in money in lieu of labour, at a certain fixed rate per day; but this is seldom resorted to. The road laws being thus radically bad, would require radical revision. One essential step towards effecting this improvement in our road police, and which is of the greatest importance towards the internal improvement and prosperity of the country, would be to abolish the present system of personal labour, and substitute a certain moderate rate in money per diem, in lieu thereof. The sum thus assessed in cash, and judiciously expended under proper superintendance, would be the means of improving the roads yearly, far more than the present system, and I am convinced would give much more satisfaction to the public, and the tax would be paid with cheerfulness.

At the close of the late war, the legislature with great liberality granted such a sum of money for the improvement of the principal roads in the district, which in the opinion of discerning men, would have (if judiciously expended) almost turnpiked the whole of them: but it is a melancholy fact, that much of it was expended where it was not wanted; and where improvement was actually required, in many instances totally neglected.

In mowing and harvest, the price of labour is mostly governed by the demand; but in all cases they never fail to make you pay well, for I have known in many instances, and successive seasons, two dollars per day paid to a mower or cradler.

The wages of this class of people in the district of Niagara, (for I do not confine my observation to this parish alone) are exorbitant, and far beyond what the present prices of the products of the country will or can bear; hence the necessity of bringing all these species of labour to a proper level, by giving encouragement to emigration into the province of this class of people.

In your queries there are a number of the mechanics whom you have not noticed, and whom you may probably not conceive as necessary to your purpose, but who, I assure you, deserve as conspicuous a place in your statistical pages as any other. Among them I may enumerate weavers, tailors, shoemakers, &c. I have often heard my neighbours assert, that it was full as cheap to go to the store and buy English broad cloth as to make homespun, for this obvious reason, that by the time it went through the hands of the carder, the spinner, the weaver, the fuller, and the dyer, it cost him more per yard than the English, and generally of inferior quality.

A woman has from six to eight dollars per month for home-work, and for spinning nearly as much. The weaver has, for weaving a yard of common flannel, from 1s. to 1s. 6d. The tailor has from four to five dollars for making you a coat, and in proportion for other garments; and a shoe maker will ask you three dollars for a pair of shoes. From this statement you will not be much surprised at the rapidity with which all kinds of mechanics accumulate property, and slip as it were at once into a state of ease and affluence unknown to the European mechanic of the same description, who very frequently has not, when Saturday night comes round, to afford from his labour wherewithal to afford a scanty pittance to pass the Sabbath before he again resumes his weekly toil. These are the sort of people whose emigration to this country ought to be encouraged in preference to most others, for they would become doubly useful, first, as being the means of reducing the price of mechanical labour, and secondly, as ultimately becoming good settlers, from the knowledge they would acquire of the customs and habits of the country, and at the same time enriching himself by his trade.

Although there are large tracts uncultivated in the township, yet literally speaking, there is little or none for sale. The uncultivated tracts, belonging mostly to the early settlers, who, perhaps, anticipating a numerous offspring, prudently provided, when in their power, for what is to come. Nor, has their foresight been ill judged, for their lands are now more or less falling under cultivation, almost daily, by their children. The price, however, of wild land, may be taken at from three to six dollars, according to situation and quality, but oftener over than under these prices. At the commencement of the settlement, lands may be said to have had no value; but from the year 1794 to 1800, the price was from 25 to 100 dollars for 200 acres; since which it has been progressively rising, so that the same cannot now be bought at an advance of from 6 to 800 per cent.; and as the government grants diminish, there is no saying to what height they may attain; but more especially if American emigration is permitted.

The late war having drained the country of horses, horned cattle, and sheep, their prices have continued high; but the stock being now nearly equal to what it was, prior to that event, they have declined.

Your obedient Servant,

WM. CROOKS.

Grimsby, January 12th, 1818.

TO MR. ROBERT GOURLAY, *Queenston.*

Pelham

8th. In this township there is one fulling mill, and one carding machine. The price of inch boards (pine) is 5*s*. per 100 feet, 3 quarters ditto, 3*s*. 9*d*. per 100 feet; when timber, taken to the mill, sawyers charge 2*s*. 6*d*. per 100 feet for inch boards. The price of wool carding has been 6¼*d*. per lb. this season.

9th. The northern part of this township is rather uneven, or it may, perhaps, more properly be denominated hilly, but watered with excellent springs: the southern part is very even, or level, and not so well supplied with water. With respect to soils, we may name them in the following order: sand, loam, clay, and gravel.

10th. There is a variety of timber produced in this township; among the most useful kinds we enumerate the following: beech, white oak, pine, sugar maple, elm, chestnut, ash, hickory, and poplar.

11th. In the southern part, iron ore, of that kind denominated bog, has been discovered in small quantities: we know not of any other minerals, except a small sulphur spring.

12th. In the northern part of the township are immense quarries of limestone, and two quarries of freestone have been opened lately.

15th. The price of an axe, 12*s*. 6*d*.; the price of a hoe, 5*s*.; shoeing a horse, 2*s*. 6*d*. per shoe; making log, or ox chains, 11*d*. per lb.

17th. Price of mowing grass, 3*s*. 9*d*. per day; reaping, 3*s*. 9*d*. per day; cradling, 5*s*. per day.

26th. On low lands, where the growth of timber has been principally beech and maple, grass seed is sown with the first crop of wheat, and the land kept under grass, either for pasture or mowing, for four or five years, or until the roots are sufficiently decayed to admit of ploughing; it is then broken up, and sown with wheat, and then put under grass for two, three, or four years. On high sandy or gravelly lands, where the growth of timber is chiefly oak, pine, and chestnut, the land is sown with rye immediately after the first crop of wheat is taken off; but where the quantity of cleared land is so small, there is scarcely such a thing as a regular course of cropping; the necessities of the farmer will seldom admit of it. Little attention has been paid to the manuring of land in this township; one farmer, the last season, made a trial of plaster of Paris, brought from the Grand river (on a small scale), both on wheat and grass; the success was such as to encourage a future trial. When manure is used, it is generally to promote the growth of Indian corn and potatoes.

27th. Letting land upon shares is not practised to any extent; when let, the landlord reserves one-third of the produce.

28th. When the settlement of this township commenced, wild land was selling at 61. 10s. per one hundred acres; in the year 1800, at 10s. per acre; the present price is 40s. per acre. The quantity of land for sale now does not seem to be easily ascertained, though we believe the quantity to be small.

30th. The roads in this township are not in a great degree of forwardness, but capable of great improvement at a small expence.

AMOS CHAPMAN,	ELI BRADSHAW,
ZENAS FELL,	AMOS SCOTT,
ELIJAH PHELPS,	JOSEPH WILLSON,
GEORGE BRADSHAW,	LEWIS WILLSON,
PETER BECKETT,	THADDEUS DAVIS.
SAMUEL BECKETT,	STEPHEN BECKETT,
JESSE WILLSON,	JOHN MCGLASHEN.
JOHN TAYLOR,	

Pelham, Dec. 6, 1817.

Postscript

The ridge, as it is called in this township, is the highest land in the district, being 500 feet higher than lake Ontario: it commences about half a mile east of the eastern limit of the township, and extends westwardly nearly four miles; the base is generally two miles in width; the ascent on the northern side is mostly pretty abrupt, but on the southern side much more gentle and easy. The soil upon this ridge is generally, and for the most part, of the coarsest kind; when first cleared, yields excellent wheat, though not in large quantities; it produces rye, buckwheat, and Indian corn. From the same point, on the eastern extremity of this ridge, may be seen the two great lakes Erie and Ontario; and in calm weather, the mist of the cataract, rising like a cloud in the eastern horizon. It was over this section of this township the dreadful tornado, on Sunday, the 1st of July, 1792, passed, which laid prostrate almost every tree that stood in its course. Before this, it was covered with chestnut, oak, and some pine timber, and was reckoned, on account of its openness, being entirely free from underwood, the handsomest tract of land in the township. Since the hurricane, it has frequently been burned, which destroys the young timber, a majority of which is a kind, here denominated, asp or aspen.

> I am, your most devoted Servant,
> ELI BRADSHAW.

Mr. Robert Gourlay.

Thorold.

We the inhabitants of the township of Thorold, at a meeting held at Thorold for the purpose, give the following as a true description of the said township.

The face of the land is level: the chief part of the timber beech and sugar maple, with plenty of white pine and oak; black walnut; and a variety of other timber.

The soil chiefly clay and loam; produces, besides wheat, pease, good oats, barley, rye, Indian corn, and buckwheat. Our meadows generally yield from one to three tons of timothy and clover hay per acre; and our fields afford good pasture from the 1st of May to the 1st of December, four months being the ordinary time for feeding cattle in the winter.

The price of beef is five dollars per 100 lb. There is in the township one oil mill, and 2 carding machines.

The present price for an improved or cultivated farm, say 200 acres, with good buildings and orchard, from 15 to 25 dollars per acre.

To Mr. ROBERT GOURLAY.

This short and simple statement of the above township, is at your service to correct and publish, if you think proper, as it is attested by twelve of the most respectable inhabitants.

GARRET VANDERBURGH, *Town Clerk.*   JOHN DECOU,
JACOB UPPER,   ANTHONY UPPER,
And nine others.
Thorold, 26th Nov. 1817.

Crowland.

Crowland, Dec. 23, 1817.
MR. ROBERT GOURLAY.

SIR,

PURSUANT to your inclination, and anxious to facilitate the good
of our country, I offer the following reply to your address of the
30th of October last. Being unable to obtain a meeting for the
purpose, I took the task on myself, which I could wish to have
been performed by an abler hand. I have taken the subsequent
signature of a few creditable inhabitants of this township, who
casually fell in my way.

JOSEPH CURRANT,
Town Clerk.

9th.   The soil is various, and much given to grass, consisting
of white, blue and red clay, black and grey sand, in spots, coming
near to gravel itself, black mould, and yellow loam; all these are
sometimes found in the compass of an acre, but clay is most
prevalent. The surface remarkably level, except two spots near the
southern limit, where it approaches to small eminences.

10th.   The ground in its uncultivated state is timbered with
white oak, swamp white oak, Spanish or red oak, sugar and red
maple, bass or linden, beech, hickory, and iron wood, and in
some places, heavy growths of white pine; in others, a species of
sycamore, some butternut, black walnut, elm, and black and
white ash.

11th.   The only mineral found here is bog iron ore in small
quantities, frequently in marshy places; springs of a saline tincture
are frequent.

15th.   Ox chains and irons, &c. are sold for 1s. 3d. per lb.
Carpenters have 10s. per hundred for framing; bricklayers, 7s. 6d.
per day, and 10s. per 1000 for laying.

16th.   Women's wages, per week, for house work, 7s. 6d.;
for spinning, 6s. 3d. The cradler's wages, per day, for cutting

wheat, is one bushel of the same, or its price; the reapers three-fourths; the mowers of grass for hay the same.

18th.   Wood lands are cleared and fenced for 31. 2s. 6d. per acre, board, lodging, and the use of team, given withal.

26th.   Manure is best applied to land in winter, while in grass.

27th.   A cropper on new lands, customarily takes three successive yearly crops for his labour, of clearing and fencing; when the cropper breaks the land from grass, the owner of the soil commonly claims one-third of the crop.

A farm let on shares brings to its owner one-third of all the grain, with half the hay it produces; this is little practised, as most people can have land of their own.

28th.   A farm of 100 acres, nearly continguous to mills, with about 40 cleared, and very mean buildings, was lately sold for 312l. 10s.

As a price would purchase all the lands in the township, so the quantity for sale is limited. Most of the public roads are capable of beneficial improvement, at a tolerable expence.

30th.   Lyons creek, a sluggish stream of blackish water, rises in the swamps and marshes of Humberston and Wainfleet, near lake Erie, and entering Crowland at its southern limit, passes through at a north-easterly direction, falls into Chippawa one mile above its mouth in the township of Willoughby, from whence it is navigable for boats and batteaux seven miles up, where it furnishes an excellent mill seat, occupied by Cook's mills. Here is a town in embryo; this spot claims notice as being the place of a brisk action between a detachment of the British army and that of the Americans, on the morning of the 19th Oct. 1814. Two miles above this, on the bank of the creek, near Humberston, is a spring whereof salts have been made, reputed to be equal in quality, as an aperient, to Glauber's salts. This spring is capable of producing large quantities.

Nature invites art, in strong terms, to open a canal between lake Erie and this creek, promising the expence to be inconsiderable, as well as reduce the carriage of commodities, from about 42 miles to 19, and render the navigation entirely safe, besides conveying pure water through this part of the country, which is a very desirable object.

31st.   Lack of money, and something to expel a torpid spirit, most impedes the improvement of this township, and perhaps the province in general; plenty of cash in circulation, and a proper stimulation to enterprise, it is believed, would be the best applicable remedy.

CALVIN COOK,
SAMUEL YOKOM,
RICHARD YOKOM,
And eight others.

Wainfleet.

20th Dec. 1817.

SIR,

WE the undersigned, according to the request of your circular letter of October, called a meeting of the inhabitants of the township of Wainfleet, and resolved on the following answers to your queries.

9th.   Generally clay soil.

10th.   Timber – beech and maple, interspersed with hickory, oak, walnut, pine, black and white ash.

11th.   No minerals discovered; a great quantity of limestone of the very best quality.

12th.   Abundance of building stone of the best kind, at 10s. per toise.

16th.   Women servants per week for house work 5s.; spinning 3s. 9d.

17th.   Price of mowing and reaping 3s. 9d.; cradling wheat 5s. per day.

25th.   The quality of our pasture is principally white clover and timothy; this most generally rises spontaneously.

26th.   When cleared, the land is sowed without ploughing, only harrowed in; after this first crop, it must remain three years in pasture, in order to rot out the roots; the land is sufficiently strong to bear 10 or 15 years without manure.

28th.   There are 22 square miles of marsh land owned by government, which if drained, would be preferable to any other land in the province for growing hemp, &c.; its soil or surface is three feet deep; it lies almost as high as the highest land between it and the river Welland, which river is 15 feet lower than the said marsh, at the distance of two miles therefrom, and several creeks of considerable magnitude run out of said marsh into the river Welland, and also to lake Erie: if the heads of these creeks were opened a small distance into said marsh, it would sufficiently drain the land for a considerable distance around them; at each and every of those creeks so running from said marsh, would be excellent mill seats, that would be of the greatest consequence; the whole expence of draining this marsh would not exceed 60s. average the whole per acre.

29th.   There is about four thousand acres of land owned by individuals for sale.

30th.   Our roads are in a bad state, but capable of much improvement, at a moderate expence. On the north side of township is river Welland; the depths of the river 15 to 25 feet, and breadth on an average 300. It is a complete water conveyance; also there might be a canal cut from the said Welland across the marsh. To Morgan's bay, in lake Erie, the distance is 6 miles and 28 chains: said canal commencing 16 miles from mouth of said Welland, which would be 20 miles short of the present route: we are of opinion that said canal might be furnished with water out of said marsh, sufficient to carry craft fully 20 tons burden: said canal would not require to be cut exceeding 6 feet deep; also an excellent road naturally would be made with the earth thrown out of said canal, which would be of the greatest service to this and the adjoining townships, as it at present prevents any communication without going the distance of 23 miles, whereas it could be accomplished by the short route of 6 miles and 28 chains, by said road passing along said canal.

31st.   The above described marsh divides our township into two separate settlements; the one on the shore of lake Erie, and the other on the south side of the river Welland, which marsh, if opened as described, would remove this obstacle.

As to the province in general, a number of causes might be assigned; but one great obstacle is the tardiness of emigration from Europe; whereas if our country was peopled according to its extent, we then would calculate on manufactures to be set on foot for the employ of artisans and mechanics, which would give more encouragement to the husbandman to prosecute his labours, and would become a reciprocal interest to both parties.

(Signed)

DAVID THOMSON, *Assessor,*
THOMAS PRIESTMAN, *Clerk.*
STEPHEN M. FARR, *Collector.*
SHUBAL PARK, *King's Deputy Surveyor.*

Niagara District.
Summary of Population, &c.

The Statistical Table exhibits 11 townships, containing	People. 8398
1312 houses, make an average of 6⅖	
Humberstone contains, houses . . . 75	
Wainfleet 72	
147	
Which, multiplied by 6⅖, gives	941
	9339

The townships of the district not reported, are Niagara, Clinton, Gainsboro' and Wedderburn. The three first being old settled townships, may average with the above at 763 each

2289

But we must add to the population of Niagara township that of its two villages Niagara and Queenston. In 1817 the former contained, houses 85
The latter, ditto 27

112

On the supposition that in villages such as these the number in family is increased by servants, shopmen, &c. it is fair to multiply by 8

896

Wedderburn has been settling these two last years; but in 1817 I presume it did not contain more than four families

24
12,548

The greater part of Wedderburn is occupied with what is called Cranberry Marsh, wholly unfit for cultivation till extensive drainage is executed. It extends into Wainfleet. The late Hon. Robert Hamilton, of Queenston, offered to complete the drainage, for half the land given to him in recompense; but this liberal offer, which would have greatly benefited the country, was refused by the land-board!! It remains a harbour for wolves, and otherwise a great nuisance.

For the reported population of 9,339, there appear to be eight places of worship and ten preachers: viz. five Methodists; one Menonist; one Quaker; two Presbyterians; and one Episcopalian. There are six medical practitioners; 46 schools; and 33 taverns.

STATISTICAL

Composed of Extracts from the Township

Names of Townships.	When Settled	Inhabited Houses.	No. of People.	No. of Churches, or Places of Worship.	No. of Preachers.	No. of Medical Practitioners.	No. of Schools.	Fees per Quarter.	No. of Stores.	No. of Taverns.	No. of Grist Mills.	No. of Saw Mills.	Price of Books per 100	Prices of time per bushel.	WAGES OF Blacksmiths per month and day.	Masons per day.	Carpenters p. day.	Common Labour ers per Annum.
								s. d.						*s. d. s. d.*	PrM. £ *s.*	*s. d. s. d.*		£. *s.*
Humberstone ..	1787	75	..	1 Men.	1 Men	0	2	13 9	2	2	1	1	37 8	..	5 0	10 0 10 0		30 0
Bertie ..	1784	200	1600	1 Q.	..	1	6	11 3	8	7	3	5	30 0	1 3	..	8 9 6 3		27 6
Willoughby	1784	63	441	0	0	0	1	12 6	1	2	0	2	30 0	..	4 10	6 3 6 3		..
Stamford .	1784	165	1200	1 P.	1 P.	2	5	15 0	8	5	1	2	30 0 0 7½	4 10	6 3 5 0		25 0
Grantham	1784	200	1200	1 P.	..	2	6	12 6	3	6	3	4	30 0 0 7½	5 0	10 0 7 6		27 10
Lowth ..	1787	130	700	0	0	0	3	12 6	3	3	2	5	30 0 0 7½	6 0	6 8 6 8		25 0
Grimsby .	1787	142	805	1 E.	1 E. 1 M.	0	3	12 0	4	2	4	6	25 0 0 7½	5 0	.. ..		25 0
Pelham ..	1790	130	776	1 Q.	0	0	5	12 6	2	1	3	6	25 0 1	0 5 0	6 3 5 0		25 0
Thorold..	1788	150	830	1	1 P. 1 Q. 2 M.	0	9	..	4	2	1	4	.. ..	PrD. *s. d.* 6 3	6 3 6 3		..
Crowland.	1788	84	600	1 M.	0	1	2	10 0	1	1	1	1	37 6 1 3	5 0	7 6 5 0		30 0
Wainfleet ..	1800	72	..	0	0	0	2	10 0	1	1	0	1	30 0 0 10	12 6	7 6 5 0		25 0
Canboro' and Caistor ..	1803 1789	25 23	190 156	0	2 M.	0	2	12 6	1	1	1	4	25 0 1 3	..	7 6 6 10		30 0
Totals.	..	1459 8408		8	10	6	46	134 6	38	33	20	41	330 2 8 1	23 9 & 35l.	82 11 69 9		269 16
Averaged by	..	13	11	..	..	..	..	11	..	..	..	..	11	9	3 & 7	11 11		10
Averages	..	112	772	..	..	..	12 2½						30 0	10½	7 11 & 5l.	7 6 6 4		26 19

Q. in columns fifth and sixth stands for Quaker; Men. for Menonist;

* Although I have entered this sum as it stands in the report; yet, as the reporters have calculated only from the number of houses, and allowed eight persons to each house *

TABLE.

Reports of the District of Niagara.

Wages of: ...ers per Winter month.	Wages of: Common Labourers per Summer month.	Wages of: ...mmon Labourers per day in Harvest.	Wages of: Women's wages, per week.	Cost of clearing and fencing five Acres of wild Land.	Prices of live stock: A Work-horse.	Prices of live stock: A Cow.	Prices of live stock: An Ox.	Prices of live stock: A Sheep.	Quantity of Wool per Sheep.	Price of Wool per lb.	Produce of wheat in bushels, per acre.	An Ox will gain in a Summer's run.	Price of Butter, per lb.	Price of Cheese, per lb.	Price of Land per Acre, at first.	Price of Land per Acre, now.
. d.	s. d.	s. d.	s. d.	L. s.	L. s.	L. s.	L. s.	s. d.	lb.	s. d.		lb.	s. d.	s. d.	s. d.	s. d.
40 0	60 0	5 0	5 0	..	17 10	5 0	8 10	12 6	3	2 6	15	..	0 11	..	0 6	12 6
40 0	60 0	5 0	5 0	20 0	16 10	5 10	10 0	12 6	3	2 6	15	..	1 0	0 7½	1 3	35 0
40 0	50 0	..	5 0	20 0	17 10	5 12	8 15	13 9	3½	2 6	22	190	1 0	0 6	1 0	25 0
40 0	50 0	4 4	5 0	..	17 10	5 0	10 0	15 0	4½	1 10½	20	112	0 10	0 7	1 0	50 0
45 0	62 0	4 4	6 3	..	15 0	5 0	8 15	12 6	3½	2 6	20	..	1 0	0 7½	0 7½	50 0
10 0	50 0	5 0	5 7	20 0	15 0	5 0	8 0	17 6	3	2 3	20	175	1 0	7½	1 3	50 0
0 0	50 0	..	..	25 0	12 0	4 0	..	15 0	2½	2 6	..	..	..	..	2 0	..
5 0	50 0	5 0	5 0	18 15	15 0	4 0	8 0	12 6	3	1 10½	15	..	0 11	7½	1 3½	40 0
5 0	65 0	5 0	5 2	..	15 0	5 12	10 0	18 9	5	2 0	..	..	7½	7½	0 7	50 0
0 0	60 0	..	..	..	20 0	6 5	10 0	12 6	3½	2 6	20	$\frac{1}{3}$	11¾	11¾	1 6	20 0
5 0	55 0	..	..	18 15	15 0	4 12	8 0	11 0	3	1 10½	20	250	1 0	0 7½	5 0 5 0	20 0 12 6
0 0	70 0	5 0	5 7	..	15 0	5 0	10 0	12 6	2½	2 6	15	275	1 3	1 0	..	..
0 0	682	38 8	47 8	122 10	191 0	60 11	100 0	166 0	40	27 4½	182	932	10 6	6 9¾	21 0	365 0
12	12	8	9	6	12	13	11	12	12	12	10	5	11	10	12	11
0 10	56 10	4 10	5 3	20 8	15 11	5 1	9 2	13 10	$3\frac{1}{3}$	2 3¼	18	186	11½	0 8	1 9	33 2

P. for Presbyterian; E. for Episcopal; M. for Methodist.

allowance quite too much, I have taken the liberty, in summing up, to deduct 100, that
ay not pervert my average calculations.—R. G.

Improvement is said to be retarded in five reports by want of people: in three reports by want of money: in three reports by large tracts of land owned by non-occupants: in two reports by the prevention of emigration from the United States: in two reports by bad roads: in one report by the crown and clergy reserves: in one report by giving away land instead of selling it: in one report by the land being all located, and no buyers: in one report by the war.

The Home District.

FROM this district I did not receive a single reply to my address, although it was first published here, and had the cordial approbation of the head magistrate of the province, as well as of every body with whom I held converse.* This may be ascribed to two causes: first, the opposition of a monstrous little fool of a parson, who, for reasons best known to himself, fell foul of the address which I had published, abused me as its author, and has ever since laboured, with unremitting malignity, to frustrate its intention.

This man, unfortunately, was a member of the executive council; and his efforts, from that circumstance, were but too successful. In another place his name, history, and machinations, shall be fully displayed.

The second cause may be traced to the low condition of society in the Home District, owing to the peculiar *state of property*. The foregoing reports sufficiently demonstrate how the farmers of Upper Canada have been baffled in their improvements by the large tracts of unsettled land; but, in the Home District, they have suffered most from this; and not only has it dulled the edge of husbandry, but in a remarkable degree, clouded the rise of intellect and spirit among the inhabitants. . . .

To carry on my estimate of population, I suppose that Little York might contain, in 1817, of people, I shall not say souls,   1,200. There are 13 organized townships in the district; that is, such as hold town meetings for the choice of town office bearers, and to these, three others are united, each containing a few inhabitants. If to these 13 townships, with their additions, are allowed 500 people each, the full number, I think, will

---

* The "head magistrate", also described as "President" by Gourlay, was Samuel Smith, the senior member of the Executive Council, who in the absence of Lieutenant-Governor Gore was Administrator of the province. [Ed]

be obtained as it stood in 1817 6,500
   The above   1,200

   Total white population   7,700

There is an Indian reserve west of York, which extends from the lake to the wilderness, between Toronto and Etobekoke, and on which some Mississaga Indians are stationary, perhaps 200. They employ themselves in fishing, and shooting wild fowl, chiefly ducks, which frequent York harbour in myriads. In still, clear weather they have a mode of killing fish with a small javelin, which they use standing upright in their bark canoes with a dexterity and ease that is delightful to witness. In 1818, a purchase was made from the Missassagas of part of their reserve, and a vast extent of the wilderness, which has since been surveying and settling, with emigrants from Britain and Ireland, British subjects from the United States, &c.

In travelling through the Home District, I observed yellow pine in two places: viz. on Holland river, which runs into lake Simcoe, and east of York a few miles. The timber of this tree is very superior to the white pine, which prevails through the province, being much more resinous. . . .

Newcastle District. Township Reports

Haldimand.

NAME, Haldimand: situated on the lake shore: extent of the township, nine miles east and west; and 12 miles north and south.

The soil appears to be very excellent throughout this township: the land being well timbered of such as beech, maple, basswood, &c. &c. &c. as well as a sufficient quantity of building timber, suitable for the purposes which we require it for.

These are streams sufficient for mills · of any size: various living springs also generally throughout.

The country began to be settled in the month of June, 1797: the quantity of land, 70,000 acres, of which is under cultivation 6,258. Persons whose property is rateable, 154; number of grist mills, 3; of saw mills, 4; of carding machines, 3; of stores, 5; of taverns, 4; meeting houses, 1; preachers of various sects, such as Baptists, Methodists, &c.; of schools, 4; teachers' fees per quarter, 12s. 6d.

The rate of grinding (as is customary) every 12th part; price

of boards at the mill, 35s.; bricks, at the kiln, 35s. each, per 1000;
lime at the kiln, 1s. 3d. per bushel; prices of labour, viz. blacksmiths per month, 20 dollars; of clearing land, 10 dollars per acre;
for common labourers, for six months in summer season, 14
dollars per month; day labourers, in harvest, 5s.; carpenters, per
day, 6s. 3d.; masons, per day, 7s. 6d.; of labouring women, per
week, 5s.; price of a horse, four years old, 60 dollars; an ox, 40
dollars; a milch cow, 20 dollars; a sheep, three dollars; 3lbs. of
wool per sheep, at 2s. 6d.; butter, 1s. and cheese, 7½d. per lb.
Time of turning out cattle to pasture about the 1st of May; of
taking into stable about the 20th November; sleighing season,
three months: ploughing in spring, about the 20th of April; of
seeding wheat, 1st September; reaping of grain, the month of
August; wheat, sown per acre, one bushel; produce 25 bushels.
Lands let upon shares, one-half the profits arising. At the first settling of the township, lands were worth 5s. per acre; at the present
time in good situations, 15s., and in ordinary situations, 10s.

NATHAN BURNHAM,   JOHN RUNGER,
EBENEZER ALLEN,   JOHNSON MERRIAM,
JOHN BROWN,   WILSON RUS.

Newcastle District: Summary of Population, &c.

THIS district has, like the last, been made the spoil of power, and
large blocks of unoccupied land every where hem in and distress
the industrious settlers. It contains excellent land, finely watered.
I had from it only the report of Haldimand; and my only data for
calculating the population is from the assessment roll, which, in
1818, gave the following account of persons liable to district
taxes:

During the last three years many emigrants have been settled
towards Rice lake, in this district, of whom I take no account.

In the Township of Percy			34
Ditto	ditto	Murray	124
Ditto	ditto	Cramahe	136
Ditto	ditto	Haldimand	162
Ditto	ditto	Hamilton	155
Ditto	ditto	Hope	120
Ditto	ditto	Clark and Darlington	58
			789

> Supposing each of the above persons to be the head of a family of   6
> The total will be   4734
> And admit that poor persons, who are not on the roll, amount to   266
> The population will be   5000

Midland District, Township Report

Kingston.

To ROBERT GOURLAY, ESQ.

November 28th, 1817.

SIR,

IT is impossible for an inhabitant of this province, who has at heart either the interest of the colony, or mother country, to read your address to the landholders of Upper Canada, without feeling a most sincere interest in the success of your arduous undertaking.

This communication, Sir, the result of that address, is made by a society yet in its infancy, which has for its object the mutual improvement of its members in the arts and sciences, and the dissemination amongst their fellow men of such useful knowledge as by their exertions they may be able to attain. Anxious to contribute our mite to the promoting so desirable an object as the laying open the valuable resources of this vast country to our fellow subjects on the other side of the Atlantic, we have taken every pains in our power to obtain correct information on the subject of your queries, as regards the township of Kingston. Should the annexed replies therefore be found in any way subservient to your laudable purpose, they are most cordially at your service, to be used as you may think proper.

Our society, Sir, whilst it confesses its inability to pay any adequate tribute to the patriotism and philanthropy of your present exertion, begs particularly to express its approbation of your plan of publishing in German as well as in English, as the Germans, from their industrious habits and attachment to our government, generally make valuable settlers.

We subscribe the names of all the members of our society in town, and remain, with warmest wishes for your welfare and property.

Your most obedient Servants,

CHAS. SHORT,	ANTONY MARSHAL,
H. C. THOMSON,	JOHN M. BALFOUR,
ROBT. STANTON,	THOMAS GRAHAM.

2d.   The first English settlement was made in the year 1783, though the French had a small garrison here, while in possession of the country. The number of inhabited houses now is about 550: population about 2,850. This enumeration includes the town of Kingston, which contains 450 houses and 2,250 souls.

3d.   There are four churches, or meeting houses, viz. 1 Episcopalian, 1 Roman Catholic, and 2 Methodists: there are 4 professional preachers, viz. 1 Episcopalian, 1 Presbyterian, and 2 Methodists. This enumeration does not include a chaplain to the army, and one to the royal navy.

5th.   Eight schools, the fees of which are various; viz. three at 40s: four at 22s. 6d.; and one conducted on the Lancastrian system at 10s. per quarter.

6th.   There are 67 stores and shops in the town and township. This includes the different denominations of shops kept by mechanics.

7th.   There are 41 taverns, inns, hotels, and coffee-houses in the town and township.

8th.   There is a machine for carding wool, at the rate of 9d. per lb.; generally paid in wool at the current price.

9th.   The soil of this township is chiefly of a clayey nature, covered in its original state with a stratum of rich black vegetable mould. The soil rests on a bed of limestone, and is of various depths: a small part is rather thin, particularly round the shores of Kingston bay and the bay of Quinté, and a great number of small stones remain on the surface, though they could be all removed at a trifling expence of labour: neither do the farmers use lime or manure upon their lands: yet they are all in good circumstances, and a few years of industry would make them all rich, they being near the market of Kingston, where a large garrison is kept; besides the royal naval establishment: also, a number of merchant vessels which belong to the port. There are numbers of natural meadows and small lakes in the township; and it is well watered with rivulets and creeks. Four-fifths of the land is still covered with forest trees.

10th.   The timber most abundant is the different kinds of maple: the curled and bird-eye maple is remarkable for making the most beautiful cabinet furniture. A grove of sugar maple trees with proper care will produce on an average, each spring, five lbs. of sugar per tree.

The other trees as they most abound are beech, ash, elm, the different species of fir, the walnut, butternut, hiccorynut, basswood, ironwood, birch, cherry, white and red cedar, poplar, elder, oaks, black and white, prickly ash, hazle, shittim wood, willows, hemlock tree, and the locust tree, &c.

11th. The whole of this township lays on a stratum of limestone, at the depth of from one to six feet. There has been iron ore found on the banks of a small river near Kingston mills, and also a salt spring tolerably strong.

12th. The blue limestone of this township makes very handsome and durable building stone: it has been sold at a quarry within the limits of this town, the last and present years, from two to three dollars per toise.

15th. The wages of mechanics are at present extravagantly high: they may, however, be considered on the decline, which will keep pace with the increase of the population.

Journeymen's wages at present are as follows:

Carpenters, on an average, winter and summer, 8s. 6d. per day, and found in board and lodging.

Blacksmiths, do 3s. 6d. per day, with board and lodging. Masons, 9s. to 12s. 6d. – not found.

The price of shoeing a horse all round is generally from 8s. to 9s. iron found. Most of the farmers make their own ploughs and harrows, the wood work of which is of little value; the iron of a plough cost generally from nine to twelve dollars, according to weight, or 1s. per lb.; harrow lines 10d.; chains, steeled wedges, &c. 1s. 3d.

18th. Clearing land covered with timber, prepared for the harrow at 3l. per acre is £15 0 0

Fencing do. at 7s. 6d. per acre, is 1 17 6

Total for five acres £16 17 6

21st. The usual time of turning beasts to pasture is about the 20th of April, and the time they are generally taken into a yard (as the farmers of this township are not in the habit of stabling their cattle, horses excepted) is about the 20th of November.

22d. The sleighing season generally commences about the 1st of January, and terminates the latter end of March. Ploughing is usually commenced about the 20th of April.

23d. What is termed winter wheat and rye is generally sown about the 10th of September. All kinds of spring grain – such as oats, wheat, peas, barley, and rye, are generally sown from the 3d to the 20th of May. The usual time of reaping spring grain is from the 15th of August to the 15th of September.

25th. A cow will give (including summer and winter) in the course of one week 21 quarts of milk, which will make three lbs. and a half of butter, or four lbs. of cheese.

26th. No general system of cropping is observed. The ordinary mode with new land is to put in a crop of wheat, and continue this from year to year as long as the land will bear it: it is then laid to grass for two or three years: after which it is cropped, without observing any general system of husbandry. Manure is seldom used, excepting now and then for a potatoe or Indian corn crop.

27th. The system of letting lands on shares is not extensively practised in this township. When it is done one-half of the proceeds is considered a sufficient compensation to the farmer, the proprietor providing farming utensils, oxen, and seed, for the first crop.

28th. Few or no actual purchases of land were made by the original settlers, as their situation entitled them to grants from government; many of these people, however, in a few years, got into the books of the merchants, and from that period we may date actual sales: from 10 to 20 years ago, lands sold to liquidate debts, may be stated at from 2s. 6d. to 10s. per acre. Since that period, it has not come to our knowledge that many sales have been made, excepting in the way of barter, the price of which generally yielded to the circumstances of the seller. Within the last month a sale of 600 acres of wild land has been made 6 miles from Kingston; the estimated price is 13s. 4d. to be paid for, part cash and part barter. Farms of 200 acres, with, perhaps, 60 or 80 acres cleared, with a house and barn, and within a range of 10 miles of this town, may be worth from 2l. to 5l. per acre.

29th. If there were purchasers in the market, we believe the quantity for sale to be very considerable.

30th. In the remote concessions of this township the roads are very bad, chiefly owing to the country being so thinly inhabited, and to the crown and clergy reserves: likewise, a principal cause of the bad roads is owing to the large tracts of land held by non-residents, as they are not compelled by law to contribute their share of the expence towards the making and improving roads: generally speaking, the materials exist in great abundance throughout the township for the making of roads, and if wise legislative and municipal laws were adopted and enforced, we might have as good roads here as in any part of the world, and not at a greater expence than they have them in countries where the price of labour bears any proportion to what it is here. Water communication is not very common, except on the front of the township; but it might be extended and improved by means of canals, &c.: however, this species of improvement would require capital and a condensed population.

31st. There are three prominent causes which tend to retard the improvement of this part of the country: first the original settlers were (generally speaking) discharged soldiers, whose habits were, and continue to be, foreign to the quiet and peaceful pursuits of industry: there is likewise another class of settlers, consisting of regardless characters, chiefly emigrants from the United States.

The second cause, which in our opinion retards the agricultural improvment of this township, is the crown and clergy reserves. If they could be disposed of, so as to allow good roads, and a free communication from one concession to another, it would tend, in our opinion, much to the improvement of the township.

The third cause is the immense tracts of land held by non-residents. We cannot pretend to give you a correct account of the quantity of land so held; but we are certain that we do not exaggerate in stating the number of acres at from 12 to 15,000, exclusive of the crown and clergy reserves, which are two-seventh parts of the whole land in the township.

Kingston. – Second Report.

At a Meeting of a respectable Number of Yeomen, Farmers, and others, held at the Village of Waterloo, in the Township of Kingston, on Monday, February 2, 1818, when Major John Everett was unanimously called to the Chair, and Mr. John Vincent was requested to act as Secretary to the Meeting, Mr. Gourlay's Publication to the resident Landholders of Upper Canada, was read and approved. It was then resolved that his Queries be taken into Consideration, and Answers returned thereto.

PASTURE good. A lean ox will sometimes gain two cwt. in a summer's run. A good cow yields seven pounds of butter per week. The cows are smaller, and badly managed to what they are in England.

At the first settlement, many sold their 200 acre lots for the value of a few shillings: 12 years ago, land a few miles from Kingston sold for 2s. 6d. per acre; and lately, in the same situations, for 30s. or 40s.; but the fire wood alone will be soon worth as much as that.

For cash a number of improved farms might be bought.

The roads are very indifferent; but if properly undertaken, might, at a little expence, be made good, as stone is at hand.

What contributes to the neglect of the roads is that the business is mostly contrived to be done by sleighing.

In answer to the last question, what, in our opinions, would most contribute to the improvement of the province, and what retards the same, the following answers were proposed, and unanimously approved of.

1st. The want of capital, which is partly caused by the arrival of so many poor emigrants from the mother country, with scarcely money sufficient to support them a month, and yet expect to undertake a farm, because the land is given them, quite forgetting they want it cleared, with a house, barn, horses, cows, and every implement in husbandry, together with provision till they can raise their own: but, it is true, most of the present farmers commenced with small means; but they better understood the nature of the country, and to be a good labourer it requires a year or two's practice to get expert in the method of farming in this country.

We would recommend men with a suitable capital to enter into farming, to take them under their protection, or by forming small colonies for the purpose of settling, and then introducing men of the country among them to instruct them; and we venture to declare, under suitable management, Upper Canada would answer any reasonable expectation to farmers, and nearly every useful artisan: the latter should not remain at the sea-ports, but proceed up the country, where they are wanted. We wish also that some method could be adopted at the sea-ports, to give such people information where they would find employment.

For want of capital the greatest object remains neglected, that is, the removing the obstacle to the navigation of the river St. Lawrence. The expence of this object, it is generally considered, would be less than it cost government to bring up the stores during the last war. The benefits we should receive are immense, when our remote situation is considered. At present every article we want from the sea-ports is brought to us at great expence, time, and risk: the same may be said of any article we have to export. We sincerely hope some spirited men of capital, in England, may turn their attention to this object, and we have no doubt but they would be well remunerated for the money they expended, by the increase of population and trade up and down the river.

The great quantities of land in the fronts and public situations that remain unimproved, by being given very injudiciously to persons who do not want to settle on them, and what is most shameful and injurious, no law is made to compel them to make or work any public road; but this is to be done by industrious people, who settle around. Such lands remain like a putrid carcass, an injury and a nuisance to all around: at the same time, to the owners, this land increases in value, without their being made to contribute towards it, at other men's expence. Our worthies a few years ago passed an act, that required a poor man to work three days upon the public roads, and these overgorged landowners but twelve days, and others, with twenty times as much property, doing no more. It would excite surprise at Governor Gore's signing such a bill, if it was not known that the parliament voted him £3,000 to buy a piece of plate.

Mr. Gourlay takes it for granted, that the restraints to improvement will be speedily removed by government. This assertion ill comports with the notice given by the Board of Trade to our merchants, to set a duty on timber from British America. We do express our belief, to think it impossible so much injury to the people of these provinces can be intended, to please a northern despot, or to answer any policy. If such is the intention, we may be assured, more, like Bute and North, are in council, who, by their arbitrary measures, lost to us the, now, United States. Our loyalty and regard for the mother country was strongly proved by the severe military duty we performed during the late war; and common gratitude would entitle us to every fostering care the mother country could bestow to the encouragement of our commerce, and other local interests.

We think an indiscriminate admission of people from the United States greatly injurious to the province; many of these people come among us solely from gain, without any respect for people or country, who would, at a favourable opportunity, join their countrymen against us; and if we were sure of their attachment, are they not filling the country where the surplus population of Britain might plant themselves with advantage and honour?

The want of success at the depot (Perth New Settlement) arises from the badness of the system pursued, and the conduct of the agents employed, and not from the country or settlers. The agents should be fatherly men, who understand the management of such business; instead of which, a parcel of ignorant proud puppies were put there, who were too indolent to give the strangers directions to find their land: but if government will take the trouble to hear, it will be explained to them in every particular.

JOHN VINCENT.

Earnest-Town, Including Amherst Island.

2d. Itinerant tradesmen, from the United States, when occasional, or rather periodical improvements require their services, in the erection or repairing of buildings, in the clearing and culture of lands, and in the disposal of implements of husbandry, often augment the actual population by some hundreds.

3d. There is only one resident professional preacher in the whole township, and he is of the Methodist society. But the respective churches are occasionally served by non-resident and itinerant gentlemen from the United States, and from the adjacent townships, especially from Kingston; which place, from its being the naval, military, and commercial capital of Upper Canada, is well supplied with religious establishments and ministers.

5th. There is one parochial academy in the village, and thirteen common schools over the township. The fees may average 10s. per quarter.

8th. There are two carding and one fulling machines. One barley hulling mill, together with a water blast furnace. Carding is 5½d. per lb. and fulling 6d. per yard.

9th. The general character is good.

10th. The timber, in order as it most abounds, is, beech and sugar maple, basswood, white pine, white oak, black ash, water elm, white cedar, red oak, white walnut, spruce, black and white birch, iron wood, tamerack, butternut, balsam fir, &c. &c.

11th. Iron and sulphur strongly indicated: limestone is universal. Plaster of Paris has lately been found in an uncalcined state, and strongly impregnated with lime. Several springs have been found charged with salt and other minerals not yet defined.

12th. There are several quarries of excellent building stone, which may be obtained for 10s. per toise.

15th. Blacksmiths, piece-work, viz. horse-shoeing, 8s.; plough shares, 15d. per lb. wrought; felling axe, 10s.; hoe, 5s.; and the general practice in working iron for the farmers' utensils (with the exception of plain work, such as harrow teeth, &c.) is charged at the current price of iron per lb.

25th. The pasture is universally good, consisting of white clover and timothy, natural and rich. The cows yield excellent milk, and the quality of the butter is luscious, and that of the cheese mellow, much resembling Dunlap cheese. Pork and poultry of every description are raised with ease and abundance, while the adjacent waters furnish a great variety of delicious fish and fowls, and the woods contain many species of game, which help to save the farmer's stock.

26th. The course of cropping is wheat, rye, grass broken up

for fall wheat, or pease. When sown with wheat, the pease or oats follow; when with pease, wheat or barley follows. Manure is applied with advantage for all crops; but generally only used for potatoes, Indian corn, flax, and barley.

27th. Land is sometimes let on shares, but not to any great extent. The ordinary terms are about one-third to the proprietor of the field produce.

28th. At the first settlement the value of wild lands was merely nominal. They have progressively risen, and their present price may be computed at £1. 5s. per acre. The average price of 100 acres of land, one half improved with tolerable buildings thereon, may be valued at £3. per acre.

29th. From the prosperity of the township, there are hardly any lands for sale, except when cases of emergency urge a disposal.

30th. The roads are tolerably good; but might be considerably improved at a moderate expence. The water communication to all parts of the province is free from the front of the township. If the improvement of this township can be said to be retarded, it is for want of more skill in husbandry, and the dearth of labourers; and it may be added, that although this township is generally considered one of the best settled, and most prosperous in the Upper Province, yet the introduction of men of capital and enterprise, and those versed in a superior knowledge of husbandry, would be a great acquisition, and contribute to its ultimate prosperity.

R. MACKAY,
Secretary to the Meeting.

Adolphustown.

9th. The general character of the soil is clay.

10th. The timber most abounding, is oak, hickory, beech, maple, pine, elm, and bass.

26th. The ordinary course of cropping upon new land is to sow it with wheat in the fall, and with rye the ensuing season; it is sometimes let lay, and sometimes sowed with pease in the spring after the first crop is reaped, and again with wheat in the fall. Manure is applied on orchard ground, and for corn and potatoes; sometimes for wheat and barley.

27th. Land is sometimes let on shares, but not practised to a great extent in this township: the ordinary terms are, the owner to furnish team, seed, &c. and take one-half when gathered.

28th. At the first settlement of this township, land could be procured at 1s. per acre. It rose gradually to 5s. 10s. 15s. 20s. &c. At this moment there is no land in the township could be procured for less than 4l. per acre, and it is believed few would sell at any price.

29th. None.

30th. The roads of this township are surpassed by none in the province. No township has greater advantages as respects water conveyance; every concession has communication with the bay leading to Kingston.

31st. In our opinion what retards the improvement of the province in general, is the great necessity which still exists in it for improvement of the St. Lawrence, the very unequal road tax, the great quantity of land held by landholders residing out of the province, and the want of a provincial bank. Could these objects be accomplished, and an emigration of enterprising settlers from home, men of capital and abilities, take place, no doubt rests with us that it would greatly advance prosperity.

JACOB HOVER,	WILLET CASEY,
THOMAS COOK,	WILLIAM MOORE,
PHILIP ROBLEN,	ARCH. CAMPBELL,
DAVID PETERSON,	*And 25 others.*

Sophiasburg.

3d. There are no churches. The Quakers, Methodists, and Presbyterians, have meetings at private houses.

8th. One carding machine: 6d. per lb. carding wool.

9th. Clay and loam: surface tolerably level.

10th. Pine, oak, maple, beech, ash, elm, cedar, and basswood.

12th. There is no building stone, except limestone, which can be had at a very trifling expence.

18th. From 8 to 12 dollars per acre, employer finding a team.

25th. Quantity of pasture is small in proportion to the size of the farms; quality tolerably good.

26th. Wheat is always the first crop, both on new lands, and on land broken up from grass. Pease, corn, or oats, the next crop; then wheat again. Manure is seldom used, and only that from the barnyard.

27th. But few farms are let on shares.

28th. At first settlement, about 1s. per acre: there is little wild land for sale here: last sales made from three to five dollars per acre. No sales of improved farms have lately taken place.

30th. State of the roads generally good. The township being situated on the bay of Quinté, is very convenient for water communication.

ORTON HANCOX.

Hallowell.

14th Feb. 1818.

At a Meeting of the Justices of the Peace, and principal Inhabitants, held at Eyre's Inn, the Proposals of Mr. Gourlay were considered, and the following Replies agreed to.

HALLOWELL is almost wholly good soil, generally of a loamy nature, yielding excellent winter wheat, and also all other kinds of spring and summer grain, such as pease, oats, Indian corn, barley, potatoes, turnips, &c. Flax, when properly attended, being raised also of an excellent quality. The township being generally level, is cultivated with ease, and is handsomely proportioned with meadow land. Orchards also begin to thrive.

We have one Methodist, and one Quaker meeting house in the township: preparations are making also for a Presbyterian meeting house. The former is attended by a circuit preacher every two weeks. The latter by a Quaker speaker every Sabbath.

One carding and one fulling machine: carding wool, 6d. per lb.; and 2s. per yard for fulling, colouring, pressing, and shearing cloth.

The timber produced is beech, maple, white and black ash, basswood, birch, white and black oak, iron wood, cedar, and a suitable proportion of white pine for building, and sawing into boards. There are various ridges which abound with limestone, which could be obtained at a very trifling expence. Excellent clay is found in different parts of the township, from which the best of bricks are made; two brick houses being finished in the township.

The course of cropping upon new lands is generally thus: the owner of the land will find team to do the work, and board the person cropping: they will labour equally, and the cropper will receive one-third of the wheat. On old lands various ways are practised, according to the circumstances of the person wishing to take or rent a farm or piece of land; but generally much to the advantage of the cropper. Old land generally drawing one-third of the produce without any labour of the owner: he finding one-third the seed, and receives his share, harvested or not, as may be agreed upon in the field. Manure is generally drawn out in the fall upon ground to be planted, with Indian corn in the spring, or for other grain, as may be required; farms being let upon shares, or leased from one to three years in general.

Farms of 200 acres, with from 30 to 50 acres cleared, having a comfortable frame dwelling house and barn, are worth from 600l. to 800l.

The roads are good, and yearly improving. Within the limits of this township lie two small lakes, called East and West Lake: the former upwards of 12 miles in circumference, the latter upwards of 16, both communicating with Ontario by outlets, which are navigable for boats, and are settled on all sides by industrious farmers. These waters abound in bass, and other fish, which are taken at pleasure.

Settlers, able to distribute money among us, would be of the greatest benefit to the township and vicinity in general; as also by instructions as to the modes of agriculture at home.

EBENEZER WASHBURN,
Chairman to the Meeting.

Thurlow.

IN the first concession of this township, and on the eastern side of the river Moira, is situated the town of Belville, composed of part of a plot which was originally a reservation to the Missassaga tribe of Indians, for the purposes of encamping and fishing. In the spring of 1816, it was by order of government surveyed and formed into a town-plot, consisting of upwards of 300 lots of half an acre each.

3d.　The Gospel is dispensed almost every Sabbath of the year, in different parts of the township, by itinerant preachers of the Methodist and Baptist sects.

8th.　There are two carding machines, and two fulling mills. The rate of carding wool, 6d. per lb.; and of fulling and dressing cloth from 7d. to 10d. per yard.

9th.　The general quality of the soil is light loam, or marl. The surface, in some few instances, is broken; but generally level, smooth, and even.

10th.　The most common timber is maple, and in succession, beech, basswood, oak, pine, elm, birch, iron wood, spruce, fir, and cedar.

11th.　No minerals have been discovered; neither does the soil indicate any impregnations; limestone is found in abundance, and can be quarried for 30s. per toise: there are no remarkable springs.

15th. Blacksmiths charge for a plough,   £1 17 6

    Do.   for a hoe, ... 0 5 0

    Do.   narrow axe, ... 0 12 6

    Do.   shoeing a horse, ... 0 7 6

25th. Pasture fields are generally composed of white and red clover, herds grass, spear grass, and blue joint, all considered of good quality. On such, an ox of four years old, would gain from three to four hundred pounds during a summer's run.

26th. The ordinary mode of cropping upon new lands is to deposit the seed as soon as the land is cleared of the timber, and harrow the land three or four times, in order effectually to cover the seed. Upon old land to break it up with the plough early in the season, say the month of May; cross plough and harrow it at different times through the season, and have it ready for the seed in September. Manure is applied in the month of November, and to such land as is intended for pease, oats, corn, potatoes, and flax.

27th. The practice of letting land on shares is common, &c. Where farms are leased for a given sum, 25l. per annum is the customary rent for a farm of 200 acres, possessing ordinary advantages and accommodations with, say, one quarter part improved.

28th. Farms situated near the bay of Quinté, consisting of 200 acres, one-third improved with a comfortable farm house, and necessary out-houses, considered worth from 3l. to 5l per acre.

29th. There are probably from 15,000 to 20,000 acres of land yet for sale.

The township comprises about 55,000 acres; 25,000 of which is in the possession of actual settlers; about 14,000 are reserved by government, and the residue is yet to be disposed of.

30th. Roads in general are tolerably good; but require and are capable of much improvement, which could be effected at the average expence of 5l. per mile. The river Moira is the only stream in the township worthy of remark. It has its source in Hog lake, which is situated about 30 miles north of the township. It abounds in valuable mill seats, and discharges itself into the bay of Quinté, at the town of Bellville.

31st. The circumstances which retard the improvement of the township may be considered as extending to all parts of the province, and proceed from the want of a much more extensive population of yeomanry, and a monied capital directed in a general and liberal manner to agricultural pursuits.

JAMES MC NAB, J. P.   JOHN W. MYERS,
SIMON MC NAB,   JOHN HUBBARD,
ROBERT SMITH,   JOHN CANNEFF.

Feb. 6th, 1818.
Midland District.

General Report.

Kingston, 26th Nov. 1817.

SIR,

I did not receive your circular until the day before yesterday, and observing, that you intend leaving the country soon, I have committed to paper, what I know myself, and what I could collect from my neighbours: if I had been informed, at an earlier period, of your intentions, I should have been able to have answered more of your queries.

The soil of the Midland District, is generally a dark coloured clay and yellow loam; both kinds good for wheat and every other grain. It is well timbered with white pine, white and red oak, maple, beech, hickory, birch, basswood, ironwood, butternut and poplar: there are no plains of yellow pine and oak: there are no mountains or hills of any height: the country is quite level. No mines have as yet been discovered; but from the difficulty which surveyors have met with, in running parallel lines, owing to the variation of the needle, there can be no doubt of the existence of iron mines. The produce of an acre of new land, is from 25 to 30 bushels of wheat, and of old, from 15 to 20: it would however produce more were the farmers to manure and till the ground well. The sowing season commences about the middle of April; and harvest about the middle of July, and continues to the latter end of August before all the grain is housed. Labourers get from 10 to 12 dollars per month, and in harvest, from four to five shillings per day, and found.

The stock of cattle was very much diminished during the war, being bought up for the army.

The assess roll gives about 3,600 horses, above two years: 100 oxen, above four years: 6,185 milch cows: 1,654 head of young cattle, above two years: 900 houses: 88 merchants' shops: 24 store houses: 24 grist mills: 40 saw mills: there are also some fulling mills and carding machines.

There are in Kingston, three clergymen of the church of England; one Presbyterian, and two Methodists: in the country the clergy are mostly Methodists. Clergymen and churches are much wanted.

Since the legislature has appropriated a sum of money for common schools, they have increased very much in the country: in Kingston there are six; two grammer, three common, and one for young ladies.

This country was settled in 1784: lands were, of course, then of no value: they rose from 15d. to 2s. 6d. per acre: are now worth from 10s. to 5l. the acre, unless distant, and of an inferior quality. The Midland District, upon the whole, contains a fine body of land, and possesses many local advantages, and only requires settlers that have some property to begin with, to make it one of the most flourishing districts in the province. Kingston must eventually become a populous town. At present, the country is but thinly settled, and to fill it up by its natural increase will require a very long period.

If I have not been able to answer all your queries. I believe the most essential ones are taken notice of, and hope they may contribute in carrying your very laudable plan into execution.

I am, Sir,
Your very obedient Servant,
THOMAS MARKLAND.

MR. ROBERT GOURLAY.

Midland District:
Summary of Population, &c. &c.

THE reports from this district being few in proportion, and several of these irregular, I cannot give an exact estimate of population; but the following will not be far wrong.

Kingston, Earnest-town, Adolphustown, and Thurlow, contain	7083
Sophiasburgh, having 101 inhabited houses, may contain	606
Total	7689
Deducting from this amount the population of the town of Kingston, viz. 2250, the average of the country population of these townships is 1068, and this average may be allowed to Fredericksburgh, Marysburgh, Hallowell, Ameliasburgh, and Sidney, which are all regularly organized townships	5340

Pittsburgh, with Wolf Island, Loughborough, Portland, Camden, Richmond, and
Rawdon, though some of them are organized,
will not average above 300 each   ¹1800

In Huntingdon I heard only of four set-
tlers, say   24

And of none in Hungerford, Sheffield,
Hinchinbrook, and Bedford.

               Total white population, 14,853

The Indians, on the Mohawk reserve,
amount to nearly   200

    Total population   15,053

This tract is now, I believe, bought up by government, and
will make an excellent settlement, being generally composed of
capital land, with a fine mill stream passing through it.

For the reported population of 7689, there appear to be 11
churches, and 5 resident ministers: viz. 1 Episcopalian, 1 Presbyterian, and 3 Methodists. There are 10 medical practitioners, 34
schools, and 78 taverns. In reflecting upon this extraordinary
number of taverns, it must be considered that there are, perhaps,
near 1500 military and naval people about Kingston, who are not
reckoned in the population.

Improvement is stated in *four* of the above reports to be
retarded by the great quantity of land held by non-occupants,
untaxed. In *two* reports, by want of capital: in *two* reports, by the
bad state of the St. Lawrence navigation: in *one* report, by crown
and clergy reserves: in *one* report, by want of labourers: in *one*
report, by want of enterprise: in *one* report, by the bad habits of
the original settlers, who were soldiers, and bad characters from
the United States: in *one* report, by the indiscriminate admission
of people from the United States: in *one* report, by want of skill in
husbandry: in *one* report, by want of emigrants with capital: in
one report, by the great number of poor emigrants: in *one* report,
by the want of a provincial bank.

A canal has been talked of to connect the head of the bay of
Quinté with lake Ontario; but on looking to the ground, I found
that the execution would be more difficult than was represented;
neither would it be of much use in a commercial point of view.
In war-time it might assist in playing at bo-peep along the shore,
should the Americans gain command of lake Ontario; but in that
event the game would be of short continuance.

The same cause which has surrounded Little York with a
desert, creates gloom and desolation about Kingston, otherwise
most beautifully situated; I mean the seizure and monopoly of the

land by people in office and favour. On the east side, particularly, you may travel miles together without passing a human dwelling; the roads are accordingly most abominable to the very gates of this, the largest town in the province; and its market is often supplied with vegetables from the United States, where property is less hampered, and the exertions of cultivators more free, accordingly.

Johnstown District.
Township Reports.

Wolford.

January, 1818.
ANSWER to Query 1st. The township of Wolford, on the river Rideau, is situated north of Kitley; south-west of Oxford; twenty miles east of the town of Perth; and is 10 miles square.

2d. The township was settled in 1797. In the census taken in the year 1817, the population contained upwards of 300 of both sexes, and the number of inhabited houses is 55.

3d. Divine worship is performed once a fortnight in one of the school houses, by a professor of the episcopalian Methodist church.

4th. One medical practitioner at present.

5th. Four common schools; three are paid 100 dollars per annum by the province; the other is paid by the inhabitants: the average price per quarter to each scholar is 15s.

6th and 7th. Four taverns and stores.

8th. Three mills for grinding grain, four mills for sawing timber, and one for carding wool. The price for grinding grain is ¹⁄₁₂, for sawing timber ½, and for carding wool, 5d. per lb.

9th. The soil is variable; but generally a sandy surface.

10th. Oak, maple, beech, pine, hemlock, ash: but chiefly maple.

11th. None, except limestone and iron ore.

12th. Large quantities of limestone can be obtained at two dollars a toise.

13th. Very few have been made, except for private use; but large quantities of clay, near the surface, of excellent quality.

14th. None for sale; some for private use.

15th. Blacksmiths, masons, carpenters, &c. 7s. 6d. per day.

16th. During the winter months, seven dollars, and the summer, from 10 to 12 dollars. In harvest, generally a dollar per day, or a bushel of whatever grain he is hired to reap.

Women generally a dollar per week.

17th. Mowing or cradling an acre of grass or wheat, 2s. 6d., including board.

18th. Clearing and fencing an acre, 4l.; the person contracting finding himself in board, &c.; if found in board, 3l.

19th. An horse, 15l.; a cow, 5l.; an ox, 8l.; a sheep, 7s. 6d., if bought after shearing; if not, the price various.

20th. Three pounds, and sells for 2s. 6d. per lb.

21st. Beginning of November, and first of May generally.

22d. Commences in December, and generally ends in March: begin ploughing latter end of April, or beginning of May.

23d. Fall wheat generally sowed in September; spring wheat in beginning of May, and reaping commences, – winter wheat in the beginning of August, and spring wheat, and other grain, about the first of September.

24th. A bushel and a peck, Winchester measure. An average crop, when well cultivated, 20 bushels per acre, and sometimes 25.

25th. If the pasture is good, and the ox not worked, he will in general gain three cwt.

26th. A man who takes shares of crops on new lands, if found ⅓ of the crop. Manure is generally applied for all kinds of crops.

27th. Answered in the last.

28th. The price of wild land at the first settlement of the township, 1s. 3d. per acre, provided it was remote from any settlement. According as the township became settled, and increased in population, wild lands enhanced in proportion, so that at present it is worth 5s. per acre.

29th. Unknown.

30th. In tolerable repair, and passable in summer and winter for any kind of carriage. In spring and autumn they are rather bad; but are capable of great improvement at a moderate expence. The water conveyance could be made passable for boats of any burthen, without the assistance of locks, &c. The government of this province have it in contemplation to erect a canal along the river Rideau, and continue it to Kingston, which, if it succeeds, will be a great acquisition to this part of the country.

31st. According to the number of settlers now established in this township, the township has improved in proportion. The province, in general, it is not in our power to answer the cause that retards its improvement. The only thing that would contribute to the improvement of the township would be to send out new settlers, distribute the crown and clergy reserves, which occupies ⅔ths of every township. — STEPHEN BURRET, JOSEPH HASKINS, SEN., WM. MERICK, JOSEPH HASKINS, Jun., JOSEPH KNAPP, ASAHEL HURD, WILLIAM N. EASTON, HENRY BURRET, CALVIN BURRET, RICHARD OLMSTED, BENJAMIN MARKER, WM. DAVIS, (Capt. 2d. Regt. Grenville Militia), DANIEL BURRET, (Lt.-Col. 2d. Regt. Grenville Militia), J. H. DAVIS, (Town Clerk, DANIEL THOMAS, (Adjt. 2d. Regt.), NATHAN BROWN, EDWARD MCCRAE, STEPHEN MERICK, THOMAS MCCRAE, JAMES MCLEAN, LUTHER CLIFTEN, EL. COLLER, EDMUND BURRET, HARLEY EASTON, ABELE ADAMS, DANIEL MCCARTHY.

ADDITIONAL
To Mr. Robert Gourlay.

Wolford, 26th Jan. 1818.

SIR,

YOU will see our names to a former letter addressed to you from this place. After a more serious consideration of query, number

30th. The water communication of the river Rideau is capable of great improvement by canalling, which may be done at small expence, for boats of three tons, as most of the materials may be obtained on the spot.

31st. On the first settlement of this province, or shortly after the disturbance in Europe commenced, and no emigration took place from that country, the government of this province made proclamation for settlers from the United States: a number applied and obtained such titles as the government were at that time giving, and sold them, and returned to the states; and the purchasers have obtained titles of the same, and hold their lands at so high a price that the poor are not able to purchase. This is the reason that we have to offer, and what impedes the settlement of this province, or this place.

From the mouth of the river Rideau to Perth, on the Tay, is a distance of about 70 miles, and a small part a good settlement, and the other part land good for settling, and the river affords a number of excellent mill seats.

We are, with respect,
Your very humble Servants,

STEPHEN BURRET,   WM. MERICK,
DANIEL BURRET, (Lt.-Col. 2d. Regt. G. M.) HENRY BURRET.

Landsdown

INFORMATION, answering certain queries proposed in a paper transmitted to the inhabitants of Landsdown, county of Leeds, U.C. from Robert Gourlay, dated Queenston, 1817, respecting the local situation, soil, produce, agricultural improvements, &c. &c.

1st.   Township of Landsdown, situated on the river St. Lawrence, in width six miles in front and rear; in depth, 16 concessions, or ranges of lots about one and a quarter mile in length, and about 80 rods in width.

2d.   This town was laid out in June, 1788, as was Leeds above, and part of the township of Yonge below, at that time a wilderness of 30 miles, and first lot taken up and first settled under the patronage of Lord Dorchester, of Quebec, by Oliver Landon, whose family then was a wife and six boys, with a gift of 200 acres of land, called Lord Dorchester's Bounty: the same man now living in this town with nine sons, six sons' wives, nineteen grandsons, and twelve granddaughters, and also three daughters, with two children, being 31 grandchildren, and total 59 of his family. Inhabitants in the front of this township, 205. Houses, 36, and all in first and second concessions.

3d.   One school house, and for public worship, Methodist every Sabbath, and occasionally Baptists and Presbyterians; but no settled preachers.

4th.   `Medical practitioners none.`

5th.   Schools, one assisted by government, 25l., and by the people, 45l. annually.

6th.   Stores, one.

7th.   Taverns, or inns, three.

8th.   Mills; one saw mill.

9th.   Soil composed of sandy loam and clay, and the surface level, and well watered with small streams and springs, and may be considered as an excellent township for wheat and grass, as well as oats, pease, and flax, potatoes, &c. All kinds of produce flourish, but much depends on the husbandry of the land.

10th.   Timber: oak, pine, ash, maple, birch, beech, walnut, hemlock, black spruce, alder, willow, and elder; apples and plums, together with cherry, will thrive here.

11th.   Minerals, no discovery.

12th.   But one quarry of building stone, and obtained by digging, and that with ease, and of good quality.

13th.   Bricks have been made here, and the materials abundant; are worth about six dollars per 1000.

14th. Limestone has not been discovered in this town; but abundantly supplied in the township of Leeds adjoining.

15th. Blacksmiths' work: axes, 10s.; horse shoeing, 10s.; chains, per lb. 1s. 3d.; masons, 5s. to 10s.; carpenters the same, and boarded.

16th. Labourers: from 120 to 150 dollars per year; 5s. per day in haying and harvest, and boarded.

Women per week, 5s. house-work and spinning.

17th. Mowing grass, 2s. 6d. per acre. Reaping, 3s. 6d.; cradling, 2s., board and lodging.

18th. Clearing and fencing five acres (for the harrow and seed, for this is the way for the first crop) 15 dollars per acre, not boarded.

19th. Present price of good work-horse, from 50 to 70 dollars; good saddle horse, sometimes 100 dollars; cows, from 16 to 30 dollars, according to size; oxen, from 70 to 100 dollars; sheep, 10s. to 15s.

20th. Average crop of wool from sheep in spring, from 2 lbs. to 5 lbs.; price of wool, 2s. to 2s. 6d. per lb.

21st. Cattle will do well in the woods at large, if in good order, from the first of April; but the grass in fields is not a support till the month of May. Time of taking in to feed from 15th November to 25th Dec. most general 1st Dec.

22d. The ordinary time of snows fit for business is three months, and that generally steady, and much to the advantage of the labouring teamster, as well as for the convenience and pleasure of life.

23d. We commonly begin ploughing about the 15th April, for spring crops, and mostly have in our spring seed in the month of May: winter wheat last of August, and first of September: reaping wheat the month of August, first half; oats and pease last half.

24th. It is common to sow one bushel of wheat on new land, if early; and 1¼ on old land; with respect to the quantity much depends on tillage, from 20 to 40 bushels per acre.

25th. The pasture enclosed is common and natural to white clover and English spear grass, and on moist land, of which this town abounds, yields an abundance very great. Cows will produce 120lbs. of cheese, and 80lbs. of butter, in the season; and oxen are raised from six to seven feet round the girt, and will weigh from 600 to 1000lbs.; 60 to 100 weight of tallow.

Butter per lb. 1s. 3d.; cheese, 7½d.; the market good; valuable mills that never fail; 7½ miles good road.

26th. Cropping on shares is various, and little done here:

manure serves well on all lands; but is mostly applied around the barn and stable where made.

27th. Land is rented at four dollars per acre; this is the worth annually. *(Some mistake here.)*

28th. Price of wild land; at the first settlement, it was sold at 5l. per 200 acres, and has gradually risen to one dollar per acre at a distance from the settlement; but on the road or river it may be valued at three dollars per acre, and that without any improvement; in the centre of the town, from three to six dollars per acre.

29th. The quantity of land for sale 50,000 acres.

30th. The main road leading through this town from the province of Lower Canada is at present quite passable for waggons in summer, and for sleighs in winter, and will not need great expence to keep it so.

31st. The principal impairment which prevents this township from being settled is the want of spirited and industrious men, who having money, might apply it with safety and profit.

Witness by us the first settlers,

OLIVER LANDON,
BENJAMIN LANDON,
JOSEPH LANDON,
OLIVER LANDON, Jun.

And six others.

Elizabethtown, Yonge, Landsdown, Leeds, Kitley, Bastard, and Crosby.

Elizabethtown, Dec. 1817.

SIR,

BY accident I saw your address to the landholders of Upper Canada, and though I have not the good fortune to come under that class of subjects, I am not on that account less interested in the improvement and prosperity of the province. Your plan of laying before the British public the true state of Upper Canada, in a statistical form, is a good one, what I have long wished to see, and as you are embarked in the laudable design, I wish you all possible success. After a residence of nearly seven years in the province, I am convinced that the truth, relative to the country, in regard to its climate, soil, and productions, together with its facilities of trade and commerce, are only required to be fairly stated, and extensively known, to induce a respectable class of emigrants to settle in the country, and cast in their lot with ours.

No assertion can be more true than the one you have made, in your address respecting the ignorance which prevails in England, in regard to the fertile regions of Upper and Lower Canada. The want of information relative to Canada, I believe is more general in England than either in Scotland or Ireland. Perhaps in Germany, from whence it would be exceedingly desirable to draw settlers, the country is little known but as the habitation of savages, and the regions of beasts of prey. The publication therefore of the statistical account in the language of that country, is highly important.

You have indeed undertaken a laborious work; but I hope, as you have "put your hand to the plough, you will not look back." Allow me, Sir, to cheer your mind under your toilsome work. Be not discouraged by the supineness of some on the one hand, or the envy and malignity of little minds on the other. Keep in view the end of your work, and contemplate the satisfaction you will experience, in not only forwarding the happiness of numerous families in Britain, and on the continent of Europe, and the essential benefits you will render to the parent state, and to these long – too long neglected provinces. Yes, Sir, in passing through the country, you have seen a powerful empire in embryo, and its own natural resources are calculated to raise it to wealth and prosperity. May God grant, that when cultivated farms, populous villages and cities, shall deck the face of the country, and the arts and the sciences spread their benign influence, the inhabitants may exemplify all the virtues of love of country, and piety.

I conceive it a duty to transmit to you some account of this part of the country, in case you should not be supplied with a better. I shall commence with ELIZABETH-TOWN, which is the ninth township in ascending the river St. Lawrence. It is of the usual dimensions, about 10 miles on the river in width, and about 14 from front to rear. It was settled in 1783. From the line of the township, about two miles below the village of Brockville, the front presents a handsome and gradual slope to the river, which flows with a gentle current, and is nearly two miles in width. A few islands deck the bosom of the St. Lawrence, which affords a pleasing relief to the eye, in viewing the expanse of water. In some parts of the front the land is stony; in others it is sandy. But in general the soil is good, and rather preferable in the back parts of the township. Limestone every where abounds, excepting on the front above Brockville, where the face of the country undergoes a considerable change. High banks, huge and impending rocks, composed of a hard granite, producing but little vegetation, excepting in the intervals, and in the cracks and crevices, where a few stunted pine and hemlock raise their never-changing foliage; these, together with the morse and large masses of rocks, present a gloomy and romantic view to the traveller. The rocks, however, are of an excellent kind for mill stones. The land immediately back of the rocks (and these only occupy a few acres in front), is of a very superior quality, for all kinds of English grain and pasturage.

The forests abound with oak, maple, basswood, beech, birch, ash, pine, hemlock, cedar, iron wood, elm, &c.

The village of Brockville is named from the gallant chief who fell in the battle of Queenston. It is beautifully situated on the banks of the river, and is considered one of the handsomest villages in Upper Canada. There are 16 two story dwelling houses, and 44 of various other dimensions, a number of which are built with elegance and taste; three of them are built with brick, and two of stone. In all, there are 64 dwelling houses and retail stores.

The court house is an elegant brick building. It is built on the rise of ground, from which there is a beautiful and regular declivity to the river, and commands an extensive prospect of the adjacent country.

The Presbyterian church is erected on the west side of the court house. It is a stone edifice, 60 feet by 40. It is considered the most stately public building in the province. It presents an elegant front, with a projection of two feet; the corners of the projection, the doors and windows, and the two front angles of the building, are composed of cut or wrought stone.

Brockville is a place of considerable trade, it being the outlet of a rich, extensive, and well settled country back. It is likewise opposite the grand turnpike road, which leads to Utica, Albany, Sackett's Harbour, and other important places in the United States. Large stores and wharfs have lately been erected to conduct the forwarding trade on the river and lakes. Various mechanical employments go forward; blacksmith's work (there are three blacksmiths), carpentering, tanning and currying, saddle and harness making, shoemaking, tailoring, &c. There is one grist, and one saw mill in the village; 1 grist mill, 1 carding machine, and 3 saw mills, in the vicinity; these, with other things of minor importance, keep the place in considerable life.

Near the centre of the township is a salt spring; but no use has ever been made of it, excepting that the cattle and deer frequently resort to it. About two miles from the west line of the township, there appears, from some specimens of stone which lie on the surface, to be a quarry of freestone; but the quarry has never been sought for, and of course no buildings have been raised with them.

Iron stone is found in some places, and from the appearance of a metallic substance that has been found between the first and second concessions among the rocks, lead, or copper, or perhaps silver, is likely to be deposited. The substance referred to, has the appearance of gold, or rather like some pieces of coal of a glossy yellow, but much heavier. Some of it has undergone chymical process; but it evaporated with a sulphureous smell. From what, however, the writer of this article has learned, the experiment was hardly satisfactory. It is also reported that several boat loads of it have been taken away by some Americans.

The roads in this township are pretty good for Upper Canada: speaking of them generally, they are the best I have seen in any town in the province. The whole of the front road is pretty good in dry seasons; and the road from front to rear, leading to Perth, Bastard, &c. is almost all turnpiked: roads, however, capable of great improvement. Ditching, a thing much neglected throughout the province, has, in some places, been tried with good success; but it is by no means general. What is called turnpiking, or throwing up dirt in the centre, is much more common. The roads made in this manner, are by far too narrow to admit two loaded waggons or sleighs to pass with ease and safety.

In the vicinity of Brockville, lands have risen 400 per cent. The price of lands in the rear, however, has not risen so high; for fifteen years, perhaps, they have not risen more than 50 per cent. In some parts of the township, lands may be bought at three dollars per acre. In this township there are one Presbyterian church, and one Methodist meeting house; nine saw, and five grist mills; two carding machines, and two fulling works.

The Presbyterian minister preaches every sabbath in Brockville; the Episcopalian minister every other sabbath; but there is no church; the congregation meets in the court house.

Price of lime at the kiln, 6d. per bushel; price of bricks per thousand, 1l. 10s.; building stone, per cord, 7s. 6d.; wages of masons, carpenters, blacksmiths, &c. from 5s. to 7s. 6d. per day: price of butter is. 3d.; of cheese 7½d. per lb.

YONGE is the tenth in the front range of townships in Upper Canada: it was settled in 1786. To Yonge is now added the Gore, formerly called Escott, so that this town is about five miles wider on the river than it is in the rear. In the back parts of the township, limestone is found in great abundance, and, in some places, iron stone. The soil is various; in general it is good, excepting on the front, where it is broken and rocky. The rocks are composed of a white stone, with a number of sparkling particles: it is probable that quarries of marble may be found, but the attention of the people is chiefly devoted to agriculture, and every thing not immediately connected with this, is not an object of inquiry or enterprise. The river St. Lawrence is about five miles wide in front of the town. On Bridge island, opposite the township, is the blockhouse, which commands an extensive prospect of the river.

In this township there are farms of one and two hundred acres, with ten or twelve acres of improvement, and a log house, which have been, and are yet for sale, at three dollars per acre.

In Yonge there are ten saw and four grist mills; two carding machines. The timber the same as in Elizabethtown.

LANSDOWN is the eleventh in ascending the St. Lawrence. It was first settled in 1786. The front is broken and rocky, the soil rather poor, and the farms in a bad state of cultivation, for want of industry and energy of the occupiers.

The land improves much in the rear, where there are some excellent farms in a praiseworthy state of cultivation. The price of land from a late actual sale is two dollars per acre. The front road through this town to Kingston is very bad; the back is rather better. Lime and ironstone are found in various parts of the township. The timber the same as Elizabethtown, and Yonge. In the river, which is very wide, are some large islands, of a very superior quality in point of soil, and from whence large supplies of oak and pine timber for the Quebec and Montreal markets have been had. The temperature of the air on the islands in the St. Lawrence is milder than on the main continent, as the tender vegetables thrive more, and come to fuller maturity. This may be owing to the humidity of the atmosphere, occasioned by the large body of water in which they are enveloped. There are some inhabitants on the Grand isle, which is about eight miles long, and on Grindstone island, and some others; but they have no title to the soil. They are generally a poor and shiftless set of people, spending too much of their time in fishing and hunting during those seasons of the year when they ought to be cultivating the land.

The rear of Lansdown is a good deal overflowed by the chain of lakes, called the Ganannoque. The large lake of this name has its chief seat in this township. The scenery around this beautiful sheet of water is surprisingly grand: the water of the lake is remarkably clear: the shores of the lake are various; in some places a gradual slope is presented; in others, shelving rocks, with a variety of trees and bushes; but where the foot of man never trod. In other places perpendicular rocks of an immense height strike the mind with terror, in the cliffs of which the eagles build their nests; and in their dreary caverns, beasts of prey have their dens. In viewing the various objects which nature has scattered in wild abundance, the mind is overwhelmed with a kind of pleasing horror. Yonder, a few small islands present themselves, rising out of the bosom of the water: here, the rocks extend into the lake, and form a variety of bays and promontories: as far as the eye can reach hills rise upon hills, and mountains upon mountains*, till they mingle with the distant horizon, and are lost in the clouds. The human voice reverberates from rock to rock. Nature is here seen in her wildest dress, and the imagination is left without control, while it wanders from object to object; indeed, every thing is on a scale of magnificence; sublimity reigns in all her glories; it only requires the hand of industrious man to add the beautiful. It may however be said, that sublimity reigns in terror, for amidst all her grandeur, the eye has to stretch far beyond the banks of the lake, and then only we indistinctly discover a few spots of cultivation.

The lake is about three or four miles wide; its margin (and that of all in the neighbourhood) is rocky. Vast numbers of wolves, bears, &c. inhabit this quarter of the country. The waters abound with great quantities of excellent fish: oak, pine, and other timber trees are found in abundance, together with vast quantities of juniper bushes, bearing a large and excellent berry; also sumach, a species of white wood used for cabinet inlaying. The lake in many places is shallow.

The township of LEEDS is the twelfth from the province line on the St. Lawrence. It was first settled in 1785. The land for some distance from the river is exceedingly broken and rocky; the soil

* My duty, as a statistical compiler, obliges me here to check my Rev. Correspondent's poetical licence. There is no such thing in Upper Canada as a mountain, according to English idiom. The highest ground in the province, I believe, is "the ridge," described in the report of Pelham township, to be 500 feet high. I have traversed much of the country above described, in which is Ganannoque river, its lakes, and many others. There is throughout a wildness, irregularity, and romantic beauty, very peculiar. There are scenes approaching to "the Troshack's wildest nook;" but there is no Benvenue, Benlomond, nor Benmore. There is enough to inspire the Muse, and give her delightful sensations; but nothing of the sublime, even though the cliffs afford security to the eagle. In the remote parts of the province, towards lake Superior, &c. there are lofty mountains; but I speak only of the settled parts, and the vicinity. – R. G.

of an indifferent quality throughout the township, though there are some patches of good land here and there between the rocks; the surface in general is uneven; the township is thinly settled, and cultivation has made but slow progress. In the rear there are some farms in pretty good order. Lime, iron, and freestone are found in great abundance, and there is a stone which withstands the action of fire.

In the river Ganannoque is what is called marble rock, and no doubt there is a great bed of this valuable material. It rises above the surface of the water in the middle of the river. No use has been made of it, except in making inkstands and other trifling articles.

On the same river are the iron works, which belonged to the late Ephraim Jones, Esq.: they are in a state of ruin, and no great use was ever made of them. The height of the fall, the constant supply of water, abundance of ore, and other advantages, render it matter of regret that so valuable a property is not put to use.

At the mouth of the Ganannoque, on the St. Lawrence, is a village of the same name; the number of houses small, one of which is two stories. In the village are two grist and two saw mills. The grist and saw mill on the east side of the stream belong to Sir John Johnston, but are in bad repair. The saw mill on the west side, erected by Charles M'Donnel, is of a very superior kind, supposed to be the best in the two provinces.

In this village are two blacksmiths' shops; one hatter, and two retail stores: timber as in other towns.

KITLEY is in general a good township of land; but poorly watered, and in many places the soil is shallow. It is fast increasing in population. Limestone abounds in it.

The timber, excepting great quantities of rock elm, is the same as other townships.

BASTARD: soil very superior, and many farms in excellent order. Limestone, ironstone, and freestone are all found in this township.

The Rideau lake extends into the rear.

In this township is the village of Stone Mills: the mill here, belonging to W. Jones, Esq. is unquestionably the best building of the kind in Upper Canada. Besides the large grist mill, there is one carding machine, one saw mill, three stores, and one blacksmith's shop. The main road through this township is pretty good. Timber as usual.

SOUTH CROSBY, is well watered by the Ganannoque waters; it is very rocky and uneven, but there is some land of excellent quality. It is very thinly settled, and the roads bad. Timber as in the neighbouring townships.

The following replies to your queries will answer for all the above mentioned townships.

14th. Prime of lime at the kiln, 6d. per bushel.

16th. Wages of common labourers, eight dollars per month in winter, and thirteen in summer; day in harvest 4s., or one bushel of wheat; women 5s. per week; mowing grass, 5s. per acre.

18th. Clearing, fencing, and preparing new land for sowing with grain, fifteen dollars per acre.

19th. Price of a good work horse, sixty dollars.

21st. May and November.

22d. Sleighing commences about the 20th of December: ends in March.

23d. Sow wheat in September; reap in August.

25th. Price of butter, 1s. 3d. per lb.

27th. Terms of letting land on shares, half the produce.

SIR,

I am sorry that I am not able to send you a sketch of all the townships I intended. Kitley, Bastard, and South Crosby are not so full as I intended. To these I meant to have added Montague, Elmsly, Burgess, North Crosby, and the four new townships in the Perth settlement, viz. Bathurst, Drummond, Beckwith, and Gouldburne; but a throng of ministerial duties, sickness in my family, and a disappointment in the sources of information regarding some of the towns, have prevented me from doing what I wished. I shall, however, still keep the object in view. Should you make it convenient to honour me with a call at my house, four miles and a half above Brockville, I shall be extremely happy to see you.

I am, Sir,
Your's truly,

WILLIAM SMART,

Minister of the Presbyterian Church, Brockville, and Missionary from the Missionary Society, London.

To ROBERT GOURLAY, Esq.

Johnstown District.
Summary of Population, &c. &c.

Having no materials from reports whereby to calculate the population of this district, I must depend chiefly on my own guessing, with the qualification of having travelled at different times in various directions through it.

Elizabethtown is one of the best cultivated and most populous townships in the province, and I shall venture to set down its population at	2,000
Yonge may rank next, at	1,400
Augusta	1,200
Edwardsburgh	1,000
Bastard	1,000
Leeds, Lansdown, Crosby, Kitley, Wolford, Oxford, and Gower, at 300 each	2,100
Burgess, Elmsly, Montague, and Marlborough, together	500
	9,200

In the year 1816, a settlement of emigrants began, under the direction of the military, in Bathurst, Drummond, Beckwith, and Gouldburne; and emigrants were also located in various vacant places throughout the first mentioned townships of this district; but of these I take no heed in the above estimate of population.

A few Indians reside in the islands, which are thickly scattered in the river St. Lawrence, opposite to the townships of Yonge, Leeds, and Lansdown, in this district; but they are too unimportant to be of consequence in an estimate of population, even if their numbers could have been ascertained. Their chief occupation is fishing. Now that the boundary line has been settled between the United States territory, and that of Britain, through among these islands, the Indians will probably be soon either driven off, or have their right of soil, where they claim it, purchased from them.

It will excite a smile when I plead excuse for imperfect knowledge of the population of Upper Canada, by mentioning that in various quarters of the province, a report was spread that I was an agent of the prime minister of England, sent abroad to ascertain how far the people could bear taxation; and after the ministerial clamour was raised by the York parson, public offices were closed against me, and it was only with much trouble that I could ocassionally get hold of an assessment roll! My present endeavours, however, will clear the way to a more accurate account of this benighted corner of the British empire, when low ideas will be extinguished, and party pique put down.

It was the military settlement at Perth, which first engaged my particular statistical inquiries in the province of Upper Canada. I reached that place the 29th of June, 1817, and spent several days there. At that time my intention was to have returned to England in September following; but that intention being delayed, I despatched the following letter and statistical table, with directions that it should be published in the newspapers, and a copy presented to Lord Bathurst.

*To the Editor of any British Newspaper**

Queenston, Upper Canada, Sept. 15, 1817.

SIR,

It will be remembered by many of your readers that in the spring of 1815 proclamations were widely circulated, inviting settlers to Canada.

Having myself occasion to visit this country, I was curious to know what had been the result, especially as I found, at Quebec and Montreal, very discordant accounts respecting it; most people asserting that the scheme had failed of success, and that the settlers were in a state of great discomfort and discontent.

To ascertain the truth, I diverged from my route about fifty miles, and spent some days at Perth, situated on the waters of the Rideau, to which a considerable body of the people, who accepted the invitation of government, had been conducted. Here I traced the reported discontent to some neglects in the general management, and some ill conceived petty regulations, capriciously exercised towards people tenacious of their rights; but in the main, universal satisfaction prevailed among the settlers, and a strong feeling of the good intention of government towards them.

The opportunity being a good one, of ascertaining the progress which a promiscuous body of settlers make in a given time, I constructed the annexed table, and had each man's signature attached, at once to prove the correctness of his statement, and satisfaction with his situation.

Should you think this worthy of publication, you are welcome to insert it in your paper. It may draw attention to a most

---

* This letter, with the Table, was published, I find, in the Salisbury Journal of November 24, 1817, and other Newspapers.

STATISTICAL

Shewing the Commencement and Progress of Improve-

Original Profession of Settlers.	Wife.	Children.	From what County.	From what Parish.	Date of leaving Home. 1815.	Date of Embarkation. 1815.	Date of Disembarkation. 1815.	Date of taking Possession. 1816
A farm grieve ..	0	6	Perth	Callender	May 15	June 24	Sept. 1.	May
Son of the above, 19 years old....	0	0	Ditto	Ditto	Ditto	Ditto	Ditto	Aug.
Weaver	1	6	Ditto	Ditto	June 21	Ditto	Ditto	May
Dyer and Clothier	1	5	Lanark	Carronwath	May 31	Ditto	Sept. 15	May
Shoe-maker	1	5	Murray	Rothes	April 20	Ditto	Sept. 1.	May
Ship-master	1	3	Ayrshire	Kelbride	April 27	Ditto	Ditto	Ditto
Weaver	1	5	Lanark	Glasgow	June 24	Ditto	Sept. 1.	May
Mason	Wife & 1 child left at home.		Forfar	Dundee	June 1	Ditto	Sept. 12	Ditto
Millwright	0	0	Ditto	Ditto	Ditto	Ditto	Ditto	Ditto
Farm-labourer ..	0	0	Forfar	St. Vigin	Ditto	Ditto	Ditto	April
Mason	0	0	Dumfries	Dunscore	June 24	June 27	Ditto	Aug.
Ship-Carpenter..	0	0	Lanark	Glasgow	Ditto	June 24	Ditto	Ditto
Schoolmaster....	1	5	Dumfries	Hutton	May 26	Ditto	Ditto	June
Farmer	1	5	Ayrshire	Kilbirnie	June 30	June 30	Ditto	April 1
Whitesmith	1	3	Edinburgh	New Greyfriars	May 19	June 24	Ditto	April 2
Farmer	0	7	Perth	Callender	May 15	Ditto	Sept. 1	June
Weaver	1	2	Lanark	Glasgow	June 24	Ditto	Sept. 15	May 1
Farmer	1	6	Lanark	Glasgow	Ditto	Ditto	Ditto	May 2
Farm-labourer ..	1	3	Lanark	Glasgow	Ditto	Ditto	Sept. 16	April
Widow of William Holderness	0	6	Yorkshire	Boobwith	April 9	Ditto	Sept. 15	May
Farm-labourer ..	0	0	Berwickshire	Coldenholm	June 26	July 3	Ditto	April 2
Shopkeeper	1	1	Edinburgh	Canongate	April 1	June 22	Sept. 17	June 1
Clerk in Property-tax	1	1	Ditto	Corsdorfin	June 13	June 24	Sept. 15	April
Gardener	1	1	Ditto	Ditto	Ditto	Ditto	Ditto	Ditto
Totals	15	74	0	0	0	0	0	0

The original table contained double the number of settlers exhibited above; but the

TABLE.

ment, in 12 months, of the Emigrant Settlement at Perth.

Dimensions of House erected.	No. of Acres chopped.	No. of Acres cleared.	No. of Acres in Wheat.	No. of Acres in Oats.	No. of Acres in Potatoes, &c.	No. of lbs. of Maple Sugar made.	No. of Cows, &c.	No. of Oxen.	Declaration and Signature.
18 feet by 20	9	4½	2	1½	1	100	2	0	Well satisfied—Peter Mc Pherson.
0	4	3	2	0	1	0	0	1	Well satisfied—William Mc Pherson.
21 by 18 and ½	10	7	4	1	2	102	3	1	Well satisfied—James Mc Laren.
26 by 21	9	8	3½	1¼	3¼	15	2	0	Well satisfied—James Taylor.
20 by 18	13	8	4½	½	3	25	3	0	Well satisfied—John Simpson.
21 by 17	7½	5	4	0	1	0	1	0	Well satisfied—James Miller.
25 by 20	6	4½	3½	½	1½	35	1	0	Well satisfied—Hugh Mc Kay.
26 by 19	9	8½	4	2½	2	20	1	1	Well satisfied—For Wm. Spalding, and self; Wm. Rutherford.
12 by 10	6½	6	4	0	2	0	0	1	
18 by 15	6	5½	3	¾	1¾	0	0	0	Well satisfied—John Hay.
alf of 29 by 22 Ditto	7	6	2	0	8	20	0	0	Well satisfied—For self and partner, Thos. Mc Lean; Archibald Morrison.
32 by 19	7½	0	3	½	3	50	0	0	Well satisfied—John Holiday.
23 by 16	9½	6½	2½	½	2½	25	3	1	Well satisfied—Alexander Mc Farlane.
22 by 14	5	4	1½	0	1	20	1	0	Well satisfied—James Mc Donald. His X mark.
24 by 21	6	5	2½	½	2	30	1	0	Well satisfied—John Ferguson.
21 by 18	6½	4½	2	½	2	25	1	0	Well satisfied—John Flood.
22 by 18	8½	4½	3½	0	1	15	1	0	Well satisfied—William Mc Gillevry.
18 by 16	8	6	4	0	2	40	0	1	Well satisfied—John Brash.
22 by 20	7	5½	4	0	1½	20	1	0	Well satisfied—Ann Holderness.
ase burned down	7½	4½	4	0	½	0	0	0	Well satisfied—John Miller.
16 by 16	10½	7	4	½	2¼	20	1	0	Well satisfied—Wm. Old.
18 by 13	5½	3½	2¼	½	¾	50	1	1	Well satisfied—Francis Allan.
18 by 12	6	5½	3½	¾	1¼	12	0	0	Well satisfied—Thomas Cuddie.
0	174½	128½	72¼	11¾	41¼	624	23	7	

re sufficient for the present purpose. The account was taken 1st and 2d July, 1817.

important subject, the colonization of this province with British subjects; and should it reach Scotland, it may afford satisfaction to many individuals who may not otherwise know the condition of their friends.

The scheme which government adopted in 1815 was expensive. The settlers had a free passage, rations, and tools: next year, rations and tools were furnished to those who came out; and this year multitudes of poor people have come to Canada in expectation of being favoured in the same way, but are disappointed, having nothing given but the land (100 acres each), which many of them, from poverty, are unable to occupy.

Having made it my study, during three months residence here, to inquire into the nature of the country, and into every particular respecting settlement, I am convinced that very simple measures might be adopted, by which the redundant population of Britain could by conveyed, by a regular flow, into Canada, instead of being wasted, to the great prejudice of British interest, over the whole of America: and were such measures adopted, this province could, in a very few years, be quite equal to its own defence in war, against the United States.

ROBERT GOURLAY.

There are several reasons for my requesting the reader's particular attention to the above tables. First, he may compare the condition as to stock, and other circumstances, of these emigrants, with those of the settlers in the former tables, a matter which I shall, in another place, particularly remark upon: he may mark the monstrous waste and want of good arrangement in this instance of a government attempt to settle Upper Canada with British subjects, by inspecting columns 6, 7, 8, and 9, of the first table. From the two first of these columns it appears that the settlers were, one with another, more than a month from leaving home till they embarked: and from the other columns that they were more than a year before they got possession of their lands in Upper Canada, – more than a year living upon government allowance, altogether idle, and sickening with idleness! . . .

Eastern District.

1st. CHARLOTTENBURGH is the second township in the province of Upper Canada: bounded in front by the river St. Lawrence; on the east by the township of Lancaster; north by the township of Kenyon; and west by the township of Cornwall. It is

12 miles square, including a strip of Indian reservation on the west side.

2d. The first settlement was commenced in the year 1784, by a part of the Royal Yorkers (principally Scotchmen). The population is 2,500, exclusive of a great number of emigrants from Great Britain since the month of June last. The number of inhabited houses is about 500.

3d. The churches and meeting houses are one church, and three meeting houses of the church of Scotland; one church (now building), and one meeting house of the church of Rome. Both churches are of stone. The clergy are, one minister of the church of Scotland, and two priests of the church of Rome.

4th. Two medical practitioners.

5th. Schools 12: average fees per quarter to each schoolmaster, 15l.

6th. Stores, 12.

7th. Taverns, 18.

8th. Mills: four grist mills, with two additional pairs of stones, one of which additional pairs is for hulling barley and oats: rate of grinding $\frac{1}{12}$: saw mills, six: rate of sawing, one half: carding mills, one: rate of carding, 6d. per lb.

9th. The soil generally is a black deep loam, generally level, with some swamps.

10th. The kinds of timber are pine, oak, maple, beech, elm, basswood, cedar, fir, hemlock, ash, butternut, walnut, &c.

11th. No minerals yet discovered, but some appearances in different places. Limestone in great abundance throughout the township: no remarkable springs yet discovered.

12th. Building stones to be had throughout the township: no price is paid for them, so that the expence in getting stone is no other than digging, carting, &c. to the building ground: quality, lime and grey sand.

13th. Bricks; average price, 1l. 10s. per 1000.

14th. Lime, from 6d. to 9d. per bushel.

15th. Wages of mechanics per day, being found by the employer, viz. blacksmiths, from 7s. 6d. to 8s. 9d.; masons, from 7s. 6d. to 10s.; carpenters, from 5s. to 10s. Rate of their piece-work: blacksmith (finding himself) for making plough irons, chains, &c. from 1s. to 1s. 3d. per lb.: masons, for building six feet square, 10s., and 3s. for each foot in height, of a single chimney in a wood or frame house. Carpenters, for flooring 10 feet square, 10s., and 2s. for each panel in a framed door: 4d. per light for making window sashes.

16th. The wages of labourers per annum is from 25l. to 36l.:

per winter month, from 35s. to 60s. per summer month, from 50s. to 80s.: per day in harvest, from 3s. to 5s.: for women servants, per week, for housework, 5s.; and for spinning, from 5s. to 7s. 6d. per week, being found.

17th.   Mowers' wages: for mowing grass, per day, 5s.: for cradling, from 7s. 6d. to 10s. per day: the kinds of grain generally cradled, and wheat, oats, rye, and barley.

18th.   For clearing and fencing five acres of wood land (that is to say, cutting, logging, burning, and fencing), ready for seed, 20l.

19th.   The price of a good work-horse, four years old, is from 10l. to 15l.: of a good milch cow, 4l. 10s. to 6l.: of a good ox, at four years old, 10l.: of a good sheep, from 15s. to 17s. 6d.

20th.   The average quantity of wool yielded by sheep, is from 5lbs. to 6lbs.: price thereof, from 1s. 8d. to 2s. per lb.

21st.   The ordinary time of turning out beasts to pasture is about the 25th April: of taking them home to the yard, or stable, about the 15th Nov.

22d.   The ordinary endurance of the sleighing season is from the 15th December to the 1st April; and that of ploughing, from the 15th April to the 15th November.

23d.   The ordinary season for sowing fall-wheat is from the 1st September to the 15th November: of reaping the same about the 1st of August: sowing spring-wheat, from the 15th April to 10th May; and of reaping the same, about the 15th August.

24th.   The necessary quantity of seed is about one bushel of wheat to an acre on new lands, and little less than one bushel and a half to an acre of old land: the average crop per acre is from 15 to 20 bushels.

25th.   The quality of the pastures is generally good, being seeded with timothy, red and white clover. An ox, of four years old, will gain, in the course of a season, in pasture, about ⅓ more. As respects milk, and the quantity of dairy produce, it will average from four to six lbs. per week for each cow: the price of butter is from 1s. to 1s. 3d. per lb.; and cheese, from 5d. to 8d. per lb.

26th.   The ordinary course of cropping new land: wheat is generally the first crop sown in dry land, and oats in low land, seeded also with timothy, and will yield four to five crops of hay before it requires to be let out to pasture: after pasturing a few years, it is then ploughed up, and will answer either for fall or spring wheat, and will yield three crops, and then requires manuring, or letting to pasture. Manure is necessary to produce a crop of potatoes, or Indian corn, except in new land, or the first crop after pasturing. Manure is frequently used for a crop of wheat also, in more sandy soil.

27th. Lands let out on shares, team, utensils, and seed being furnished, one-half the produce; and nothing being furnished, one-third to the landlord.

28th. The price of wild land for the first period, say six years of the settlement, was from 1s. to 5s. per acre; and at present, is from 20s. to 30s. per acre. A lot of 200 acres, with 30 acres clear, under good cultivation, with a framed house and barn, with shade, &c. is worth from 500l. to 600l.

29th. The lands now for sale are a number of valuable tracts in the front of the township along the river St. Lawrence, and a number of lots in the different concessions, amounting to several thousand acres, together with a number of crown and clergy reservations, which are leased to settlers at a moderate rent.

30th. The state of the public highways is greatly advanced within a few years past, and can be improved at a moderate expence, the ground being generally suitable for roads throughout the township. There are two main roads through this township, leading to the province of Lower Canada; one in the front, and the other near the centre of the township, and both are sufficiently good for any carriage whatever. The water conveyance is on the river Aux Raisins, navigable for boats about five miles from the St. Lawrence, and could easily be continued to the adjoining township of Cornwall, by building locks at the different rapids on said river.

31st. Not having the front main road completed through the first township in the province, called Lancaster, is a great bar against the improvement of this township: the road is already so as to allow the mail stage to run within three miles of the province line: there are also five miles of the province of Lower Canada without a road to join this main road, which makes eight miles in all to complete the land conveyance between the two provinces on this route, which, if completed, would be of infinite convenience to the province in general, as well as to the inhabitants of the adjoining townships: also the want of a few locks being erected along the river St. Lawrence, between the towns of Cornwall and New Johnstown, in the following places, viz. Long-Sault, Galleaus, and Rapid Aux Plau, (which might be done with little expence) greatly retards the improvement of the province at large. Another great detriment, both to the commercial and agricultural societies in the province, is the want of *capitalists* becoming settlers therein.

Charlottenburgh,
5th Jan. 1818.

JOHN CAMERON, M. P.	DUN. MC KENZIE,
ALEX. MC KENZIE, J. P.	ALEX. CAMERON,
ALEX. FLETCHER,	JOHN WRIGHT,
JOHN MC KENZIE,	D. MC PHERSON,
PETER FERGUSON,	LEWIS CHISHOLM,
PETER MC INTYRE,	A. FRASER,
ALEX. MC GRUER,	DON. MC KENZIE,
JOHN MC MARTIN, M. P.	JAMES CUMMING,
JOHN MC LENNAN,	ALEX. MC GILLIES,
WM. MC LEOD,	ALEX. CLARK,
HUGH MC DONELL,	ALLAN MC DONALD.

Eastern District.

Summary of Population.

THE above exhausts the budget of regular Township Reports put into my hands by the inhabitants of Upper Canada, for publication in England. Having but a single one from this district, I can by no means give an accurate estimate of its population.

By the Report, CHARLOTTENBURGH contained, in 1817	2,500
CORNWALL, including its village, may be reckoned to hold as many	2,500
LANCASTER though double the ordinary extent of townships (now by statute divided into two), and partly well settled, contained, till 1816, a large portion of unoccupied land. Its population cannot, therefore, be reckoned at more than	2,000
OSNABRUCK, WILLIAMSBURGH, and MATILDA, being front townships, and among the earliest settled in the province, are pretty populous. Osnabruck is settled back to the eighth and ninth concessions; Williamsburgh to the seventh: Matilda is marshy and unsettled through a considerable portion of its extent. The three together, I shall suppose, contain	4,500

MOUNTAIN and FINCH are regularly
organized, and have considerable settlements:
WINCHESTER few or none; and ROXBURY but
few: altogether we shall say

$$\begin{array}{r} 1,200 \\ \hline 12,700 \end{array}$$

There are a few families resident on the islands of the St.
Lawrence, opposite to this district; but having neither a precise
estimate of their numbers, nor knowing how the boundary line
between the United States and Canada has determined their
cession to the one or the other country, I avoid giving them any
place in the estimate. The tract belonging to the St. Regis Indians
is now almost entirely in the hands of white people, who hold by
lease, and are reckoned among the inhabitants of Charlottenburgh
and Lancaster.

It is painful for me once more to make excuse for so imperfect an
account of a considerable district of Upper Canada, by referring
to the illiberal jealousy which orginated at the capital, and had
peculiar aids in spreading itself from thence downwards to this
place, where it did not rest in mere sullenness; but ultimately
broke out into fury and outrage. There was no secret as to the
cause of this. The parson of York had for a series of years kept a
school in the village of Cornwall; and here he had whipped a very
considerable portion of the youth into due submission, before he
was doubly installed in the pulpit and executive council. Thus
situated, no talent was required but that of activity, to deal out
favours in such measure as to ratify an authority among men
which had been acquired over them when children. Magistrates,
members of parliament, and militia officers, besides the attorney
and solicitor general, had sprung up in the school of Cornwall,
and were all zealous in the cause of their master.

The above Report of Charlottenburgh was intrusted by the
body of subscribers to be forwarded to me by two members of
parliament, both worthy honest men, and from one of whom I
had received the greatest civilities; but such became the solemn
hum of suspicion – such the impression from the ministerial, or
rather clerical awe and dread, after the Augusta parson had
proclaimed that my first address contained "principles inimical to
the peace and quiet which the inhabitants of this province so
happily enjoy," that this Report, dated fifth January, 1818, was
not delivered till the month of April, and then only at the
instigation of another member of parliament, whose letter, stating
the doubts which had weighed against the surrender, I still hold
as a curiosity.

Under similar influences, other Reports were withheld, and

two, if not more, withdrawn from the post office of Kingston, where I had directed they might lie for me till called for. An attorney withdrew one of these, and finding afterwards that I was to be prosecuted by Government, had the impudence to disperse over the district wherein I was to be tried circular letters by the dozen, declaring that I had "sinister motives," and this too while, by his own shewing, he was in expectation of pleading against me at the bar. The people of the Township whose Report was thus withdrawn, when they saw what had been done, furnished me with another, and publicly expressed in the newspapers their disapprobation of the attorney's conduct, who was, in fact, a notorious fool and blackguard. The other Report was withdrawn by a person of a very different character, a worthy magistrate. Being assured that pure simplicity of fear had been the moving principle in this case, I called on his worship, dined with him, and held the "sinister motives" so cheap, to say nothing of the "principles inimical to the peace and quiet which the inhabitants of this province so happily enjoy," that we parted very good friends; the magistrate having reported to me some acts of a late governor, not very creditable.

By giving place to these incidents, I do not merely apologize for insufficiency of local facts; but I hope they distinguish features growing out of the political circumstances of Upper Canada not unworthy of notice. It never can be right to hide even weakness, if by exposure the cause can be removed, especially if that cause originates in superstition or the delusions of power.

Ottawa District.

THIS district, recently formed out of part of the Eastern District, had no communication by land with the other parts of the province, till 1816, when some Scotch emigrants were located in the upper part of Lancaster, and assisted in opening roads. At great hazard I crossed to it through the new settlements, the first week of June, 1818, on horseback, and spent a couple of days there.

The only settlements were in Hawkesbury and Longeuil; and I do not suppose the whole population could amount to more than 1,500; probably not so many. Much of the landed property being held by merchants in Montreal, &c., the farmers in Hawkesbury were so kept at arm's length by untaxed lots that they could do little in union for public good or their own relief. In Longeuil, a party of people from the United States were settled more compactly, and shewed signs of vigorous improvement. In passing northward from Lancaster, the Ottawa river presents itself in grand style; and the woods of the Lower Province rising from its opposite bank, upon hills, varying in their aspect, and some of them steep and lofty, produce an effect very agreeable to him who has long been accustomed to the greater tameness of Upper Canada. On an island in Ottawa river, opposite the higher part of Hawkesbury township, are erected saw mills of the best construction, and upon a scale superior to any other in the province. They were first owned by Mr. Mears, of Hawkesbury; but are now the property of Mr. Hamilton, from Ireland; and the business seemed to be carried on by him with great spirit; about fourscore people being employed in the works on the island. Nothing can be better situated than these mills, either as it respects the command of water, as a moving power for machinery, or as a conductor of the log timber to the mills. The Ottawa river, a little way above the island, expands into a noble sheet of navigable water, extending as far as the eye can reach: at and below the island, for eight or nine miles, it is rapid. In my sketch of the practicable watercourses, inserted upon the large map attached to this volume, I have introduced a canal for getting over this rapid, and the accomplishment of this upon a proper scale, is an object of high importance both for public good, and the benefit of those who possess lands to the west and north. The Ottawa, indeed, for nearly two hundred miles, could be made navigable for large steam boats, with little else than locks, were this, one of the most considerable rapids, got over; and into it flow the rivers Petite Nation, Rideau, Mississippi, and others, all capable of being navigated with an expenditure, quite moderate, considered in proportion to the vast commerce which the naturally fertile regions on their banks, well cultivated, would surely generate.

There is, at the extremity of that part of Ottawa river, called the lake of the Two Mountains, a considerable current, but not such as to impede navigation; and when I left Canada, it was said that a small steam boat was established, to ply regularly from La Chine, near Montreal, to the lower part of Hawkesbury township. How glorious might be the day, and that day may be within twenty years from the present time, when, by the union of British capital and Canadian capability, steam boats of 500 tons burden, could take their departure from Quebec and Montreal, pass up the St. Lawrence or Ottawa into lakes Superior and Michigan; excite industry and honest ambition by the display of British manufactures, and return loaded with the produce of the distant and widespreading shores!

STATISTICAL

Composed of Extracts from Township Reports of the

Names of Townships.	When Settled.	Inhabited Houses.	No. of People.	No. of Churches or Meeting-Houses.	No. of Preachers.	No. of Medical Practitioners.	No. of Schools.	Fees per Quarter.	No. of Stores.	No. of Taverns.	No. of Grist Mills.	No. of Saw Mills.	Price of Bricks per 1000.	Price of Lime per bushel.	Blacksmiths per men. and day.	Masons per day.	Carpenters p. day.	Common Labourers per annum.
								s. d.					s. d.	s. d.	L. s d	s. d.	s. d.	L.
Haldimand ..	1797	..	..	1	..	..	4	12 6	5	4	3	4	35 0	0 3	5 0	7 6	6 3	..
Thurlow	1786	240	1700	..	..	2	4	10 0	16	7	4	6	30 0	1 8	5 0	6 3	6 3	30
Sophiasburg ..	1790	101	..	0	..	1	5	12 6	4	7	5	5	27 6	0 6½	Pr. D. s. d.	8 9	8 9	31
Hallowell	..	..	..	1 M. 1 Q.	1 Q.	2	4	13 9	9	4	4	6	27 6	0 9	8 9	8 9	8 9	31
Adolphustown ..	1784	..	..	1 M. 1 Q.	..	0	3	..	1	2	0	6	35 0	1 0	7 6	7 6	7 6	25
Ernesttown ..	1784	..	2450	1 E. 2 P. 1 M 1 L.	1 M.	3	14	10 0	9	21	5	13	23 9	0 7½	..	7 6	7 6	25
Kingston	1783	550	2650	1 E. 1 R. 2 M.	1 E. 1 P. 2 M.	4	8	27 6	..	..	1	3	30 0	1 0	..	..	8 6	27
Lansdown	1788	36	205	..	..	0	1	..	1	3	..	1	20 0	..	..	7 6	7 6	33
Wolford	1797	55	320	..	1	4	15 0	..	..	3	4	..	..	..	7 6	7 6	7 6	..
Charlottenburgh	1784	500	2500	1 E. 3 P. 1 R.	1 P. 2 R.	2	12	..	12	18	4	6	30 0	0 7½	8 1	8 9	7 6	30
Totals	..	1482	9525	19	9	15	59	101 3	57	66	29	54	278 9	7 5½	31 10	70 0	76 0	233
Averaged by	..	6	6	..	..	..	..	7	..	..	..	..	9	8	4	9	10	8
Averages	..	247	1587	..	..	..	14 5	..	..	..	..	..	30 11	11½	7 11	7 9	7 7	29

Composed of Extracts from Township Reports

															P.day			
Sandwich	1750	200	1000	1 R.	2 R. 1 E.	2	3	..	13	8	9	0	45 0	..	..	10	10 0	31
Malden	1784	106	675	1 R.	1 R.	2	3	20	12	5	2	..	40	1 3	10	10	10 0	30
Raleigh	1792	55	273	0	1 M.	0	1	15	5	1	2	..	37 6	..	5	10	5 7	..
Dover, &c.	1794	133	795	..	..	1	4	15	7	4	2	1	35 0	..	7 6	10	7 6	30
Totals	..	494	2746	2	5	5	11	50	37	18	15	1	157 6	1 3	22 6	40	33 1	91
Averaged by	..	4	4	..	..	..	..	3	..	..	..	..	4	..	3	4	4	3
Averages	..	123	686	..	..	..	16 5	..	..	..	..	..	31 10	..	7 6	10	8 3	30

In Columns five and six, E. stands for Episcopal ;   Q. for Quaker ;

TABLE,

Newcastle, Midland, Johnstown, and Eastern Districts.

Wages of					Prices of live stock.											
Common Labour per Winter Month.	Common Labourers per Summer Month.	Common Labourers per day in Harvest	Women's Wages, per week.	Cost of clearing and fencing five Acres of wild Land.	A Work Horse.	A Cow.	An Ox.	A Sheep.	Quantity of Wool per Sheep.	Price of Wool per lb.	Produce of Wheat in Bushels, per Acre.	An Ox will gain in a Summer's run.	Price of Butter, per lb.	Price of Cheese, per lb.	Price of Land per Acre at first.	Price of Land per Acre now.
s. d.	s. d.	s. d.	s. d.	L. s.	L. s.	L. s.	L. s.	s. d.	lb.	s. d.		lb.	s. d.	s. d.	s. d.	s. d.
..	70 0	5 0	5 0	12 10	15 0	5 0	10 0	15 0	3	2 6	25	..	1 0	0 7½	5 0	12 6
40 0	67 6	6 3	5 0	11 5	20 0	5 10	10 0	12 6	3	2 9	20	350	1 1½	0 8½	4 0	32 0
47 6	80 0	..	5 6	..	18 15	5 0	10 0	12 6	3½	2 6	22½	..	1 0	0 7½	1 0	20 0
45 0	65 0	6 3	5 7	..	17 10	5 10	9 7	17 6	3½	2 6	22½	60	1 3	0 8	3 9	32 6
40 0	55 0	5 0	5 0	12 10	..	..	..	11 0	3½	2 6	20	250	1 0	0 6¾	1 0	80 0
37 6	50 0	5 0	4 0	12 10	15 0	5 0	9 10	12 6	3	2 0	17½	113	1 1	0 7½	..	25 0
40 0	55 0	5 0	6 3	16 17	13 10	5 0	8 0	15 0	2⅔	2 6	22½	112	1 6	0 7½	..	..
..	..	5 0	5 0	18 15	15 0	5 15	10 7	12 6	3½	2 2	..	..	..	..	0 6	14 2
35 0	55 0	5 0	5 0	20 0	15 0	5 0	8 6	..	3	2 6	22½	336	..	..	1 3	5 0
47 6	65 0	4 0	5 0	20 0	12 10	5 5	10 0	16 3	5½	1 10	17½	..	1 1½	0 6½	3 0	25 0
332 6	562 6	46 6	51 4	124 7	142 5	47 0	85 4	124 9	33	23 10	190	1220	9 1	5 0	19 6	246 2
8	9	9	10	8	9	9	9	9	10	10	9	6	8	8	8	9
41 6	62 6	5 2	5 1	15 11	15 16	5 4	9 9	13 10	3⅓	2 4	21	203	1 1½	0 7½	2 5	27 4

of the Western District.

45 0	67 6	5 7	6 1	12 10	12 10	5 0	7 10	20 0	3½	2 6	..	120	1 10	1 2	..	12 6
50 0	75 0	5 0	7 6	25 0	16 0	6 0	7 0	17 6	3½	2 3	27½	..	1 3	1 3	1 6	25 0
50 0	82 6	5 0	6 3	24 0	14 8	5 8	..	20 0	2½	2 6	20	..	1 3	1 2	..	..
40 0	70 0	5 0	5 7	..	14 0	6 5	10 0	17 6	3½	3 1	25	200	1 3	1 3	2 6	20 0
185 0	275 0	20 7	25 5	61 10	56 18	23 13	24 10	75 0	13	10 4	72½	320	5 7	5 0	4 0	57 6
4	4	4	4	3	4	4	3	4	4	4	3	2	4	4	2	3
46 3	68 9	5 2	6 4	20 10	14 4	5 13	8 3	18 9	3¼	2 7	24	160	1 5	1 3	2 0	19 2

M. for Methodist; R. for Roman Catholic; L. for Lutheran, and P. for Presbyterian.

As I have no regular report from Ottawa district, and only one from that which lays alongside of it, I shall here introduce accounts of some seigniories and townships on the opposite side of Ottawa river, and otherwise on or near the boundary of Upper Canada, from Bouchette's Geographical Description of Lower Canada.

These seigniories and townships appear in my map, and an account of their soil, state of settlement, tenure, &c. may be of use to him who thinks of emigrating to the provinces. I shall make no invidious comparison between Upper and Lower Canada; but this may be said for the latter, that its proximity to market, considerably compensates for severity of climate; and all within the compass of my map may be occupied by British emigrants, without any risk of their early habits unfitting them to contend with that severity. The fact is, that the winter cold of Canada greatly exceeds that of Britain, looking to the range of the thermometer, yet it is much less painful to the feelings than that which proceeds from our moister atmosphere; and it is exceedingly healthy and invigorating. Indeed I would not wish to dictate as to the emigrant's choice of situation any where in the country between Montreal and Sandwich.

I ought, of course, to have had Mr. Bouchette's leave for extracting so largely as is done below; but this at present being impossible, I shall trust to his pardon. My object is to make this country known; and the following specimens of his publication may attract readers to his work, but cannot injure its sale. His geographical descriptions of Lower Canada are no doubt correct, from his capacity of Surveyor General of that province. Should a second edition of his book appear, the NOTES on Upper Canada should be revised.

General Summary, &c.

HAVING produced the whole regular information concerning Upper Canada, which the inhabitants put into my hands, and having from place to place introduced SUMMARIES of such facts and opinions as seemed of most consequence to bear in mind and arrange, I shall now combine these, and make out a general abstract of information.

The amount of population has been the first object of attention, and results stand as follows:

Western District 4,158
London ditto 8,907
Gore ditto 6,684
Niagara ditto 12,548
Home ditto 7,700
Newcastle ditto 5,000
Midland ditto 14,853
Johnstown ditto 9,200
Eastern ditto 12,700
Ottawa ditto 1,500
                                     ───────
                                      83,250

The writer of the Sketches (page 139) calculates, that in 1811, the province contained 76,984 people. The grounds of his calculation were the number of people, taxed multiplied by 8, the number which he had found to be the proportion to the number taxed in a particular township. Without having looked back to his reckoning, I assumed the number of people taxed in the Newcastle District as my ground work, multiplied that number by 6, as the average number of each family whose head member was taxed, and added 266 persons for untaxed families and individuals, to make up the even number of 5,000 as the total. Had I calculated by 8, the total would have been 6,312, or 1,312 above my fixed result. Were the rule of calculation adopted by the writer of the Sketches generally correct, my error would be in assuming too small a number of untaxed people, viz. 266 instead of 1,578, and this would be a great error indeed; but it is well to investigate error for the sake of coming at truth. My assumption of 6 for a family was fair. The assumption of the number 266 was purely hypothetical, and in the Newcastle District may not be so far wrong as it would appear to be from the above contrast. The writer of the Sketches assumes the number 8 for each name on the assessment roll, from his certain knowledge of one Township, viz. Ernestown. Now Ernest-town was one of the first settled Townships, and in 1811 perhaps the most flourishing in the Province. In such a Township the proportion of untaxed persons will be much greater than in a thinly settled one, and where improvement is proceeding with spirit. Spirited improvement requires many hands, and attracts them from other places; and so we find it said in the Ernest-town Report, that "itinerant tradesmen from the United States often augment the population by some hundreds," none of whom would be entered on the assessment roll: besides, as a settlement gets old and wealthy, the number in families increases from an increased number of children, domestic servants, shopmen, &c. – Newcastle District was not early settled, is remote, thinly settled, and in consequence has had little spirited improvement, each farmer doing his own work with little assistance from hired labourers, &c. Indeed, when I viewed the number of people which resulted from my calculation, and considered the proportional estimate which I had in my mind, by travelling through it, with that of other Districts, I was more afraid that the result was above than below the mark.

Comparing my estimate of population with that made out in 1811, viz.: 83,250 with 76,984, the increase may at first sight appear too small for six years; but circumstances should be considered. In 1812, when war was declared by the United States, a proclamation was issued by the person administering the government of Upper Canada, desiring those persons to depart the Province who were not heartily resolved to espouse the British cause. In consequence of this, some who had settled but a few years, did go off quietly, and others at different periods of the contest followed them; some from dread, and some traitorously. Thus, and by the waste of war, there must have been a diminution of several thousands.

Immediately after the war, in 1815 and 1816, a tide of emigration from the States was setting into the Province, which had then acquired reputation as a place of security, not only from the gallantry of its own people, but from the zealous efforts manifested by the British government in its defence. Many Americans at that time, soured with their own government, and exasperated by party violence, were anxious to retreat into Canada; and there, undoubtedly, would have become the most loyal subjects of the king. This tide, however, had only begun to move, when it was stopped by orders from the Lieutenant-Governor, not only in the face of ancient statutes, but contrary to common sense and the best policy. In 1817 not a creature could safely settle in the Province from the United States; and partly from discontent, partly from a succession of bad seasons, there was a disposition in many of the provincials to sell off their property, and move further to the south, into Indiana and the Illinois.

Having thus reasoned and explained, I shall give in so far. I think the amount of population, as it appears from the Township Reports, and otherwise by analogy, must be below the mark. Some of the reporters, I suspect, have given me the population from assessment rolls alone, without taking into account the untaxed part of the community, and perhaps 90,000 is not too many to estimate as the total amount. In a recent publication I have seen it stated at 94,000, even so early as 1814. This, I am convinced, was too high, and Heriot's estimate, made out in 1806, must have been greatly so.

The chief end of these observations is to draw attention to the subject in future. Nothing can be easier than for the rulers of any country to obtain correct returns of population, births, deaths, &c. annually, from which interesting conclusions may be drawn.

Of the Indian population my account is vague, but it is of little consequence.

Western District	1,000
Gore ditto	1,859
Home ditto	200
Midland ditto	200
Total domiciled in or near the surveyed tracts	3,259

Throughout the wilderness there are many more; but every where they are decreasing in number, and since the treaty of Ghent, by which the independence of the Indian nations between Detroit and the Mississippi was given up, Canada must no longer trust to the tomahawk for defence in war – a consummation not to be regretted.

In the above estimate of population, as it stood in 1817, no notice has been taken of the *mass* of settlers from the United Kingdom since the war. Upon a mere surmise, and I have nothing else for it, these emigrants may have amounted

In 1816, to	2,000
In 1817, to	3,000
In 1818, to	6,000
In 1819, to	8,000

By a late newspaper account there have arrived this year (1820) at Quebec, 11,239 emigrants, about 1,200 less than last year; but supposing the arrangement for settling the country improved, perhaps fewer of these have passed into the United States; say, that actual settlers have amounted to

	8,000
	27,000

Of discharged soldiers settled since the war, and abiding, I have still a less perfect knowledge; but for the sake of being corrected by those who know, we shall suppose, with women and children

6,000

Of settlers, on purchase, from the United
States, for three years, 1818, 1819, and 1820,
we shall, in the same way suppose   2,000
 Settled population estimated above, 1817 90,000
 Natural increase of these in 3 years   6,000
 Indians   3,259
              134,259

There are generally about 2,500 military and naval people
occupying the various forts, &c. throughout the Province. In
order of importance these are, Kingston say 1,500*; Niagara
500*; York 150*; Amherstburgh 100*; Drummond's Island 50*
(near Michilimackinac); Fort Wellington 20*; Fort Erie, Chippawa, and Queenston: Mouth of the Grand River and naval
establishments, Penetangushene: several block houses have been
abandoned entirely.

From the statistical tables of the Western, London, Gore, and
Niagara Districts, it appears that 42 townships contain 24,734
people; and supposing these townships to average 100 miles
square, there are not 6 people to a square mile; while these
townships are better settled than many intermixed with them.

Supposing that there were in Upper Canada, in 1817,
100,000 inhabitants, including emigrants and discharged soldiers;
and supposing 160 townships then surveyed contained 100 square
miles each, there would not be quite seven persons to the square
mile; a miserably thin population. England, with all its wastes,
averages 200 souls to the square mile, and some of the thickly
peopled counties upwards of double that. Canada, under good
cultivation, could, I am convinced, maintain a third part more
people over the same extent than England; and at such a rate,
that part of it laying between Lakes Ontario and Erie, northward,
so far as Lake Nipissing, might nourish 15 millions of people.

For the reported population of 26,977 in the Western, London, Gore, and Niagara districts, there appear to be 20 places of
worship and 35 resident preachers, of whom
15 are Methodists
 5 Baptists
 4 Quakers
 3 Presbyterians
 3 Roman Catholics
 3 Episcopalians
 1 Tunker
 1 Menonist.

 * These numbers are given chiefly to denote the proportional importance
  of the respective stations, and with no pretension to accuracy as to the
  number of the military and naval people.

For the same population there are 20 medical practitioners, 132 schools, 114 taverns, 130 stores, 79 grist mills, and 116 saw mills.

AVERAGE PRICES, throughout the province, appear to be as follow –

	£.	s.	d.
School fees, per quarter	0	13	8
Bricks, per thousand	1	10	11
Lime, per bushel	0	1	0
Blacksmith's wages, per day	0	7	8
Do. – per month	5	14	0
Masons, per day	0	8	4
Carpenters, per day	0	7	9
Common labourers, per annum	28	16	0
Do. per winter month	2	3	3
Do. per summer do.	3	5	2
Do. per day, in harvest	0	5	2
Women, for house work, per week	0	5	6
Spinning, generally 1s. more.			
Cost of clearing and fencing five acres of wild land	19	4	0
Price of a good work horse	15	11	0
Do. a good cow	5	5	0
Do. an ox	8	16	0
Do. sheep	0	14	3
Do. wool, per lb.	0	2	5
Do. butter, per do.	0	1	1¼
Do. cheese, per do.	0	0	10
Do. wild land, at first	0	3	9
Do. in 1817	1	4	0

N.B. *Wheat in* 1817 *was* 6s. *per bushel; now* (1820) *it is* 3s.

An ox will gain in a summer's run . . . . . . 171⅖ lbs.

Average produce of wheat, per acre . . . . 21 bush.

Do. of wool, per sheep . . . . 3½ lbs.

TIMBER TREES may be supposed to abound most, as they are most frequently mentioned in the Reports; thus:

MAPLE (hard and soft) 53 times: OAK (white, red, black, swamp) 52: BEECH, 48: BASSWOOD, sometimes called WHITE WOOD (page 292), sometimes LYNDEN (page 389), 45: ASH (black, white, and swamp), 45: PINE (white), 44: ELM (white and red), 38: HICKORY, 34: WALNUT (black and white), 29: BUTTERNUT, 21: CHESTNUT, 19: CHERRY, 18: IRON WOOD, 15: CEDAR, 12: BIRCH, 8: HEMLOCK (of the fir tribe), 7: POPLAR, 5: SPRUCE, 5: TAMARACK (a species of larch), 4: PLUM, ELDER, WILLOW, HAZLE, and

CRAB TREE, *twice:* BUTTON WOOD, ALDER, TULIP TREE, QUAKING ASP, SHITTIM WOOD, SYCAMORE, CYPRESS, MULBERRY, THORN, LOCUST, SASSAFRAS, and DOGWOOD, *once.*

N. B. DOGWOOD, *and some others here quoted from the Reports, should not properly rank as timber trees.*

PLOUGHING begins generally about the 1st of April: some seasons not till the 15th or 20th.

SOWING WHEAT chiefly in September; but sometimes so early as the middle of August, and so late as the 10th of October.

REAPING WHEAT end of July and beginning of August; occasionally so late as September.

CATTLE are turned out to pasture generally the 1st of May, and taken in the end of November: they can *browse* in the woods from the 1st of April till the end of December.

SLEIGHING begins, throughout the upper part of the province, about the 1st of January, and continues two months; in the lower parts of the province it begins about the 15th of December, and lasts three months.

MOWING grass for hay and REAPING, from 3s. 9d. to 7s. 6d. per day.

CRADDLING wheat, 5s. to 10s. per day.

The customary terms of LETTING LAND, or, as it is called, letting it on SHARES, is for the land-owner to have one-third of the produce. If the land-owner furnishes seed and team, he gets one half; and if he furnishes every thing but manual labour, he gets two-thirds. . . .

A GOOD FRAME FARM HOUSE costs from £125 to £250.

A GOOD FRAME BARN, £125.

A LOG HOUSE, £25.

BLACKSMITH'S work, iron, at the rate of 7½d. per lb. common work; making chains, 1s.

AN AXE costs 12s. 6d. a HOE, 5s.; SHOEING A HORSE, 10s.

CARDING WOOL, 7½d. per lb. and from 5d. to 9d.

A TAILOR charges, for making a coat, from 20s. to 27s. 6d.; and 10s. for pantaloons.

SHOEMAKERS charge 3s. 9d. for making a pair of shoes; and a WEAVER has, for weaving a yard of common flannel, 1s. to 1s. 6d. SAWING, 2s. 6d. per 100 feet, or half the timber.

THE AVERAGE PRODUCE OF WHEAT per acre being 21 bushels for one of seed, speaks sufficiently for the fertility of the land. The average produce of England does not exceed 18 bushels per acre for 3 bushels of seed. In Canada the husbandry is in general very bad; in England it is the reverse: but the natural superiority of Canada, in point of soil, over England, rises to greatest excess, when we consider, that from one end of the province to the other there is scarcely two acres of sterile ground to be seen side by side, while England has its mountains, its moors, its poor downs, and its barren sands.

Opinions

As to what retards the improvement of the Province.

1st.	In	24	Reports, lands of non-occupants.
2d.		19	do. crown, clergy, and other reserves.
3d.		14	do. want of people, especially men of capital and enterprise.
4th.	In	8	Reports, want of money.
5th.		5	do. shutting out Americans.
6th.		4	do. bad navigation of the St. Lawrence, and remoteness from market.
7th.		3	do. bad roads,
8th.		3	do. lands of Indians.
9th.		2	do. want of emigration, and of a liberal system of emigration.
10th.		2	do. difficulties opposed to emigrants, and poverty of beginners.
11th.		1	do. damaged sustained by war.
12th.		1	do. want of liberal and indiscriminate admission of settlers from the United States.
13th.		1	do. indiscriminate admission of do.
14th.		1	do. want of incentive to emulation.
15th.		1	do. defect in the system of colonization.
16th.	In	1	Report, lands in the hands of individuals unwilling to sell, and minors who cannot convey.
17th.		1	do. remoteness from market, and difficulty of communicating with the lower province.
18th.		1	do. People, who got land, from the United States, and went off after selling it.
19th.		1	do. want of spirited and industrious men.
20th.		1	do. want of a bank (now supplied).
21st.		1	do. want of skill in husbandry.
22d.		1	do. bad habits of original settlers, soldiers, and bad characters, from the United States.
23d.		1	do. want of rousing up.

Review.

THE work of compilation is now finished. I have placed before the reader documents not only authentic and interesting as they concern Upper Canada, but from which conclusions may be drawn of the utmost importance otherwise.

In the course of this work I have abstained, as much as possible, from intruding my own opinions, that those of the reader might form gradually as facts presented themselves, without prejudice or bias. My purpose now is to look back on the materials collected together, and discover what is most worthy of notice, and whence we may derive knowledge for decision and future transaction. . . .

The fancy of giving to Canada the British constitution was a good one: about as rational as to think of cultivating sugar canes in Siberia, or to entertain hope from grafting a fruit twig on an icicle. The British constitution is a thing which circumstances have generated, and which only can be upheld while peculiar circumstances exist. Notwithstanding all our boasts, chance and necessity have had more to do in its maturation than reason and truth; and while we look back into history, and survey the world around us, we have much reason to be thankful that it is, as it is. To assume it as perfection, and palm it upon a distant country without consulting first principles, afforded little chance of success. At home, the British constitution would be all-sufficient if we had it; and were we ourselves perfect, we may have it in perfection: abroad, it cannot possibly be had. Mr. Pitt is so far excusable as he brings forward the measure only as one of trial. He is framing an act of parliament, which, at any time, can be repealed or new modelled; which is wholly *"subject to revision:"* and here the Canadian has advantage over the British constitution. The latter, suspended by the cobwebs of antiquity, cannot be taken down, cleansed out, and hung up again, without dirt and danger. The former, fresh in all its bindings and appointments, can be unloosed, examined, and altered at any time with the utmost safety. Church and State are not indissolubly joined together in Canada, as some say they are at home. Church, indeed, in Canada, is not yet thoroughly established and defined; nor does it appear to have any connexion with Church at home. Church at home is not responsible for Church abroad; and would lose neither credit nor security, though never united to it. As to ruling colonies, we know that Church can be dispensed with. Church has little to do with the government of the West Indies;

and nothing at all with that of the East. We know, what is of more consequence still, that the Church of Christ never was meant, by its founder, to be connected with government.

As to establishing hereditary nobility in Canada, it is a thousand pities, that Mr. Pitt's notion had not been carried into effect. Nothing could have so well exposed the absurdity, as actual trial and consequent ridicule. By this day we should have witnessed many a pleasant farce. We should have seen, perhaps, the Duke of Ontario leading in a cart of hay, my Lord Erie pitching, and Sir Peter Superior making the rick; or perhaps his Grace might now have been figuring as a petty-fogging lawyer, his Lordship as a pedlar, and, Sir Knight, as a poor parson, starving on 5,000 acres of clergy reserves.

As it is, the Legislative Council of Upper Canada must soon come into contempt. It can never rise above the value of a bundle of well tried sycophancy and passive obedience. The characters of the Governor's *elect* are perfectly known before their appointment for life; and, I doubt, if a single instance has yet occurred, where any one councillor has ever, in a manly manner, opposed the *dictum* of his Excellency. But Upper Canada has not suffered so much from its legislative councillors as from its assembly men. The councillors have generally been better educated than the representatives of the people, and have had greater regard to outward appearances. The Honourable William Dickson, for instance, being bred a storekeeper, could write a good hand and keep accounts, with which accomplishments, and some practice as a clerk to a district judge, he was made lawyer by act of parliament, and then dubbed with the *honour* which he now bears. He is of course so far superior to Isaac Swayze, Member of Assembly, who can scarcely write his own name, and for whom no employment was too mean, even that of collecting fowls for the Lieutenant-Governor's table, who had no blush for palpable malice and perjury, and who was notorious for the commission of most shocking crimes, in capacity of spy and horse provider to his Majesty, during the revolutionary war of America.*

But this superiority of the Councillor does not go beyond external acts, and, so far as morality is concerned, every suspicion

---

* Isaac Swayze of Niagara was the man who brought an accusation against Gourlay under the Alien Act. A Loyalist and, at least after his own conviction for sedition in 1795, an active supporter of government, he had also brought a motion in the Assembly for slander against an earlier critic, Joseph Willcocks in 1808, and had begun the libel action that imprisoned Gourlay's Niagara publisher, Bartimus Ferguson. [Ed.]

must sink him below the Assembly-man. The act of the one manifests brutal ignorance, that of the other results from cunning. Dickson's superiority over Swayze, in point of education, his profession of lawyer, and the very feeling which his *nominal honour* should have bestowed, all militate against him, and point at the willing abettor of perjury. The law, even though applicable to me, did not require that a direct assertion should be made that I *was* seditious. An oath as to the *belief* of this would have done equally well, as appears more particularly from inspection of the original Sedition Act; and which kind of swearing was in constant practice in Canada, for the arrest of debtors suspected of intention to leave the province. The man who could sufficiently read and write, the lawyer, and the legislative councillor, could not be ignorant of this. He could not be ignorant that Swayze subjected himself to a prosecution for perjury; but he felt *himself* secure from danger, and therefore winked at the iniquity. In cunning he was superior to his cat's-paw. The Councillor and Assembly-man, in these their acts, do but too exactly exemplify proceedings in their respective Houses, which may by-and-bye appear. The House of Assembly has always been made the *prominent* instrument of gross performances in the political drama of Upper Canada. The Legislative Council has assisted only behind the scenes, or come forward after the way was smoothed by the pioneers.

This question will naturally arise, how could such a man as Isaac Swayze be elected, and repeatedly elected, by the people as a representative in Parliament? and, to be sure, the people must bear reproach. I shall say the best I can for them: simplicity abounds in Canada. Swayze could cover all the stains upon his character, before my time, with hypocrisy. I once heard him tell, *at the table of a Legislative Councillor,* by what means he gained favour with his constituents. "When electioneering," said he, "I pray with the Methodists;" and were it not wandering from my present subject; I could satisfy the reader how it came about that jesting with religion and honesty could be endured in such a situation. The fact is, that till I resided in Upper Canada I did not believe that there were, on earth, men so thoroughly destitute of shame as I found among the *higher ranks*, Legislative Councillors, and Assembly-men, of that province. Swayze is now put out of the Assembly; but I am sorry to say, that, from another quarter, men have been returned to it, even of a more dangerous stamp to decency and the hope of good. The first session of a new Parliament has passed over without the grand essential of inquiry being carried. The Commons have voted down the Sedition Act, but the Legislative Council has put a veto on its repeal.

The Legislative Council of Upper Canada has considerably declined, in point of respectability, since its first institution. Originally, there were some gentlemen nominated, who had no previous trial and training in mean and dirty things; and who justly bore a high character. Now, and as necessity increases for making the Governor's arbitrary will secure, – for strengthening *his* influence, I do not say the crown influence, for the influence of a provincial governor goes quite beyond that, we may well imagine what it will come to. In short, the existence of the British constitution in Canada, was, from the beginning, a mere delusion, and experience has given proof of its being a mischievous one. . . .

It does not appear that there was much call on the part of the Canadians, for a constitution, when British ministers tasked themselves with the fabrication of one for the colony. Perhaps it was thought, that as constitutions were beginning to wither in Europe, and a rank young one, self-sown, was springing up in America, it was time to stick in a sucker by the side of it, torn from the root of our old plant, to try if it might not prosper and overshadow the seedling of nature and independence: perhaps it was thought time to be making a shew of liberality; but sham liberality cannot lcng hide the cloven foot. Sure I am it would have been better, both for Canada and the parent state, had there been no attempt to transplant the British constitution,—much better for Canada to have had no parliament up to the present time. Had ministers, simply and sincerely, considered, that all, of government, which is required to make people happy and contented in a young country, is only security for person and property: had they, with this single object in view, chalked out certain rules to be observed by a governor and council; and devised right plans for the disposal of wild land, the provinces might have flourished far beyond what they have done, been free of all discontent, and run no risk from invasion. The wild lands economically managed, might, from the beginning, have yielded profit, and enabled government to have executed every design without calling upon the inhabitants for a single farthing, in the shape of tax; might have saved them from the shame of enacting laws for which their predecessors, the savages, would have blushed. . . .

Nothing can be more pusillanimous – more treacherous to nature and truth, than to maintain that, because kings and nobles got established in days of darkness and superstition, they should be established for ever. The doctrines of Burke would go to this; and, while the representative system of France was yet concocting, and had not gained fair trial, our most loyal politician would misrepresent its tendencies, and ridicule all expectation of its success. It was from no fault in the plan of representation that the horrors of the French revolution proceeded: they proceeded from the bad *material* which the ancient reign of kings, and nobles, and priests had generated. Frenchmen were vain, and volatile, and vicious: they were brutal and base, because they had been cradled in corruption, canopied by the wide spreading iniquity of an absolute monarchy. They needed, perhaps, all the chastisement they have received, to purify them from the filth of age, and fit them for the enjoyment of rational freedom. They needed, perhaps, such monsters as Danton and Robespierre, to give them an outward view of their own hearts. They needed, perhaps, a Buonaparte to exhibit to them their vain glory, their false views of liberty, and their despicable prostration to military despotism. They needed, perhaps, their present subjugation to a family they despise, to train them in, by humility and calm reason, to act like men. But, bad as the French were at the commencement of their revolution, they might, I doubt not, have accomplished it in peace, but for such writings and speeches as those of Mr. Burke, which bolstered up pride, kept alive resentments, and riveted prejudices, which imposed upon common sense, and confounded reason: – but for the combined powers of church and state, the high blown conceit of princes, and the wrath of a sinking priesthood. They will yet accomplish it. The present is a useful breathing-time – a time when the world quietly, and to profit, can study the acts and declarations of the Holy Alliance.

Had Mr. Burke been an impartial reasoner on the rights of man, he would not have connected them with the delirium of the French revolution: he would have sought for their genuine worth, as exemplified, and fairly brought to issue, in that of America. This was the quarter to which he should have looked for precedent, when framing a constitution for Canada; but from this quarter he averts his eye, that he may gaze upon the darling idols of antiquity – that he may divert attention from reason and common sense, to superstition, to vanity, and all the delusions of ancient misrule.

The States of America had enjoyed constitutions founded on the rights of man for fifteen years before Mr. Burke run riot against these sacred rights. They have since enjoyed them twice fifteen years, and what has experience taught us? Have we seen the poor rising against the rich in America? Have we seen life or property insecure? Have we seen government unstable? – Quite the reverse. During forty years, while the people of each State had a constitutional liberty, to assemble at any time and remodel their form of government, this has been resorted to only in one instance. I was in Connecticut while a constitutional reform was decided on by the assembled people; and it was decided upon and carried into effect, without the smallest commotion.

It is pretty clear that Simcoe was sent out to govern Upper Canada, without any control in the disposal of land. Only a year after his arrival in the Province, war broke out with France, and thenceforth, till the American invasion, that country was little thought of. As soon, indeed, as the war in Europe began, England had full employment for her people, and Canada was of no consequence as a receptacle for redundant population. Simcoe's plans were all ruled with an eye to military operations, and, so far, they were judicious. In business he was energetic. And, as remarked by Rochefoucault, the greatest obstacle to success rested in his purpose of returning to England at the expiration of five years. He was recalled even within that period, and as soon as he was gone, not only were all his schemes set aside, but the engagements which he had entered into were grossly violated. Men of capital and enterprise, who had come into the Province duly furnished with cattle and implements to commence the settlement of townships, granted on condition that they should be settled, had these taken from them, and 1200 acres of land offered in lieu thereof. Some accepted of this, and remained: others went off in disgust, to proclaim through the United States the perfidy of the British government. Whether the scheme of settling Upper Canada by such contracts was politic, it is not now necessary to determine; but it was at once impolitic and dishonourable to run from solemn agreements, made in the name of his Majesty. Governor Simcoe had sent forth proclamations liberally inviting settlers into Upper Canada, and all that he did should have been ratified. One of his schemes was in every way judicious, yet most wantonly marred. He had lined out a grand highway, which was to run from one extremity of the province to the other, connecting his military posts and naval establishments. This he called Dundas Street, and part is represented on my map. He had no money wherewith to open this; but his purpose was to grant its margin to actual settlers, on condition of each making good the road, so far as his grant extended. Settlers sat themselves down at different parts, along the line of this proposed grand thoroughfare, and fulfilled their engagements only to be grievously disappointed. The moment that Simcoe was recalled, the ungranted lots along Dundas Street were seized by people in power, and the actual settlers, up to 1817, remained in little communities, cut off from each other, and unable to make good the grand communication, the completion of which had, at the outset, promised them such advantages, and tempted them so far into the wilderness. I have spoken of this before, but it cannot be too much reflected on, as the beginning of just complaint and discontents in Upper Canada – discontents which have ever since been kept alive by similar outrages on the part of administration. Only think of a dozen or a score of poor men going into the woods, fifty or sixty miles from connected settlement, expending their labour, for four or five years, clearing farms and erecting buildings, in the assurance that, before long, they should have an outlet to market, and a reward for extraordinary exertions and privations. Only think of these people, after five or six years perseverance and hope, being suddenly chilled with disappointment, and left imprisoned in the woods. They cannot dispose of their farms: they cannot afford to abandon them; and they pine on, from year to year, deploring their fate, and uttering reproaches against government. . . .

This is plain language, but really I know of none other adequate to throw light on the subject; to account for the horrible policy and misrule which prevailed in Canada when I went out to it; which had prevailed ever since the time of Simcoe; and which is yet far from being corrected as it should be. . . .

While I was in Canada, men of education, talents, and experience, came from home to settle there; but it would not do, and many of them have left the province. A country surgeon at home has hard work of it. What may he be supposed to have where population does not amount to seven *bodies* to the square mile? and where fees must be received per the barrel or the bushel; perhaps in *lumber*. For my part, I see no occasion to have any restraining law as to the practice of physic or surgery in any country. Instances of mischief from unlettered empirics have no doubt occurred; but law will not prevent such; while perfect freedom in this, as in trade of all sorts, has many advantages. If a medical man has obtained a diploma, so much the better for him. It will give confidence to his first employers; but it must require practice on his part, and experience of his success on that of the public, to establish his merits. An invalid, in short, should be allowed to choose his own doctor; and, as his purse will allow, to pay a five guinea or five farthing fee.

Mankind, in all ages and countries, have had an avidity to legislate over-much. The sumptuary laws of some countries, and innumerable absurdities on the British statute-book, witness this: but I have descanted more on the instance immediately before us, to draw attention to the misery and inconvenience which result from a new country, being settled as Upper Canada has been, – planted with people at the rate of one family per mile square.

No less than *ten* ACTS have been made for securing *titles to lands, registering deeds,* &c. &c. . . . When we look back into the history of old countries, and observe how landed property was first established; how it was seized upon, pulled about, given away, and divided, in all sorts of ways, shapes, and quantities; how it was bequeathed, burthened, entailed, and leased in a hundred forms: when we consider how dark were the days of antiquity, – how grossly ignorant and savage were our remote forefathers, we cannot be so much surprised at finding ourselves heirs to confusion; and, that, in these old countries, entanglement continues to be the order of the day. But when civilized men were quietly and peaceably to enter into the occupancy of a new region, where all could be adjusted by the square and compass; and where order, from the beginning, could have prevented for ever all possibility of doubt, and dispute, and disturbance; how deplorable is it to know, that in less than a life-time, even the simplest affairs should get into confusion! and so it is already in Upper Canada, to a lamentable degree. Boundaries of land are doubtful and disputed: deeds have been mislaid, lost, confounded, forged: they have been passed again and again in review before commissioners: they have been plotted and blurred: they have got into the repositories of attornies and pettifogging lawyers; while courts of justice are every day adding doubt to doubt, delay to delay, and confusion to confusion; with costs, charges, cheating.

Things are not yet beyond the reach of amendment, even in the old settlements. In the new, what a glorious task is it to devise plans for lasting peace and prosperity! – to arrange in such a way, as to bar out a world of turmoil in times to come!

The present very unprofitable and comfortless condition of Upper Canada must be traced back to the first operations of Simcoe. With all his honesty, and energy, and zeal for settling the province, he had really no sound views on the subject, and he was infinitely too lavish in disposing of the land – infinitely too much hurried in all his proceedings. In giving away land to individuals, no doubt, he thought he would give these individuals an interest in the improvement of the country, – an inducement to settle in it, and draw to it settlers; but he did not consider the character and condition of most of his favourites; many of them officers in the army, whose habits did not accord with business, and less still with solitude and the wilderness; whose hearts were in England, and whose wishes were intent on retirement thither. Most of them did retire from Upper Canada, and considering, as was really the case, their land grants of little value, forgot and neglected them. This was attended with many bad consequences. Their lands became bars to improvement: as owners they were not known; could not be heard of; could not be applied to, or consulted with, about any measure for public advantage. Their promises under the Governor's hand, their land board certificates, their deeds, were flung about and neglected. But mischief greater than all this, arose, is, and will be, from the badness of surveys. Such was the haste to get land given away, that ignorant and careless men were employed to measure it out, and such a mess did they make of their land-measuring, that one of the present surveyors informed me, that in running new lines over a great extent of the province, he found spare room for a whole township in the midst of those laid out at an early period. It may readily be conceived, upon consideration of this fact, what blundering has been committed, and what mistakes stand for correction. . . .

In short, numerous mistakes and errors of survey have been made and discovered: much dispute has arisen therefrom; and I have been told infinite mischief is still in store. It occurred to me, while in Canada, and it was one of the objects which, had a commission come home, I meant to have pressed on the notice of government, that a complete new survey and map of the province should be executed; and at the same time a book, after the manner of Doomsday-book, written out and published, setting forth all the original grants, and describing briefly but surely all property both public and private. I would yet most seriously recommend such to be set about. It might be expensive now; but would assuredly save, in time to come, a pound for every penny of its cost. To proprietors of Canadian lands, who reside in Britain, I would more particularly advise the forwarding of this necessary measure, for they may depend upon it that blazing may be outblazed, and absentees ousted by roguish residents. How easy, even for a single axeman in the lone and remote wood, to cut down the originally blazed timber, and blaze afresh in a very different direction! The Lawyers of Upper Canada will have an abundant harvest before them, if nothing is done to cure this evil. I do my duty in presenting it as a very great one. A new survey, Doomsday-book, and well-ordered registries, might, after a little exertion, settle for ever, all disputes as to boundary lines, land deeds, &c. in the old settlement; and wholly prevent them in the new. Then *one* ACT of Parliament would be a good substitute for the *ten* pointed at above. . . .

The first tax raised by statute in the province, was appropriated to pay the members of Assembly, and this is provided for by five ACTS. Supposing that parliaments, for the twenty-five years in which the foregoing statutes were passed, sat six weeks upon an average, and had twenty members in attendance at 10s. per

day, the amount of charge would be 10,500l. In 1801 the salaries
of the officers of Parliament stood thus; per annum:

	£.
Clerk of the Legislative Council	145
Usher of the Black Rod	50
Master in Chancery, attending the Legislative Council	50
Chaplain of the Legislative Council	50
Door-Keeper of Ditto	20
Speaker of the House of Assembly	200
Clerk of Ditto	125
Serjeant at Arms	50
Chaplain of the House of Assembly	50
Door-Keeper of Ditto	20
Copying Clerks	50
	£. 805

These salaries were afterwards increased: that of the Speaker
to 400; and, together with contingent expences, were provided for
by *twenty-one* ACTS. A regular estimate of government expences,
with the neat annual supply, is not published in Upper Canada;
and neither the one nor the other can be ascertained from what
appears in the Statute Book. After my friends of the Assembly
peruse this I hope they will be so good as have these matters
annually laid before the House, and published. Supposing the
above 805l. was made up to 1000l. for contingent and other
expences, annually incurred by the sitting of the legislature, then
we have 35,500l. at least, to reckon upon as the cost of the 293
statutes of Upper Canada, whose titles are given above. Are they
a good bargain? Or must we look to the whole concern through
the "gross of green spectacles," for which the younger son of
Parson Primrose sold the old mare? No, I have yet in hold *one*
ACT to be particularly noticed, which is worth all the money, and
more, say 50,000l. which I doubt not the statutes of Upper
Canada cost up to 1817, including increased salaries, a house for
the accommodation of the legislature, the statute book of England, a library, and printing of the statutes: I mean the ACT for
establishing common schools, number 281. The other ACTS, numbers 72 – 143 – 165 and 244, are of inferior stamp. Number 72
provides for the education and support of orphan children. It
allows the town-wardens of any township, with the consent of two
justices of peace, to bind and apprentice children deserted by
parents; males till twenty-one, and females till eighteen years of

age. It also allows mothers to do the same, where the father abandons his child; but in case relations of any child or children are able and willing to bring them up, then no power rests with town-wardens; and none having attained the age of fourteen years are liable to be apprenticed, unless he, she, or they consent thereto. This ACT seems humane; but it is just one of those *meddling* laws which have done so much mischief in England, in the poor-law system, and would better be expunged. In Scotland there are none of these legal interferences, and I never heard of an orphan that was left destitute. Numbers 143 and 165 regard the District Schools. These could not benefit the mass of the people who were taxed to maintain them. They were complained of, and produced little good. The institution of these before common schools was beginning at the wrong end. . . .

Having said thus much as to the lesser acts of Upper Canada, which regard education, it is with infinite delight I call attention to the great one . . . [the Common Schools Act of 1816]. This ACT was worth £50,000 to the people of Upper Canada, as before said; and it would be worth ten times that sum to England, if adopted next session of parliament, instead of the monstrous stuff lately shaped into a bill by Mr. Brougham. When I heard that Mr. Brougham had corresponded with *fifteen thousand parsons*, on the subject of educating the poor of England, it puzzled me to think what would be the result. Now I am satisfied. Mr. Brougham, I conceive, wished first to get the good will of the parsons to the general measure, and then give them the go-by. He has, since his bill was introduced into the House, spoken fairly out, and declared that there was "too much religion in the schools of Mr. Owen at New Lanark," as much as to say, that religion should have nothing to do with public schools; and certainly the dogmas of particular sects should have no control over those supported by the public purse. Young people are allowed to be initiated into every trade – to be taught every mechanical art without the interference of the clergy. So, also, may they be taught the art of reading and writing with equal freedom and safety. When parish schools were first instituted in Scotland, during the 17th century, the great mass of the people were of one way of thinking in religion, and there was no objection to giving ministers and elders of the kirk a charge over the schools. Now, it is altogether different; and Mr. Brougham has found the dissenters adverse to his scheme; as well they may be. Will dissenters – will any sensible class of people object to public schools on the plan of the Canadian ACT? I cannot think it. This plan admits of every sect suiting itself out of the common fund. If Episcopalians can bring forward a sufficiency of scholars,

they may have the stated allowance for a schoolmaster; and
nobody will interfere with their cramming into their children the
Athanasian creed. If Presbyterians can bring forward the requisite
number of scholars, then they will have the allowance, and be
suffered to go on with the apostles' creed, only: while Quakers
will do without any creed, nobody troubling them. In England,
£30. a year, instead of £25. might be allowed as school-master's
salary; and forty scholars instead of twenty be required for
obtaining it. All this, however, would be easily settled. In twenty
years, I am convinced, legal provision for schools might be
dropped. Legal provision is only required till the mass of the
people become sufficiently enlightened; and then they will best
educate their children without either aid or interference. Was the
provision for parish schools in Scotland now withdrawn, I question if schools would become either less respectable or fewer in
number. I would hope not.

The Canadian plan could be adopted and acted upon at the
same moment. It requires no immediate vote of money. It needs
but a guarantee that the money will be payable when called for
under the declared stipulations, and this would come on gradually. It requires neither money nor consideration for providing
school-houses. The people would take care of all this, and suit
themselves, as taste, convenience, and situation required. The
whole business would regulate itself, and go on smoothly: it
would proceed just so far as the public feeling was inclined to
carry it: a fair opportunity would be given to all; and, the ACT
might be amended or repealed without occasioning either extraordinary bustle, or unnecessary expense.

The Upper Canada school ACT was, I believe borrowed, in
substance, from the state of New York; but, is no worse for that;
and we need not be ashamed to borrow at second hand from one
of our own colonies, knowing that "out of the mouths of babes
and sucklings proceeds knowledge." Dr. Bell brought his system
of education from the East Indies: it flags. Let us now draw
refreshment from the west. With a few modifications, the Canadian ACT would suit England delightfully. . . .

At an early period of British dominion in America, blocks of
wild land were set apart, to make provision, by a future day, for
public institutions, judged essential to the well being and perfection of society. Since the revolution, the United States had followed out, in part, this practice, by allotting land for schools, and
in Canada whole townships have been appropriated for the same
purpose, to say nothing of the crown and clergy reserves. It is
altogether delusive; and has been productive of much annoyance

and disappointment. It is indeed truly surprising that the fallacy of such a measure has not been perceived by Americans. People on this side the Atlantic may be excused. Here we see land set aside for all sorts of purposes – for maintaining schools, hospitals, churches, and what not? We see land thus appropriated answering the end; and, without considering the difference of circumstances, fly off with a conclusion that appropriations of land in the wilderness of America, will prove equally effective as at home. The Edinburgh Review has given in to this error. Not long ago I read in that oracle of wisdom, an approval of the American plan of setting out land, to secure the benefit of education to future generations. The plan is wrong in every way. It creates a species of entail; a barring out from the market, property which should be left to the operation of free trade: it presumes to dictate where there is no right to dictate: it puts restraint upon the free course of nature and improvement. Were the Jews in the Stock Exchange to get possession of half the land of England through mortgage, and then to indulge a whim of appropriating all the rents to teaching Hebrew, and re-establishing Judaism, what would be said? But this view of the matter is not what I now particularly wish to call attention to. I wish to draw attention to a grossly stupid piece of policy, which does a mighty deal of mischief, without the chance of accomplishing any good. I allude to the practice prevalent in America, of setting apart wild land for the maintenance of contemplated public institutions; and I should be glad to have the Edinburgh Review convinced of this error in political economy, that a strong arm may be put forth for its correction.

All land in Britain will bring a certain clear rent in money, owing to the great demand from our confined and dense population. In America land is so abundant, that it can be let only on *shares*. None but poor men will take it; and they must generally be assisted with stock by the proprietor. It was once so in Scotland under the name of *steel bow*. The tenant is little else than a labourer for the proprietor. He is only hired in a particular way, which saves the trouble of tasking and oversight. He is a tenant at will – his *own* will, and makes but a temporary convenience of the farm he rents. As soon as he gets a little money, and becomes able sufficiently to stock a farm, he will no longer submit to be a tenant. He can immediately get land of his own on credit; and after a very few years can pay its price out of the profits of his industry. Under such circumstances, and such circumstances must long exist in America, there can be few or no mere money renters – no farms let as with us, without trouble to the landlord, and for a series of years.

In America, the landlord who lets must be close at hand, supplying seed, implements, cattle; or, in the very simplest way, ready to take into his barn the various kinds of produce for rent as they are harvested. Now, when wild land is appropriated for any public purpose, what is it to produce? who is to stock it, or gather together rent in raw produce? who is to take it for cultivation without assistance? especially if it lays together in great quantity. Setting aside whole townships, as has been done in Upper Canada, for schools, was absolute folly; and, it is perfectly astonishing how men on the spot could not discover this. Even the more cunning plan of intermixing every two hundred acres of crown and clergy reserves with the gifted lands has not succeeded. These reserves have drawn but a mere trifle in money – a few dollars per lot, and that only for the sake of the timber which, during war time, had a value, but now is worth nothing. In Canada, excellent wild land could be purchased, when I left the country, for a dollar an acre, or could be had for a mere *promise* of a little more to be paid by instalments. Now, any man that can occupy a crown or clergy reserve, can occupy a lot on purchase, and no man but an idiot would choose the former. A purchaser, to a certainty, if he is at all industrious, can clear the price of his land in six or eight years; and be settled for ever, without further change or charge, while the tenant of a reserve must yield up every thing at a given term – fields which he has cleared, and buildings which he has erected. The poor man who rents on shares is better than he. His labour is bestowed on fields already cleared; and he can quit at any time without regret for what he leaves behind. Some large proprietors of land in America have tried to lease out their lands, but it does not succeed. To have profit, they must sell it outright; and *they* have made most who have most freely sold. In short, land in America, or in any other new country, can have little value till it becomes private property, and is occupied by the owner. This is an important truth, – a truth which I am anxious should be attended to, not only for the sake of establishing a right principle for the settlement of Canada, but of our immense territories in every quarter of the globe. The British nation is the greatest landowner in the world; but up to the present time we have fooled away our foreign possessions: we have marred our settlements: we have made them sinks for wealth, instead of sources from which it may be drawn. Nay, what is worse than waste of treasure, we have rusticated, and enfeebled, and vitiated our transplanted stock of men, – all from inattention to certain simple truths which regard the state of property. Let this be well understood, and well regulated, then wonders may be effected; – every other good, indeed, would follow of course. Mankind do not require coercion for improvement so much as is thought. It is not necessary for this generation to pre-scribe for the good of the next, so far as property is concerned. Let that go free from father to son; and it will be put to better and better use, as society advances in knowledge and refinement. The School Act of Upper Canada is a glorious proof of the natural disposition of mankind to promote education – of what may be expected from voluntary effort.

Considering that the Canadians are the poorest people of North America, the vote of money for that purpose is liberal in the extreme; and pity it is that the state of property should render the effort in any respect abortive. It has greatly done so. In many parts, population is so thin that the required number of children cannot be got together, to give those willing to take advantage of the ACT an opportunity of benefiting by it. It has hence been complained of; and it was thought might even be allowed to expire. I hope it is revived; and that it will be maintained till property is well arranged, and society strong.

In the United States, opposite to Canada, where property has been exposed to free sale, where it has not been gifted away to drones, nor held back from cultivation by reserves for church and state, public institutions are in the most thriving condition. In every quarter excellent schools are established, and in every vil-lage we see an elegant church, in some two, in some three; all well endowed, and occupied with zealous, well-educated ministers, solely from the voluntary contributions of the people: In Canada, which began to settle eight or ten years sooner, and had all along assistance from the British government; in Canada, cursed with reserves and unoccupied lands of all sorts, we withness a melan-choly difference: from end to end, schools feeble even with liberal provision, and not a single place of worship approaching to elegance, – neither a steeple nor a bell. These effects, so different, have resulted mainly from the difference in the state of property; and could I succeed in rousing attention to the simple governing principle, – in bringing about a complete change of policy, so that a people hitherto enveloped in darkness and unnecessary toils, could see the light and get free, little indeed should I grudge all the miseries I have sustained in making the attempt. It is the simplicity of my remedies which warrants hope; yet there seems a continual warfare among mankind against simplicity in govern-ment. Let me repeat, nevertheless, that the right ordering of property, and an effective system of taxation, can accomplish every desirable end.

In conjunction with the common schools of Upper Canada, the District Schools, if well appointed, might be productive of much good; and I should propose measures by which the maintenance of these, out of public funds, would be fair and politic, which is not the case at present, while only the wealthier classes, and a few others residing near those schools, can have benefit from them. I should propose that one boy, the best scholar of each township, should be annually sent up to the District Schools, and there educated at the public charge for one year: at the end of which time to have an opportunity of gaining another year's education at the public expense, and so a third with superior merit, ascertained by fair competition and impartial decision: the scheme to carry forward a certain number of the best scholars to a free attendance at a British University. Thus, suppose 200 boys from 200 townships, sent up to ten District Schools, at the cost of 20l. per annum each,

	£. 4,000
100 of these boys kept on a second year	2,000
50 kept on a third year	1,000
25 sent annually to Britain, to remain at the public expense four years, at the rate of 100l. per annum, including travelling expences to and from	10,000
	£.17,000

Does this scheme seem extravagant, or vain, or hopeless? I think not; and the only question I would further put, on the part of my friends in Canada, is this: would it pay? There is no doubt but it would. We must not look to the improvement of the youths who have the benefit, direct. We must consider the sum of excitement which would be produced in all the schools; the laudable ambition, the industry, the effort, which would be communicated throughout, upwards to Dux, and downwards to the greatest Dult.

It has been proposed to have a college in Upper Canada; and no doubt colleges will in time grow up there. At present, and for a considerable period to come, any effort to found a college would prove abortive. There could neither be got masters nor scholars to ensure tolerable commencement for ten years to come; and a feeble beginning might beget a feeble race of teachers and pupils. In the United States, academies and colleges, though fast improving, are yet but raw; and greatly inferior to those in Britain, generally speaking. Twenty-five lads sent annually at public charge from Upper Canada to British universities, would draw after them many more. The youths themselves, generally, would become desirous of making a voyage in quest of learning. – Crossing the ocean on such an errand, would elevate their ideas, and stir them up to extraordinary exertions. They would become finished preachers, lawyers, physicians, merchants; and returning to their native country, would repay in wisdom what was expanded in goodness and liberality. What more especially invites the adoption of such a scheme, is the amiable and affectionate connexion which it would tend to establish between Canada and Britain. But it will not do at present to follow out the idea.

From my banishment here at home, a home which yet carries the palm of superiority in arts and sciences, before the whole world, I dedicate the hint to those Canadians who may yet think well of me; and, since the province has the honour of having framed one excellent ACT of legislation, may it continue to mount to excellence, by fostering liberal sentiments, without which man is inferior to the beasts that perish. . . .

The Indians can now, happily, be no longer looked to by Canada, as allies in war, and within the province will soon be extinct. Yet, it is well to note, in the history of the country, of what consequence they were considered, and how they were treated at the first settlement. . . .

To attempt any improvement with grown-up individuals would be of no avail. Near Quebec, near Montreal, on the Grand River, &c. churches have been erected for the reform of such poor people, but no change has been effected for good. Their children grow up, wild, irregular in their habits, and altogether useless members of the community.

Here the push should be made. Well-ordered and efficient establishments should be erected for training up the youth. They should be taught not only to read and write, but be bred in to industry and regular business. There are ample funds for this. Government need no longer throw away presents on Indians living beyond Detroit River, or maintain a useless Indian department, with a view to conciliate and hold on the Indians for a war time. The speedy civilization of those within the surveyed bounds should be the sole object, and in ten or twelve years it could be completely effected. The Indians of the Grand River have monied means of their own, to accomplish this under proper management; and the rising generation could be portioned off with land as they grew up, qualified to improve and enjoy their inheritance. Speaking of the Grand River Indians, it may not be improper to say a few words in defence of their right of soil, which has been encroached upon by the Provincial Executive Government. These Indians, who retired to Canada after the American revolutionary war had, by written grant, a tract of land assigned to them, extending from the mouth of the Grand River to its source, averaging six miles in width from the river, on each side. It will be observed, by inspection of my map, that the source of the Grand River lies beyond the farthest survey; viz. the township of Nichol. Soon after Sir P. Maitland arrived in the province, orders were issued for extending surveys in that quarter, and lands have been granted away, which, in fact, belonged to the Indians. The Indians complained, but were denied compensation. Their right, I hope, will only need to be made known at home, to admit of justice being done.

In Wentworth's Account of New South Wales, we are informed that attempts are making, and with success, to educate the savages of that country. I question if this is advisable. Our own breed, I suspect, is a better one; and with due encouragement, we can stock the whole earth as fast as the improvement of morals and civil government makes it desirable that it should be stocked. Many considerations urge to an extraordinary exertion being made to advance the Indians of Canada, who are now interwoven with civilized society as fast as possible, into a condition to amalgamate – to mix and be lost in that society: but I repeat, that with all other Indians, savages, the best policy is to keep them as distinct as possible, and always on the outside of settlements. Of all things Government should guard against allowing these primitive beings from being vitiated and led on to crimes by ruffians escaping out of civilized society. What shocking consequences appear even already to result from this in Van Dieman's Land and New South Wales, according to Wentworth's account. Indeed, what we there read, makes us deplore the whole system of colonizing from our gaols, and wish it put an end to. It is expensive: it holds not up the best scare to wickedness: it appears to be any thing but a corrective to the vices of individuals; but when we think of its furnishing the seed of crime and misery to distant and hitherto unpolluted countries, when we think of the worst of our convicts escaping into the woods, becoming more hardened and determined villains than ever, and rousing up the passions of savages to war, and bloodshed, and revenge, it is hideous. Good God! can we not keep our villains at home, wall them in, give them plenty of fresh air and exercise, while they feed in proportion as they exert themselves with solitary labour – labour that may be made to defray the cost of their maintenance. Colonization is yet, I hope, to become the means of improving society, instead of lending aid to barbarism. We have honest men willing to emigrate, and rogues only should be restrained from it. . . .

Having exhausted my remarks on the compilation of this volume, I shall now look back to the first; and review what is there most worthy of notice. With an eye to this, I collected together, at the close of that volume, the heads of opinions as to what retarded the improvement of the province, and numbered these for more ready reference upon this occasion.* The simplicity of these opinions should not lessen their importance, but give value to it. They should be weighed even by the statesman, while he studies the future fate of a very extensive portion of the British empire – a portion which must be with us, or off from us, just as opinion turns, and as respect is paid to it. My strictures shall begin with the last, and proceed backwards in order.

The improvement of Upper Canada, according to opinion 23d, is retarded by a want of *rousing up;* and in page 448, vol. 1st, it is said, "something to expel a torpid spirit" is wanted. I suspect my worthy reporters confound effects with causes; or, to use a farmer's phrase, "put the cart before the horse." The Canadians had three years of a powder and shot war; and then they had twenty months of a paper bullet war: they had a time of high prices and brisk trade; and now they have low prices and dull trade; but with all this commotion and variety improvement is still retarded, and we must infer that something more is wanted than *rousing up;* the fact is this, that people immured in woods, and scattered about at the rate of half-a-dozen to the square-mile, even though roused up, can do little; and very naturally sink down into despair, and become torpid. They can live: they can procure bread; but man was not made for "bread alone."

The *bad habits of original settlers,* &c. (22d), have certainly operated considerably against the improvement of Upper Canada. For many years there were no schools, and there are now many of the people woefully deficient in education. Indeed, I suspect that civilization has, upon the whole, retrograded in the province. Schools, and dense population, will rouse up the people, expell the torpid spirit, introduce *skill in husbandry* (21st), and give *incentive to emulation* (14th). *Spirited and industrious men* (19th), will then make their appearance: and after them *men of capital and enterprise* (3d), with *money* (4th), and *banks* (20th).

A bank was set up in 1818; but money has since become more and more scarce. A chartered bank may now be established, the royal assent having been given to an ACT of Parliament for the purpose; but even this will be of small avail till the greater matters of the law are attended to. This is all that I shall say of opinions 22d, 21st, 20th, 19th, 14th, 4th, and 3d.

Opinions 18th, 16th, 8th, 2d, and 1st, all relate to the over-whelming abundance of unoccupied land, and the grand cure is to

* For the tabulation, see p. 293. [Ed.]

be found in a new system of taxation, laying the whole burden upon land, and making that burden as heavy as possible, while the proceeds are judiciously applied to public works.

Opinions 17th, 7th, and 6th, relate to matters of first-rate consequence, which can only be provided for, as they ought to be, from the new system of taxation, which, by and by, will be particularly spoken of.

The *defect in the system of colonization* (15th), is great indeed. My chief ambition in this work, is to throw light upon the subject. I shall endeavour to shew how *emigration* may be promoted on a *liberal system* (9th), how *difficulties opposed to emigrants* may be removed, and how the *poverty of beginners* (10th), may be overcome.

There are two opinions (13th and 12th), directly opposed to each other. I am decidedly for *liberal and indiscriminate admission of settlers*. Something is wrong with the government of that country, which cannot let Americans and all others come in and go out as they please. It is part of the excellent policy of the United States to receive into citizenship people of all nations and persuasions, Gentiles and Jews. There, "charity thinketh no evil;" and evil never came of it. But behold Upper Canada, jealous even of a British subject, imprisoning, torturing, and banishing, all upon the oath of a perjured villain. Behold such a country, and say what retards its improvement!

The 11th opinion regards *damages sustained in war*. Much damage was sustained, especially in the Niagara district; and everywhere the stock of the country was nearly exhausted; but the improvement of the country, as I wish it understood, did not, in the main, suffer much retardment from this. . . .

The only remaining opinion, which rests for consideration, regards the *shutting out of Americans* after the war; and it is well that this comes last to notice, as it should engage most serious attention, and remain for every in fresh recollection.

Under the last head, I said that the improvement of Upper Canada was not much retarded, comparatively, from the damages sustained in war. I now say, that the effect of the war was in many respects favourable to the province; and had it been duly taken advantage of, might have outweighed the evil of losses sustained by individuals, even unpaid, a hundred times over. By the war many disaffected persons were got rid of: by the war the gallantry of the inhabitants was proved, as well as the desire of the British government to support that gallantry, and to protect the province: by the war an important and pleasant truth was established, that settlers from the United States were to be depended upon as loyal and faithful subjects.

This was pleasant, as it determined an important fact regarding human character; in as much as it was found to be true to principle, and to prefer honour to interest, nay even to the ties of country and kindred. Three-fourths of the people who defended Canada from invasion were settlers from the United States; but, strange to say, the war had scarcely ceased when settlers from that country were looked upon with suspicion by the administration; and by and by were generally refused admission; that is to say, they were not allowed to take the oath of allegiance, as formerly, for the purpose of ratifying their settlement, and enjoying common privileges. The writer of the Sketches says that such jealousy was natural. I say, it was much more foolish than natural. What can induce settlers to come in from the United States to Canada *after the war*, but a prejudice in favour of British government, an inclination to live among a people who had bravely defended themselves, and a desire to be out of a country where political rancour had become so intolerable that federalists could scarcely be safe in the neighbourhood of democrats. Canada, after the war, seemed to be a place of refuge from party persecution; but strange to say, and order was sent out to Canada by the British Ministry to check the ingress of American settlers. Was this done in contemplation of saving room for British emigrants? No: In the year 1815 a shew was made at home of encouraging emigration to Canada, but what has appeared in the management of the Perth settlement? – waste, and finally, total neglect. What have I to say of the treatment of emigrants from Britain in the year 1817, the very year in which all settlement from the United States ceased, from the effect of arbitrary decrees. During the year 1817 the treatment of poor British emigrants in Canada was worse than mockery – was infamous. The provisions and tools given to those who had emigrated the two preceding years, were now denied, and the poor people had, to use the words of one of the Township Reports, (page 378, vol. 1st), to "dance attendance at York," for weeks and months together, before they could get a hearing from the land-granting department; and when at last they were heard, their fate was to be sent 20 or 30 miles into the wilderness, where even native Americans could scarcely exist. When our home government had once gone so far as to expend many thousand pounds on an *experiment* for settling Canada with British subjects – an experiment which they followed out to no good: – when the British Ministry had gone so far as to order the ingress of Americans to cease, surely it was their duty to give orders to the land-council of Upper Canada to be civil and attentive to poor British emigrants; but it was far otherwise. I witnessed the miseries of emigrants who had left home in hope of being kindly treated in the king's dominions, and it was impossible not to be touched at the heart with what I saw – with what I felt from bitter experience. Soon after my arrival in Canada, I wrote home, highly pleased with the natural appearance of the country, and while I was yet altogether unacquainted with the dirty ways of Little York. My brother, sixteen years younger than myself, who had nearly served out an apprenticeship to a writer to the Signet in Edinburgh, with the expectation of inheriting an estate in Fifeshire, had retired from his business, and resolved to go abroad to the East or West Indies.... To please our father, then an old man, and afraid of my brother's health, he relinquished this design, and came out to me in Canada, in consequence of the favourable report I had sent home of the country – its fine climate and fertile soil. He arrived the very day after I had published the address which gave rise to this work, and while I was yet sanguine of all going well. As soon as I found him resolved on settling in the country, I dispatched him to York – I mean to Little York, with introductions, and he there took the oath of allegiance, and paid fees, demanded preparatory to presenting a petition for a grant of land. His petition was in course presented. It was respectful: it was every way correct; but what happened? Instead of getting land, he had, after remaining in the province more than two months, a most insolent reply. He remained in the province nearly a year, and, getting no land, left it, for want of employment, to go to Demarara, where he now is. I had done nothing in Upper Canada to offend when my brother was thus treated, save publishing my first address, which had offended the Rector of York, a member of the land-council; and my brother, on no occasion, either before or after his refusal of land, gave offence to any body. He was known at home as a peaceable, quiet young man, and both in Fifeshire and Edinburgh must still be remembered by many respectable persons to have been so. As to politics, he was totally different from me, and was always indeed averse to intermeddle with any thing of the kind. His plan was to have occupied a farm, and at the same time to have kept a store of merchandise. A relation had offered him a thousand pounds to begin with, and he had connections ready to procure for him credit in Montreal.

This young man, twenty-three years of age, driven from home by adversity, every way qualified to have done well for himself in Canada, and with every recommendation as one who would have been faithful and true to British interests – to British government and British feeling; – this young man had insult in return for a respectful petition, and at last went empty away from a country to which he was really partial, disgusted with neglect, and the abuse of power. Before my brother was insulted, I had been fully charged with abhorrence of the treatment of emigrants in Upper Canada. I had been roused to a full sense of the mean, selfish, unprincipled, and unfeeling conduct of the Provincial Government: his wanton and altogether undeserved treatment, brought me to decide that it was duty to expose the damning system that prevailed, and I did launch forth against the creatures in office – the loathsome things of the land-granting department. I attacked Little York: I fluttered the Volsci in Corioli; and in less than two months it was observed by the country, and I trust is still remembered, that a goodly reform was brought about. People having business at the Land Office were attended to, and afterwards the emigrants had something like civility shewn to them, though, even now, there is nothing like system or comfort.

But I must not forget the main question, that of *shutting out Americans*. This was the deadliest thrust ever made by folly at the prosperity and welfare of Upper Canada. It had created most serious reflections, and engendered a deep-seated disease in the province, before my arrival there. It had worked up the resolutions of Parliament recorded page 289, and led the agitated Lieutenant-Governor to hasten, in the most indecorous manner, to dismiss that body in the midst of the most sacred and most urgent deliberations that had ever been before it.

It was not for some months after my arrival in the province that I gave any serious attention to this subject, though those with whom I was most intimate, particularly. William Dickson, were furious, whenever it came into discussion. I was three months in the province before my mind was made up as to settling in it; and the question of shutting out Americans engaged very little of my attention. After publishing my first address to the resident landowners, I travelled through all the western part of the province, to inform myself personally of its topographical and agricultural state, as well as to afford time to the people to reply to my queries. On this journey I found that four-fifths of the settlers had come from the United States, and that there was not one British-born subject among twenty. I found that the very best people were of those called Yankees, and saw that wherever improvement was advancing with most spirit, that these people had the chief hand in it. I learned, besides, that in war they had acquitted themselves well, and could find no reason whatever for the absurd interdict against others, such as them, coming freely into the country: indeed, where there were settlements of Europeans, a due mixture of Yankees was truly desirable. They were active, intelligent, friendly; and adepts in the art of settlement. The monstrous conduct of the Government, forbidding free ingress from the States, had keenly wounded the feelings of these people. It was to them most unmerited reproach, and was rather deeply felt than openly complained of. This impressed the matter on my mind as of more dangerous tendency; and when I came to peruse the Township Reports, the impression became more strong. As a cause which retarded the improvement of the province, the *shutting out of Americans* was at this time the greatest beyond all comparison; and but for a hope of extraordinary emigration from Britain and Ireland, seemed to me altogether fatal to prosperity. From bearing a high price, which land did in Canada for the two first years after the war (that price, by the by, quoted in all my Reports), there was now no demand whatever. During the winter 1816-17, some settlers had continued to come from the States on permission, and prices were nominally kept up; but now the Americans had been apprized of the check to free admission, and of the slur cast on those who had gone before them into Canada. Democrats laughed at their neighbours who in the heat of party disputes had threatened to retire under British protection, after the war. "You have now a sample," said the former to the latter, "of the steady, generous, and noble government you so much admired: get off with you, and *beg* of them to take you in." The taunt was severe; but there was now no help for it, save by endurance or flight to Indiana or the Illinois.

Notwithstanding the fact that shutting out Americans was, at the time that the Township Reports were written, by far the greatest and most obvious cause of retarding improvement, five only of these Reports notice it; and the reporters, in all these five cases, are either native-born British subjects, or of the oldest settlers. They had been stung with no reproach, and could speak out on the subject. They deprecated the act of shutting out Americans, but did not feel sore on the subject, as did the settlers from America. The feeling of these I had observed while travelling through the country: it was palpably marked by the silence of the Reports; and I repeat was of dangerous tendency, especially when kept smothered.

On the part of some of those who do speak of the shutting out Americans, there is a feeling of a different kind; but also well worthy of notice. The fate of Upper Canada should be staked to no slender or unseen twig. No doubtful, timid sentiment should be suffered to lay undisturbed. All should be disclosed which may lead to false hopes and deceitful conclusions: every thing should be removed which stands in the way of important and necessary decision regarding the policy which rules over a country so situated. Those who speak on the subject of shutting out Americans are impressed with no indignant feeling touching their characters as loyal and true men. Their interest as land-owners is alive to the subject; but this again had to struggle with a dread of offending the higher powers. It still remained undecided whether the Executive Government would insist on barring out Americans, or whether the Assembly, when again met, would resolutely declare the law, and insist on the removal of restraints to free ingress of all settlers. The dread of speaking out on this, then ticklish question, was strongly marked to me in the Report of Nichol, page 381, vol. 1st. It is there said, "On this head we decline giving our opinion." Now, whence was this diffidence? Thomas Clark, who wrote the Report, was a Scotsman, a legislative councillor, and a great land speculator. He had been touched to the quick by the *veto* against the free admission of settlers. It had entirely cut down his hope of turning his land purchase to profit: it was truly provoking: it was ruinous; and though he declines publicly to give an opinion on the grand cause of his and the country's misfortune, he asked me passionately, before delivering the Report, if the conduct of administration, "would not justify rebellion." Surely it is better that the home ministry should know such truths – should be frankly informed of the mischief done by their ill-judged, arbitrary mandates to exclude Americans from Canada, than that false delicacy should muffle up most serious facts, and that blundering should go on till the most loyal people, and even legislative councillors, should be driven to the point of rebellion. . . .

As, before the war with the United States, the settlement of Upper Canada depended chiefly on people coming in from that country, certain magistrates throughout the province were commissioned to administer the oath of allegiance to such, that there might be no delay on their coming to settle, – no impediment to their holding property and possessing all the privileges of native-born British subjects; but after the war, the following CIRCULAR was addressed to the Commissioners.

Lieutenant-Governor's Office,
York, 14th Oct. 1815.

SIR,

It is deemed expedient that the Executive Government should be informed of the number and character of ALIENS coming from the United States, or elsewhere, into this province. I am therefore commanded by his Excellency the Lieutenant-Governor, to desire that you would report to this office, the names and designations of all such as may now be resident within your district, and known to you, or of whom you can obtain information, as also of all such as may in future come to reside therein, in any capacity, either as *preachers, schoolmasters, practitioners in medicine, pedlars,* or *labourers.*

The Lieutenant-Governor is pleased further to require that you do not, hereafter, administer the oath of allegiance, to any person not holding office in the province, or being the son of a U. E. loyalist, without a special authority, in each case, from this office.

I have the honor to be,

Sir,

Your most obedient, humble servant,

(Signed)

WM. HALTON,
Secretary.

Now, supposing the Governor, who issued this CIRCULAR, had the undoubted right to dictate to Commissioners under his appointment, and supposing him quite liberal in granting his "special authority," as to administering the oath of allegiance, it is evident that the process of obtaining his authority would very much impede settlement. A settler, we shall suppose, crosses Detroit river to Sandwich, or the St. Lawrence to Cornwall, and applies to a Commissioner to administer to him the oath of allegiance, that he may safely purchase land in the province, and settle upon it. The Commissioner tells him, that it is necessary first to procure *a special authority* from the office at York. It is applied for. Doubts as to the character of the person wishing to purchase and settle arise. He is required to produce evidence as to the soundness of his character, which he may not be able to obtain immediately: much time is thus wasted, and still there is doubt: the settler is kept waiting in suspense; and is at last, perhaps, refused. Say that he *is* refused. Has the *Governor* any right to refuse administering to him the oath, as a person willing to become a settler? The Governor appoints Commissioners for the execution of the law. He makes and can unmake them. He has their existence under his command; but can he say, I will be altogether arbitrary in my *will* as to administering the oath of allegiance? I *will* let aliens settle in the province, or not, *just as I please.* This is a most important question to have settled, and we must consult statute law on the subject. The Members of the Provincial Parliament thought that the statute law had something to do with the question, and they resolved, . . . 1st, *"That an ACT was passed in the 13th year of George the 2d for naturalizing such foreign Protestants and others therein mentioned, as were then or should thereafter be settled in any of his Majesty's colonies in North America."* They resolved, 2d, *"That an ACT was passed in the 30th year of his Majesty's reign, (George 3d), entituled, an ACT for encouraging new Settlers in his Majesty's Colonies in America."* . . .

There is no difficulty whatever in deciding what was the intention of these ACTS. It was good: it was politic: it was liberal: it went to encourage the people of all nations to settle in our colonies. With the *first* ACT in his hand, a Frenchman or Jew, or a *Turk*, (if he took the sacrament, &c. as required) might enter our colonies with confidence that he would have all the benefits of British subjects as soon as he had resided seven years, and taken the oath of allegiance. Could he doubt that the chief judge, or other judge, would refuse to administer to him the oath after he had resided seven years in the colony? – would it be warrantable for the judge so to refuse? and if the judge refused, could the alien insist that the oath should be administered to him, by which he might be put in possession of all "the advantages and privileges which natural-born subjects enjoy?" Certainly he would be entitled to have the oath administered to him; and the judge could not in duty refuse to administer it when called upon. The *second* ACT is still more liberal as to the admission of aliens; but its benefits are confined to subjects of the United States. To subjects of the United States this Act, it is clear, dispenses with the seven years residence; seeing that it *requires* any such person coming to reside to take and subscribe the oath of allegiance to his Majesty *"immediately after his arrival;"* and if the first ACT imposed it as a duty on judges to administer the oath to any foreigner, after seven years residence, this ACT does still more clearly impose such a duty upon "the Governor, Lieutenant-Governor, or chief magistrate of the place where such person shall arrive." This ACT admits of subjects of the United States coming into Upper Canada, and insisting on having the oath of allegiance administered to them. They may come in or stay away, as they choose, but there is no choice to the Governor, Lieutenant-Governor, or chief magistrate, as to administering or not administering the oath. It requires of the settler *"immediately after his arrival,"* to take the oath, and of course the oath must be administered by those competent and specially named for the performance of that duty. That the duty is imperative upon them is more obvious from their being restricted as to the amount of fees for performing it.

Neither of the acts say any thing of commissioners being

appointed to administer the oath of allegiance to settlers. The *first* ACT names "the chief judge or other judge" as the person whose duty it is to administer the oath: the *second* names "the Governor, Lieutenant-Governor, or chief magistrate of the place." The appointing of commissioners to administer the oath of allegiance was a capricious whim of the rulers of Upper Canada, and the "special authority" was *arbitrary authority*, which the law did not warrant. When I went out to Upper Canada, there was much doubting, demurring, and disputing, about these express and clear ACTS of the British Parliament; and there were some persons so confused in their notions that they argued in behalf of the Governor's arbitrary will, from a clause more especially made to encourage settlers, viz. that which gives them a release from duties on certain imported goods. This clause speaks of settlers "having first obtained a licence," and the wise-acres inferred from these words that settlers themselves could not come in *without* licence. The licence was to clear their goods from duty – a licence which could not be refused when regularly applied for; which, in fact, instead of being intended to bar them out, was to give greater encouragement to their coming in.

Notwithstanding the Governor's CIRCULAR of 14th October, 1815, certain of the commissioners appointed to administer the oath of allegiance did not very strictly regard the "*special authority*." They were land-owners, and could not well afford to have the sale and settlement of their land impeded by arbitrary punctilio. They administered the oath without leave in "each case," from the Lieutenant-Governor's office. Here then was a fine display. The Governor issuing orders, and petty magistrates holding these in contempt. This contempt naturally spread forth, and excited a general sneer; and this again provoked and awakened the jealousy and ire of creatures of the Government. They saw sedition on every side; and the country, which had held out against powerful invasion for three years, was now thought in jeopardy from internal plots. Armies could not conquer it in war; yet there was dread from solitary unarmed individuals in the time of peace!! such are the natural consequences of exercising power wilfully and capriciously: such are the results of ignorance and illiberality.

After the Assembly had been dismissed by the Lieutenant-Governor, for DARING *to resolve* that certain British statutes were in existence which admitted of free settlement from the United States, the non-conforming Commissioners did not the more respect the Governor's CIRCULAR, but continued to administer the oath of allegiance to settlers from that country. This, however, was soon put a stop to. The Governor could make and unmake commissioners; and to be sure he sent forth a second

CIRCULAR

Lieutenant-Governor's Office,
York, 16th April, 1817.

"SIR,

"I am commanded by his Excellency the Lieutenant-Governor to inform you, that the commission constituting and appointing the Honourable Robert Hamilton, Benjamin Pawling, Peter Tinboak, John Warren, William Dickson, Robert Nelles, Richard Hatt, Samuel Hatt, and Thomas Dickson, Esquires, Commissioners, to tender and administer the oath of allegiance to all persons within the district of Niagara, has been suspended, and that a new commission has issued appointing the Honourable William Claus, Thomas Dickson, Robt. Nelles and Ralph Clench, Esquires, Commissioners for that purpose.

"The new commission has been transmitted to the Clerk of the Peace of the District of Niagara, of which you will please take notice, and govern yourself accordingly.

"(Signed)

D. CAMERON, Secretary."

After this, the CIRCULAR of 14th October, 1815, was again issued under date 8th May, 1817, and the business was completed. The Governor had now selected Commissioners who were quite submissive to his will; not a settler could come in from the United States without his "special authority;" and, by and by, none came to trouble themselves about the matter. . . .

The British ministry, I have said above . . . sent out an order to Canada to check the ingress of American settlers. They had done so without thinking that they were proceeding in the teeth of statute law: they had acted upon very erroneous information as to any necessity for what they did, even though they had been entitled to dictate: they did so with a bad grace indeed, when they took no pains to make arrangements for the comfortable reception and accommodation of British emigrants; and in doing so they manifested a thorough ignorance of the state of property in the province, of the system of management which had all along prevailed there, and of the real means of rectifying the mischief which that management had incurred. The executive government had an unquestionable right to give away or withhold waste lands of the crown, unchallenged by the British parliament, and unhappily parliament had never gone into discussion upon, or even thought of interfering with, this right. The executive government had been lavish in giving away land, so much so that their lavish gifts had totally marred the progress of prosperous settlement. Actual settlers were stuck in at this place and that; but no sooner were they fixed down than they were surrounded with reserves, and blocks given away to drones and absentees. Now, in the first place, it is necessary to consider that after the waste land was given away, it had certain rights attached to it. Its owners were entitled to claim all the benefits which were originally granted to the province by the constituting statute of 31st Geo. III. and these benefits were great. The constituting ACT, while it existed, secured to private property every advantage which could be found in the British statute book prior to its date. It secured to it the benefits of the statutes given above at length, viz. the 13th Geo. II. and 30TH GEO. III.* Upon the faith of having the benefit of these statutes, the chief value of lands in Canada rested; and upon this faith purchases were made, and speculations set on foot with confidence. Land speculators in Upper Canada had seen, since the beginning of Simcoe's government, up to the invasion, the most liberal admittance of people from the United States. They had seen these people invited in by proclamation, and treated with land for the payment of fees, little more than adequate to defray the expences of the survey and grant. They had speculated; – they had purchased land on no other hope whatever, but to retail out such land to American settlers; and they had ACTS of the British parliament to ratify their hopes. Was there ever, then, such a breach of faith, such a departure from ancient custom, such a criminal counteraction of law as that of the British ministry putting restraint on the admission of settlers from the United States? They had a perfect and unquestioned right to cease giving away the wild lands of the crown to Americans or others; but they had no right on earth to interfere with legalized commerce – with the rights of property established on the most sacred basis; and if there had been a spark of sense, determination and vigour in the parliament of Upper Canada, there would have been an impeachment moved against the men, whoever they were,

* 31 George III, c. 31 is the Constitutional Act of 1791. 13 George II, c. 7, the Naturalization Act of 1759, provided for the naturalization as British subjects of foreign Protestants settling in British colonies, 30 George III, c. 27, an Act of 1790 to encourage American settlers, required them to take an oath of allegiance but exempted their household goods (including slaves) from duty. [Ed.]

whether home ministers or provincial ministers, who dared to take such liberties as were taken. If it could be proved to be fact, that the ingress of Americans, after the war, was dangerous and incompatible with the continuance of British rule, then there were two constitutional methods of proceeding, to put a stop to that ingress. *First,* it might have been proposed to the provincial parliament to repeal the statutes 13th Geo. II. and 30th Geo. III.; and if the provincial parliament did repeal these, the point was settled, legally and constitutionally settled. If the provincial parliament refused to repeal these statutes, then the British parliament might have interfered, – might have repealed the statute 31st Geo. III. and then have constitutionally and legally dictated as to the coming in of American settlers, or any thing else, which the inhabitants of the province would submit to without rebellion. Had the statutes 13th Geo. II. and 30th Geo. III. been allowed to take their course; had governors, and judges, and chief magistrates, done their duty, and no more; had they administered the oath of allegiance to every Frenchman, Jew, or Turk, who had resided seven years in the province, and fulfilled other conditions; had they administered it to every subject of the United States who simply presented himself before them *"immediately after his arrival,"* – then I am most thoroughly convinced that Upper Canada would, by this time, have been, without all exception, the most flourishing spot in America, from Cape Horn to Hudson's Bay. Some of the best people of the United States would now have been settled in it; and many of those intelligent and wealthy emigrants, who have gone, and are still going from this country to America, would have given it a preference. I myself could have directed thousands to the province, had I found public faith respected and maintained, – had I found person and property safe, the two grand objects of good government; but who could recommend a country where all was the reverse? who could put in comparison independent America with a province abused in every way as Upper Canada has been, its good laws trodden upon, and its execrable Sedition ACT taken advantage of to imprison and banish a British subject, whose greatest glory would have been in its prosperity, and who is still toiling to rescue it from poverty and shame? Yes! it shall be the last effort of my life to persevere and requite good for evil, – to gain for Upper Canada independence, peace, and prosperity.

What harm could possibly have resulted from administering the oath of allegiance to subjects from the United States, or to the people of any other nation? Does the oath of allegiance protect any one in Canada who has committed crime from punishment; quite the reverse. It renders him more amenable to every law that is consistent with reason, which is rational and fair; but here was the secret? it gave him protection from the execrable sedition act; and there is a record to justify my suspicion. On turning over the file of the Kingston Gazette, I found the following article:

UPPER CANADA.

GEORGE THE THIRD, BY THE GRACE OF GOD, OF THE UNITED KINGDOM OF GREAT BRITAIN AND IRELAND, KING, DEFENDER OF THE FAITH.

"WHEREAS it has been represented to us, that divers persons who withdrew from the protection of our government, immediately previous to the late declaration of war, by the United States of America, or during actual hostilities, are about to return to our province of Upper Canada. We have found fit by and with the advice of our Executive Council, to call upon the members of the Legislative and Executive Councils, the judges and others commissioned to carry into effect the provisions of a certain statute made and passed in the forty-fourth year of our reign, entituled, 'An Act for better securing this province against all seditious attempts or designs to disturb the tranquillity thereof,' to be vigilant in the execution of their duty, under the authority of the above recited Act.

"In testimony whereof we have caused these our letters patent to be made patent, and the great seal of our province to be hereunto affixed, witness our trusty and well-beloved Sir George Murray, Knight Grand Cross of the most honourable military Order of the Bath, Lieutenant-General commanding our forces within our province of Upper Canada, and provisional Lieutenant-Govenor of the said province, at York, this sixteenth day of May, in the year of our Lord, one thousand, eight hundred and fifteen, and fifty-fifth year of our reign.

"W. JARVIS, Secretary.

G.M."

Here is the secret disclosed: here is the wheel within a wheel – the *imperium in imperio*. In order to retain arbitrary power: in order to keep the hold which the provincial parliament had given to governors, judges, and magistrates, by passing the sedition act of 1804, it was found necessary to put under restraint the accustomed licence of the commissioners, who had hitherto freely administered the oath of allegiance to aliens. It must have soon become obvious, after the above proclamation was issued, that while outlawed persons and aliens could go to a magistrate, and upon their desire have the oath of allegiance administered to them, that they got immediately out of the toils of the sedition ACT of 44th Geo. III. Alas! alas! how miserable are the shifts of tyranny! Was it to keep hold of such power as that of the sedition ACT, to which the wise, the liberal, the excellent statutes of the British parliament for encouraging the settlement of our colonies were sacrificed: – was it for this, alas! alas! that Upper Canada was disgraced, impoverished, and ruined? It must have been for this, and for this alone; but, let us calmly consider the wretched policy which is now folded and seen through. In page lxxxii of my GENERAL INTRODUCTION, I have observed, "How easily could thousands of aliens or others, having seditious designs, steal into the province, and by renting tenements for six months, unknown to government, get beyond the action of the sedition law." With six months residence, there is no need of the oath of allegiance to get clear of its hold. All that the sedition ACT can accomplish is banishment, and it cannot take hold of one in the hundred who may be suspected of sedition for this end. When any man had taken the oath of allegiance, sedition, on his part, then became crime; nay, he could be prosecuted as a traitor within the province: while on the other hand, an alien having got beyond the power of the sedition act by six months residence, without taking the oath of allegiance, was really not so easily to be kept in check by fear of the common law; and so it was absolutely to *gain a loss* that the rulers of Upper Canada were niggard in administering to subjects of the United States the oath of allegiance, – to gain a loss in two ways. They lost thereby the power of duly punishing sedition and treason, if such really existed; and they gained the tremendous loss of preventing money and the best possible settlers from coming into the province! Were weakness and crime ever so completely associated as in such policy? a wretched law acted upon for no purpose whatever, and truly good laws sacrificed that this wretched law might have a chance to be put in action!!!

How little did I imagine, when writing my first address to the Resident Landowners of Upper Canada, that their "fine country" had such terrific canker-worms gnawing at the root of its prosperity. On my journey through the western parts of the province, the reserves, the lands of non-occupants, the poverty and ignorance of the people, the manner in which many of them had been blocked up in Dundas Street, and elsewhere; – all appeared palpable bars to improvement. On this journey, too, I had an immediate, a clear, and well-authenticated proof of the total disregard of good faith and duty on the part of the Executive Government, and was constantly hearing complaints of the land-granting department: yet still I thought all resulted from the sloth, the ignorance, the infatuation of Little York. I then thought that nothing more was required for the correction of evil than that a true and plain statement of facts should be laid before our home ministers, and I despatched repeated letters to England, to be presented to Lord Bathurst, as frank as they were sincere and unsuspicious. Alas! I had not then sufficient experience of human nature, nor had I fully reflected on what tyranny could effect. I had not been imprisoned, maddened, and banished. . . .

I have now to record my most remarkable experience, with regard to the *shutting out of Americans*. On returning from my Western Tour, it was my design immediately to set off on my way to England, when a most trivial circumstance contributed to delay my departure. The magistrates of Niagara had been the first publicly to patronise my proposals of publishing a Statistical Account of Upper Canada, and some of them, with other inhabitants of that township, had met and drawn out for me a Report. This Report of Niagara Township, was lodged with William Dickson, who was to finish it by replying to the 31st query, and attaching his signature. My brother was employed writing out duplicates of all the communications sent me, and which I intended to leave behind at Queenston, lest accident should befall the originals, on my way to England. I asked Mr. Dickson for the Niagara Report; but he put me off, and for some reason which I then could not fathom, deferred finishing it. I asked it again and again, but in vain. This trivial matter, actually first disconcerted my arrangements; and, I have often called it to mind, in considering by what slight accidents the whole of one's fate may be changed. I have often reflected upon the fact, that the very man, who ultimately drove me from Upper Canada, had first contributed to my stay. He it was, indeed, who first drew me into political discussions, and worked me up to the strong feeling which induced me to call for inquiry into the state of the province. The train of circumstances which led on to this shall be recounted. On my return to Queenston from my tour, the first week of Jan. 1818, sleighing had commenced, and during the sleighing time, it had been usual for settlers from the United States to come into the province. I have said, that in the winter, 1816–17, a few had come in by permission, and while there were magistrates still on the commission for administering the oath of allegiance, who would not yield passive submission to the orders of the Governor. Now, not a creature appeared; the stream of settlement was entirely dried up. This made the question, as to *shutting out Americans*, become every day to be more and more talked of. Legislative Councillor Clark, who signs the Report of Nichol Township, and Legislative Councillor Dickson, my particular friends, were of all others most violent on this subject. They were great land speculators, and Dickson, especially, had recently launched forth in a purchase of 94,000 acres of Indian land (the township of Dumfries), which being free of crown and clergy reserves, was greatly preferable to other parts of the province for settlement. He had made the purchase for less than a dollar per acre, and had every reason to suppose he might retail it out for three, four, or five dollars. His settlement had just begun, winter 1816 – 17, when Governor Gore's "special authority" had taken effect, and Dickson was one of those Commissioners who had been thrown out by the nomination of 16th April, because of disobeying orders. Though deprived of his power of giving legal admission to settlers, he continued to advertise his land for sale in the American newspapers up to the winter of 1817 – 18, trusting that he might still obtain purchasers; but he was completely disappointed. Not a single settler would move into the province from the States, and the settlement of Dumfries was wholly at a stand. I could not help sympathizing in Dickson's calamity. He was then my friend: by marriage I was related to him; and his case was cruel in the extreme. Hearing him constantly exclaiming against Governor Gore's administration, I entered keenly into political discussions, and began to make more minute inquiries into the policy which had subsisted in the province. My convictions on the subject became strong, and I was at last convinced in my own mind that nothing but open and full inquiry, with a complete change of system in the government, could ensure any thing like permanent good; and with such impressions, I felt that I could not go home and invite settlers to Canada till I saw a fair prospect of necessary change. Parliament was summoned to meet on the fifth of February, and as I had pre-determined to take my route home by York and Kingston, I now resolved to wait, and by petition, bring seriously into consideration the question of inquiry, which had been hinted at during last session. The firm support of my two friends, Clark and Dickson, I had no reason to doubt, and nothing appeared wanting but a complete *rousing up* of the public mind to a just sense of mal-administration, and a clear view of the fact, that without inquiry and reform the province could not long remain an integral part of the British empire. Mr. Clark's question to me, whether the conduct of the provincial government would not "justify rebellion" has been already incidentally noticed. He further assured me, that Upper Canada would not remain a British province for five years, managed as it was; but Dickson was still more loud in complaint, and getting tipsy at a mess of the 70th regiment, let out the secret by declaring, that he would rather live under the American than British Government. Under all circumstances, it was hit or miss with me. My plans could only be successful under British government, and for that I became zealous, and even enthusiastic. I had a scheme for establishing a land agency in union with a newspaper, both of which were dependent on British connection, and I indulged a hope of rendering Upper Canada the grand receptacle for the redundant population of England. This last idea brightened in my imagination more and more, while nothing appeared wanting to its fulfilment but a right knowledge of the state of the province, which might gain for it the attention of the British public. Mr. Clark furnished me with a copy of the statute 30th Geo. 3d, and Dickson pointed out what was most worthy of notice in that of the 13th George 2d, having made discovery of this in Anderson's Commerce. To attract notice to the subject which I determined to handle, I sent the 30th Geo. 3, to be published in the Spectator newspaper, with the following introduction.

To the Editor of the Spectator.

SIR,
As I believe the British Act of Parliament, 30th Geo. III. chap. 27, has never been published in this province, I herewith send you a copy, and trust you will find room for its insertion in your next newspaper, as matter of *utmost importance* to be considered by the inhabitants of Upper Canada at the present moment. Had I seen this act prior to writing the letter which appeared in your paper of 20th November last, I might have corrected my first opinion of the resolutions brought forward towards the end of last session of parliament. Instead of characterizing them as "able resolutions," I might have said that in some cases doubting was weakness, and ignorance a fault. Of the spirit of the act I was well informed; but conceived that some ambiguity had arisen from its wording, which called for the language of courtesy to an over-officious Executive.

I am, &c.

ROBERT GOURLAY.

Queenston, 26 Jan. 1818.

A few days after this was published, I wrote the following Address.

To the Resident Land Owners of Upper Canada.

Queenston, February, 1818.

GENTLEMEN,

I did myself the honour of addressing you through the medium of the Upper Canada Gazette, of the 30th October last, and my Address has been since widely circulated over the province by various other channels. Its object was to gain the most authentic intelligence concerning this country, for the information of our fellow-subjects and government at home. The object was important: the means employed were simple and fair: the effect to be produced was palpable.

To lull the spirit of party, and quiet every breath which might stir against a measure so chaste and efficient, I forebore all allusions to political concerns. Conscious of being moved by the purest intentions, and desiring alike the welfare of this province and its parent state, I dispatched a copy of my Address, as soon as published, to be presented to Lord Bathurst, and trusted, that by calm and dispassionate statement at home, the supreme Government would be best persuaded to amend the errors of original institution. In these, I conceive, lay the chief obstacles to the prosperity of the province: in Canada I thought there was but one interest: in simplicity I said, "Here we are free of influences."

Since then, three months have passed away. In this time I have travelled more than a thousand miles over the province. I have conversed with hundreds of the most respectable people: I have gravely and deliberately considered what I have heard and seen: I have changed my mind; and most unwillingly, must change my course of proceeding. This country, I am convinced, cannot be saved from ruin by temporizing measures, nor by the efforts and reasoning of any individual. If it is to be saved, reason and fact must speedily be urged before the throne of our Sovereign, by the united voice of a loyal and determined people: if it is to be saved, your Parliament now assembled must be held up to its duty by the strength and spirit of its constituents: a new leaf must be turned over in public conduct; and the people of Upper Canada must assume a character, without which all Parliaments naturally dwindle into contempt, and become the mere tools, if not the sport, of executive power.

It is but recently that I searched the public journals, and otherwise made inquiry as to what was going on before my arrival in the province. Your public men, I find, were most lovingly attached to your late governor. He was praised for his "mild administration," when he had done nothing; and in the midst of mischief he was fondled, he was fattened. While yet he must have been laughing in his sleeve at the subservience of the last Parliament, he found the present one willing to stifle the remembrance of subserviency; and while it should have been moving impeachment against himself, wrangling about the expulsion of one of its own members for having inadvertently published the truth. Sure of his friends, in favour and in office, he could even dash off his last card with eclat; and, dismissing Parliament, in a style unheard of since the days of Cromwell, he could carry home as much flattery as secured to himself a snug retirement in Downing-street.

Though I thus speak, let it not be thought that I have any personal pique to gratify. I never saw your Governor: I never conversed with any one of your parliamentary disputants: I have drawn my picture, not from a partial but full view of the subject: I wish not to flatter, and certainly I do not fear. Of all things, let it not be imagined that I would stir up any one to anger, or to contempt of constituted authorities. It is my opinion, that in all countries the goodness of government keeps pace with the virtuous spirit of the people; and in no country has this spirit less to contend with than here. – Since matters have been allowed to go so far wrong, I would have the people of Canada take home to themselves every particle of blame for the past, and remember what has happened, only as a guard for the future. Wherever I have inquired, Governor Gore's private character has been spoken of with respect; and so it is with many private characters at York; but is it not also true that the conduct of public affairs has become a standing jest? Nay, if allowed, I will prove the fact before the bar of your parliament, that good faith has been trifled with, and that the rights of property have been violated, by the very functionaries appointed to render them sacred and secure.

In my humble opinion, Gentlemen, there ought to be an immediate parliamentary inquiry into the state of this province, and a commission appointed to proceed to England with the result of such inquiry. This measure should not be left to the mere motion of Parliament: it should be pressed by petitions from every quarter, – from individuals and public bodies; it should appear, if possible to be the unanimous desire of the whole population. This would give confidence to Parliament to proceed without bias, hesitation, or dread: – it would ensure success to the cause.

Before we heard of Governor Gore's favourable reception at home, there was sufficient call for the declaration of public opinion and for some energetic move through the whole province, to rescue it from thraldom and infatuation. This intelligence, only now received, leaves not a doubt as to the necessity of the case. It shows that the gross manner in which the Canadian Parliament was dismissed, had been misrepresented in England; and that ministers labour under the most fatal mistakes as to the laws and policy which have made and sustained this country.

Gentlemen, the British ACT of Parliament for encouraging the settlement of the colonies was made over to you with your constitution; and *your* Parliament alone, in conjunction with the British Sovereign, had a right to alter it. This ACT was framed in wisdom, and under its auspices the desert wilds of Canada began to unfold their treasures for the use of civilized man. It theoretical opinions could have been entertained as to the policy and soundness of this ACT before the late war, that trying crisis should have dismissed them for ever. Is it not a fact that three-fourths of the population here emigrated from the United States since the revolution? Is it not a fact that one half of these people came invited by proclamation, and with this ACT fresh issued from the British Parliament as their security? Is it not a fact that many of these men stood foremost in battle defending British rights? Is it not a fact, recorded even in the speech of your late Governor, that this province owed its safety, during the first year of invasion, entirely to the loyalty of its own militia? How, in the name of God, could all this have happened, had the law been impolitic, – had people from the United States been unworthy of its adoption? – That there were unprincipled villains in Canada was indeed proved by the war; but who were they, and from whence did they come? Has it been shewn that the majority were Americans? – Is it not true that the basest of all were Europeans born?

The swaggering declaration of a war minister, founded on the dogmas of antiquated lawyers, has said that we cannot change our allegiance; but this great question, for the comfort of individual right, was long ago set at rest by British Acts of Parliament, in the face of which declarations and dogmas are but empty sounds. The good sense of our ancestors established this principle, and in language the most perspicuous, declared its object and its end: witness the following extract from the 13th of George the Second, chapter 7th, a statute *"for naturalizing such foreign Protestants and others as are settled, and shall settle in any of his Majesty's colonies in America."* The words of this statute run thus: "Whereas the increase of people is the means of advancing the wealth and strength of any nation and country; and whereas many foreigners and strangers, from the lenity of our Government, the purity of our religion, the benefit of our laws, the advantages of our trade, and the security of our property, might be induced to come and settle in some of his Majesty's colonies in America, if they were made partakers of the advantages and privileges which the natural-born subjects of this realm do enjoy;" *therefore* it was enacted, "that from and after the first of June, 1740, all persons born out of the legiance of his Majesty, who shall have resided, or who shall hereafter reside, for the space of seven years or more, in any of the colonies in America, and shall not have been absent from thence above two months at any one time, and shall take the usual oaths of fidelity, or if Quakers, shall subscribe the declaration of fidelity, or if Jews, with the omission of some Christian expressions; and shall also subscribe the profession of their Christian belief (Jews excepted), as directed by a statute of William and Mary, &c &c., shall be a sufficient proof of his or her being thereby become a natural-born subject of Great Britain to all intents and purposes."

Gentlemen, when I read this law, my blood warms within me, with the feeling that I am of that nation which promulgated it, – that nation which did not even allow such a monstrous supposition to appear in its civil code, as that men could not change their allegiance, – that nation whose Parliament could boast of inducing foreigners to give up their native allegiance, and accept of our's, from *the lenity of our Government, the purity of our religion, the benefit of our laws, the advantages of our trade, and the security of our property.* These, Gentlemen, were glorious boasts, such as none but the British nation could maintain: these were liberal and worthy rewards, to draw people to our colonies, and thereby *to increase the wealth and strength of our country.* Such modes of seduction – such boasts and rewards, are not only innocent but useful in the most exalted sense. They tempt individuals to fly from beneath the rod of oppression, and thereby diminish the power of despots: they excite nations to emulate each other in virtue and peace. Compared to these, what are the boasts of war – what the rewards of conquest? They do not seduce but force men from their allegiance: they instigate and keep alive every furious passion: they weaken and impoverish, not our country only, but our kind.

The grand purpose of government is the protection of our persons and property; in return for which we owe it our allegiance, even unsworn. When we remove, in a becoming manner, from beneath this protection, our allegiance is reasonably and fairly at an end. Before I myself sailed for Canada, I was importuned by friends to emigrate along with them to the United States. We never thought of its being crime to pass from beneath the protection of the British to that of the American government; and my chief reason for preferring to come to Canada was that I had here a wider circle of connexions. I knew that my person and property would be protected any where in America; and as to the form of government, I gave it no thought, perfectly agreeing with the poet, who says –

> "For *forms* of government let fools contest,
> "Whate'er is best administer'd, is best."

Wherever I abide I shall bear true allegiance to Government: to whatever country I belong, I shall endeavour, by every honest means, to advance its prosperity: where my treasure is, there also shall be my heart.

Although British statutes, and the practice upon them, have for generations recognised and guaranteed the right of individuals to change their allegiance from one government to another, they have not yet sufficiently defined the terms under which the change may be effected. Tacitly, however, all good men admit that this change is not to be trifled with; and a valuable moral lesson was given on this head, in the treatment of those people who deserted from the province during the war. It was determined, and most properly, that persons deserting their property, in such circumstances, should lose it; and, further, that if they aided or assisted the enemy, they should be hanged. This lesson was valuable to the province in the event of other wars. After such a lesson, weak or wicked men would think more seriously of desertion; and the free admission of foreigners was rendered much more safe. Canada had indeed, in many respects, gained by the war. Before that event, every one must have doubted her ability to hold out against hostile attack. The issue gave confidence on this important point; and it is notorious that many of the most upright citizens of America were on the wing to settle here, as soon as peace was declared. They had found that even pure democracy was not immaculate: they had been oppressed with taxation, to sustain the ambition of conquest: they had seen this unrighteous ambition foiled in all its movements, as if by the hand of an offended Deity: they had seen liberty giving birth to a thousand angry passions, and sending forth, under her mask, the demon of licentiousness: they had been terrified with the mobs of Buffalo and Baltimore. When all this was fresh in recollection; – when such people had become not only willing but anxious to be *made partakers of the advantages and privileges which the natural-born subjects of this realm do enjoy,* then, forsooth, was the time for your executive to quash the liberal spirit of existing law, to erect an odious barrier between kindred nations, and bring contempt and dishonour on the British name.

Gentlemen, I should not dwell so long on this revolting subject did it concern only the business of the present day, – did it concern only the value of your property, which would have been double at this moment, but for the narrow policy which has been pursued, – did it concern only the dignity of your Parliament, which was turned adrift merely because it ventured to open the statute-book, and resolve between right and wrong. The present time is on the wing: you and your property will soon be parted; and it may be said that a parliament, which permitted the laws to be set at nought for two long years, could suffer little diminution in dignity. The subject before us demands attention, for reasons infinitely more important than these. It demands attention for the sake of principles which govern and direct all things for good, now and for ever; – principles which have long been the pride and support of the British constitution, – which have nursed up all that is yet valuable in civilized life.

Our constitution, which has been refining for ages, and the spirit of which is purity, has been often lauded, for its effects are irresistibly impressive, but it has been seldom understood. It is that beautiful contrivance by which the people, when perfectly virtuous, shall become all-powerful; but which reins back their freedom in proportion to their vice and imbecility.

The British constitution sets the law above all men; and that the law may be reverenced and implicitly obeyed it has anointed a king to be its grand Executor. That we may look to this personage with unceasing faith and respect, he is clothed in fiction, and it is acknowledged by the law itself that he can do no wrong. In courtesy and fiction every thing belongs to him: in fact, little or nothing; and, though he can do no wrong, his ministers, through whom every act must proceed, are open to our censure, and amenable to justice. Nay, in proportion to the intensity of sentiment which directs our love and regard for the King, should be our watchfulness over those delegated by him to discharge the sacred trust of the laws, and preserve them inviolate.

At home, this watchfulness has ever given employment to the most able and virtuous of our statesmen, and but for their unceasing efforts the ambition of those in authority, would convert their sacred thrust to purposes of selfishness; they would set aside the laws to gratify their own whims and caprice. Here we have had an example: we have been unwatchful, and experience the consequences. Blame not therefore the constitution, neither withdraw from honouring the King; but brace yourselves up to the performance of your individual public duties, and all may yet go well. After what has happened, it is not for the people of Canada to be vindictive: it is not for them, who have been culpably negligent, or pusillanimous, to be inveterate accusers. They should drop impeachment against their late Governor; but while they seek not blood as an atonement for the mischief he has done, they may yet very properly extort his tears.

In thus addressing you, gentlemen, I can have no little selfish object in view – no passion to gratify, but that of seeing the land you inherit prosperous and happy. From the day that I first set foot on Upper Canada, now seven months ago, my mind has been devoted to the contemplation of its resources, and the benefits which might accrue to the whole British nation, were these called forth by a liberal system of management. The more I have known, the higher have I estimated these, both in a moral and political light: but the more I become acquainted with the conduct of public affairs, the more am I afraid that all will be thrown away, unless an immediate and determined stand is made against little policy and reigning abuse.

I have not descended to the exposure of peccadilloes which you all know to be innumerable and base in the extreme. I have struck at great leading principles, and the conduct of your leading man. The mischief he has done is irretrievable; but if his acts receive a due mark of reprobation from the mass of the people of the province, it will greatly re-establish confidence: it will make future governors more circumspect; and shake "the insolence of office" to its lowest grade.

In all past times provinces have been the sport of arbitrary power. Want of public spirit in the people, and a desire to tyrannize, which is greatest in little men, have jointly contributed to this effect. It is an evil, however, by no means unconquerable, and it will be worthy of a British colony to be the first in surmounting it.

This province, indeed, can no longer be trifled with: it must prosper or fall. You resisted invasion for three years: you staked your lives: you sunk your fortunes: you exposed your wives and children to every privation; and for good cause you did so. You are here as free, if you will, as any people upon earth: you have the power of taxation in your own hands, while Britain, the most generous of nations, bears many of your burdens, and has shed her best blood in your defence. After all this, are you to look back upon the struggle of war as mere foolishness? Having repelled an enemy with the sword, are you to suffer a more deadly foe to waste and destroy you? Are you to pine in ignominious sloth, and desert a cause which now only wants reason to maintain it? Gentlemen, the prosperity of this province needs nothing more than your peaceable exertions to procure respect for the laws, and to introduce a new system of management.

I have been told, that were Canada united to the States, your property would rise to twice its present value, and it is true; but it is also true, that if a liberal connexion with Britain was established, and a system of business introduced into public offices here, instead of a system of paltry patronage and ruinous favouritism, the same property would rise to ten times its present worth.

The day after writing the above, I chanced to breakfast with a magistrate, a native of Connecticut; and while the beef steaks were getting ready, I handed to him my manuscript for perusal. He had not read far, when he began to tremble, being a nervous man. "What is the matter?" said I. "This will not do," said the magistrate. "What is the matter?" I repeated. "This must not be published," said he; "I must take notice of this: it is my duty to take notice of it." "Surely," said I, "you will not take notice of it till printed; you will not consider it a publication till then." I could not appease the native Connecticut, heir direct of the blue-laws. He said he was bound by an act of parliament to arrest my purpose of publishing the paper he had read; and getting his waggon to the door, moved off to hold consultation with his neighbour Councillor Clark. I mounted my horse, and proceeding to Niagara, gave in the three first paragraphs to the editor for insertion in his newspaper, bidding him announce the continuation for the following week. This I did that magistracy might have time to cool and consider. From the printing-office I proceeded to Councillor Dickson's, and read my address to him. The Honourable Legislative Councillor, with land in the market, took a different view of the subject from his worship of Connecticut, who had a matter of consequence still resting with the good graces of Governor Gore in London. I had no sooner finished reading than Dickson called me into a private room, and warmly addressing me, said, "Mr. Gourlay, you must accept from me a Deed for five hundred acres of land."

My address had thrown him into ecstasy. Though he had bitterly inveighed against shutting out Americans; though he had scanned over the British statutes, which were framed for their admission, and abused Governor Gore for counteracting these, still he knew the overwhelming power of the Executive, and had reason to suspect that it might overtop the Legislative branch. A panic, or rather stupor, had very generally pervaded the country since the bold stroke of Governor Gore, in dismissing the Assembly. Both the people and their representatives were at a loss to think what would become of the question, and the grandees of Little York were decidedly for shutting out Americans: nay, one of them gave me his opinion, that even British subjects, who had travelled in the States, should be shut out – such was the existing madness and dread. . . .

Though Dickson could fume, and bluster, and even expose himself at Niagara in the agony of disappointed hopes; he had still a hazardous card to play at Little York. He had still interests to attend to, which roosted at home. He was a legislative councillor: had received this honour, of which no man could be more vain, through the good graces of Governor Gore: had been long a partisan of provincial administration: knew well its sinuous ways; and could form just estimates of its wrath and its favour. For the latter he had still much and immediate need in more ways than one. *One* I shall exhibit, as it will throw light on his conduct towards me, – his extraordinary conduct of first offering me reward, and then pursuing me with revenge, – first patronizing and then persecuting.

Just before my arrival in Upper Canada, he and Councillor Claus had laid their heads together for a shameful adventure. Claus was the head of the Indian department at Niagara – a department which had long been notorious for the grossest delinquencies. Presents to the Indians, to great amount, were at the disposal of this department; and through means of these most commanding influences were acquired, – all-commanding, indeed, whether for love or for money; – whether to swindle the Indians out of their property, or to procure for lust the prostitution of their wives and daughters.

The Indians submit themselves and their affairs, in time of war, to War chiefs, who inherit such honour – in time of peace, to Council chiefs, who are elective. By means of the presents it was no difficult matter to sway the election of Council chiefs; and these, when chosen to the liking of Councillor Claus, could very easily be prevailed upon to obey his will. Constitutionally, the Council chiefs should be chosen at the *Council fire-place* in the *long house* of each Indian village. For political purposes, this constitutional practice of the Indians was changed; and elections were held elsewhere, that the temptation of presents and the power of liquor might be more commanding. In this way I was told by a most intelligent chief of the Grand River Indians, did the Honourable William Claus get a party of Council chiefs to make over to the Honourable William Dickson 6000 acres of their most valuable land: that tract which appears in the Niagara Canal Sketch, enclosing the naval establishment at the mouth of Grand River. This was not only valuable because of its being capital land, but being a situation likely to become the site of a town; and for what was it given? It was given in recompence for trouble which Dickson had taken (as a lawyer) in drawing out certain accounts for the Indians; but the lawyer's bill was so monstrously overpaid that the country talk was loud against the transaction; and Dickson's own brother made it subject of ridicule. It made little impression upon me, who had my eye chiefly engaged with surveying abuses of more public concern. The transfer of land from Indians to any one likely to settle it, was indeed no public grievance, but the contrary, by whatever means the business was settled. A combination of circumstances brought the transaction into a different light. While it was still notorious that strong complaints existed among the Grand River Indians against the unfair means which Claus had taken to procure for Dickson their valuable land; while Dickson could not but feel that his right to it was far from being valid or honourable, he applied to Sir John Sherbrooke, the Governor-in-chief, to make interest for him at court, and get the Prince Regent's consent to the issuing of a royal patent in his favour for the land, by which all that was unfair and complained of might be overawed and silenced. He told me of this manoeuvre. It struck me as reprehensible in a high degree; but still, I was no common informer. In a few days after, when the whole government of the country was dissolved by the folly of its members: when Dickson himself had been a chief actor in this folly: when the cause of inquiry, which he had at first seemed to patronize, could no longer have the aid of Parliament; and when I took the only and best remaining constitutional step for effecting this great, this necessary, and still essential, measure, for good; – then, forsooth, Councillor Dickson was in arms against the cause, – not openly, but meanly, using his friend Clark as a cat's paw, to stir up the fire of party spirit, to alarm with the cry of sedition, to repress the general ardour for inquiry, and put down the most valuable of public rights. Then my eyes were opened: then I saw into the whole system which had from the beginning biassed and regulated his conduct. He had been keen for the admission of Americans, and for that alone. That point carried, he was of all men most opposed to general inquiry, because of all men he dreaded it most, and for powerful reasons. It might expose his manoeuvres with Claus: might deprive him of his Indian gift; and, perhaps, let our secrets still more fatal to his interest and his ambition. I received from him, as no secret, his application to the Governor-in-chief, nor would I, as a secret, have received it. But the man who will this day inspire confidence, stimulate, and push on to adventure; and the next day betray that confidence, impeach the motives, and blast the character of his friend!____what is he?

This was the conduct of Mr. William Dickson to me; and this laid open the whole arcana which governed him. This made exposure duty; and, because of exposure, he became more hostile to inquiry, and, to me, who urged it, inveterate. . . .

Let us now leave Mr. William Dickson and the Sedition Act; and bestow more particular attention on the conduct of the other magistrates, who figure before us. These I acquit of all malevolence towards me; and though in duty I shall be perfectly free in exposure, I could wish them to be assured that any thing but personal dislike urges me to expose. Mr. Thomas Clark and Mr. Samuel Street, for that is the name of my Connecticut friend, (and I use the word, as I wish it to be understood, in sincerity) were partners in one of the largest mercantile and *milling* concerns in Upper Canada. They were proprietors of what have been called "Birche's Mills," now "Street's Mills," and had a right to the whole water power of the rapids of Niagara. They were adepts in business; and both the one and the other very superior, in point of common sense, to Councillor Dickson, who had, however, a most unaccountable influence over them. A better hearted man than Clark I never knew. During the years 1812 and 1813 he over-exerted himself in the King's service, and came home wounded and worn out, to recruit among his relations. He stood connected with me as Dickson did. He was second cousin of my wife, and spent some weeks with us in Wiltshire, summer 1814. I cannot imagine to myself two men better qualified than Clark and Street were to do good in the world, both to themselves and others. They had also the means: they were substantial men in trade; and saving their dependence on Government patronage – their hanging upon Governor Gore for favours, would have been in every way respectable. This wretched dependence rendered them worse than useless in public affairs. It deadened; it corrupted their public spirit: it rendered them at once treacherous to themselves and others. . . .

Now that I have done with the Sedition Act and the abettor of perjury, I wish not to fret myself or the reader with more than enough of the disagreeable. The ruinous effects of Gore's government can be illustrated even with a good-humoured parable. – A certain rich man had a pig, which he was ambitious to make as fat as the pig of his poor neighbour. He spared no cost in the purchase of viands known to be palatable to pigs, and he flung these viands into the pigstye incessantly from night to morn; but nevertheless his pig remained lean and sickly. By-and-by he was advised to alter his system of pig-feeding. He cleaned out the stye: let the pig find the bottom of its stomach: kept its appetite sharp; and by ceasing to overdose, was speedily in possession of an excellent porker.

At Queenston there was a most valuable public property, the best landing-place for goods on Niagara river. This property had been promised away to a relation of Mr. Street . . . but the grant had not yet been confirmed, when Mr. Street stood in the shoes of his deceased relative. The confirmation of the gift still rested with Governor Gore. I wish not for a moment to say that Mr. Street's claim to the property was not good, yet *favour* was at the bottom of the transaction, and *fear* was the consequence. The fear of offending Governor Gore undoubtedly urged on Mr. Street to a desire of checking the *freedom of opinion*. By-and-by I shall shew the infinite need there was for the freedom of opinion, for discussion, and inquiry: here I shall only notice, that if the public property in question had been put to use, as Government could have done, its value might have been raised a hundred fold: it might have been publicly useful. To this hour I presume Mr. S. has not drawn from it a farthing, or put it to any good purpose; nor can he do what I allude to, as Government could have done.

The rapids of Niagara would have given motion to a thousand mills. These rapids are entirely in the hands of Clark and Street: given away by thoughtless patronage and favour, only to encourage monopoly, and deprive the public of fair competition;

to say nothing of laying the owners of them under restraints and obligations at variance with truth and public spirit. A lawsuit was pending, which sprung out of a lease of part of the water privileges. It was thought that procuring a king's patent to the property in fee would strengthen the lease, and affect the issue of the suit. To obtain this patent became another object of favour and fear; and so the thing goes on, like sin and death, in eternal abomination.

The individuals in question were, in every way, the most respectable in the province. In their situation, who might not have acted as they? who might not have been blind and infatuated? My complaint is against the system of public management, not against the men. Thousands throughout the province were operated upon by the *system* in worse ways than *they*. *They* fell in my way: *they* thrust themselves before me; and while I regard their worth as private men, I hesitate not to hold them up as examples for public instruction.

About a fortnight after Mr. Street's absurd rising against my Address, he got still more alarmed with an appearance of being connected with me in politics. He wrote a letter, which he desired me to get published for him in the newspapers. I remonstrated seriously against his desire; that he might not expose the infatuation under which he laboured; and when serious remonstrance failed, I tried to laugh him out of his intention; but all to no purpose. Then again, Mr. Clark, after being my warmest, and, I thought, most trusty friend, started off in a moment, at the bidding of William Dickson: he not only attacked my public principles, but openly, before a multitude, run down my veracity: and from shaking of hands, was at daggers drawing! Neither then, nor now, did I look to such conduct as proceeding from malevolence. It was infatuation – provincial madness; and, in these needy times, it is no joke, if, by putting down this madness, which rages more or less all over the provinces, half a million of money may be saved out of the taxes of England, and perhaps half a million more brought to a profit account only by putting down *madness*, and substituting common sense and *management*!

The physical strength of Canada, and I would wish this constantly to be kept in mind, is to be improved by the *right arrangement and proper disposal of property*. Its moral worth is sadly abused by *magistracy*; and as better opportunity may not occur, I shall here glance at the state of the province in this respect.

The *genus*, magistrate, in Upper Canada, has, in its composition, a large proportion of ignorance and vanity; and the different species most deserving of note may be thus statistically ranked, in order as they most abound throughout the province.

1st.	*Simple magistrates,* in proportion of 50.		
2d.	*Loyal-mad magistrates,*	do.	25.
3d.	*Ruffian magistrates,*	do.	15.
4th.	*Big-bugs,*	do.	10.

My friends Clark and Street did not rank under any of these denominations. Free of Government influences, they would have been highly respectable, even in this country. Free of Government influence, such men would be a host in the provinces for all that is good. They were active, judicious, honourable in their dealings, and had a proper sense of decorum in all civil and religious observances. There was nothing in the AIR of Upper Canada that had maddening effects, so far as I could discover. There was in the province less morbid melancholy than in England, and less *daffen** than in the county of Fife. All that was wrong, indeed, in Upper Canada, could clearly be traced to the cursed, useless, wasteful influences of Government.

Your *simple magistrates* were scattered throughout the whole province, from Hawkesbury, on the Ottawa, to Amherstburgh, on Detroit River. Distance from neighbours, from schools, from churches, from books, from newspapers – all tended to make simple magistrates most abound. They were very good sort of men; but, as magistrates, really worth nothing; and, when afraid of their character, as loyal men, being put in hazard, very considerably worse than nothing, as I found to bitter experience, even in the district of Niagara. I had only been confined a fortnight in Niagara jail, trusting that I should, at least, have fair play by the time that any charge against me was brought before a jury; but here Messieurs Clark, Dickson, and Co. were too much for me. They got up no less than three fulsome and most insidious addresses to the Lieutenant-Governor, in order to injure me in the public mind, and save themselves: brought these into consideration at a quarter-sessions court held right over the cell where I was confined: had the Parson of Grimsby to blow up the fears of simple magistrates on the subject of sedition, and a full dozen of

---

* The *folk* of *Fife* will understand me; but, for the instruction of others, I must note, that *daffen* means *merriment*, in its general application. Applied to a certain inherent or hereditary quality in the *lairds* of Fife (landed 'squires), the word *daft* must be taken with a tincture of innocent madness. "The *daft lairds of Fife*" are well known over all Scotland. . . .

my friends, simple magistrates, who had been the first to support my proposals for inquiry, signed these addresses, and made the country ring with "for shame!" and, *for shame*, say I still, after two years have gone by, and I am removed more than 3,000 miles, from the cowardice and treachery of simple magistrates of Upper Canada. Jesus Christ was crucified on false charges of sedition and blasphemy; but nobody said he did wrong in calling the provincial governor a *fox*, and holding meetings. The simple magistrates of Niagara district deserted me, because I asked them to meet for consultation as to instructing members of Assembly in their duty, and, very good-humouredly, called the provincial governor a *babe!!!*

Your *loyal-mad* magistrates were composed of half-pay officers, officers of the militia and U. E. loyalists. These were good-hearted gentlemen; but singularly wrong-headed. All Americans, with them, were *Yankees* in the bad sense; and the revolutionary war of America, which procured for them and all the other North American colonists, the valuable consideration of not being subject to taxation, but by their own consent, was uniformly called by them the *rebellion*, and spoken of with symptoms of detestation. The loyal-mad, though 15 per cent. in 1818, will, I am convinced, wear out rapidly.

Ruffian magistrates abounded along the banks of the St. Lawrence from Brockville to Cornwall inclusive; and, while the Lieutenant-Governor is held in leading-strings by the Parson of Little York, they will be kept up in full strength and number, no doubt.

Big-bugs, were mostly confined to the town of Kingston. In Niagara district there was but one Big-bug: viz. Councillor Claus.

Little York contained a peculiar sort, with characteristics bearing affinity to those of an animal still more familiar to man than a bug; and no dishonour to Little York, for "your louse is a gentleman." Their number is too contemptible to give them place, as a species. There was but one NON-DESCRIPT among the magistrates of Upper Canada, for all that is above said by no means conveys an adequate conception of *the Honourable William Dickson, Esquire, Legislative Councillor, lawyer, land-jobber, and Justice of the Peace.*

This sketch I have drawn out, to call attention to the urgent necessity of reform in Upper Canada, in the appointment of magistrates. It may excite laughter; but my own impressions sink rather into melancholy: and I am truly serious in wishing that no feeling but what is respectable and grave, could be associated with the character and conduct of Canadian magistrates; nor, is it impossible.

The policy of strengthening the Executive branch of Government by letting the Governor have undivided and uncontroled power in making and unmaking of magistrates, is attended with the most woeful consequences. The Governor never can be personally acquainted with a tenth part of those who must be put on the commission, and he is surrounded with people who have neither character themselves, nor care for that of those they recommend to notice. There were on the commission, while I was in the province, some magistrates who would disgrace St. Giles'; men who never would have had countenance, either from the most stupid or depraved Governor, could he have had personal knowledge of their conduct and character, altogether subversive of every purpose of policy. Ignorance, I have said, pervades the whole *genus* of magistracy, and no wonder, considering the wretched state which society must be in, where there are not seven souls to the square mile. Thus situated it is no discredit to be ignorant. Men secluded from opportunities of gaining information must be so. What I want to observe more particularly, is the effect produced by the conjunction of ignorance with the other prevailing quality – vanity. An ignorant man, set above his neighbours by a Provincial Governor, has every innate particle of common sense blown out of him by the inordinate swell of vanity. The silly conduct of the *simple magistrate*, in particular, whether puffed up with vanity, or trembling in dread of being put out of the commission, is absolutely sickening, or what is still more ruinous to authority – laughable. The jealousy, the false notions of duty, and the foolish zeal of the *loyal-mad*, all heightened with the swell of vanity, does infinite mischief; while the same quality blinding all sense of shame in the *ruffian* magistrate, makes him stick at nothing either in court or out of it. The people in general through the province are peaceable, willing to obey lawful authority, and docile, – susceptible, indeed, of being trained to perfection; yet I witnessed, during my stay, some of the most shocking outrages, and in every case there were either committed or countenanced by magistrates: nor is there a possibility of an ordinary individual getting redress for wrong. Mr. Birkbeck has, in his Letters from Illinois, given a sad account of the ferocity and lawlessness of some of his neighbours in the woods. I never observed in Upper Canada any thing of this sort unless on the part of magistrates or creatures of the Government. Now, what I wish to be particularly attended to is this fact, that, sinking every other consideration, it is bad policy for Government to have magistrates appointed as they now are. Nothing, indeed, sours the people with the Government, or makes them so contemptuous of constituted authority, as the silly, mad, and ferocious conduct of magistrates. The corrective is obvious and simple. The people ought to have a voice in the appointment of magistrates. The people, left entirely to themselves, would not select the fittest characters to have authority over them; and this has been proved by practice in the United States; but were they to choose a certain number of individuals from among whom only the Governor could appoint; or could a magistrate be removed from the bench upon the regular application of a certain proportion of the people of the township or district wherein he resides, very great benefit would thence accrue. No very ignorant person would remain on the bench if the people had an eye to it, with such controul as I have pointed out; and that most contemptible of all qualities – that quality most at variance with the exercise of authority, as well as respect for it – the quality of vanity, would be completely kept down. I cannot, perhaps, leave on the reader's mind, a better or more lasting impression as to the vanity of Canadian magistrates than what will appear from the following account of the Big-bugs.

Big-bugs, I found, chiefly congregated in Kingston. They were shopkeepers, who during the war had become wealthy, and from looking at, or perhaps associating with, British officers, had acquired an outward shew of gentlemen, while the interior was stuffed with all sorts of selfishness, vulgarity, and rottenness. These gentlemen could do what they liked, but under the influence of deep-rooted ignorance, put their hand to nothing which they did not bungle. In the exercise of their brief authority, they bit keenly and capriciously; and this, with a certain impression made upon the olfactory nerves by the view of ill-put-on pomposity, had, I suppose, acquired for them the above very significant appellation; which, however nauseous, when duly considered, had nevertheless, by use and wont, if not by pleasure and profit, become enviable. One day I had occasion to call on a simple magistrate, some way in the woods out of Kingston, in company with two farmers. Speaking to the magistrate, of the opposition which had been stirred up against inquiry, I chanced to say, "You Big-bugs oppose us unreasonably." The eye of his worship instantly brightened: I felt that an advance was made in his good graces; and, on our departure, my brother farmers, laughing, said, that I had hit upon the very charm of charms in applying the term Big-bug!

One person on my list still demands attention, Chief Justice Powell. This important person of the drama was, I believe, a native of Boston. He has friends still there, as well as in England. Though a shallow lawyer, he is quite the deepest man in the province – *a man of the world*. I have, for want of better, applied to him a Scotch word, as most descriptive of that knowingness for which he has been noted – the word *pawkie*; but, then, as all my readers are not my countrymen, I must define the word, thus. Suppose a personage having purloined your sugar-plum, sucks it till both his mouth and eyes water with gladness, making you all the time think that such gladness proceeds from the pleasure of your company, instead of the sweet relish of your unseen and lost sugar-plum; then you have some idea of the term *pawkie*; and it will help you on to comprehend, though not altogether, the Chief Justic of Upper Canada: it will give you more favourable impressions of him than I received from certain magistrates of Niagara district in 1817-18; one of whom very positively assured me that he "was at the bottom of all the mischief in the province."

It is said that he was once arrested, put in irons, and hurried from top to bottom of the province, on suspicion of carrying on a treasonable correspondence with Americans; but I myself acquit him of all mere suspicions, knowing how villanous they are under provincial jurisdiction. I shall try Chief Justice Powell upon something more tangible, legal, and logical. After getting clear of the handcuffs, he continued under a cloud, but at last got into favour with Governor Gore, and by that favour gained his seat on the bench, and many more *favours*. . . .

I exhibited above what were the consequences of Government influence with two of my especial friends. Now I have got deeper into the slough of corruption, for here it is, fore and aft; above, below: and over head and ears. The Chief Justice of Upper Canada gets himself out of the cloud of suspicion, feathers his nest with flattery, and then with his brood sits basking in the sunshine of court favour, totally regardless of truth, good policy, or statute law! – aye, of the most invaluable of British rights! – Was all this from ignorance!!

Let us now try him a little further by his own chronicles. When we have sufficiently reflected upon his false and fulsome addresses to Governor Gore, so far as they ratify and approve the arbitrary measures taken to *shut out Americans,* let us take into consideration "*the* WISDOM *of the measures by which you have preserved this province to be a* TRULY BRITISH COLONY, *and the solicitude with which you have watched over the welfare of his Majesty's subjects:*" – let us take this into consideration, and contrast it with his remanding *me,,* a British subject, to goal; – *me,* who had applied to him, by my constitutional and unalienable right of *habeas corpus,* to be set free: – let us contrast his doing so with his approving of *shutting out Americans,* contrary to law, and then canting about the *"truly British colony,"* and the *"welfare of his Majesty's subjects"!!* Lastly, let us see him sitting on the bench at Niagara, with a little cocked hat stuck over the top of his sugar-plum countenance, putting me on my trial of *guilty*, or, not *guilty*, of the *fact* of having *refused to obey Councillor Dickson's order, founded on the oath of Isaac Swayze, Member of Parliament,* that I was *seditious,* nearly twelve months after I had refused Dickson's land, for upholding British statute law, in opposition to this Yankee's cant: after I had voluntarily suffered imprisonment for nearly eight months, in order to go home in triumph to my friends as a thrice-tried British subject, with a THIRD *honourable acquittal* from false charges of *sedition:* let any one keep all this in view, and it is not a tenth of what I could present; – let any one keep all this in view, and imagine himself brought into the fresh air, after six weeks close confinement, during the dog-days of Upper Canada, with an imagination more lively by weakness, and the powers of reasoning totally unmanageable; – let any one suppose himself brought forth and insulted with the mockery of justice and all that was decent, by such a man as I have described, asking me if I was *ready for trial*, and he will be cruel, indeed, who would not grant indulgence to the utterance of contempt. It was in this feeling, – in this maze of digust that I lost myself. – Thank God, I am now in the calm enjoyment of reason; and setting aside all feeling – all passion, I would, in sincerity, put this question to everyone who has an interest in, or any regard for, our national honour and prosperity, if Chief Justice Powell is a man calculated to advance either the one or the other, – if his conduct has not added to the many reasonable demands for inquiry into the state of Upper Canada? . . .

To close this subject of *shutting out Americans*, I shall now make a few remarks on my second Address to the Resident Landholders of Upper Canada, which assisted to open the door for free ingress according to law. That Address was by far the boldest thing published by me in Canada; but it was imperiously called for in all its parts; particularly where it decides as to the principle and law of allegiance. It is perfectly clear, that though orders had been sent from home to exclude Americans from freely settling in Upper Canada, that the provincial legislators, not excepting my *faithful* instigator Councillor Dickson, were one and all of them to blame as to the counteraction of the British statutes 13th Geo. 2d. and 30th Geo. 3d. All of them joined in giving the £3,000 to Governor Gore within six months after he had issued his CIRCULAR of 14th October, 1815; and it was even said that the Resolutions which caused Parliament to be hastily dismissed would not have been brought forward had Governor Gore continued sufficiently loving to certain of his favourites. Caprice, it was said, assisted to frame the Resolutions, which should have been framed and passed one year sooner; and certainly, prior to bestowing any gift on the Governor. Councillor Dickson himself did not run restive from any zeal to support statute law against the encroachment of executive power, or any clear perceptiosn of law. He got sulky only after he began to *feel* consequences; and had no right whatever to abuse Governor Gore for putting restraints on the free ingress of American Settlers. He had, for a year at least, countenanced the unwarranted presumption of executive power, in issuing the first restraining CIRCULAR; and, under circumstances, Governor Gore did perfectly right to turn him out of the commission. Governor Gore had an undoubted right, at any time, with reason or none, to make or unmake him a magistrate, and his acquiescence in the general measure of restraint, justified Governor Gore in the particular act of depriving him of power which he used to contravene the spirit of that measure. Mr. Councillor Dickson did not seem to care one farthing though Americans were *shut out*, in general: did not seem to care one farthing for the law, as it was essential to public interests, provided he could have a special leave to benefit himself and settle Dumfries with Americans. The Councillor would say this to his Excellency, "Take you, Governor Gore, £3,000 of the people's money for the purchase of silver spoons*, and indulge yourself in a thorough search of every man and woman also, that comes to settle in Upper Canada: annoy the men and kiss the women, by all means, coming in to settle other people's land; but throw not the smallest obstacle in the way of male or female proceeding to Dumfries. Let me remain on the commission to swear in my settlers without annoyance, and in that case, do whatever you please. I care only for *myself.*"

As to me, I had not been in the province many days before I saw into the absurdity and impolicy of making harsh and odious distinctions between British and American settlers; but I knew little of the laws on the subject till a week or two before I took up my pen to support the principles on which they had been framed. As to self-interest in the affair, that did not move me in the least degree. I had some landed property in Upper Canada, which had

---

* The vote of Parliament to bestow on Governor Gore £3,000 by address, for the purchase of plate, was humourously called by the people, "*The Spoon Bill.*" They saw through the thing perfectly; but thought it best to console themselves with a laugh.

become unsaleable in consequence of the *shutting out* of *Americans*, and in drawing out a petition to the Provincial Parliament, and otherwise, I took advantage of this to ground upon it my plea of complaint; but the consideration of loss upon that property, in consequence of the counteraction of law, did not actuate me in the slightest degree when I wrote my second Address to the Resident Landowners of Upper Canada. If I had regard to any private interest in this way, that of Mr. William Dickson was nearest my heart, for I did think his situation a very cruel one. In some respects, the *shutting out of Americans* promised rather to be favourable to my own private views. Looking to the business of land-agency which I proposed to establish, it gave hope that the home ministry might be more disposed to countenance emigrants to Canada, and patronise my efforts, when once convinced of their error, in order to make amends for the mischief done to that country by stopping the accustomed stream of settlement. . . .

It is worse than usless to promulgate a law which cannot be enforced, even though that law is not at variance with abstract, natural, and indefeasible right; and, if any law exists, whether a law of nations, or any other, which experience and growing knowledge demonstrates to be wrong, that law should be repealed, openly and expressly. It is, in fact, repealed, tacitly, the moment that it cannot be enforced, for power to execute a law is a necessary part of it. When the power ceases the law must, from the nature of things, cease to exist. It may be said that our Government, when they relinquished their design of trying, as traitors, those native-born subjects of Britain who were found fighting against the King in Canada, – who had sworn allegiance to the Government of the United States, might have been tried and put to death, for the ancient law of allegiance had not yet been dropt, and our Government *had* the *power* to enforce it: it may be said that the ancient law still exists, because our Government, only for the time, yielded to *expediency*. I say, no: the ancient law of allegiance is *dropt* – is *annulled for ever*, as an international law between Britain and America. It *is*, and *ought to be* dropt. The intercourse between America and Britain is now so great; and so many natural-born subjects of Britain have become sworn subjects of America, and becoming sworn subjects of America, and will continue to become sworn subjects of America; – so much intercourse has taken place, is taking place, and will continue to take place, between Britain and America, that the very idea of maintaining, that the ancient law of nations, regarding allegiance, now subsists between these nations and countries, is absurd; and, what is now required – imperiously required, when we look to the relative situations and close connexion of America and Canada, is, that between these countries there should be an *immediate* understanding on the subject, – that between these countries, at least, there should be fixed terms to regulate practice as to the rights, duties, and obligations of allegiance. The subject should immediately be brought under discussion before the British Parliament; and, after grave determination there, our ministers should confer with the American Government, in order to have a rational international law decided upon and mutually proclaimed.

After my Address on the subject of allegiance was published in Canada, I observed, from American newspapers, that the question was agitated in Congress; but it was quashed, or laid aside. It ought not to be laid aside, or neglected. The consideration of it is most pressing, as it concerns Canada and the United States – Britain and America; but, it would be well if every nation on the earth could be brought to a unanimous decision for general good – to a plain, well-defined, and well-understood international law on the subject of allegiance.

Mankind are every day becoming more and more enlightened; and as they become enlightened, the intercourse between nations will increase: it will increase, I hope, till all nations become one as to allegiance, and every law on the subject shall be void for want of object – when a free and unrestrained intercourse and fellowship shall universally prevail. In barbarous times, and while mankind were not yet in possession of the printing press – when they could not converse together beyond limits prescribed by tyrants – when they could not find opportunity to learn and be agreed upon these great truths, that bad government had mainly promoted *national* antipathies; that the interest, of governors only, was served by war; and, that, that of the people was to join hands from all sides for the suppression of tyranny; – in these times it was indeed fitting to declare that the bond of natural allegiance could not be shaken off; that, if born in Turkey, we must worship Mahomet; that, if born in Hindoostan, we must fall down before Jaugernout; that church and state were indissoluble; and that natural allegiance must give eternal sanction and support to superstition and tyranny. O! to be sure, these were all choice and necessary maxims for the days of darkness: these, indeed, were the maxims of antiquity, which Edmund Burke, thirty years ago, wished us to adopt, and to entail on posterity. Thank God, that, after thirty years have passed away, we can laugh at the frenzy of Burke, give full swing to speculative opinion, and stand up as staunch and determined supporters of abstract right. . . .

The grand essential for the improvement of man and government, is *freedom of opinion*, which blue-laws would put down; but which, thank God, has now, from the aid of the printing-press, got beyond controul – got fairly a-head of superstition and tyranny; at least in the United States of America; and, with discretion, even here, in London.

A case can scarcely be supposed to exist which required, nay demanded *freedom of opinion*, more urgently than that which induced me to put it to use by the publication of my second Address to the Resident Landowners of Upper Canada. Orders had come from home to check the ingress of Americans into that province, clearly without knowledge or regard of statute law, and still more so, of other circumstances. The Provincial Executive had acted upon these orders, under the countenance of the legislature; and nothing but sore experience and a vast depreciation in the value of property, had awakened *feeling* to any consideration on the subject. . . .

This frightful state of things, as it concerned the question of allegiance and others of the highest importance, which I clearly saw into, and which could only be settled by the British Parliament, stimulated me to be bold and determined in the measures I took, in writing my second Address to the Resident Land-owners of Upper Canada, and in urging an immediate inquiry to be made, with a view of submitting the whole state of the province to liberal and superior consideration – to the British Parliament, which alone could settle matters of such tremendous consequence; not only regarding the properties but lives and liberties of many thousands of people; we may say, the whole inhabitants of the province. My address produced effect; but by no means, the full effect which I desired. It served the purpose of Mr. Wm. Dickson, indeed; but to this day, I am convinced that even *he* remains blind to the question of allegiance, as I have now represented it; and which I am most anxious should be taken into the serious consideration of my readers in this country, better qualified to judge than the weaklings of a province. The conduct of Dickson and Claus, Legislative Councillors of Upper Canada, in arresting and imprisoning me, a native-born Briton, under colour of the alien sedition law, as well as that of Chief Justice Powell, in refusing me liberty, applied for on writ of *habeas corpus*, most clearly proves that these men were blind on the subject of allegiance. They neither appreciated justly the value of *natural* allegiance, nor understood the distinction between that and *local* allegiance, which alone their sedition law regarded or could regard. And here it is necessary to explain. I have said that the law of *natural* allegiance has ceased, as it concerns people emigrating to America, and becoming citizens of the United States; and, I *do* say so. It has ceased as an international law, from necessity; and its cessation in this character, has been manifested by the act of our Government setting at liberty native-born Britons, *sworn* citizens of America; but, it has *not* ceased, as an international law otherwise; far less as a national law. Its cessation, as an international law, between Britain and America, has not taken away its power over a British subject while he remains within his Majesty's dominions; neither, I trust, are my most valuable rights and privileges held under it, to be taken away at the arbitrary will of Councillors Dickson and Claus, aided by Chief Justice Powell: no, nor even by my own act of submitting to a trial while my powers of reasoning were weakened by the oppression and cruelty of provincial tyranny, no doubt enforced by the orders of Sir Peregrine Maitland. By a right understanding of the law and principle of allegiance, the Canadian Sedition Act, infamous as it is, can yet be made perfectly consistent, so far as British rights are in question. Let it be understood that, the oath of allegiance which it requires to be taken, is merely that which confirms *local* allegiance, and all difficulty, in its interpretation, is done away – all inconsistency is at an end. With this understanding, it merely says to aliens and outlaws, take care of yourselves till the oath of *local* allegiance has put you under the protection of the British Government; and it makes a clear distinction between these persons and native-born subjects, who, of their own right, have a claim to that protection. Further, an alien cannot be tried for treason till he takes the oath of allegiance. The native-born subject, who has neither been outlawed, nor has sworn allegiance to a foreign government, can be tried for sedition and treason, though he has not gone through the ceremony of swearing allegiance, seeing that his natural allegiance subjects him to prosecution for such a crime. The Canadian Sedition Act empowers governors, and others, to order aliens to depart from his Majesty's dominions, and to imprison them in case of refusal, that they may not carry on seditious and treasonable practices with impunity; but, it never empowered them, nor was it ever necessary to empower them, to order native-born subjects, thus arbitrarily, out of the province; for the moment they could be convicted of sedition, they could be punished for that crime; – the moment they could be convicted of treason, they could be put to death. They could, under accusation for the first offence, have liberty till trial by finding bail. On a special charge of treason they could not find bail; yet they could not be condemned till an overt-act was proved on trial by two witnesses.

I now come to the grand practical requisite for Upper Canada, – the matter of first importance for the British Parliament to determine, as to the obligation of allegiance; and, it is very simple. It is to fix a certain time within which a person having sworn allegiance to the King, in Canada, shall not lawfully throw off such bond of allegiance, and fight against the King, say, one year, two years, three years, or more. The confiscation of property upon desertion, in time of war, is one just and necessary principle of practice; and, thus fixing a time to restrict persons as to changing sides, and taking part in warlike operations, would complete all that is required. Under existing law, any man in Canada who has become a British subject, merely by taking the oath of allegiance, can unquestionably step into the United States, take the oath of allegiance to the Government of that country, and return immediately, in time of war, to fight in Canada against his Majesty's crown and dignity. I appeal to every rational being, if this is not an awful state of affairs: I ask, whether this alone did not call loudly for consideration, and whether it does not now imperiously require the attention of the British Parliament? I ask, if the necessity for settling this single point did not justify my first political Address in Upper Canada; – did not prove the value of opinion being free; and, does not demand inquiry into the state of the province?

Parliament, and the People.

AFTER Councillor Dickson was so well satisfied with my Address, in favour of the free ingress of American settlers, as to offer me 500 acres of land for writing it, my hope was, that he would finish the Niagara Township Report, sign, seal, and deliver it; nor did I cease to entreat of him to do so. But, no: the Report was doomed to remain in the honourable hands to which it was committed by the worthy magistrates and others who drew it up. He and Councillor Clark went off for Little York, to be present at the opening of Parliament, 5th February, 1818; and, my purpose was to follow them, on my way to England, as soon as the Address was published at length in the Niagara Spectator, which it was the 12th February. On that day, and while the newspaper was preparing for press, the Gazette arrived, containing the President's speech; from which I extract the following clauses:

"His Royal Highness the Prince Regent has been graciously pleased to devote the proceeds of the estate vested in his Majesty, under the provisions of the statute to declare certain persons therein described aliens, to compensate the loss of individuals by the invasion of the enemy."

"To carry into effect the gracious intention of his Royal Highness, some further legislative provisions may be required."
    "*Honourable Gentlemen, and Gentlemen,*

"His Majesty's Government having countenanced a migration from the United Kingdom to the provinces of Lower and Upper Canada, it is expected that great benefit will result to this colony from the accession of an industrious and loyal population, and I recommend to your consideration how far it may be expedient to assist the emigrants by providing the means to defray the expense of the location and grant of land bestowed upon them by his Royal Highness the Prince Regent in his Majesty's name."

The reader will not, at first, see any thing very wrong in these clauses of the opening speech of his Honour the President of Upper Canada; but I would wish him to read them over again; and, by way of puzzle, question himself on the subject before perusing my remarks, which will be severe: not wantonly, but, in duty, severe. Deceitful, and often unmeaning, slang, has injured Upper Canada beyond all conception; and the above extracts will prove good examples for illustration.

Having said, that I shall be severe in my remarks upon these clauses of the President's speech, it may be well, in the first place, to say something of the President himself.

Colonel Smith served his Majesty in the American revolutionary war, and afterwards settled in Canada. I had but two or three short conversations with him, and my first impressions, that he was a good, well-meaning man, never changed. As a President he was nothing. He obtained that honour merely by routine, on the departure of Governor Gore; being one of the Executive Council. There were senior Councillors; but one of these held a permanent lucrative situation; and the other was disqualified, from being a catholic. A half pay Officer, after more than 30 years retirement in the wilderness, with little incentive to action, and very little communication with enlightened society, must be an extraordinary man indeed if he does not sink into sloth and inanity. I shall describe the residence and neighbourhood of the President of Upper Canada, from remembrance, journeying past it on my way to York from the westward, by what is called the lake road through Etobicoke. For many miles not a house had appeared when I came to that of Colonel Smith, lonely and desolate. It had once been genteel and comfortable; but was now going to decay. A vista had been opened through the woods towards lake Ontario; but, the riotous and dangling undergrowth seemed threatening to retake possession, from the Colonel, of all that had once been cleared, which was of narrow compass. How could a solitary half-pay Officer help himself, settled down upon a block of land, whose very extent barred out the assistance and convenience of neighbours! Not a living thing was to be seen around! How different might it be, thought I, were a hundred industrious families compactly settled here out of the redundant population of England! The road was miserable. A little way beyond the President's house, it was lost on a bank of loose gravel flung up between the contending waters of the lake and the Etobicoke stream. This bank was partially covered with bushes. My pony sunk over the pasterns, and got afraid with the rattling gravel: he shyed at every bush; and was as foolish as a loyal-mad magistrate, alarmed with sedition: he was absolutely provoking. The half-spun appellations of Sterne's nuns would have been lost upon him. I cursed Little York for it; spurred, remounted, dragged, remounted, and spurred twenty times over, losing five minutes of time for every step of advance. It was my anxious wish to get through the woods before dark; but the light was nearly gone before the gravel bank was cleared. There seemed but one path, which took to the left. It led me astray: I was lost; and there was nothing for it but to let my little horse take his own way. Abundant time was afforded for reflection on the wretched state of property, flung away on half-pay officers. Here was the head man of the province, "born to blush unseen," without even a tolerable bridle-way between him and the capital city, after more than twenty years possession of his domain!! The very gravel bed which caused me such turmoil might have made a turnpike; but what can be done by a single hand? The President could do little with the axe or wheelbarrow himself; and half-pay could employ but few labourers at 3s. 6d. per day, with victuals and drink. After many a weary twist and turn, I found myself on the banks of the Humber, where there was a house and boat. A most obliging person started from his bed to ferry me across the river; but the pony refused to swim. With directions to find a bridge near at hand, I was again set adrift, lost and forlorn! The bridge was at last found; but a third time, lost! was the word, and that, too, in the very purlieus of Little York; for even to the church of that poor, dirty, and benighted capital, there is nothing like a direct and wellmade road! No less than seven hours were thus wasted in getting over as many miles!! The first improvement of every country should be the making of roads; and, after that, speeches from the throne may be patiently listened to. I blame not the poor President; but I lost every particle of patience with the clauses now to be examined.

The worthy President, I am convinced, had no concern in the fabrication of the speech. Judge Powell was *guessed* to be its author; but to save the modesty of Little York, I *fathered* it, to use Councillor Clark's expression, on "some half starved clerk in London." But what, now, is so very objectionaable in these extracts before us? Gentle reader! be patient, and I will shew you, by and by, that these extracts, plain and simple as they may seem, with fewer *gracious* phrases in them than usual, do, nevertheless, contain that description of humbug (I can find no other word for my meaning) by which the august Assembly of Upper Canada has, from its nativity, been kept in precious stupefaction. Whether to give *design* any credit for this description of thing, and call it court policy, or whether it is a direct and natural sequence of mere silliness, under certain modifications, I am quite dubious; but, certainly, it could produce *effect*. I know that, by its instrumentality, business and common sense, nay, even truth and justice, have been blinked, and blinded, and overturned. A speech from the provincial throne is never questioned. In the Assembly there are no butts, called Ministers, against whom Opposition has a natural inclination to shoot a bolt. What falls from his Majesty's Representative falls, as it were, from heaven, immaculate; and, in faith, must needs be received as gospel. The speech all-courtly must needs have a courtly reply. The speech of his Majesty's Representatative can thus become at once both butt and barbed hook, for "*the Honourable Gentlemen, and Gentlemen.*" In Upper Canada the opening speech invariably takes its fish. The poor fish generally plays about a week or two of the session quiet enough. Then some little twist of the angler gives him pain. He flounces: he flounders; and, at last, perhaps, snapping the line, rather than be *taken in, takes* himself off to the tune of Yankee Doodle! My figurative language may not, perhaps, convey, rightly and completely, an idea of the meeting, sitting, and breaking up of the august Assembly of Upper Canada; but only three more words shall be wasted upon it, characteristic of the beginning, middle, and end: flattering – fighting – flying.

The session, opened with the speech from which the above extracts are taken, completely answered this description. Most gracious and courtly replies were made to the opening speech; but not one piece of business was adjusted which might not as well have been let alone, saving that the *fourth* resolution of the former session was passed, confirming the fact, that "subjects of the United States may lawfully come into, and settle in this province, hold land, and be entitled to all the privileges and immunities of natural-born subjects." For the last two or three weeks a most deadly feud went on between the Legislative Council and House of Assembly, the former maintaining that they had a right to alter and amend money bills: the latter denying this. His Honour the President, at last seeing that seed-time was coming on, and that Members of Parliament would be better employed at the plough than in Little York, "came in state to the Legislative Council Chamber, and being seated on the throne, the Gentleman Usher of the Black Rod was sent to require the attendance of the House of Assembly. His Honour was pleased to close the session with the following SPEECH."

"Honourable Gentlemen, and Gentlemen,

"When I called you together in obedience to the law, it was in full expectation that you would assiduously labour to bring up any arrear of public business.

"The ready pledge offered by your cordial addresses, in answer to my suggestions from the chair, confirmed me in that hope.

"I the more regret to have experienced disappointment, and finding no probability of any concert between the two houses, I come reluctantly to close the session, its business unfinished.

"I do most earnestly entreat you to weigh well, during the recess, the important effects of such a disunion, and that you may meet, resolved to conciliate and be useful."

Having sketched the general character of an Upper Canadian session of Parliament, and let the President tell for what good end it sat nearly two months, and then *run away*, (for, it must be known, that the above closing speech from the *chair*, was not delivered to a House, but only to part of a House) I shall now take on hand to make good my charges against the President's opening speech by calm and fair criticism – by exposure and proof.

On the subject of the two first paragraphs I have already dilated. ... My present concern with them will go only to mark the *manner* in which the people of Upper Canada have been humbugged (here this vulgar and odd-looking word must again be excused) – humbugged and bilked of their fair and well-authenticated claims for losses sustained in war, by decitful slang. A stranger would, of course, suppose that when "the Prince Regent had been graciously pleased to devote," that he *devoted* something. It was known to all, save, perhaps, the Prince Regent, who probably knew nothing of the business; – it was known to all that nothing was devoted. It was known particularly to the Commons House of

Assembly that their constituents could get not one farthing from the confiscated estates, yet they returned thanks for "the gracious offer," ...

The third paragraph, that which regards emigration, next comes to be considered. It sets before us these words: "His Majesty's Government having countenanced a migration," and, of course, means that countenance was *still* given, for the President recommends the House to "*consider of assisting the emigrants with means to defray the expense of location.*" Now, every word of this can be proved to be idle and worse than idle; untrue, deceitful, mean, and insulting. In using these words, I wish not a syllable to be construed as personal to the President who read them. Perhaps, even the writer of them did not think any thing of their import. I suppose the President, for the sake of charity, to be dreaming and acting with as much innocence as an automaton made to enter a church, and throw dirt about till the whole congregation flies from the worship. The speech of the President of Upper Canada is not a whit less indecent than would be such an exhibition; and a thousand times more mischievous. The automaton's performance might neither be indecent, nor without its merits, its good intention, or its very good effect. Were they worshippers of the Devil, every good Christian, would, *in this case*, not only find excuse for, but applaud the performance of the automaton. If they were hypocrites, pretended worshippers of God, then it would be a hundred times more meritorious, and indecency itself would be out of the question, as it was when Christ overturned the tables of money-changers in the temple, and whipped out of it every one who dealt in filthy lucre. Having sufficiently worked up my picture for comparison, and strongly guarded against all idea of personal insult to the President of Upper Canada, I shall now make as free with his speech as I would think it my duty to do with the speech of a British Minister, for President, Lieutenant-Governor, or Governor-in-Chief of Canada can be considered as no other, in respect to free remark and censure of words and actions: nay, by the term which was applied to Herod, so expressive of the character of provincial governors in general, we are authorized to use the strongest figurative language when such men are to be spoken of and censured. I say, then, that every word of the passage quoted from the opening speech of the President of Upper Canada is idle and worse than idle; untrue, deceitful, mean, and insulting. When I first read this passage, it filled me instantly with disgust, and was a mean of changing the whole course of my conduct and fate. Let me now take it to pieces, and expose it, bit by bit; nor for its own sake; not for any mischief that was occasioned by it; not as a passing matter; but as an illustration for general use, a corrective for future evil. Before any assertion is made, it is proper in every case to consider whether that assertion is true, and according as the assertion is deliberately and formally made, so much the greater care should be taken as to this most essential point. An assertion made from a throne should of all assertions be the most guarded, because the whole nation listens to it, confides in it, and regulates the most important concerns thereby. An assertion made from a provincial throne, as to any act or intention of the Supreme Government, rises in importance, should be particularly guarded, should be most minutely correct. The assertion with which the clause, now before us, extracted from the opening speech of the President of Upper Canada, commences, is not only untrue, but deceitful in many ways. His Majesty's Government certainly did countenance "migration" to Canada in the year 1815 to a certain extent; but we have any thing but proof that this countenance was continued. We afterwards found emigration to the Cape of Good Hope, &c. countenanced, but not to Canada. What I have stated with respect to the Perth settlement is indicative of Government having ceased to countenance emigration, having neglected that settlement, even as an experiment, having given it no fair trial. . . .

I do not think it necessary to dwell on the extreme childishness of these clauses: but to shew still further how much more ridiculous, and contrary to all common sense and business rules, this Governor's schemes and practices went, I shall here insert a letter which I wrote to him, with the reply.

TO HIS EXCELLENCY SIR JOHN SHERBROOKE, &C. &C. &C. QUEBEC.

Queenston, Upper Canada, Sept. 14, 1817.

SIR,

I am a farmer from England, and have visited Canada, to ascertain how far it would be profitable to cultivate the land here.

On my first arrival, I went to the new settlement of Perth, on the Rideau, to make inquiries there, and had much attention shewn me by Captain Fowler. He intimated that I might have land granted me at Perth, but in no greater quantity than one hundred acres together. As this would not suit my views, having been accustomed to extensive operations, I then gave up thoughts of the matter; but it has since occurred, that as Government is particularly desirous of peopling that quarter, and much is expended in the accomplishment, a contract might be formed which might at once suit me and forward the wishes of Government. Captain Fowler informed me, that the settlement of Perth lay entirely under the direction of the military department, which has induced me directly to address myself to you. The question shortly is, would Government furnish land to any extent in proportion to the clearance made, buildings erected, and number of people settled, during a given time, allowing the farms to be regulated as to size, and the buildings to be placed as the contractor should incline?

You will excuse, I trust, the liberty now taken and oblige me much by directing a reply to the post-office, Queenston. If favourable, I should be happy to communicate more fully on the subject.

I have the honor to be,
Your's, respectfully,

ROBERT GOURLAY.

To MR. ROBERT GOURLAY, QUEENSTON, UPPER
CANADA.

Quebec, September 29, 1817.
SIR,
In answer to your letter of the 14th inst. addressed to the Commander of the Forces, I have received his Excellency's directions to acquaint you that it does not appear to him that the mode proposed by you of settling and clearing land on the Rideau, by contract, would be desirable. Land is granted at that settlement to emigrants from Britain, in proportion of one hundred acres to each man, and this quantity will be increased, according to the means and the industry of the settler, from time to time, and which will be ascertained by an inspection of the progress made on the first grant.

I am, Sir,

Your most obedient Servant,
(Signed)   CHRISTOPHER MYERS,
Col. D. Q. M. Gen.

. . . Captain Fowler actually offered me a thousand acres of land if I would settle at Perth; and on my objecting to the lots lying asunder. "O!" said he, "that is more in your favour, as it becomes valuable from the efforts of the other settlers;" and here indeed is the secret. It answers very well, indeed, for half-pay officers to get their 500, their 700, and their 1000 acres so located; because not one in ten of them ever cultivate their land, and if not intermixed with the farms of the poor settlers, it would never bring them a farthing. The officers let their land lie waste in lots of 100 acres or 200 acres all over the country in this way, till, by the efforts of the industrious, it fetches money to them, the drones. This is the way that Canada has been impoverished, first and last; and yet the trashy speeches from the throne go on, year after year, insulting common sense. Lord Dalhousie, the present governor-in-chief, has been trifling with agricultural societies and stuff of this sort, for years, both in Nova Scotia and Canada; while the great obstacles to improvement are untouched, – while clergy reserves, and lands gifted away to drones, render improvement almost hopeless. In his opening speech of last winter, 1820 – 21, to the Parliament of Lower Canada, the governor-in-chief said:

"The settlement of the waste lands is a subject to which I feel it my duty to point your attention in a particular manner. The great tide of emigration to these provinces promises to continue, and the experience of several years has shewn the want of some measure to regulate, and give effect to this growing strength. Many of these people arrive in poverty and sickness, many also with abundant means, but the settlement of both descriptions is impeded by the want of legislative aid."

Now, what legislative aid does he want? His provincial parliament cannot do the needful – cannot get quit of a seventh part of lumber land, set aside for supporting a Protestant clergy, in a country where nine-tenths of the people are Roman Catholics, and quite willing to pay their clergy without government interference. Can there be any thing so monstrous as to bore the French of Lower Canada with *Reserves* for a *Protestant Clergy?* No legislative aid but that of the British parliament can set aside this curse: no legislative aid but that of the British parliament can check the governors, themselves, from marring improvement by gifting away land, in all directions, to good-for-nothing favourites and sycophants.

I have instanced my brother's ill-treatment, which was manifested at the very time that President Smith was suggesting a vote of money to pay fees for emigrants into the land offices. He had not, I am convinced, a single atom of hope that the thing could ever be thought of for a moment by the Assembly. The very idea was ridiculous; but it went to make believe that emigrants wanted such relief; whereas their great want was ready service on the part of the Land Council, and land in situations where it was possible to clear it. At this very time, when money was asked for parliament, hundreds of emigrants were going from the Province from the mere sloth and indifference of men paid salaries to give attention to business in the land-granting department.

It was by the merest accident that I remained another week at Queenston; and that week determined a much longer stay. During that week, seriously reflecting on the usage which both I and my brother had experienced, I resolved to throw before the public a correspondence which I had carried on for near three months, with the folks of Little York, without getting the smallest satisfaction. I resolved calmly to address the President when exhibiting these letters, but several incidents occurred which really put me out of all temper towards the end of my epistle. It was now notorious that the parson of Little York had been using every effort to mar the purpose of my first address to the resident land-holders. I found other beside the Niagara Report withheld after preparation, and I had not a doubt but he had been the cause of my brother's denial of land. At this moment, when he was flying in the face of the very best interests of the province, and neglecting his duties at the Land Board, for which he was paid; – at this time, when all should have been business in the capital, he advertised, in the style of a store-keeper, that the *subscriber* would lecture on philosophy, *to get the school-house painted!* My second address, too, I found was to have serious opposition, notwithstanding the great authority of Dickson in its favour. A half-pay major was my opponent; but he was evidently set on by some one deeper than himself. He carried to the Spectator Office two letters; one written by himself, weak in the extreme; another, anonymous, by a different hand, malignant and ungentlemanly. Having seen these letters accidentally, I apprized the major that it was not fair to attack *motives*, and begged of him to withdraw so far, as that was illiberal. He was obstinate, however; and it was not for me to let the cat's-paw of a villain escape with impunity; and none but a villain would have written the anonymous letter. To be accused of improper motives, in writing my second address, was accusation of crime of the deepest dye – of treason. It could not be less, if my motives were impure; which they were as opposite from as day from night. If it cost me another week's delay, I was fully resolved to defend the ground which I had taken in so dread a question as that of allegiance. While my letter to the President was yet unfinished, – while the parson's busy malice, and the major's unwarrantable and low suspicions, were together on my mind, a letter from my wife arrived from England, stating circumstances of the most serious import, and expressing such fears for my safety, as threw me into an absolute fever of care, perplexity, and feeling. I ought to have been in England by the first of October; but two months ailment had first detained me. A month after that was spent in recovering health, on an excursion in the United States. The statistical inquiries next caused delay, then Dickson's politics, and now, war. In a tumult of feeling, – in a paroxysm, I sat down to finish my letter to the President. I thought of my wife's anxiety – I thought of hundreds of emigrants who had been vexed and disappointed, and torn to pieces, by the vile, loathsome, and lazy vermin of Little York. I attacked the whole swarm, and flung into my letter an extract from that of my beloved and distressed wife. The bolt was discharged, and kindled unextinguishable flame.* Little York! Little York on fire!!! Dickson and Clark, misjudging the warmest impulses of a convulsed heart, deserted my cause in the capital, and went, sneaking, forsooth, to the President to make an apology – to the President, whose speech was so matted with meanness and mischief! Clark wrote me to get out of the Province by a by-path. That was too much: it caused a revulsion: completely righted my bark, in the public mind; and even brought back my friend Clark to temper. I was attacked. I had to defend; and a controversy of two months ensued. My constant aim was *inquiry into the state of the province.* Without that, the province, I saw, was nothing. I was right: it is nothing: it yet remains worse than nothing, – a sink of all that is vile. Though I offered to appear at the bar of parliament, and sent up petitions for presentation to parliament, nobody would *"father"* these. The conscript-fathers had not courage; but a motion was at last made for inquiry in the Commons House of Assembly. A committee was appointed, with power "to send for papers and persons:" but alas! all hope was soon over. The feud above spoken of broke out between the Assembly and Legislative Council, and nothing more could be done. After two or three weeks of strife between peers and commons, *we, the people* of Niagara, heard a round of great guns go off in the direction of York. It was immediately conjectured that parliament was broken up. It was the first of April, and the people said that, the *fools* had been dismissed on their own proper day.

On the 2nd, our Councillors and Assembly-men arrived in a vessel at Niagara. I immediately waited on William Dickson, and found him full of the dispute with the Assembly. The Legislative Council had insisted on *altering* money bills. The Commons stiffly resisted this; and neither would yield. Dickson said, "What! shall we allow bills to come up to us with bad spelling

* Gourlay is referring here to letters he published in the Niagara *Spectator*, 17 February 1818, beginning with an account of his own applications for land and ending with bitter criticism of the policies and personalities of the provincial government. He ridiculed Strachan's lecture series (meant to raise funds to paint his church: it is to this series that Gourlay's passage about painting the school-house refers). The "bolt" is sometimes taken, not accurately but quite reasonably, to refer to his "Third Address to the Resident Land-Owners of Upper Canada," 2 April 1818, which is printed below, p. 367.[Ed.]

and bad grammar, and not alter them? No: it would never do to disgrace the statute book in this way." He had submitted to the Legislative Council certain resolutions, which, he said, breathed the true spirit of that august body; but, the pawkie Chief Justice had got something more smooth and soothing substituted. . . .

That Dickson had a chief hand in this squabble between the Peers and Commons of Upper Canada, I have not the slightest doubt, as it was quite in character for him to be *great* and presumptuous. The Dominie of Little York had thought the Legislative Councillors wrong, in attempting to encroach on the privileges of the Commons; and to this hour I see, in imagination Dickson storming against him, and with his mouth screwed up, to mimic the Aberdeen brogue, repeating the Dominie's words, "they're *wraung* – they're *wraung*."

Upon returning to my lodgings, I wrote a third Address to the Resident Land-owners of Upper Canada, advising them to choose Representatives to meet in convention; subscribe, every man a dollar, and send home a Commission to entreat enquiry into the state of the province.

The first meeting was held at Niagara, a Member of Assembly in the chair; and this meeting having chosen a Committee of Management, every thing went quietly and peaceably on till Councillor Dickson instigated Councillor Clark to raise the cry of sedition; and, strange to say, Clark, who but a few days before shook me by the hand, not only alarmed the country with insinuations against my public measures, but read from a paper, at a public meeting, the grossest attack upon my private credit and character. I have mentioned this before, and I mention it again, as a most extraordinary instance of that fury and fanaticism (I cannot find a right word for my meaning), which could make a man like Clark, naturally good-hearted and sensible, forget common decency, friendship, and faith, in a gust of political zeal blown up by such a jumble-brain as Dickson. Even Dickson himself seemed in good humour, and free of all low suspicion for more than a week after my third address to the resident land-owners was published, advising the people to meet in convention, and send home a commission. I carried to him the proof sheet, and made a small correction to humour him. He joked about sending his black servant to the first Niagara meeting, and I returned the joke, by assuring him that the black servant with a dollar in his hand, should be considered as good a man as himself: and now, truly, I would not put them in comparison, to the honour of the black outside, be it spoken. Had these two men, Clark and Dickson, behaved to me with singleness of heart, and steadiness of purpose; had they assisted in carrying into execution the objects of my *third* address, as keenly as Dickson commended my *second*, which proposed the very same end, viz. a submission to the British parliament of the whole affairs of Upper Canada, what blessed consequences might now have resulted! I know that my plans, executed, would have enriched these very individuals: but we know not what, ultimately, may be best.

Niagara district was completely and almost instantaneously organized under my plan. A pamphlet was printed, setting forth, *principles* and *proceedings*. As soon as this was printed, four persons were dispatched on horseback to lodge it for sale and distribution through different quarters of the province. One person went out to the Western district, one to the London district, one to Gore, and one to Newcastle and the Home districts. I, myself, having, all along, had it in contemplation to complete my tour of the province, by visiting certain parts north and east of Lake Ontario, took on hand to spread the pamphlet in these parts. Crossing Lake Ontario, to Kingston, I found an attorney, who very completely did the business of the Midland district. I travelled to the extreme point of the Eastern district in a waggon, and thence over to the district of Ottawa on horseback, so as to do every thing in good time: and never, perhaps, were the people of so extensive a tract so speedily roused up and organized – a tract nearly 600 miles in length. In the Districts where my writings had been circulated by newspapers, viz. Niagara, Gore, and the Midland districts, the organization was complete, and the full number of Representatives returned to the Convention.

Niagara district	full	4 members	
Gore do.	do.	2 do.	
Midland do.	do.	5 do.	
Newcastle do.	do.	1 do.	
Johnstown do.		1 do.	short 1
London do.		1 do.	do. 1
Western do.		1 do.	do. 2
Home do.		0	do. 1
Eastern do.		0	do. 4
Ottawa do.		0	do. 1
. . . .		15	10

The leading people of Ottawa district declined sending a member to the Convention because of the extreme distance from York; but, they agreed to support measures by subscribing money to support the cause in equal proportion to other districts.

The London district, which contains some of the most spirited people in the province, would have mustered well, but for efforts made against the cause by Colonel Talbot and his surveyor, Colonel Burwell; for which the people have little to thank them. Little York kept down the poor people of the Home district; and the Dominie of York, with his fellow-labourer, the priest of Augusta, kindled up into madness the fanatics of Cornwall.

On the day of the general election, the 6th of June, 1818, I was at Johnstown, on my return to Kingston. To avoid all concern in the affair, I hired a horse, and spent the whole of that day surveying the country backwards towards Spencer's Mill, Grant's Mill, and into the township of Oxford, with a view of ascertaining the levels of the country in connexion with the St. Lawrence navigation, and its junctions.

In my General Introduction, I have stated that I advised the Convention to refer its cause to the Lieutenant-Governor and General Assembly, who woefully misused our trust; and, enacted a law to prevent, in future, all meetings by deputy!! But this will not do: the people of Upper Canada will, in a few years, get out of every treacherous snare: they will shake from their limbs every fetter which their base Representatives have hung round them.

To shew what was the spirit of the people while acting free of unworthy terror or base sycophancy, I shall here introduce the pamphlet of *Principles* and *Proceedings* – together with Minutes of the various regular meetings which took place throughout the province. These will not be destitute of interest, as part of the history of Upper Canada. They will evince the genuine spirit of the people. They will demonstrate how readily – how peaceably – how effectually men may unite for their common interests, while yet in possession of natural and just rights.

As to my advising the people to choose Representatives to meet in Convention, and send home a commission for inquiry, it was the thought of a moment. My third address to the resident landowners of Upper Canada was written at a downsitting, without the smallest premeditation, immediately after hearing Dickson's account of the rupture between the Legislative Council and Assembly. In writing this address, my intentions were as distant from any thing seditious as heaven is distant from hell; yet this address was the mean of subjecting me to trials, persecution, and misfortune, altogether without parallel – and altogether springing out of the selfish, guilty, and gloomy soul of William Dickson.

My intentions are such as can yet be made clear – intentions not only pure but exalted; at once devoid of selfishness, and big with benevolence – intentions which may yet be realized in the accomplishment of infinite good to my country and fellow men.

PRINCIPLES AND PROCEEDINGS

OF THE

INHABITANTS

OF THE

DISTRICT OF NIAGARA,

FOR ADDRESSING

HIS ROYAL HIGHNESS THE PRINCE REGENT

RESPECTING

CLAIMS OF SUFFERERS IN WAR,

LANDS TO MILITIAMEN,

AND THE GENERAL BENEFIT

OF

UPPER CANADA.

PRINTED

AT THE NIAGARA SPECTATOR OFFICE.

1818.

Price – One Shilling, Halifax.

*To The Inhabitants of Upper Canada.**

St. Catharine's, District of Niagara, 5th May, 1818.

FRIENDS AND FELLOW SUBJECTS!

We lay before you the Principles and Proceedings of the People of this District, and example being better than precept, we have now only earnestly to entreat you to join in the cause. You will here find that we have been opposed, but opposition has strengthened us. It would swell too much this little Publication to give a List of Subscribers, but, they will be found week after week, in the Niagara Spectator *as room will admit. They already amount to upwards of nine hundred, and are daily increasing. Many have waited for the Address, which is only this day prepared, and will be found below.*

ROBERT HAMILTON,
WILLIAM ROBERTSON,
CYRUS SUMNER,
JOHN CLARK,

Representatives for
the District of
Niagara.
A true Copy.

WILLIAM J. KERR, Secretary.

To the Resident Land-Owners of Upper Canada

Niagara, April 2d, 1818.

GENTLEMEN,
Your Parliament is broken up! – a second time broken up, from employment of the most vital import to the honor and well-being of the province!! – Good God! what is to be the end of all this?

For my own part, Gentlemen, *I had little hope of satisfaction from the sitting of Parliament, after perusing the Administrator's speech from the throne; and this little was entirely extinguished with the disgusting* reply made to that speech by your Representatives. That a man who had spent the best part of his life in Upper Canada, – whose every interest and affection rested here, should even read a speech, not only containing mean sentiments, but notifying a measure provoking in the extreme to the feelings of a large body of his suffering countrymen, was indeed heart-sickening: yet this was not all: – what could we expect – what sensation

---

* This pamphlet, originally issued in Niagara, was the basis for the second unsuccessful libel action brought against Gourlay by the Attorney-General. [Ed.]

could swell in our breasts, when we found men, employed and *paid* by these very sufferers to guide their affairs and watch over their interests, bowing down to kiss the rod of affliction, and, in return for a most insulting offer, granting a receipt in full for demands, equally just and well authenticated?

Gracious heaven! Did we, the offspring of early civilization – the first hope of genuine liberty – the favoured wards of divine revelation, come to this new world, only to witness the degradation of our kind, and be humbled beneath the rude savage who ranges the desert woods? Surely, British blood, when it has ebbed to its lowest mark, will learn to flow again, and yet sustain, on its rising tide, that generous – that noble – that manly spirit, which first called forth applause from the admiring world.

It has been my fate to rest here nearly two months, viewing at a distance the scene of folly and confusion, – by turns serious, and by turns jocular, that the serious might not sink into the melancholy. I have advised – I have in duty offered services, but in vain: on went the sport, till yesterday, when the cannon announced to us that the play was over; and now we have the second speech of the Administrator, who has appropriately sunk down from the throne to the chair!

Gentlemen, *the constitution of this province is in danger, and all the blessings of social compact are running to waste. For three years the laws have been thwarted, and set aside by executive power; – for three sessions have your Legislators sat in Assembly, and given sanction to the monstrous – the hideous, abuse.* A worthy catastrophe has closed this farce of government; – your Commons and your Peers have quarrelled, and, the latter would assert, that the constitutional charter of Canada may be trifled with. What is to be done? Do you expect any thing from a new Governor? – you will be disappointed. Do you expect any thing from a new set of Representatives? – here again you will be deceived. Your Members of Assembly are now at home: compare their characters with those around them, and you will find them equally honest – equally wise – equally independent. Now that they are returned to society, as private individuals, I should be the very last man to call in question their worth or their probity: they are probably every way above par. It is not the men, it is the *system* which blasts every hope of good; and, till the system is overturned, it is vain to expect any thing of value from *change* of, Representatives, or, Governors.

It has been the cant of time immemorial to make mystery of the art of Government. The folly of the million, and the cunning of the few in power, have equally strengthened the reigning belief; but, it is false, deceitful, and ruinous. The people of every nation may at any time put down, either domestic tyranny or abuse, – they may, at any time, lay a simple foundation for public prosperity: they have only to be honest, and, in their honesty, bold.

In my last address to you, I said that the British constitution was "that beautiful contrivance by which the people, when perfectly virtuous, shall become all-powerful." Did you mark these words? – did you weigh them? – they are as important as they are true. We, of all men, have least to oppose us in correcting the errors of our constitution. The British constitution has provided for its own improvement, in peace and quietness; it has given us the right of petitioning the Prince or Parliament; and, this right, exercised *in a proper manner*, is competent to satisfy every virtuous desire.

My present purpose is not to dwell on theory; but to recommend and set example in the practice of using this glorious privilege. As individuals, we have a right to petition the Prince or Parliament of Britain: and we have a right to meet for this purpose in collective bodies. My proposal now is, that a meeting be forthwith held in each organized township throughout the province. I shall take upon me to name the day for the meeting of the people of this township of Niagara; and say, that on Monday Next, the 13th inst. I shall be ready by 12 o'clock noon, at Mr. James Rogers' coffee-house, to proceed to business with whoever is inclined to join me. The people of each township should, I conceive, at meeting, choose a Representative and Clerk. The Representatives should assemble from the several townships, within each district, on an appointed day, to draw up a petition to the Prince Regent: and, which could, soon after, be got signed by every well wisher to the cause.

The district meetings should, without delay, hold conference by representatives, each respectively choosing one, to meet in a provincial convention, and who should arrange the whole business, dispatch commissioners to England with the petitions, and hold correspondence with them, as well as with the supreme government. Two or three commissioners would suffice; and the necessary cost of carrying the whole ably and respectably into effect, would require but a trifling contribution from each petitioner. It is not going out of bounds to reckon on ten thousand petitioners, and a dollar from each would make up a sum adequate for every charge. I should recommend the subscriptions and payments to commence at the first township meetings; the money to be paid to the clerks, who should keep in hand one-seventh for local and incidental disbursements, and pay over the remainder to a treasurer, to be appointed in each district, by the representatives, at their first meeting. Beyond making choice of representatives and clerks, the less that is done at township meetings the better: debate, of all things, should be avoided. The clerks should minute transactions, and keep a list of subscribers, which should immediately be published in the nearest newspaper within the province, and week after week in the same manner, should be reported, additions. The public would thus, at once, see the strength and growth of the cause, as well as have vouchers for the payment of cash. Every transaction should be plain, downright, and open to view or inspection, – every principle should be declared – every proceeding be made known.

The simplicity of all this, and the ease with which it may be accomplished, is obvious: to go into more minute detail, at present, would be wasting time. No man, by joining the cause, can lose more than a dollar, and no responsibility whatever is incurred. As I take upon me to name the day of meeting for this township of Niagara, so that meeting may appoint days for the meetings of other townships, and, for the district meeting; seeing, that it can be matter of no consequence who settles such points, provided the business, thereby, has a fair chance of commencement, and that the whole system of petitioning may proceed without doubt or delay. No man upon such solemn occasion should say, "I am greater than another, and will not be seen acting with him:" no one should say, "I am less, and therefore presume not to set myself forward." On such an occasion, and under such circumstances as the present, every party, and every personal prejudice, should be put down, every eye should be resolutely bent on the one thing needful – a radical change of system in the Government of Upper Canada.

I address myself particularly to land-owners, because their interests are most deeply involved; but every man resident in Canada – every man who is a lover of peace – who desires to see this country independent of the United States – who desires to see a worthy connexion maintained between this province and Britain; – every man, in short, who has a spark of sincerity or patriotism in his soul, has now sufficient cause to bestir himself.

There was a time when Israel was famished with intense drought. Day after day, and week after week, the uncovered sun rose, only to frighten the nation, and open more wide the yawning fissures of the scorched earth: – there was yet however faith in Israel; and the faith of a few brought, at last, salvation to the expiring multitude. Let not the ancient record be lost to these modern days; let not the signs and figures of the material world be thrown aside as vain emblems, illustrations, and manifestations of the will, the power, and the goodness of God. He never deserts his creatures while they are true to themselves and faithful to him, – while they honourably put to use the divine gifts of rationality. The course to be pursued by the people of this province, at the present juncture, is so clear, that he who runs may read: they have only to put trust in the success of their own virtuous endeavours; and, success will as surely follow, as day succeeds to night – yes, worthy inhabitants of this township of Niagara, you may begin the necessary work with confidence: – the little cloud which rose from the horizon, at first no bigger than a man's hand, gradually expanded – mantled over the relentless face of a burning sky, and at last showered down refreshment on the thirsty land.

The good which may result, not only to this province, but to the general cause of truth, should these proposals be *cheerfully* and *alertly* adopted, surpasses all calculation. It would be needless for me now to descant on the subject. If there is really no public spirit in the country, I have already thrown away too much of my time: if there is, let it now be shown, for never was occasion more urgent. If the people of Canada do not *now* rouse themselves, they may indeed have plenty whereon to exist; but to that "righteousness which exalteth a nation," they will have no claim. The farmer may plod over his fields, – the merchant may sit, drowsy and dull, in his store; but the life, the vigour, the felicities of a prosperous and happy people will not be seen in the land: – the superiority of public management in the United States will bother all hope of competition: America will flourish, while Canada sinks into comparative decay; and another war will not only bring with it waste and destruction, but ignominious defeat.

In the scheme proposed I will accept of no appointment; but persons acting in it shall have my utmost assistance, and I shall make clear to them every course to be pursued. As soon as matters come to a head, all information, collected by me, shall be at the disposal of the commissioners; and even better consequences may be expected from this popular movement, than any that could have followed from the parliamentary inquiry, had that been allowed to proceed. It will shew, that though the rights of Parliament may be trifled with, those of the people of Upper Canada are not so easily to be set at defiance.

The Assembly of the Lower Province is to petition the British Parliament as to their trade: your representatives are to petition the Regent as to their privileges: when I found my petition set aside and despised at York, I dispatched one immediately to be presented to the House of Commons in England, to call attention there, to Canadian affairs: – all this will go for little, if something else is not done. You have read in the newspapers of my scheme having been discountenanced by Ministers at home: you have read of speculations upon making the best bargain with the United States for these provinces. I know whence all this proceeds: I know what would open the eyes of the people and Government at home to the true value of the Canadas, and put an end to such unnatural – such disgusting surmises; and all this I shall be happy to explain, as soon as explanation can be useful. One thing I am very sure of, that if the people of Canada will only do their duty as honest men, and as brothers, in unity, not only every just claim may be paid by next Christmas, but a foundation may be laid for this province becoming speedily the most flourishing and secure spot on the habitable globe.

ROBERT GOURLAY.

Niagara, April 13, 1818.

WHICH day a numerous meeting of the inhabitants of the township of Niagara, having been held at the house of JAMES ROGERS, and DAVID SECORD, Esq. M.P. being called to the chair, the Address of Mr. Gourlay to the Resident Land-owners of Upper Canada, dated April 2d, 1818, was read over, and its whole tenor and sentiments unanimously approved of. In conformity to the recommendations therein contained, the meeting proceeded to elect a representative and clerk, when *Robert Hamilton*, of Queenston, Esquire, was appointed to fill the former situation, and *John Ross*, of Niagara, Esquire, the latter. A committee also was appointed to forward the views of the meeting, viz. *Timothy Street, John Hagan, Wm. G. Hepburne,* and *Robert Moore,* Esquires.

Monday, 20th of this present month, was named as a proper day for the meetings of other townships within the district of Niagara, and Monday 27th for the meeting of the representatives from the various townships, to be held at SHIPMAN'S Tavern, St. Catharine; the Committee duly to advertise the same, and take such steps as to them shall appear requisite for furthering the good cause.

The thanks of the meeting were then unanimously voted to David Secord, Esq. for his public spirit in coming forward, on this occasion, and liberally fulfilling the duties of the Chair.

DAVID SECORD, *Chairman.*

A true Copy, JOHN ROSS, *Clerk.*

Grantham, April 20, 1818.

This day a numerous meeting for the inhabitants of the township of Grantham having been held at the house of Paul Shipman, and Geo. Adams, Esq. being called to the chair, spoke in substance as follows:

"GENTLEMEN,

"I am happy to see so many of you assemble here this day on the present occasion. You have heard the address of Mr. Robert Gourlay read: you have likewise heard the address of the Hon. Thomas Clark, and as it has been your unanimous vote, that I should be called to the chair, I beg to make a few remarks on the business before us. I assure you, Gentlemen, if there was the least appearance in any one sentence of Mr. Gourlay's address tending to sedition, I would be the last person to come forward to support it. You observe, Gentlemen, that in the address of the Hon. Thos. Clark, to the public, he endeavours to impress on your minds, that our meeting together tends to sedition, but allow me to say, it is an erroneous opinion.

"I have been acquainted with you twenty-four years, and so has that Hon. Gentleman, particularly in the late war with the United States of America, when you all went forward and exposed your lives and property in defence of your King and Country. Gentlemen, your loyalty is not, and *cannot* be shaken by the address of Mr. Gourlay, or any other individual – neither ought you to be intimidated by the address of the Hon. Thomas Clark, wherein he states, it was necessary for the Parliament to suppress seditious meetings. But the Hon. Gentleman should have recollected that the meetings alluded to were entirely of a different nature from our's – at a time when the greatest part of Ireland was in a state of open rebellion, and when preparations for the same were going on in Scotland. This, Gentlemen, is not the case here, and God forbid it ever should be; for I am certain there is not now, a more loyal people in the British dominions, than you in the township of Grantham. It would be doing Col. Clark the greatest injustice, were you not to hold him in the highest esteem, and hand his name down to posterity, for his active and zealous conduct, in frequently exposing his life and fortune in defence of the province. But, Gentlemen, you have all done the same, and I do not think he has any more reason to doubt your loyalty, than you have his. I conceive, Gentlemen, our object for meeting here to-day is to endeavour peaceably and quietly, to petition the Prince and Parliament of our mother country, and let them know the state of the province. You have suffered privations, and have lost property during the late war, which we have a just claim to ask for."

The meeting then proceeded to elect a representative and clerk, when WILLIAM HAMILTON MERRITT, Esq. was appointed to fill the former station, and GEORGE A. BALL, the latter. – A committee was also appointed to forward the views of this meeting: viz. *William Chisholm, Charles Ingersol, Robert Campbell, Amos M'Kenny* and *James Dedrick.*

The thanks of the meeting were then voted to Mr. Robert Gourlay, for the disinterested manner, in which he has come forward in endeavouring to promote the prosperity of this Province.

The thanks of the meeting were also voted to George Adams, Esq. for his spirited address on this occasion, and his able and impartial conduct in the chair.

GEO. ADAMS, *Chairman.*

GEO. A. BALL, *Clerk.*

When the meeting had finished business and were about dispersing, Mr. Gourlay, who had been visiting some townships, to advise delay till the aspersions cast on his conduct and the right of the subject to petition, were proved to be unfounded, accidentally arrived; whereupon a dinner was ordered, and Mr. G. being invited to partake, a large party sat down, and spent the evening in the most convivial manner.

The following toasts were given, – by the Chairman.

"The King," (with cheers.)

"The prosperity of the province of Upper Canada."

By William Merritt, Esq. – "May every township contribute its aid to the prosperity of the province."

By Mr. G. A. Ball. – "May the navigable waters of the province be speedily improved."

By J. Clark, Esq. – "May the adherents of Mr. Gourlay, be ever encouraged in their virtuous proceedings."

By Geo. Adams, Esq. – "The Administrator."

By Mr. Gourlay – "May the Representative of his Majesty in Upper Canada, ascend from the chair to the throne."

Some of the company desiring an explanation of this toast, Mr. G. rose and replied, that, as unworthy views had been attributed to him, and as such meetings as they had this day held – meetings for the pure purpose of petitioning the Sovereign, had been stigmatized as illegal and seditious, he gave this toast as the most loyal which he could possibly think of for the occasion. The Administrator having, in his speech to Parliament, expressed himself as addressing that body "from the *chair,*" had virtually deprived the province of the royal presence, and let down the dignity which it was his duty to maintain.

This was a matter of more consequence than might at first be supposed. On the part of ministers at home there was a glaring indifference to the concerns of these provinces; and when public prints ventured to hint at the bartering them away to the United States for their value in cash, it was high time for the people here to support their own dignity by marking every step towards their degradation. True loyalty did not consist in mere passive submission: it consisted in watching over every part of the constitution, at once, with jealousy and affection.

By G. A. Ball. – "May our Representatives undergo a reformation."

By the Rev. Mr. Williams. – "May morality and religion increase throughout the province, particularly in the township of Grantham" (by a wag, in addition) "where there is so much room."

By George Adams, Esq. – "May the United Enemies of the United Kingdom of Great Britain and her dependencies be drowned in this draught." – (Cheers.)

St. Catharine's, 4th, May, 1818.

This day representatives (and clerks,) chosen by the inhabitants of the several townships of Niagara district, for the purpose of petitioning the Prince Regent, on the general state of public affairs now existing in the province of Upper Canada, met here.

Robert Hamilton, Esq. representing the township of Niagara.

Wm. Hamilton Merritt, Esq. J.P. do. Grantham.

John Clark, Esq. J.P. do. Louth.

Dr. Cyrus Sumner, do. Clinton.

Captain Henry Hixon, do. Grimsby.

Major Wm. Robertson, do. Caistor and Canbury.

Mr. John Kennedy, do. Gainsborough.

Mr. John Henderson, do. Pelham.

George Keefer, Esq. J. P. do. Thorold.

Dr. John J. Lefferty, do. Stamford.

James Cummings, Esq. J. P. do. Willoughby.

John Baxter, Esq. do Bertie.

Mr. Joseph Current, do. Crowland.

Mr. Benjamin Horton, do. Humberstone, and Lake side of Wainfleet.

David Thompson, Esq. do. Wainfleet.

John Clark, Esq. being unanimously called to the chair – the business of the day commenced by Mr. Clark's reading over Mr. Gourlay's Address to the resident landowners of Upper Canada, dated 2d April, 1818. The recommendations and principles contained in the Address, were declared to be those now generally approved of, and as constituting the basis of the present proceedings. – It was then moved and carried, that Mr. Gourlay should be called to the sitting, and invited to assist in the business of the day.

George Adams, Esq. J. P. was elected to be treasurer for this district, and, being sent for, accepted the office. William J. Kerr, Esq. was elected secretary; and these gentlemen were desired to retire with township clerks, to arrange accounts and commerce a regular journal of transactions. It was then moved, that a draft of a petition previously prepared, should be read, which being done, its general principles were approved of, and it was agreed further that consideration, as to its style, &c. be referred to a committee of four. – *Moved, and unanimously carried,* that as soon as the committee are sufficiently satisfied with the wording of the petition, they order it to be printed, with a view to it lying before the public one month, and affording opportunity for animadversion or amendment, that finally it may be so drawn out as to give the greatest possible degree of satisfaction to the people of the district – *Moved, and unanimously carried,* that the same committee do immediately publish, throughout the province, the whole proceedings of the people of this district of Niagara, up to this time; and take all necessary steps towards promoting the objects in view.

Moved, and unanimously carried, that the gentlemen of the committee advertise Saturday, 6th June, at 2 o'clock, afternoon, as a proper time for the people of other districts, to hold township meetings throughout the province, at all places where township meetings are usually held – that Saturday, the 13th of the same month, be advertised for the meetings of township representatives at the head town of their respective districts, there to choose district representatives, to assemble in the provincial convention. – *Moved, and unanimously carried,* that Monday, 6th July next, be advertised as the day of meeting at York, of the provincial convention, there to appoint a commission to proceed to England, with the petitions to the Prince Regent, and hold conference, generally, on all matters then requiring attention. *Moved, and unanimously carried,* that it is proper for each district, to send to the provincial convention, representatives, in like number and proportion as they send members to Parliament. – *Moved, and unanimously carried,* that it be recommended that the district representatives for the Western, London, Gore, and Niagara districts, do meet together, at Ancaster, on Friday, 3d July – there to tarry one or two days to consult and order with regard to any thing in these districts, that may then be discovered to be neglected. – Also, that the district representatives for Ottawa, the Eastern, Johnstown and Midland districts, do meet for the like purpose, on Wednesday, the 1st of July, at Earnest Town.

The meeting proceeded to choose representatives for Niagara district, when Robert Hamilton, Esq. Dr. Cyrus Sumner, John Clark, J. P. and Major Wm. Robertson, were duly elected. – It was then moved and carried, that these gentlemen constitute the committee above mentioned.

One of the representatives requesting to be allowed to read a paper to the meeting, the request was granted. The paper regarded certain partial proceedings, in courts of justice, and attributed the same to the present corrupt state of public affairs: The gentleman wished the meeting to take the same into consideration; but the proposal was lost, this being declared not a meeting of deliberation as to private or particular grievances, but for the pure purpose of petitioning the Prince Regent generally, as to the state of the province. It was admitted that this, or other papers respecting public grievances, might be given to district representatives, sealed up, and directed to be put into the hands of the commissioners, that they may make what use they please of the same, for the general good of the province. *Moved, and unanimously agreed,* that the thanks of the meeting be given to John Clark, Esq. for his impartial conduct in the chair.

The meeting then adjourned till Monday, 8th June, at St. Catharine's, when the petition will be finally adopted, and measures taken for its signature in the several townships of this district.

JOHN CLARK, *Chairman.*

WILLIAM J. KERR, *Secretary.*

N.B. *Should any person incline to draw out an* ADDRESS, *entirely different from the above, it is requested that a copy may be directed to* "Mr. John Ross, Niagara," *(for the District Committee,) and it is also requested that reports of township meetings, stating what persons are appointed to act as representatives, clerks, and committee men, be forwarded to the same, with all convenient speed, immediately after such meetings are held.*

Draught of an Address proposed for presentation to the Prince Regent – submitted to the consideration of the people of Upper Canada, for animadversion and amendment. *

TO HIS ROYAL HIGHNESS, GEORGE, PRINCE OF WALES, REGENT OF THE UNITED KINGDOM OF GREAT BRITAIN AND IRELAND, &C. &C. &C.

The Humble Address of Inhabitants of Upper Canada.

May it please your Royal Highness,

THE subjects of your Royal Father, dwelling in Upper Canada, should need no words to give assurance of their loyalty, if the whole truth had reached the throne of their Sovereign. His loving subjects have reason to believe that the truth has not been told.

During three years of war, Upper Canada was exposed to the ravages of a powerful and inveterate foe. The Government of the United States

---

* The draft petition adopted by the Niagara meetings was widely circulated and was adopted, or its object endorsed, by meetings in the Western, Gore, Midland and Johnstown districts between 13 and 26 June 1818. The York Convention, to which these meetings also chose delegates, decided on Gourlay's recommendation to present two addresses, one to the Prince Regent and one to the new Lieutenant-Governor, Sir Peregrine Maitland. The second asked for an early election as well as an inquiry into the state of the province; there was in fact an election in 1820, in which eight of the thirty-two assemblymen returned had at one time or another supported Gourlay's petition. Maitland forwarded the addresses of the York Convention, but refused to meet the delegation presenting them. The italicized parts of this draft petition were the grounds for Gourlay's first arrest on a charge of libel. He printed it in the first volume of the *Account,* along with the single township report from the Eastern District, because copies of it had been publicly burned at Cornwall. [Ed.]

had been long concerting the invasion of this Province: hostile preparations against it, had been long masked under other designs: and at last the accumulated torrent of violence burst on the defenceless children of the British Empire. Nor were they assailed by the weapons of war alone. An insidious Proclamation preceded the host of the enemy – forgetful of honour – regardless of humanity,; and, daring to seduce the subjects of Britain from their true allegiance. The subjects of Britain remained dauntless and firm. It was not for property that they rose against the Invader: the Invader would have spared to them their property. They flew to arms in defence of the Rights and Sovereignty of Britain. Twice had the American standard been planted in Upper Canada, while yet but a handful of British troops aided the native battalions of the Province; – twice did these raw battalions wave the laurel of victory over the prostrate Intruders on their true soil. The second year of war saw Canada contending with yet little assistance from the parent state: – the second year of war saw her sons confirmed in their virtue, and still more determined to resist. Wives and children had fled from their homes, the face of the country was laid waste, and the fire of revenge was sent forth to consummate distress and misery; – still did it burn with patriotism and loyalty.

By the third year, every risk of conquest was at an end; for now the British aids poured into the Provinces; and peace was proclaimed, when war was no longer to be feared.

It is now more than three years since there was an end of war; but, strange to say, these years of peace have manifested no appearance of affection or care from the mother country to the Canadas. Commercial treaties have been made, altogether neglectful of British interests, here: Government transactions, which used to give spirit to trade and industry, are at a stand: troops are withdrawn: fortifications are suffered to go to ruin; and rumours are abroad too shocking to be repeated in the Royal ear.

May it please your Royal Highness to listen calmly to the complaints and grievances of the people of Upper Canada, who are fully assured that your Royal Highness has been kept ignorant of most important truths, – who are well assured of the generous dispositions of your Royal heart; and of your desire that British subjects, should, every where, share equally, your paternal regard and affection.

It was matter of much provocation to the people of this Province, to see, even during the war, which afforded such striking proofs of their loyalty and valour, reports sent home, highly rating the merit of regular troops, while the tribute, due to Canadian levies, was unfairly let down. Nay the principles of the most loyal subjects here, were often stigmatized by British Officers, ignorant of human character, and still more so of circumstances which affect it, in this part of the world. It was not so with the immortal Brock. He justly appreciated Canadian worth; and his memory will happily long cherish, in the minds of the Canadian people, a due regard for the genuine spirit of a British soldier, at once generous and brave.

The loyal Inhabitants of Upper Canada would disdain to notice the misrepresentations of individuals, so contrary to notorious truth, if these had not obviously conspired, with other causes, to lessen the regard, which should subsist between British subjects, here and at home – to influence the conduct of ministers towards the general interest of the Provinces.

The loyal subjects of his Majesty in Upper Canada, suffered grievously during the war, in their property, and many were bereft of their all. A solemn investigation, on this subject, took place: the claims of sufferers were authenticated; and there was every reason to expect that recompence would immediately follow; yet nothing has followed, but delay and insult. – Surely, if there is, among mankind, a single principle of justice, this is one, that the individuals of a nation ought not, partially, to bear the weight of public calamity, – surely, individuals who have exposed their lives for government, should not be disgusted, with finding government regardless of those very principles, which it is intended to sustain. The people of this Province are well aware, that their fellow subjects, at home, are pressed hard with taxation; and far is it from their wish that relief should be afforded from thence. Canada contains, within itself, ample means of exonerating government from the claims of sufferers by war; and it is within the *fiat* of your Royal Highness to remove, by a single breath, the evil now so justly complained of. Millions of acres of fertile land lie here, at the disposal of your Royal Highness, upon the credit of which, put under proper management, not only the fair claims of loyal sufferers could be instantly advanced; but vast sums could be raised for the improvement of the Provinces, and the increase of revenue to Britain.

Another grievance, manifesting the neglect of government to the concerns of Upper Canada, is equally notorious; and must be still more abhorrent to the generous feelings of your Royal Highness.

The young men of this Province, who were armed in its defence, had, for their spirited conduct, the promise of their commanders, that land would be granted them as a reward for their services, as soon as war was terminated; and after this promise was universally confided in, the Parliament of Upper Canada passed an extraordinary law, in the face of established British principles, that the militia should pass beyond the frontier. With these promises, and in obedience to this law, the militia passed beyond the frontier with alacrity: yet, since the peace, the greater part of them have been denied the pledge of their extraordinary services, and the land is unjustly withheld.

Such ingratitude – such dishonour – such errors in policy, your Royal Highness may be well assured, could not exist, without extraordinary influences; and were your Royal Highness sufficiently informed as to these, and of the true state of Upper Canada, we flatter ourselves, most important changes would speedily take place, as well for the glory of the throne, as for the benefit of its subjects.

Permit the loyal subjects of his Majesty merely to say as much, at the present time, on this subject, as may induce your Royal Highness to order inquiry to be made.

The lands of the Crown in Upper Canada, are of immense extent, not only stretching far and wide into the wilderness, but scattered over the province, and intermixed with private property, already cultivated. The disposal of this land is left to Ministers at home, who are palpably ignorant of existing circumstances; and to a council of men resident in the province, who, it is believed, have long converted the trust reposed in them to purposes of selfishness. The scandalous abuses, in this depart- ment, came some years ago to such a pitch of monstrous magnitude, that the home Ministers wisely imposed restrictions on the Land Council of Upper Canada. These, however, have by no means removed the evil; and a system of patronage and favouritism, in the disposal of the Crown lands, still exists, altogether destructive of moral rectitude, and virtuous feeling, in the management of public affairs. Corruption, indeed, has reached such a height in this Province, that it is thought no other part of the British empire witnesses the like; and it is vain to look for improvement till a radical change is effected. It matters not what characters fill situations of public trust at present: – all sink beneath the dignity of men – become vitiated and weak, as soon as they are placed within the vortex of destruction. Confusion on confusion has grown out of this unhappy sys- tem; and the very lands of the Crown, the giving away of which has created such mischief and iniquity, have ultimately come to little value from abuse. The poor subjects of his Majesty, driven from home by distress, to whom portions of land are granted, can now find in the grant no benefit; and loyalists of the United Empire – the descendants of those who sacrificed their all in America, in behalf of British rule – men whose names were ordered on record for their virtuous adherence to your Royal Father, – the descendants of these men find, now, no favour in their destined rewards: nay, these rewards, when granted, have, in many cases, been rendered worse than nothing; for the legal rights in the enjoyment of them have been held at nought: their land has been rendered unsaleable, and, in some cases, only a source of distraction and care.

Under this system of internal management, and weakened from other evil influences, Upper Canada now pines in comparative decay: discontent and poverty are experienced in a land supremely blessed with the gifts of nature: dread of arbitrary power wars, here, against the free exercise of reason and manly sentiment: laws have been set aside: legislators have come into derision; and, contempt from the mother country seems fast gathering strength to disunite the people of Canada from their friends at home.

The immediate interference of your Royal Highness might do much to check existing evils; and might wholly remove those which spring from the system of patronage and favouritism, in the land-granting department. Other evils, however, greatly retard the prosperity of Upper Canada – evils which have their root in the original constitution of the Province, and these can only be removed by the interference of the British Parlia- ment, now most imperiously required.

Deeply penetrated with these sentiments, and most seriously inclined to have such needful changes speedily effected, the loyal subjects of Britain, dwelling in Upper Canada, now take the extraordinary step of sending home Commissioners to bear this to the throne, and humbly entreat your Royal Highness to give ear to the details which it will be in their power to relate: above all, that your Royal Highness would, immediately, send out to this Province a COMMISSION, consisting of discreet and wise men – men of business and talent, who shall be above every influence here; and who may be instructed to make inquiry into all the sources of evil.

Notes on the Author and the Editor

Robert Gourlay, a stormy petrel of Upper Canadian politics and long celebrated as a forerunner of the Rebellion of 1837, has a better claim to be remembered in his *Statistical Account of Upper Canada*. Although his ambitious plan for what amounted to a private census of provincial agriculture and settlement was interrupted by his decision to seek political reform, his pioneering questionnaire enabled him to compile the best picture of Upper Canada to be drawn before the Union.

S. R. Mealing is Professor of History at Carleton University and is the founding editor, with Marcel Trudel, of *Histoire Sociale*. He was the editor of *Jesuit Relations and Allied Documents* (Carleton Library, No. 7).

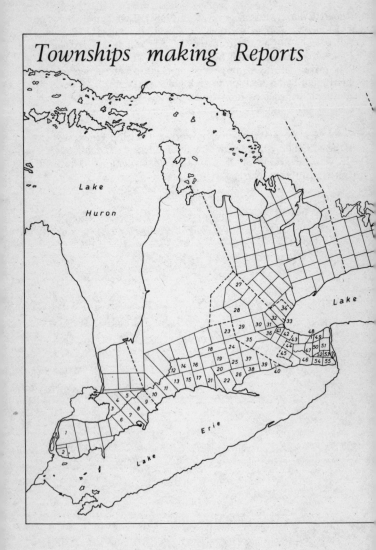

Townships making Reports

Lake
Huron

Lake

Erie

Lake

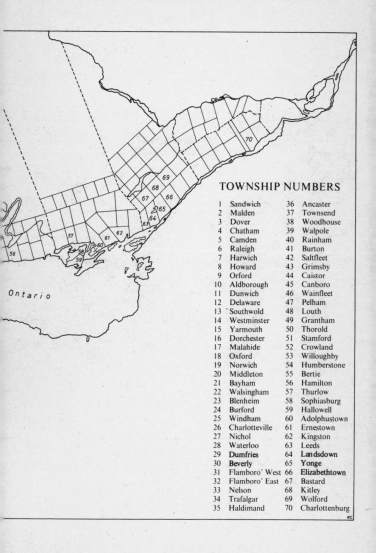

TOWNSHIP NUMBERS

1	Sandwich	36	Ancaster
2	Malden	37	Townsend
3	Dover	38	Woodhouse
4	Chatham	39	Walpole
5	Camden	40	Rainham
6	Raleigh	41	Burton
7	Harwich	42	Saltfleet
8	Howard	43	Grimsby
9	Orford	44	Caistor
10	Aldborough	45	Canboro
11	Dunwich	46	Wainfleet
12	Delaware	47	Pelham
13	Southwold	48	Louth
14	Westminster	49	Grantham
15	Yarmouth	50	Thorold
16	Dorchester	51	Stamford
17	Malahide	52	Crowland
18	Oxford	53	Willoughby
19	Norwich	54	Humberstone
20	Middleton	55	Bertie
21	Bayham	56	Hamilton
22	Walsingham	57	Thurlow
23	Blenheim	58	Sophiasburg
24	Burford	59	Hallowell
25	Windham	60	Adolphustown
26	Charlotteville	61	Ernestown
27	Nichol	62	Kingston
28	Waterloo	63	Leeds
29	**Dumfries**	64	**Landsdown**
30	**Beverly**	65	**Yonge**
31	Flamboro' West	66	**Elizabethtown**
32	Flamboro' East	67	Bastard
33	Nelson	68	Kitley
34	Trafalgar	69	Wolford
35	Haldimand	70	Charlottenburg

Ontario

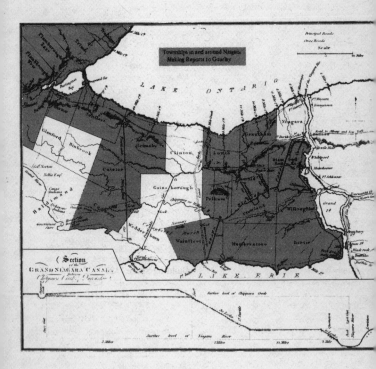

Townships in and around Niagara
Making Reports to Gourlay

Index

THE CARLETON LIBRARY